DATE DUE

BEFORE THE KNIGHT'S TALE

Imitation of Classical Epic in Boccaccio's *Teseida*

BEFORE THE KNIGHT'S TALE

Imitation of Classical Epic in Boccaccio's *Teseida*

DAVID ANDERSON

UNIVERSITY OF PENNSYLVANIA PRESS

Philadelphia

17550206
DLC

11-15-88

University of Pennsylvania Press
MIDDLE AGES SERIES
Edited by
EDWARD PETERS
Henry Charles Lea Professor of Medieval History
University of Pennsylvania

A complete listing of the books in this series
appears at the back of this volume

FRONTISPIECE: A later fourteenth-century Italian copy of the *Thebaid*, with glosses and a historiated *F*, in "Fraternas aties," representing the subject of fraternal strife. Vatican City, Biblioteca Apostolica Vaticana, MS Vat. lat. 1615, detail from fol. 1r

Copyright © 1988 by the University of Pennsylvania Press
All rights reserved
Printed in the United States of America

Library of Congress Cataloging-in-Publication Data

Anderson, David, 1952–
  Before the knight's tale: imitation of classical epic in
Boccaccio's Teseida/David Anderson.
    p.   cm.—(Middle Ages series)
  Includes bibliographical references and index.
  ISBN 0-8122-8108-X
  1. Boccaccio, Giovanni, 1313–1375. Teseide. 2. Chaucer,
Geoffrey, d. 1400—Criticism and interpretation. 3. Boccaccio,
Giovanni, 1313–1375—Influence—Chaucer. 4. Statius, P.
Papinius (Publius Papinius). Thebaid. 5. Boccaccio, Giovanni,
1313–1375. Teseide—Sources. 6. Chaucer, Geoffrey, d. 1400.
Knight's tale—Sources. I. Boccaccio, Giovanni, 1313–1375.
Teseide. II. Title. III. Series.
PQ4270.T43A54 1988
851'.1—dc19

88-4739
CIP

CONTENTS

ILLUSTRATIONS

PREFACE

Chaucer's use of the *Teseida* has long occupied a central place in discussions of the Knight's Tale, to such an extent that it is hard to think of an important reading of this poem that does not make reference to the evidence of his adopting or transforming the Italian source. Students of the Knight's Tale have not, however, been enthusiastic students of Boccaccio's humanism as well, preferring to restrict their analysis to a comparison of the *Teseida* and the Knight's Tale in isolation. By treating Boccaccio's poem exclusively as a source, rather than as an imitative poem in its own right, Chaucerians have concluded—inevitably, perhaps, in view of the nature of the investigation—that Chaucer's version greatly improves on its original. The critical approach itself implies, and the critics have often asserted openly, that the *Teseida* is a hodgepodge of narrative motifs needing the hand of a better maker, a literary embarrassment requiring our attention only for so long as it takes to see "what Chaucer has done" to it. But this is inadequate as a description of Chaucer's original, the narrative he borrowed from it, and its place in a much older literary tradition. Chaucer came third in the sequence of authors, perfecting the inventions of the second.

Consider Chaucer's references to ancient Thebes, prominent in the Knight's Tale and also in *Troilus and Criseyde*. In both poems, the legendary history Chaucer sketches into the background is also reflected in the main action. The foreground moves like the events in the background, so that the narrative structure is itself allusive. I have argued before that in the *Troilus* Chaucer uses his references to the fall of Thebes according to a double parallel: the fall of Troy is mirrored in the foreground action of the fall of Troilus, while Thebes, already fallen, is placed just a little farther back, as a historical type and an admonition. With its "olde walles wide" and its memories of civil war, Thebes looms closer to the action of the Knight's Tale, where the foreground narrative of Palamon and Arcite moves like the legendary rivalry between Eteocles and Polynices over the throne of Oedipus, the subject of Statius's *Thebaid*. The epigraph, a passage from *Thebaid* 12, seems to be placed at the head of the Knight's Tale to acknowledge a source for the opening scene and to establish a historical continuity with Statius's narrative.

Here the picture is complicated by Boccaccio's *Teseida*, which was Chaucer's primary source. He does not allude to the *Teseida* but rather repeats it, drawing characters and the main action from Boccaccio's poem. Now, the more useful one finds the concept of allusive narrative in reading the Knight's Tale, the more one has to recognize it as something that Boccaccio invented. There is, in the first place, the question of distinguishing two varieties of intertextual relations: Chaucer imitates Statius openly; he does not "imitate" Boccaccio in this sense at all. Rather his imitation of the *Thebaid* silently follows the example of the *Teseida*.

By taking a serious interest in Boccaccio's achievements as the basis for understanding Chaucer, this study aligns itself with several recent publications: Piero Boitani's *Chaucer and Boccaccio*, Barry Windeatt's edition of the *Troilus*, with facing Italian text and extensive notes on Chaucer's translations from the *Filostrato*; Chauncey Wood's *The Elements of Chaucer's "Troilus"*; and David Wallace's *Chaucer and the Early Writings of Boccaccio*. Wallace has stated the objective thus: "Any account of Chaucer's transforming art must be preceded by some consideration of the literary and historical formation of the text that Chaucer is engaged with." My account differs from these works in that it concerns the Knight's Tale rather than the *Troilus*, and especially in its greater emphasis on Boccaccio than on Chaucer. The importance of the old classical source determines this shift in emphasis. Chaucer's open imitation of the *Thebaid* in his main action suggests that, in many of its aspects, his "transforming art" was not a transformation *of* Boccaccio's work but *like* Boccaccio's work. Thus the proper study of imitation in the Knight's Tale is largely a study of Boccaccio's imitation of the *Thebaid* in the *Teseida*.

"So that this work, which has the look of something rather long, not be regretted before it is read, and with the hope of encouraging an affectionate disposition toward it in case the foregoing has not done so already, I set down for you here a brief summary of the contents of the whole book." I am reminded by this gracefully complicated sentence in Boccaccio's introduction to the *Teseida* that the summary decalogue is useful to the reader even though it may try the patience of the author, who cannot give any rein to his enthusiasm in such a small space. The present study is organized as a response to a critical commonplace, as follows:

I begin by observing the development among literary historians in the later nineteenth century of a consensus, which defined the main action of the *Teseida* as a betrayal of its epic form and consequently sought its origins in a lost "medieval romance." The Introduction takes a representative statement of that consensus and examines it at length, sorting out its underlying assumptions about Boccaccio's model of epic and his imitative strategy. Taking its clue from the earliest critical reactions to the *Teseida*, those of the fifteenth and sixteenth centuries, the Introduction argues that Boccaccio aimed not for a "faithful reconstruction" of the epic genre but for a creative transformation of a single classical epic.

The first chapter pursues the question of imitative strategy by analyzing, first, three formal similes and, next, the patterned borrowing from the *Thebaid* in the main action of the *Teseida*. It proposes that the "romance" of Palamon and Arcite develops as an extended comparison, matching the protagonists of *Thebaid* 1–4, scene by scene, with those of *Teseida* 3–6.

The second chapter examines the narrative structure of Boccaccio's second six books, where he alters the *Thebaid*-like pattern. The change is modeled on the first funeral game in *Thebaid* 6 and especially on Statius's apostrophe in the midst of that narrative, in which he proposes a hypothetical alternate ending to the history of the Theban war. By elaborating Statius's hypothesis instead of imitating the actual sequence of scenes in Statius's narrative, Boccaccio keeps his main action more sharply focused on the theme of fraternal strife and its motivating passions. The chapter then turns to *Teseida* 6 and the contribution of Boccaccio's epic catalog to this allusive design.

The third chapter takes up the question of Boccaccio's model. The model of classical epic was somewhat different in fourteenth century literary culture than it is today, and the differences have to be taken into account by any study of Boccaccio's imitation. With reference to medieval commentaries on the *Thebaid*, I suggest that Boccaccio imitated such formal features as verse arguments and chapter rubrics that were features of classical epic in medieval codices. Furthermore, Boccaccio's imitation of the *Thebaid* was mediated by an exegetical tradition that defined epic narrative in terms of "history and fable," "truth" about human events and "lies" about the pagan gods. When the model is defined in these terms, Boccaccio's imitation resembles it more closely, and his transformations can be defined with greater precision.

The final chapter comes to Chaucer, examining his imitations in a longer perspective. I characterize Chaucer's use of Boccaccio as a careful preserving, in the smaller space allowed by the frame story of the *Canterbury Tales*, of the patterns of open imitation established in the *Teseida*. Adoption of Boccaccio's allusive narrative structure places the Knight's Tale firmly in epic tradition, in the sense that it is designed to take on meaning as it is seen against the *Thebaid*, a variation on the theme and main action of this classical source, and it also sets the paradigm for the brilliant sequence of analogies and transformations in the narratives of the Miller and Reeve.

As the main focus of this study lies on Boccaccio and Statius, it is concerned with aspects of early humanism. I hope to have made good use of the work of the scholars who have cultivated those fields; they made my particular itinerary possible. Their names appear throughout the footnotes to this book, but I should like to add special thanks to some of them here and also to name some of the many persons whose good will and effort improved these pages: D. W. Robertson, Jr., Violetta de Angelis, Giuseppe Billanovich, Victoria Kirkham, Vittore Branca, Joseph Farrell, Mary Louise Lord, William Coleman, Winthrop Wetherbee, and two anonymous readers for the University of Pennsylvania Press. I was able to begin study of unpublished medieval commentaries on the *Thebaid* with a Fulbright fellowship in 1978–1979, and I transcribed the anonymous fifteenth-century commentary on the *Teseida,* quoted in the Introduction, with the financial assistance of a summer stipend from the University of Pennsylvania. My study of Boccaccio's contemporaries at the court of Robert the Wise, which makes occasional contributions to this book and which I hope to elaborate more systematically in the future, was helped by a summer stipend from the National Endowment for the Humanities in 1984. Seth Weiner, GianLuca Piotti, and Giovanni Creton have given inestimable help, especially in the early stages of the project, as has my tirelessly generous wife, Teresa Murano-Anderson. Part of the argument in Chapter 4 appeared in the *Chaucer Review* 21 (1987); many of the glosses on the altar of Clemency, discussed in Chapter 3, were published in *Studies in the Age of Chaucer,* Proceedings 2 (1987). My thanks to the editors for permission to repeat this material here and to the Vatican and Laurentian Libraries for permission to reproduce pages from manuscripts of the *Thebaid* and the *Teseida.*

The two essays referred to in this Preface are "Theban History in Chaucer's *Troilus,*" *Studies in the Age of Chaucer* 4 (1982): 109–133; and "Cassandra's Analogy," *Hebrew University Studies in Literature and the Arts* 13 (1985): 1–17. I quote from the preface to David Wallace's book *Chaucer and the Early Writings of Boccaccio,* which was published by Boydell and Brewer (Woodbridge, Suffolk, 1985).

Boccaccio's elegant *captatio voluntatis* appears in the middle of the introductory epistle "A Fiammetta," where it is followed by a summary of the main action of the *Teseida.* For the text, see the edition of Limentani, in *Tutte le Opere,* ed. Vittore Branca (Milan: Mondadori, 1964), vol. 2, p. 247: "E acciò che l'opera, la quale alquanto par lunga, non sia prima rincresciuta che letta, disiderando di disporre con affezione la vostra mente a vederla, se le già dette cose non l'avessero disposta, sotto brevità sommariamente qui appresso di tutta l'opera vi pongo la contenenza."

BEFORE THE KNIGHT'S TALE

Imitation of Classical Epic in Boccaccio's *Teseida*

Introduction

By the end of the nineteenth century a consensus had developed among literary historians that Boccaccio's *Teseida* was a conspicuously unsuccessful experiment in the imitation of classical epic. Guglielmo Volpi's chapter on Boccaccio in the scholarly *Literary History of Italy* stated the case this way: "With the *Teseida*, Boccaccio had the idea of giving Italy a vernacular poem that would be what the *Aeneid* and the *Thebaid* had been for the Romans; it is hardly necessary to point out that he was deluding himself if he thought he had attained his goal." The chronology of Boccaccio's works, which had been an object of minute attention during the later nineteenth century, placed the *Teseida* early in his career: together with the emerging critical view of the poem's failed epic design, this dating suggested that its author had been young and ambitious and had overreached his powers. There was "tension" between classical and nonclassical elements. "His learning and culture were not of the sort that would permit him to compose a true epic according to the classical models." And while the *Teseida* failed to recreate its august models in several respects, the main problem could be seen in Boccaccio's terribly indecorous choice of a main action: "A love story makes up . . . the substance of the poem. Two friends become rivals in love, they have a scuffle but the fight is interrupted and postponed, the duel converted into a joust: this is the skeletal outline, one more suited to a novella than to a long poem, which Boccaccio fleshed out as best he could to give it the majestic shape of an epic." [1] By 1912 this conventional opinion, if not in Volpi's summary version then in one of its many analogues, had already been adopted in England as the basis for comparing Boccaccio's work with the Knight's Tale, [2] and for the Chaucerians it led directly to the simple and (I suppose) satisfying thesis that Chaucer had returned the misconstrued "romance" to a more appropriate generic form; that he had disencumbered an unheroic action of its heroic apparatus; that he had, in effect, concurred with the modern view of the *Teseida* and shown his agreement by editing the twelve books of the *Teseida* into the "novella" that begins the *Canterbury Tales*.

Volpi's remarks offer a good place to enter the history of this critical commonplace. They appeared in an influential publication in 1898 at about the time the consensus first took form. His description is free of the speculation about autobiographical motives that was so common during the later nineteenth and early twentieth centuries, and which in this case was to hold that a "romance" spoiled the epic design of the *Teseida* because Boccaccio was overwhelmed by the desire to recount an affair of his own heart in the guise of Palamon and Arcite. Volpi's version makes no such appeal and focuses instead on the formal design of the poem itself. Moreover, he states the assumption, left implicit in many discussions of the *Teseida* before and after, that Boccaccio intended to compose a vernacular poem that reproduced a classical genre. Volpi makes it clear that he is not asking how the generic model appeared in the literary culture of Boccaccio's time and he is not asking if another strategy could be employed in imitating it. For Volpi, to imitiate classical epic is not to transform but to recreate. And his remarks have the great virtue of indicating just which features in the *Teseida* itself have led him to make these assumptions.

The view of Boccaccio's poem that is presented in this literary history was not very old in 1898, at least with regard to its central tenet that the poem is a "failed epic." By contrast, the accompanying assertion that the *Teseida* is a minor work of Boccaccio's youth has a longer genealogy. In fact, Boccaccio himself may be responsible for its origin. Petrarch, in the letter accompanying his Latin translation of Boccaccio's tale of Griselda (*Seniles* 17.3), refers to the vernacular *Decameron* as a rather wanton pastime of Boccaccio's "youth" containing some things of value perhaps, but not constituting what one would call a significant work of literature, comparable to Boccaccio's Latin works. It is in light of this valuation of Latin over vernacular that we may read Boccaccio's own disparaging reference to his "youthful" compositions in *Eclogue* 12 (ca. 1355):[3]

> Puero carmen vulgare placebat . . . ast nunc
> altior est etas, alios que monstrat amores.
>
> [Vernacular poems pleased me when I was young, . . . but now the age is greater and it shows (me) different loves.]

The early disciples of Petrarch's Latin humanism tend to follow this critical line, classing Boccaccio's vernacular works as trivial by comparison to
his writings in Latin even while admitting that the vernacular works were
well known. Coluccio Salutati, writing to Francescuolo da Brossano on
the occasion of Boccaccio's death in 1375, mentions not a single vernacular work while building an eloquent case for Boccaccio's literary im-
mortality on the basis of *De casibus,* the *Genealogie,* and so on. Filippo
Villani reserves a single phrase in his life of Boccaccio for all of the writings in Italian, a phrase, moreover, that echoes the language of Petrarch's
judgment in *Seniles* 17.3: these are minor works, products of his youth,
"and he composed many other minor works [*opuscula*] in the vernacular
tongue . . . in which, in the spirit of his green youth [*lascivientis iuventutis ingenio*] he ran a little wild and which he thought it best not to mention after he grew older."[4] To be sure, we are products of a very different
time, in which the story of Boccaccio's career is told with one of those
vernacular works, the *Decameron,* as the point of arrival. In our modern
arrangement, the other Italian works are considered as preparation for
the *Decameron,* while the Latin works appear as lamentable distractions.
They are infrequently read and rarely edited.[5]

Here then is the old root of Volpi's "youthful" and "minor" *Teseida,*
which in the nineteenth century had come to nourish an otherwise very
different critical plant. It is interesting to note how these disparaging epi-
thets serve to reinforce critical judgments in both instances. The scarce
attention accorded vernacular works by the Petrarchans is obviously a
consequence of literary values that have little to do with the *Teseida* per
se. When the terms reappear in the modern discussion of the poem, they
again reflect a critical judgment rather than a simple historical statement
based on evidence for its date of composition. This is apparent even in the
briefest review of what we know about the origin and early history of
the poem.

Just how "early and minor" is the *Teseida?* The terms are not very precise, but they are meaningful enough to leave one surprised on discover-
ing that its author began to compose it after he had attained a measure of
fame as a poet and after he had laid the foundations of his great erudition
in the Latin classics; and moreover that the *Teseida* was cultivated widely
and by several kinds of reader, including the learned, throughout the
fourteenth and fifteenth centuries.

Boccaccio probably began work on the poem after the middle of the
year 1339.[6] The best evidence for this date comes from the letter "Sacre
famis" (epistola IV), in which Boccaccio tells an anonymous friend that

he has been reading, with some difficulty, a new copy of Statius's *Thebaid* and would like to have a copy of Lactantius's commentary on that work. Boccaccio remarks that he has recently acquired this new copy of the text and has been reading it "without guidance or glosses," which has kept him from attaining a full understanding ("sed cum sine magistro vel glosis intellectum debitum non attingam"). Because he uses the *Thebaid* so extensively in the *Teseida* and draws on all parts of the long text, it seems unlikely that he began to write before he felt he had mastered it and likely that he began to write during this period, when he held it fresh in mind. The date of the letter is, therefore, a key to dating the beginning of Boccaccio's work on the *Teseida*. The letter was certainly written in Naples, because the copy that survives in Boccaccio's own hand bears the subscription, "scripta sub monte Falerno apud busta Maronis Virgilii, iulii kalendas iiii" (= 28 June). No year is given in the subscription, but Boccaccio's copy of "Sacre famis" appears fourth in a group of four letters that he seems to have transcribed at about the same time; the first letter in the group bears the date April 1339, and Boccaccio may have seen no need to repeat the same date in each of the following letters. If this assumption is correct, "Sacre famis" belongs to the summer of 1339, though it is possible that he wrote it the next summer, when he was still in Naples.[7]

Another piece of evidence comes from Boccaccio's use of the Lactantius commentary in the *Teseida* and the existence of a copy of the *Thebaid* containing that commentary that was in Boccaccio's possession at a fairly early date. On balance, it must be said that Boccaccio did not use Lactantius extensively in the *Teseida*, but at least one section of the poem and its accompanying gloss, in book 11, derives from that late classical commentary, which in "Sacre famis" Boccaccio says he would like to borrow and consult. Giuseppe Billanovich has argued that the request is formulaic and that Boccaccio may even have possessed the Lactantius commentary by the time he wrote.[8] But the general absence of Lactantius among the sources of the *Teseida*, coupled with its brief appearance near the end, suggests that Boccaccio's request of 1339 (or possibly 1340) was genuine, and that the composition of the *Teseida* extended over the period of time during which he came into possession of a copy.

There is no proof positive. We are dealing in probabilities. But on the basis of the "Sacre famis," it appears that Boccaccio conceived the *Teseida* and began composing it while he was still in Naples, where he lived from the late 1320s until 1341. It is then less clear when he finished. The poem represented a major undertaking; it is as long as a classical epic; and we shall be wise, therefore, to allow the possibility that he

worked on it over an extended period of years. There is certainly reason
to believe that he carried it with him when he returned to his native Florence, where he had moved by the summer of 1341. There are several references to Florence in the glosses to the *Teseida* that support this belief,
and A. E. Quaglio has argued that Boccaccio's quotations from Dino del
Garbo in the gloss on the temple of Venus in *Teseida* 7 must date from
the Florentine period.[9] More recently, James McGregor has demonstrated
that Boccaccio drew on the chronicle of Martinus Polonus in his description of the amphitheater in *Teseida* 7.[10] Boccaccio's use of this source contributes to the impression that he worked on the *Teseida* during the
1340s, though the evidence is hardly conclusive, because Boccaccio
copied the passages in question from Martinus's chronicle into a commonplace book, which has been dated to the period from the mid-1340s
to the mid-1350s. If we assume that the copying of excerpts into a commonplace book corresponds to or precedes the use of the same passages
in the *Teseida* (a large assumption, but not without merit), then either the
commonplace book must be dated earlier than it has been heretofore, or
these passages in the *Teseida* were composed in the mid-1340s. The one
surviving copy of the *Teseida* in Boccaccio's own hand—it is probably a
presentation copy, and in any case not his working copy—has been dated
to 1350 on paleographical grounds. This too opens the possibility that he
continued to work on the poem as well as the commentary during the
1340s.[11]

Some further clues to the relative chronology of Boccaccio's earlier
works have been found in his changing preferences among the different
versions of classical myths. Thus he tells the story of Jove and Alcmena in
one version in both the *Teseida* and the first redaction of the *Amorosa
visione* (1343?), but gives a different version in the second redaction of
the *Amorosa visione* (1355?) and the *Genealogie deorum gentilium* (begun ca. 1350).[12] Also, a poem attributed to Matteo Frescobaldi mentions
two characters from the *Teseida,* Ippolita and Emilia. If the attribution to
Frescobaldi is correct, we may be sure that the *Teseida* circulated before
1348, the year of his death.[13] This early reference, together with the date
of Boccaccio's holograph copy of the *Teseida,* establish a terminus ante
quem in the late 1340s.

In sum, a good deal of circumstantial evidence allows us to place the
Teseida at the end of the first major period in Boccaccio's career. By
mid-1339, he had lived in Naples for about twelve years. He had come as
a boy to train in his father's business ("for six wasted years," he was to
recall later); he had apparently held a position at court[14] and he had studied canon law (and perhaps civil law as well): "as there seemed to be

some indication that I was more disposed to literary pursuits [than bank-ing], my father decided that I should study for holy orders as a good way to get rich. My teacher was famous, but I wasted under him almost as much time as before."[15] It was in Naples during these years that Boccac-cio determined, against his father's earnest wishes, to spend his talents not in commerce or in law but in the study of poetry; in Naples he had made his first respectable essays in literary composition (the "Elegia di Costanza," "Allegoria mitologica," and "Caccia di Diana") and had written his first substantial literary works (the *Filocolo* and the *Filo-strato*). And it was in Naples that he had laid the foundations of his great erudition in the Latin classics, chronicle literature, and natural sciences. Thus even if we take the earliest possible date for the completion of the poetic text, about 1341, and assume that Boccaccio carried a full draft of the work with him when he made his way north to Florence in that year (we know that he had left Naples by midsummer, and that he had prob-ably left before Petrarch's visit to that city in the spring),[16] it is clear that he wrote not as an uncertain beginner but as a poet of some experience and some sense of his literary powers.

Relations between Naples and Florence were especially close during this period, but they were not equal.[17] King Robert of Anjou ruled from Naples one of the most important kingdoms in Europe between 1308, when he succeeded his father, Charles II, and his death in 1343. It encom-passed southern Italy (exclusive of Sicily, which had been lost during the Vespers); provinces in southern and western France (though not, after 1290, the province of Anjou), and various territories in Greece and the eastern Mediterranean, including for a time the regions of Athens and Thebes, where the events of the *Teseida* are set. One of Robert's nephews sat on the throne of Hungary, slightly more distant relatives on the throne of France. As the leader of the Guelph party in Italy, Robert or his repre-sentatives served several times as governors of Guelph city-states in cen-tral Italy, including Genoa and Florence. Although Robert earned little praise from Dante because of his anti-imperial policies (Dante refers to him rather sourly as "the sermon king" in the *Paradiso*),[18] Petrarch, Boc-caccio, and many of their contemporaries were to praise him highly for his learning and good government. Of particular importance to the early career of Boccaccio, Robert brought many of the leading scholars of the time to his capital city, which was rich in libraries. It undoubtedly proved a more stimulating place for the young Boccaccio than Florence, torn by factional strife and not yet the city of great scholars and great libraries it became by the next century.[19]

In Robert's city, Boccaccio pursued his interest in poetry and history with men like Paolo di Perugia, the royal librarian, and Dionigi da Borgo San Sepolcro, sometime papal ambassador, professor of theology, and—as must have proved especially important to Boccaccio—expositor of the classics. Dionigi had come to Naples at the king's request in 1337, sometime after publication of his commentary on Valerius Maximus, and when he was well known as a friend to Petrarch.[20] There is every indication that by the time he sat down to write the *Teseida*, Boccaccio not only had completed the *Filocolo* and *Filostrato*, but also had projected his major Latin works that were to occupy him in the middle years of his career, including his encyclopedia of classical myth and history, the *Genealogie deorum gentilium*, and its formal defense of classical poetry. Boccaccio tells us that the mythography was inspired by the *Collectiones* of Paolo di Perugia, and it is anticipated by the extensive glosses in the *Teseida* concerning mythological topics.[21] Certain motifs in Boccaccio's defense of poetry, in book 14 of the *Genealogie*, can also be traced to the influence of Paolo's commentaries on the satires of Persius and Horace, and to Dionigi's commentary on Valerius Maximus.

Whether the *Teseida* was finished as early as 1341—a date suggested by the fact that he seems to have been engaged with the *Commedia delle ninfe* and the *Amorosa visione* in 1342 and 1343—or whether Boccaccio worked on it for a number of years during the 1340s, as the preponderance of other evidence suggests, all possible measures indicate that it was highly regarded in its own time and throughout the following centuries. Something on the order of sixty manuscripts of the *Teseida* survive from the fourteenth and fifteenth centuries, and although the number of copies of a medieval work surviving today offers an unreliable guide to determining the number of copies actually produced, we may note by way of comparison that approximately the same number of copies of the *Decameron*, now considered Boccaccio's masterpiece and certainly "popular" in his lifetime, survive from the same period;[22] and again by way of comparison, that the manuscripts of Chaucer's popular *Canterbury Tales* survive in about equal numbers, while Chaucer's *Troilus*, a work resembling the *Teseida* in length, subject, and verse form, survives in fewer than half as many copies.[23] The popularity of the *Teseida* ran particularly high in the 1400s, if we judge by the Italian commentaries composed in that century, the French, English, and Greek translations, and the two incunable editions (printed in Ferrara and Naples).[24] Scenes from the *Teseida* were represented in the visual arts of the period,[25] and other writers began mentioning characters from Boccaccio's poem as early as the

1340s, though the date of the earliest such reference is, as we have seen, still debated. Such early references include one in a distinctly learned context.[26] A long gloss in the margins of a fourteenth-century manuscript of Statius's *Thebaid*, which was once in the possession of Tedaldo della Casa, contains a summary of *Teseida* 1–2.40 in Latin. Tedaldo's learning and his dedication to the Latin works of Boccaccio and of Petrarch add something to the importance of this gloss even though it is not in Tedaldo's hand. On paleographical grounds, it may be dated to the twenty years before and after Tedaldo's death in 1406, and as the manuscript remained in the library of Tedaldo's convent, it would seem to have been written at Santa Croce in Florence. If nothing more, it is a striking example of a vernacular poem being cited as an authority in explanation of a passage in a classical Latin work.

Yet the most striking evidence for the early reputation of the *Teseida* comes from fourteenth-century England, where Geoffrey Chaucer introduced it, probably after one of his trips to Italy on the king's business in the 1370s. He translated portions of the *Teseida* in his *Troilus* and in the *Parliament of Fowles*, probably in the mid-1380s. He mentioned the work in his prologue to the *Legend of Good Women;* he began and then abandoned an adaptation of it in English rhyme royal, known as the *Anelida and Arcite;* and finally, perhaps in the early 1390s, he offered a shortened version of the *Teseida* as his Knight's Tale.[27]

Even this simple account of the *Teseida* among Chaucerian sources speaks eloquently if we will let it. Chaucer was a learned poet; he knew Dante's *Commedia* and Petrarch's *Canzoniere* and made sparing use of them. He was familiar with Boccaccio's major Latin works and he must have been aware of the *Decameron,* but he gave his time and attention to the vernacular works of Boccaccio's Neapolitan period and especially to the *Teseida*. Studies of his translations and adaptations have shown that he knew the poem so well that he could run lines from distant parts together in a seamless English fabric.[28] Surely it is risky and a little irreverent to conclude that Chaucer found something overblown in need of deflation. His recourse to the *Teseida* was too frequent; his emulation of its verbal fabric, his imitation of its scenes and its main action are too elaborate. He must have found something worthy of study and of representation in English.

We are not inclined to let Chaucer's extraordinary use of the *Teseida* speak in this way because we are inclined to think of the *Teseida* itself as a baggy monster. In Volpi's literary history, the statement that Boccaccio's poem is "youthful" and "minor" joins forces with the more specific charge that it is a failed epic. But unlike its companion, this second accusation was not very old in 1898. I can trace it back about thirty years, into the 1860s. This relative newness raises a number of interesting questions, for if we consider the accusation together with the date of its appearance, it begins to look like a critical opinion that characterizes the critic better than the object of criticism. It has a lot in common with the familiar nineteenth-century statements about classical antiquity and the translation of classical literature that valued "reconstruction" over parodic transformation or creative reformation. Modern versions of the classical poems, like dioramas in the new archaeological museums, should be faithful as far as possible to the effects of the original on the original audience.[29] Matthew Arnold gave this proposition one of its most circumspect and influential expressions near the beginning of his essay "On Translating Homer":

> No one can tell how Homer affected the Greeks; but there are those who can tell (the translator) how Homer affects *them*. These are scholars; who possess, at the same time with knowledge of Greek, adequate poetical taste and feeling. No translation will seem to them of much worth compared with the original; but they alone can say whether the translation produced more or less the same effect upon them as the original.[30]

These literary values, with their odor of the academy and the excavation pit, are manifest in Volpi's assumptions as well, while the aims and situation Arnold imagines for his translator of Homer accord perfectly with those Volpi has imagined for Boccaccio. In neither is there enthusiasm for imitative strategies involving transformation; indeed neither shows much interest in the question of imitative strategies at all. It is taken for granted that the reconstruction of ancient forms must be the first aim and justification of the enterprise.

The confidence Volpi shows ("it is hardly necessary to point out . . .") derives in part from an authoritative critical tradition that had grown up before him in the 1860s and 1870s. An early expression can be found in the German medievalist Marcus Landau, whose *Giovanni Boccaccio: His Life and His Works* appeared in 1877, was reprinted in 1880, and was translated into Italian by 1881. Landau had made the same assumption and had reached the same dissatisfied conclusion we have seen in Volpi's essay published twenty years later. His analysis of Boccaccio's use of epic conventions comes to a dramatic climax with the subject of the pagan gods, where Boccaccio's failure to reproduce the dignity, the *gravitas,* of a classical model is especially evident: "Even stranger than the heroes of the poem is its machinery. Boccaccio . . . disdained the elves and dwarfs, the magic spears and impenetrable armor of the chivalric romances, employing instead the gods of the Greeks and the Romans. But just as his Emilia is not a Helen, and his Palamon is not an Achilles, so too his gods are not the gods of Homer." [31] Landau worked in the generation of Boccaccisti that included Attilio Hortis and Gustav Koerting and Francesco Macrì-Leone. In this distinguished company, he stands out more for his critical panache than for his care with primary sources, characteristics evident here in his references to Homer. [32] Homer for Landau was the great epic poet as he was for Landau's century, so that failing to reproduce the "spirit" of epic can be stated the more vigorously with reference to Homer. But it is not quite accurate—I almost said fair—to suggest that Boccaccio's sense of epic machinery might derive from Homer's epics, because Boccaccio did not have full access to Homer's works in Greek. Still, the most interesting feature in this passage is Landau's assumption in the first place that we should expect Boccaccio's gods to be like the gods of a pre-Christian author.

A brief challenge to this assumption throws its special dimensions into higher relief: the problematics of imitation are not examined here with reference to Boccaccio's literary culture in the fourteenth century, only with reference to that of the classical models themselves as Landau understands them. Landau does not consider either the possibility that Boccaccio transformed his classical model in some way (perhaps Boccaccio disapproved of that model) or the possibility that the model itself may have appeared somewhat different in the fourteenth century than it did in the nineteenth. The presence of fictions about pagan gods was in fact a subject of concern to the literary culture of Boccaccio's day, with certain quarters arguing that any cultivation of such subjects was quite undesirable. Boccaccio himself stood on the other side of the argument, defending the usefulness of classical fables when they are presented in certain ways, but even in doing so he suggested that his feeling for the "spirit" of the gods of Homer was more characteristic of his own time than of Landau's: "Yet without question poets do say in their works that there are many gods, when there is but One. But they should not therefore be charged with falsehood, since they neither believe nor assert it as a fact, but only as a myth or a fiction, according to their wont" (*Genealogie deorum gentilium* 14.13). [33] Classical fables of the gods, though they do not represent literal truth, may nevertheless serve as morally instructive examples of behavior and misbehavior, and they may teach through allegorical representation of physical, moral, or historical truths: if this is

Boccaccio's model of the "gods of Homer," Boccaccio's imitation of it may not be as aberrant as Landau believed.

If Landau's approach to the *Teseida* reflects a general tendency in the way later nineteenth-century scholarly writers approached the subject of translation and imitation, it may not be possible to trace his assumptions to earlier remarks on the *Teseida*. But as with so much Italian literary history in this period, there is precedent in the writings of Francesco De-Sanctis. Those assumptions had appeared in print several years before Landau's *Giovanni Boccaccio* and were certainly known to him. De-Sanctis had begun his monumental history of Italian literature in the 1860s and had issued a significant excerpt, covering Boccaccio's "minor" works, in the Florentine journal *Nuova Antologia* in 1870. One passage is especially pertinent:

> The success of the *Filocolo* raised the young man's aspirations
> for a higher flight; he thought about something like the *Aeneid*,
> and wrote the *Teseida*. But nothing was further from his nature
> than the epic genre, nothing further from the age than the sound
> of the trumpet. Here you have assaults, battles, conspiracies of
> gods and men, pompous descriptions, and artificial speeches,
> the whole structure and appearance of a heroic poem. But no
> feeling of true grandeur enters into its bourgeois spirit; and The-
> seus and Arcite and Palamon and Hippolyta and Emilia have
> nothing epic about them except their clothing.[34]

DeSanctis saw in all of Boccaccio's "early romances" an attempt "to fuse those two elements found in Italian society, the ancient and the modern," but a failure to unite them, so that the mixture of medieval romance and classical epic form in the *Teseida* was "more a parody" of the form than a reproduction of its "seriousness and weight."

Nourished by this critical assessment of the poem's design, the debate grew concerning Boccaccio's sources for the *Teseida*, for if Boccaccio had forced a medieval story and characters into the classical literary structure, it seemed likely that a medieval source for the story of Palamon and Arcite would come to light. The hypothesis proved to be fruitful; though no such source was in fact discovered, the debate centered on those characteristics of the assumed source thought to be evident in the language of the *Teseida* itself, and these arguments led to the single most enduring study of the poem made in the nineteenth century. It was contained in Vincenzo Crescini's *Contribution to Research on Boccaccio*, published ten years after Landau's book and seven years after the compendious work of similar title by Landau's compatriot Gustav Koerting: *Boccac-cio's Life and Works*.[35] Crescini, like Volpi after him, wrote about the *Teseida* with admirable lucidity as well as erudition, but unlike Volpi he addressed scholars rather than the well-read general public, and therefore conceived his remarks as a formal argument, thoroughly documented. His clear exposition leaves no doubt of the close relations between his critical assessment of the *Teseida* as an epic and the question of the poem's sources.

In a long appendix entitled "Notes on the Sources of the *Teseida*," Crescini traced arguments as far back as Tyrwhitt's second edition of Chaucer (1798) and Baldelli's *Life of Boccaccio* (1806), which had maintained variously that Boccaccio invented the main action himself, that he had borrowed it from a Byzantine source, and that he had borrowed it from a French source. Crescini is especially interested in the second hypothesis, which had recently been argued by Koerting: "Two scholars who labored to establish that the *Teseida* reflects, though perhaps indirectly, a Greek source, were Ebert and Koerting, with whose position Zumbini seems not to be in disagreement." Landau was on the fence, but leaning toward the French side: "Landau notes that the true heroes of the *Teseida*, Palamon and Arcite, had not been made known by any other, earlier, work, and owe their existence to our poet alone, but then he adds that it is also probable that he imitated or drew on some lost French poem, agreeing in this conjecture with Sandras."[36] Crescini now attacks the evidence proposed by Koerting for a Greek source, demonstrating that the descriptive passages in the *Teseida* that Koerting had advanced as evidence could all be traced directly to Statius's *Thebaid*. In the process of refuting Koerting, Crescini established once and for all that Boccaccio had imitated the *Thebaid* closely in several extensive passages of the *Teseida* and in the general design of *Teseida* 1, 2, and 12. The work was augmented by Savj-Lopez in an essay on the sources of the *Teseida* published in 1900.[37] But Crescini does not resolve the question of a "source" for the story of Palamon and Arcite, the "true heroes" or principal characters in the poem's main action. He falls back on the familiar explanation: this story is so ill-suited to the epic structure of the poem that it probably derived from a medieval source:

> It is nevertheless very clear, I believe, that Boccaccio reworked— if he did not invent—a chivalric story with arrogant literary ambitions [*superba intenzione letteraria*], attempting to make in the footsteps of Vergil and Statius, an epic poem. . . . We see that here, as in his other works, Boccaccio tends to dress modern

content in classical garb, which he draws from his beloved Latin
authors. Thus we have the story of Arcite and Palamon with the
machinery of ancient epic: sacrifices to the gods, divine intervention, catalogs of heroes, and battles like those in the *Aeneid* and
the *Thebaid*. Because Boccaccio's knowledge of antiquity was
imperfect, however, his sense of the ancient less than complete,
and because . . . of the disposition and taste of his public . . . a
strange conflict appears between the two elements, which he was
incapable of uniting: the classic, that is, and what I would call
the romantic.[38]

Crescini has been more careful than Landau in identifying Boccaccio's
models as specifically Latin epics, but he has followed the literary historians of the previous decades in his judgment that the poem fails to reproduce the effects of those models. In an essay that otherwise maintains
for a reader today much of its original brilliance, the confident assertion
that his age understands the classical spirit better than Boccaccio's had
gives Crescini's conclusion an amusingly archaic ring. He says that Boccaccio's "imperfect knowledge of antiquity" and the "contemporary
taste" of his audience led him to mix classical form with a chivalric tale of
love. "This disharmony constitutes a fatal flaw [*un difetto gravissimo*] for
us, who have a mature historical sense and a more sharply defined set of
aesthetic criteria." In the century of Schliemann and Grimm, which had
seen the emergence of newly scientific discipline in the fields of archaeology and philology, such confidence must have seemed fully justified to
Crescini. But its pertinence to the question at hand continues to depend
on the assumption that Boccaccio, in adopting epic conventions, intended
to reconstruct an epic faithful to the classical norms in the manner of the
archaeological reconstructions of Crescini's own time.[39]

So it appears that Volpi's discussion of the *Teseida* in a scholarly publication directed at the well-read general public summed up several decades of learned debate and assessment. Because he argues the case that
Boccaccio tried and failed to do what Vergil and Statius had done by
pointing to the features in the *Teseida* that support this assumption, it is
useful to examine Volpi's statement in extenso:

With the *Teseida*, Boccaccio had the idea of giving Italy a vernacular poem that would be what the *Aeneid* and the *Thebaid*
had been for the Romans. Its divisions into twelve books, the
solemnity of its invocation, the catalog of heroes, the intervention of the pagan gods, and the descriptions of battles and feasts

would clearly demonstrate this, even if the author himself did
not say it in these verses from the final book:

Poi che le Muse nude cominciaro
nel cospetto degli uomini ad andare,
già fur di quelli i quai l'esercitaro
con bello stilo in onesto parlare,
e altri in amoroso l'operaro;
ma tu, o libro, primo a lor cantare
di Marte fai gli affanni sostenuti
nel volgar lazio più mai non veduti.
                                         (12.84)[40]

We hear in these words the echo of a passage in the *De vulgari
eloquentia*. Dante, in book 2, chapter 2 of that treatise, says that
there are three main subjects to be celebrated by those who
cultivate the high vernacular: arms, love, and rectitude; and after
citing Cino da Pistoia as a poet of love and himself as a poet of
rectitude, he adds "Arma vero nullum latium adhuc invenio po-
etasse" (I find that so far no Italian has sung of arms). Boccaccio
alludes with *onesto parlare* to the bard of rectitude, and with
amoroso to the bard of love; he then concludes that he is the
first to entrust to the *volgar lazio* the "labors of Mars"—and his
recourse to the word *latium*, used by Dante in the sense of "Italian," is not without purpose. Arms, while giving his work
novelty, also conferred on it the characteristics of epic.

These observations on the envoy lead to the critical view of the *Teseida*
that I have been calling the nineteenth-century consensus:

It is unnecessary to point out that he was deluding himself, if he
thought he had attained his goal. His learning and culture were
not of the sort that would permit him to compose a true epic
according to the classical models. As was already the case in
French literature, the matter of antiquity came to be transvested
and transformed [in the *Teseida*]. . . . A love story makes up . . .
the substance of the poem (cf. 1 stanza 5). Two friends become
rivals in love, they have a scuffle, but the fight is interrupted and
postponed, the duel converted into a joust. . . . This is the skeletal outline, one more suited to a novella than a long poem,
which Boccaccio fleshed out as best he could to give it the majestic shape of an epic.[41]

Boccaccio's open imitation of the minor forms of epic ("its invocation, the catalog of heroes") is without doubt one of the most prominent features of the *Teseida,* along with the poem's division into twelve books on the pattern of the Latin epics; and the envoy certainly echoes *De vulgari eloquentia.* But has Volpi not rushed to the conclusion that Boccaccio therefore intended to write a poem with a martial subject just like the classical epics? *Talis qualis?* The passage in *De vulgari eloquentia* to which Boccaccio alludes is concerned with the subjects suitable for poetry in the vernacular, "love, moral rectitude, and arms." Although Dante's word "arma" (replaced in the *Teseida* by "Marte") alludes further to the tradition of Vergil's *Aeneid* and its subject ("Arma virumque"), Dante in *De vulgari* is only describing subjects or "argumenta," not genres, and the one poem he cites as an example of a vernacular work treating of "arma," Bertran de Born's "Non posc mudar," certainly does not resemble a classical epic.[42] Volpi has arrived at his conclusion by putting two observations together: first he points to Boccaccio's declaration that "you, my book, are the first to make [the Muses] sing the long labors of Mars" (12.84); and then he notes the formal resemblance of the *Teseida* to the classical Latin epics, concluding that Boccaccio "had the idea of giving Italy a vernacular poem that would be what the *Aeneid* and the *Thebaid* had been to the Romans." The unacknowledged assumption in Volpi's argument concerns the nature of Boccaccio's imitative act. Looking at the same evidence with Volpi, could we not conclude that the "love story," which he believes betrays its epic aspirations, represents the subject of "Mars" in a different way than Vergil and Statius had done? The envoy itself would admit such an interpretation as well as Volpi's.

There is considerable evidence that readers of the *Teseida* before the nineteenth century did *not* interpret the envoy as Volpi does and did not share his assumption about the nature of Boccaccio's imitative design. If we trace the topic back through the critical history of the *Teseida,* we discover that concern over its "inappropriate" main action was not expressed frequently before the later nineteenth century and seems never to have been a focus of criticism of the poem's design. There may be a hint of it in Mazzuchelli's report (1762) that "Bernardo Tasso held the opinion that Boccaccio used the title *Teseida* inappropriately" [*così poco giudiciosamente*] because it referred to an episode in the poem, not its main action. But this opinion, which was reprinted in the Camposampiero edition of the *Teseida* (1821), appears only as part of a general assessment of Boccaccio's work.[43] Mazzuchelli immediately qualifies it with general praise: "It has been judged [Boccaccio's] greatest poem by Abbot

Antonio-Maria Salvini, full of literary beauties and judicious diction, such as are not encountered elsewhere." The major concern of Salvini, echoed by the publishers of the 1821 edition, is the poor state of Boccaccio's text in printed editions, and it is to this state of affairs that any negative assessments of the work might be referred.[44] Baldelli, whose *Life of Giovanni Boccaccio* (1806) dedicates several pages to the *Teseida,* mentions nothing about conflict between the poem's main action and its classical form, though he too laments the unhappy state of its text, "available to be read only in rare printings, spoiled and incorrect, it is known only to a few lovers of vernacular poetry, for whom thereby it loses not a little of its intrinsic value."[45]

Such reputation as the *Teseida* enjoyed in the Counter-Reformation period and eighteenth century rested principally on Boccaccio's fame as the inventor of ottava rima and the *Teseida*'s place at the beginning of the tradition of Italian chivalric epics, from Boiardo to Tasso. The association of the *Teseida* with these romance epics goes back to the Renaissance. Even the Aristotelian critic Trissino (1478–1555), who had strong reservations about the departures from classical decorum evident in these poems, praised Boccaccio's *Teseida* as the origin of their characteristic verse form and as an influence on the development of this literary tradition. In doing so, he comments explicitly on the envoy to the *Teseida,* and his remarks afford a fascinating contrast to those of Volpi. In his *Poetics,* Trissino drew attention to Boccaccio's envoy and also to its source in Dante's *De vulgari eloquentia,* but he takes the implications of Boccaccio's reference to "Mars" rather differently than Volpi was to do three centuries later:

> And because no one had written of arms in our language up to
> the time in which he was living (as Dante says in his book on
> eloquence in the vernacular languages), Giovanni Boccaccio de-
> cided to treat again this part [*parve a Giovanni Boccaccio
> trattare ancora questa parte*] and he discovered ottava rima, in
> which he composed his "Palamon and Arcite." This ottava rima,
> in fact, . . . has been used by almost everyone who has written
> on the subject of arms, and that is, by Pulci, by Boiardo, by
> Ariosto, and so on.[46]

The association made here is not with the subject of arms as presented in the classical epics, but in "Pulci, Boiardo, and Ariosto," who had transformed the model while imitating it. Trissino, far from censuring Boccaccio for claiming to sing of arms in the "Palamon and Arcite," associated him with the later Italian poets who had transformed classical epic by adding "love" to "arms" as the declared subjects of their narrative poems. In his *Discorsi* (1594), with reference to the *Teseida*, Tasso would argue that "amor," like "arma," was a suitable subject for heroic verse.

I have translated Trissino's comment that Boccaccio decided to treat *again* this subject of arms, though the original might be better represented with "it occurred to him to treat *also* or *even* of arms," because the context of Trissino's remark clearly indicates that "arms" are not to be understood as the only subject of the *Teseida*. By likening the *Teseida* to such works "on the subject of arms" as the *Orlando innamorato* and the *Orlando furioso,* he implies that he understood Boccaccio's "Mars" to be one subject among others; and the envoy itself certainly allows this interpretation, especially if it is read together with Boccaccio's invocation at the beginning of the *Teseida*.

In his invocation, Boccaccio calls on "Mars," "Venus," and "Cupid," as well as the Muses (1.1–3). He adds a gloss to explain these mythological allusions, referring to the "poetic language" of the poem with the schoolmasterly tone of a Servius, as if to remind his slower readers of the obvious fact that the pagan gods have no reality and are only useful fictions: "Because [the poet] must deal with battles and with love, he invokes simultaneously the help of Mars, who, according to the ancient pagans, was god of battles, and Venus, the mother of love, and Cupid, that is, love" (in 1.3). The invocation corresponds faithfully to the narrative that follows, for it concerns a rivalry in love that leads to a fierce, if not always solemn, battle. Moreover, the two pagan gods here invoked as representatives of the subjects "love" and "war" will have prominent roles in the poetic fictions of the narrative itself, with accompanying glosses there to explain what the fictions mean in terms of human behavior and its motivating passions. If we turn to the envoy again and assume that Boccaccio was aware of the subject he has just written about, it becomes difficult to conclude with Volpi that the poet is asserting he has written a poem intended to match the martial "spirit" of a classical epic:

Since the time that the bare Muses began
to walk in view of mankind,
they have already been possessed by some
who exercised them in moral composition,
with beautiful style; others have worked them
in love poetry; but you, my book, are the first
to make them sing the long labors of Mars,
never before seen in the vernacular of Italy.

Strictly speaking, the poet only claims to have been the first to make the Muses sing of wars in Italian verse, not the first to make them sing of Mars alone. Neither does he say he is the first to sing of Mars just as Vergil and Statius had done. The relations between the *Teseida* and classical epic are suggested, as they are by Boccaccio's use of the minor forms of epic throughout the *Teseida,* but they are not defined as narrowly as Volpi believes. Perhaps Trissino's approach is the more satisfactory: the envoy may mean that the *Teseida* has "love and moral rectitude" as its subject, and even "arms" as well.

The earliest writings that mention the *Teseida* and its classical sources are as free from Volpi's concern as is Trissino in the *Poetics*. A commentary on Boccaccio's poem, apparently written in the Regno during the mid-fifteenth century and completely independent of Boccaccio's own glosses, survives in a single manuscript copy now in Paris.[47] It begins with a formal prologue that discusses the style of the *Teseida*. The literary historians of the later nineteenth century who developed the "failed epic" hypothesis did not address the question of Boccaccio's diction, which is notably mixed. And that is to say, it is different from the uniformly high style of diction in the classical epics. The academic prologues of the Middle Ages had included diction, or "style" among the topics that should be investigated in the prologue to any literary work, often introducing their remarks with the formula "quo genere stili utatur (auctor)"[48] and the anonymous commentator on the *Teseida* follows this learned tradition in a full and suggestive passage:

> The title of this book is this: Comedy [of] John Boccaccio, et cet., concerning which: there are four styles of poetic discourse, that is, tragic, comic, satiric, and elegiac. Now tragic is the style that Lucan uses, and Vergil in the *Aeneid,* which begins in happiness and ends in misery; comic is a style for treating continually of base things of diminished status and the like, where he who begins in misery ends up in happiness, as Ovid in the *Metamorphoses;* satiric is a style for treating with repetition, as does Horace or Juvenal; elegiac is a style for treating things in misery, as Boethius does. Concerning this, it could be said that this work treats of all four of these styles in various parts of the book, if you will note them well.[49]

The commentator describes both the styles and the pattern of action (and in the case of comedy the characters as well) for which each is suited. Tragedy, for example, is defined as a conjunction of high style with a pattern of action beginning in happiness and ending in misery. Epics were frequently referred to as "tragedies" in medieval tradition (Chaucer does so at the end of the *Troilus*), primarily because of their formal diction, though the main action of the three great Latin epics, the *Aeneid*, *Thebaid*, and *De bello civili*, could also be described, with some approximation, by the associated pattern of action.[50] What is interesting for present purposes is that a commentator writing in much the same literary culture as Boccaccio himself was inclined, when he took up the question of style in the *Teseida*, not to identify the work as a close imitation of classical epic: the *Teseida* is a "comedy" (despite the obvious contradiction between the application of this term to the poem and the subsequent reference to the "base" social rank of characters in comedies), because the main action of the *Teseida* ends with a marriage. Indeed, though the wheel of fortune turns several times for Palamon and Arcite, both end up in "happiness" of one sort or another. Moreover, the commentator judges the *Teseida* to be a mixture of "all four of these styles" and enjoins us to pay attention to Boccaccio's use of different styles in different parts of the *Teseida*. It is interesting to note in this regard that early commentaries on Dante's "comedy" often refer to a mixture of "tragic," "comic," and "satiric" elements as well.

The other medieval prologue to the *Teseida* was composed by Pietro Andrea de' Bassi, a scholar in the service of the d'Este of Ferrara. Like the Neapolitan commentary, it dates to the middle of the fifteenth century: unlike the anonymous Neapolitan, de' Bassi makes extensive use of Boccaccio's glosses, which do not, however, include an *accessus* or prologue. In his prologue, de' Bassi lists the topics for investigation as five and does not include "style," though he addresses this topic obliquely in the third place, under "subject." The other four are as follows: (1) author ("Zohanne da certaldo cognominato bochazo . . ."); (2) title ("theseida de le noze de emilia . . ."); (4) the "end to which the author compiled the work" ("so that by his veiled arguments, man might see the mutations of false fortune"); and (5) the "part of philosophy the present book is placed in" ("moral philosophy"). The third topic, the "subject [the author] wants to treat of," is discussed in terms that look directly forward to Trissino: "As regards the third part, we know the author wants to treat of and to be the subject: his presentation of battles, of the power of love, of the effects of Venus, which things mixed with infinite poetic fictions and histories he puts forward most elegantly, with great abundance of proper speech."[51] De' Bassi, like Trissino and the Neapolitan commentator, does not seem to see any incongruity in Boccaccio's design. The intended subjects are wars and also the power of love, not "wars" alone or wars primarily, or as Volpi, Landau, and Crescini assumed, wars in the manner of Vergil and Statius.

There is, of course, common ground in Volpi's view of the *Teseida* and that of the fifteenth-century commentators, for they are all telling us that Boccaccio did to some extent imitate classical epic, but did not reproduce *talis qualis* the features and the "spirit" of classical epic. The big difference is that Volpi assumes Boccaccio was attempting to do just that, while the earlier writers do not. The same thing may be observed in the remarks of the Neapolitan commentator on Boccaccio's envoy at *Teseida* 12.84. In several dense pages, he seeks to illuminate Boccaccio's "poetic" or fictional allusions and references, but he does so with no mention of generic imitation whatsoever. Unfortunately for us, the text used by the commentator was corrupt at lines 12.84.6–7, so that his lemma reads "Ma tucti allibro primo allor cantare / Di Marte fu . . ." rather than "Ma tu, o libro, primo a lor cantare / di Marte fai." For this reason, Boccaccio's reference to his book as the first to treat of "wars" in the vernacular is lost, and the commentator makes what sense he can of the corrupt version. But it is nevertheless clear from his discussion of the lines at the beginning of the envoy that he does not consider the passage to refer to generic models. His principal concern is to elucidate Boccaccio's reference to the Muses: "In these verses and end of his work, the author wants to come to a conclusion, which [the reader does] in these twenty-four verses [i.e., 12.84–86] cited above, where in the first he says 'Poi che le Muse,' to wit, the sciences, 'cominciaro ad conversare colli gienti,' clearly meaning that the said sciences began to be discovered among the people of this world."[52] After a long disquisition on the origins of writing and the branches of philosophy, which Boccaccio refers to as the "Muses" and their "first appearance," the commentator returns to the poet's reference to the Muses as "bare" and to the ways men have "exercised them": "But let us leave the deeds of this wise man and return to that which the author says in the verses quoted above, . . . that when the sciences showed themselves completely and came to be known in the presence of men, there were some who exercised them with beautiful philosophy, and there were others who exercised the said sciences with beautiful and sweet words, and others who dedicated themselves to and made books about love."[53] The Muses here are not the Muses of poetic genres, but all human learning, manifested in the writings of philosophers (who wrote "philosophy") and poets (who composed "with beautiful style and sweet words"). The discussion that follows is based on the corrupt text at 84.6–7 and is itself somewhat ambiguous because of the difficulties presented by that lemma, so that we do not find out exactly how the *Teseida* fits into this scheme. But it is apparent from the discussion of the "Muses" themselves that the subject of the envoy is viewed with regard to the poem's subject or "argument" and its place in the branches of philosophy, rather than its relation to classical rhetorical forms.

If there is a general characterization of the *Teseida* to be found in the early commentaries on the poem, it does not concern its similarity in "spirit" to the classical epics, but the similar difficulties that are presented to the reader by its "poetic fictions." De' Bassi observes this characteristic in his prologue, which is addressed to Niccolò III d'Este: "It pleased you to instruct me, Pieroandrea dei Bassi, long your faithful servant, to expound the obscure text of the said *Theseus* by making keys [*giose*] with which the readers may obtain substance [*cavare sugo*] from their readings; the text, because of the obscurities of its poetic fictions, is difficult to understand." [54] The language is typical of commentaries on classical poetry, particularly works like the Latin epics, which abound with allusions to legend and myth. It is these "poetic fictions" rather than lexical obscurities in the *Teseida* to which de' Bassi draws special attention, and the contemporary Neapolitan commentator makes similar observations in his prologue. [55] Even more conspicuously than de' Bassi, the other commentator takes care in his exposition to repeat and interpret the classical stories mentioned in Boccaccio's text. The sharp contrast between these early references to the classical elements in the *Teseida* and those of the later nineteenth century would be enough to cast doubt on the latter and its assumptions about Boccaccio's imitative design, even if that assumption were not so vulnerable to challenge on its own merits.

The nineteenth-century view of "tension" between the main action of the poem and its imitative form has continued to find expression in the later twentieth century, though it has taken on the characteristics of an accepted commonplace rather than a topic still considered worthy of systematic exposition. And because Chaucer's Knight's Tale is based on the *Teseida,* these commonplace views have also appeared in analyses of the way Chaucer made use of his Italian source. To the Chaucerian branch of this topic I shall return in Chapter 4. A recent echo of the nineteenth-century thesis about the *Teseida* may be heard in the writings of Salvatore Battaglia, the poem's most authoritative modern editor, who may be quoted in place of many others: "More heterogeneous [*più promiscua*] is the structure of the *Teseida* [i.e., than that of the *Filostrato*]. . . . Although the work may aspire to give to Italy a version of heroic poetry of love and war (the war of Theseus against the Amazons), it is transformed along the way into a knightly adventure of love." [56] Criticism of the *Teseida* in recent decades has been distinguished by a number of studies

that show the range of Boccaccio's sources in the poem and the sophistication with which he translates, modifies, and reunites them in its
various episodes.[57] But the nineteenth-century view of Boccaccio's "unhappy" choice of a main action for that imitative design has not been
reconsidered.

Striking as it may be that the early commentators do not support the
nineteenth-century thesis, their different concerns with the poem are even
more useful in mounting a challenge to it. First, the early commentators
give us reason to question Volpi's characterization of Boccaccio's imitative strategy. They certainly do not challenge his initial observation that
Boccaccio has placed the *Teseida* in the epic tradition, that he recalls his
model in the twelve book divisions and the minor forms of epic, from
invocation to envoy. But they decline to read Boccaccio's reference to
"singing of Mars," in the envoy, to mean that he wanted "to do what
Vergil and Statius had done." Trissino actually suggests that Boccaccio
wanted to do with the materials of epic tradition what Boiardo and
Ariosto were to do after him, while the two fifteenth-century prologues
note and approve a mixed diction and an argument one calls a "comedy."
Second, the early commentators place an extraordinary emphasis on
identifying Boccaccio's allusions to mythology and legendary history.
The difference between reading with "dottrina" and without it, says the
anonymous, is like the difference between tasting mustard whole or
ground: with knowledge of the mythographical background, "'l gusto sa
più forte," and in the commentary of the anonymous this knowledge includes traditional figurative meanings of the myths as well as their literal
sense. Identifying "stories" and occasionally conventional interpretations
of these stories is also the most prominent feature in de' Bassi, as it is in
Boccaccio's own notes to the poem from which de' Bassi draws. This pre-
occupation suggests that the rhetorical mechanisms of the *Teseida*, if not
built with an exclusively learned audience in mind, at least require that
serious attention be given to the classical stories behind Boccaccio's story
and their relation to that narrative foreground.

The following chapters pursue the two lines of investigation suggested
by the earliest critical response to the *Teseida*. They take up the problem
of Boccaccio's main action without the prejudicing assumption that Boccaccio necessarily intended to reproduce the spirit of a genre in the manner of Arnoldian translation. They propose an alternate characterization
of Boccaccio's imitative strategy based on his use of learned allusions in
the poem, especially in its formal similes and in its main action. The
much-maligned "romance" in this light appears rather as the creative
transformation of a single epic than as the reevocation of its classical

genre. And finally, they propose that the model of classical epic itself was somewhat different in the fourteenth century from in the nineteenth, and that this difference in the model goes part of the way to explaining the direction of Boccaccio's transformation.

Perhaps the most telling argument from critical history that might be cited in favor of this approach is Volpi's own uncertainty about the origin of that "medieval romance" which he believes to be the ruin of Boccaccio's epic design. If the romance has not been found in medieval sources after a century of investigation, perhaps it is time to look at the classical sources once again. And if the source turns out to be a classical epic, then perhaps the main action of the *Teseida* has more in common with the rhetorical apparatus that adorns it than Volpi—or better the consensus expressed by Volpi, with its narrow definition of imitative procedure— was able to see. In fact, the main action has a source in epic tradition in the same classical epic that Crescini showed to be the source for Boccaccio's introductory books, *Teseida* 1 and 2, but the relation of source to imitation here is analogical rather than direct. It can only be seen if one begins with an understanding of Boccaccio's practice as imitator of Statius that allows the possibility of allusive transformation.[58]

Notes to the Introduction

1. Guglielmo Volpi, *Il Trecento,* in Storia letteraria d'Italia scritta da una società di professori (Milan: Vallardi, 1898). I have used the second edition of 1912, pp. 185–186. The passage is quoted in full below, note 41. The "società di professori" included such prominent figures as Francesco Novati, Nicola Zingarelli, and Angelo Solerti (see below, note 4), who each contributed a volume to the Storia letteraria. The series has had an important place in Chaucer criticism, for W. P. Ker (1912) seems to have read Volpi, and Pratt (1948) relied on his successor, Natalino Sapegno (*Il Trecento,* in Storia letteraria d'Italia nuova edizione [Milan: Vallardi, 1933; 2d ed. 1955]). On the Chaucerians, see here below, Chapter 4.

2. For example, in W. P. Ker's Clark Lecture of 1912, "Chaucer and the Renaissance," where the characteristic word "novella" reappears: "The *Teseide* is really a short novel of the French type enormously magnified and diversified into the likeness of an epic." I quote from W. P. Ker, *Form and Style in Poetry* (London: Macmillan, 1928), p. 71.

3. For the text of Petrarch's letter, see the edition in J. Burke Severs, *The Literary Relationships of Chaucer's "Clerk's Tale"* (New Haven: Yale University Press, 1942), pp. 254–292. The full passage in Boccaccio's eclogue is as follows:

> [CALIOPES]   Non ego te vidi pridem vulgare canentem
> in triviis carmen, misero plaudente popello?
> [ARISTEUS]   Vidisti, fateor. Non omnibus omnia semper

sunt animo. Puero carmen vulgare placebat.
. . . Ast nunc
altior est etas, alios que monstrat amores.

Buccolicum carmen 12.48–53, ed. A. F. Massèra, *Opere latine minori* (Bari: Laterza, 1928), p. 57. In the passage, Boccaccio has worked a variation on Vergil's "miserum carmen" of *Eclogue* 3.27. Janet Levarie Smarr, *Giovanni Boccaccio, Eclogues* (New York: Garland, 1987), translates "vulgar song" but notes the traditional understanding of the passage as a reference to vernacular song.

4. Coluccio Salutati, *Epistolario*, ed. Francesco Novati, vol. 3 (Rome: Tipografia del Senato, 1891), xxv; Filippo Villani, in *Le Vite di Dante Petrarca e Boccaccio scritte fino al secolo XVI*, ed. Angelo Solerti (Milan: Vallardi, 1909), p. 675: "Extant et quamplura eius opuscula vulgari edita sermone . . . in quibus lascivientis iuventutis ingenio paulo liberius evagatur, quae, cum senuisset, ipse putavit silentio transigenda; sed non potuit, ut optaverat, verbum emissum semel ad pectora revocare, neque ignem quem flabello excitaverat, sua voluntate restinguere."

5. The preceding paragraph follows the arguments of Giuseppe Petronio's history of critical response to the *Decameron* in Walter Binni, ed., *I Classici italiani nella storia della critica*, vol. 1 (Florence: La Nuova Italia, 1960), esp. pp. 173–177.

6. Boccaccio was twenty-six or twenty-seven years old; see Vittore Branca, *Giovanni Boccaccio: Profilo biografico* (Florence: Sansoni, 1977), pp. 5–8 on the date of his birth; pp. 48–49 and n. 15 on the probable date of the *Teseida*'s composition. The *Profilo* appears in a slightly shorter version in Giovanni Boccaccio, *Tutte le Opere*, ed. Vittore Branca, vol. 1 (Milan: Mondadori, 1967), pp. 3–203.

7. For the Latin text, see *Opere latine minori,* pp. 118–124; and for the date of composition, pp. 313–314. On Boccaccio's manuscript of the *Thebaid* with Lactantius's commentary, see here below, Chapter 1, note 1.

8. On the conventional nature of Boccaccio's concluding request for a copy of Lactantius's commentary, see Giuseppe Billanovich, *Restauri boccacceschi,* 2d printing (Rome: Edizioni di Storia e Letteratura, 1947), pp. 69–78.

9. A. E. Quaglio, "Prima fortuna della glossa garbiana a *Donna me prega* del Cavalcanti," *Giornale storico della letteratura italiana* 141 (1964): 346–348. Quaglio (p. 347 n. 1) and Giuseppe Billanovich, *Prime Ricerche dantesche* (Rome: Edizioni di Storia e Letteratura, 1947), p. 28, suggest the possibility that not only the glosses but also the poetic text were composed in Florence after 1341. Among the features associating the poem with Florence are references to the city in glosses on 1.60, 4.12, 6.52; the name Emilia (see Billanovich, *Restauri,* pp. 119–127), and the quotation from Del Garbo in the gloss on the temple of Venus. To them might be added the theme of fraternal strife itself. In the *Trattatello in laude di Dante*, Boccaccio will cite the conflict between Polynices and Eteocles as an emblem for the rivalry between factions in the city of Florence (ed. Pier Giorgio Ricci, in *Tutte le Opere*, vol. 6, p. 464). But there is no reason to assume that Florentine affairs held no interest for Boccaccio before 1341.

10. James McGregor, "Boccaccio's Athenian Theater: Form and Function of an Ancient Monument in *Teseida*," *Modern Language Notes* 99 (1984), esp. 25–26. On revising the date of the Zibaldone Magliabechiano, or at least part of it, to the early 1340s, see Giorgio Padoan, "Petrarca, Boccaccio, e la scoperta delle Canarie," *Italia medioevale e umanistica* 7 (1964): 263–277. Many of the works copied in the second half of the codex may be associated with Boccaccio's Neapolitan period: see Aldo Maria Costantini, "Studi sullo Zibaldone Magliabechiano," *Studi sul Boccaccio* 7 (1973): 21–58; 8 (1974): 79–126; and especially 10 (1977–1978): 255–275. In a paper given at the New Chaucer Society Congress in Philadelphia in 1986, William Coleman announced that his examination of the manuscript tradition revealed three stages in the growth of Boccaccio's glosses, with the holograph (and therefore all recent editions) representing the last and fullest version. It will be interesting to see whether the Florentine references appear among the primitive glosses, or only in their final elaboration.

11. Florence, Biblioteca Medicea-Laurenziana, MS Acquisti e Doni 325. For a description, see *Mostra di manoscritti, documenti e edizioni*, Sesto Centenario della morte di Giovanni Boccaccio, (Certaldo: A cura del Comitato promotore 1975), vol. 1, pp. 32–33 and plate I. On the development of Boccaccio's hand, see Pier Giorgio Ricci, "Studi sulle opere latine e volgari del Boccaccio," *Rinascimento* 10 (1959): 3–21; and Ricci's essay in Vittore Branca and Pier Giorgio Ricci, *Un Autografo del Decameron* (Padua: CEDAM, 1962), 49ff. On the date of MS Acquisti e Doni 325, see A. C. de la Mare, *The Handwriting of Italian Humanists* (London: Oxford University Press, 1973–), p. 27 and n. 9. The description in *Mostra di manoscritti* is more cautious, giving the date as 1340–1350. See now also Edvige Agostinelli, "A Catalogue of the Manuscripts of *Il Teseida*," *Studi sul Boccaccio* 15 (1985–1986): 17–19.

12. *Amorosa visione*, ed. Vittore Branca, in *Tutte le Opere*, vol. 3, pp. 651–652.

13. Santorre DeBenedetti, "Per la Fortuna della *Teseide* e del *Ninfale Fiesolano*," *Giornale storico della letteratura italiana* 60 (1912): 259–264; Giuseppe Corsi, ed., *Rimatori del Trecento* (Turin, 1969), pp. 83ff.; F. Gaeta and R. Spongano, eds. Gianotto Calogrosso, *Nicolosa bella* (Bologna, 1959), p. 52. See also Branca, *Profilo*, p. 49, n. 15.

14. Giovanni Boccaccio, *De casibus virorum illustrium*, ed. Vittorio Zaccaria, *Tutte le Opere*, vol. 9, p. 856. "Me adhuc adolescentulo versanteque Roberti . . . in aula" and note, p. 1060.

15. *Genealogie deorum gentilium libri* 15.10, ed. Vincenzo Romano (Bari: Laterza, 1951), vol. 2, p. 776; translated by Charles G. Osgood, *Boccaccio on Poetry*, 2d ed. (New York: Liberal Arts Press, 1956), 131–132. The "famous master" to whom Boccaccio refers was no doubt a canon lawyer, one of the many associated with the famous Neapolitan Studio and Robert's court, but it is worth noting as regards Boccaccio's legal training that Cino da Pistoia lectured on civil law in Naples in 1330 and 1331, at which time he struck up a friendship with the young Boccaccio. See Francesco Sabatini, *Napoli angioina: Cultura e società* (Naples: Edizioni Scientifiche Italiane, 1975), p. 57, on Cino's year in Naples. (Sabatini's brilliant essay is also

available in vol. 4 of the same publisher's *Storia di Napoli*.) Billanovich has suggested that Boccaccio's "nearly six years" of legal study should be identified as lasting from 5 October (the beginning of the academic year) 1335 until the end of the academic year in June 1341. Boccaccio would therefore have completed the usual six years of study for a degree in canon law, but would have left without taking his doctorate (Giuseppe Billanovich, *Petrarca letterato* [Rome: Edizioni di Storia e Letteratura, 1947], pp. 72–73; cf. Branca, *Profilo*, p. 51).

Many of the writings of Boccaccio's teachers and associates at the court of Robert the Wise have yet to be published in modern editions. Sabatini's study is based in part on manuscript sources, and its great value suggests the rewards that await future investigators. Able summaries of the secondary literature may be found in Giorgio Padoan, "Boccaccio e la rinascita dello stile bucolico," in *Giovanni Boccaccio: Editore e interprete di Dante*, ed. Società dantesca italiana (Florence: Olschki, 1979), esp. pp. 36–47, and David Wallace, *Chaucer and the Early Writings of Boccaccio* (Woodbridge, Suffolk: Boydell and Brewer, 1985), pp. 23–38.

16. Boccaccio expresses his regret at having to leave Naples in a letter to Niccolò Acciaiuoli, written in Florence on 23 August 1341 (epistola V, ed. Massèra, *Opere latine minori*, pp. 125–126). Thus we may be certain that he returned to Florence by late August, though the date of his departure from Naples is uncertain. See Branca, *Profilo*, 51–55 and Billanovich, *Petrarca letterato*, pp. 72–73; but Branca's arguments for a departure in winter or early spring are convincing (pp. 51–52).

17. Émile G. Léonard, *Les Angevins de Naples* (Paris: Presses Universitaires de France, 1954), which I have used in the (slightly augmented) translation of R. Liguori, *Gli Angioini di Napoli* (Varese: dall'Oglio, 1967), pp. 261–423. Cf. Robert Davidsohn, *Geschichte von Florenz*, vol. 2, pt. 2 (Berlin: Mittler, 1908), pp. 1–151 on the seigniory of Robert's son Charles. Florence had particularly close relations with Naples in the early fourteenth century, her merchant bankers providing Robert with loans and trade while Robert provided Florence with military and diplomatic support in the struggle against the empire. Boccaccio's father was head of the Neapolitan branch of the important Bardi banking house from the late 1320s until about 1338. These relations were closest during the years of Boccaccio's residence in Naples. In 1325, threatened by Ludwig of Bavaria, the Florentines invited Duke Charles of Calabria, Robert's son and heir, to take control of their city. He accepted on 8 January 1326. At first his power was vested in a lieutenant, one Walter of Brienne, known as the "duke of Athens," but Charles himself came to Florence with a large following that same year and stayed through much of 1327. See Léonard, *Gli Angioini*, pp. 308–310. Charles died at age thirty-one in 1328.

18. *Paradiso* 8.147. Dante has Charles Martel say that Robert is better suited to preaching than to governing, referring to Robert's custom of delivering a short speech, organized around a scriptural passage, when he appeared at public ceremonies. But Robert wrote laws as well as sermons: see Walter W. Goetz, *König Robert von Neapel* (Tübingen: J. C. B. Mohr, 1910), pp. 46ff. for a list of the 289 sermons that survive; and Romualdo Trifone,

La Legislazione angioina (Naples: L. Lubrano 1921), pp. 156–282, for the 107 laws Robert is known to have written. He seems also to have been a good administrator: see Léonard, *Gli Angioini*, pp. 339ff. Petrarch called him the "most illustrious king in Europe" (*Familiares* 4.2, 12.2, 12.7), dedicated the *Africa* to him, wanted Robert to crown him poet laureate, and wrote a moving eulogy after his death (eclogue 2, the "Argos"). Boccaccio praised him for keeping his lands at peace "with the help of Pallas" (*Filocolo* 1.1.14; *Fiammetta* 2.6.21), and remarked that "he made of himself a king whose superior in learning men have not seen since Solomon" (*Genealogie* 14.9). On the fate of Robert's library, see now Luciano Gargan, "Per la Biblioteca di Giovanni Conversini," in *Vestigia: Studi in onore di Giuseppe Billanovich*, ed. Rino Avesani, Mirella Ferrari, et al. (Rome: Edizioni di Storia e Letteratura, 1984), pp. 365–385.

19. ". . . around 1300 Florence was a center of interest in classical studies . . . even though she was unusually poor in classical texts . . . [and] it was the wandering Dominicans like Trevet as well as resident notaries like Brunetto who helped to make her learning less provincial" (Charles T. Davis, "Ptolemy of Lucca and the Roman Republic," in *Dante's Italy and Other Essays* [Philadelphia: University of Pennsylvania Press, 1984], p. 267; see the same author's remarks in Charles T. Davis, "Education in Dante's Florence," *Speculum* 40 [1966]: esp. 417–419). Without wishing to overstate the relative poverty of Florentine libraries, one notes that Naples contained remarkably large and catholic collections in the royal library, the libraries of the religious orders, and those associated with the Studio. See Sabatini, *Napoli angioina*, pp. 66ff., and Fausto Ghisalberti's remarks on the references used by Paolo di Perugia ("Paolo di Perugia: Commentatore di Persio," *Rendiconti del Istituto lombardo . . .* 2d ser. 62 [1929]: esp. 541ff.) for some indication of the royal library's holdings.

20. Boccaccio calls him "il reverendo mio padre e signore maestro Dionigi" (my reverend father and lord, Master Dionigi) in a letter of 1341, written shortly after Dionigi's death (*Opere latine minori*, ed. Massèra, p. 126). Branca (*Profilo*, p. 37) remarks of Dionigi's importance to the young Boccaccio, "dovette, fra il '37 a il '40, essere per il Boccaccio non solo il persuasore a Seneca e a Sant'Agostino, ma veramente il maestro e la 'speranza' dell'anima, come [Boccaccio] dichiarava in una epistola (V)" (from '37 to '40, Dionigi not only led Boccaccio through Seneca and Saint Augustine, but truly must have been his master and that "hope" of his soul, to which Boccaccio refers in a letter). On Dionigi, see Rudolf Arbesmann, "Der Augustinereremitenorden und der Beginn der humanistischen Bewegung," *Augustiniana* 14 (1964): 250–314 and 603–639; on the reflections of Dionigi's influence in Boccaccio's early writings, see especially Billanovich, *Restauri*, pp. 57–61; on manuscripts of Dionigi's commentary, see Dorothy M. Schullian, "A Revised List of Manuscripts of Valerius Maximus," in *Miscellanea Augusto Campana* (Padua: Antenore, 1981), pp. 695–728.

21. Alberto Limentani has noted the "anticipation" of Boccaccio's *Genealogie* in the glosses to the *Teseida*. See his introduction to the *Teseida* in *Tutte le Opere*, vol. 2, p. 242.

Boccaccio writes in his *Genealogie* of Paolo di Perugia, "Advanced in

years, of great and varied learning, he was long the librarian of the famous
King Robert of Sicily and Jerusalem. If there was ever a man possessed of
the curiosity of research he was the one. A word from his prince was sufficient to send him hunting through a dozen books of history, fable, or
poetry. . . . He wrote a huge book which he called *The Collections;* it included much matter on various subjects, but particularly his ingatherings of
pagan mythology from Latin authors, together with whatever he could collect on the same subject from the Greeks, probably with Barlaam's help. I
shall never hesitate to acknowledge that when still a youngster . . . I drank
deep of that work. . . . But to the very serious inconvenience of this book of
mine, I found that his saucy wife Biella, after his death, wilfully destroyed
this and many other books of Paul's" (*Genealogie* 15.6; Osgood, p. 114).
On Paolo's life, see Francesco Torraca, "Giovanni Boccaccio a Napoli,"
Archivio storico napoletano 39 (1914): esp. 664. On his surviving works,
see Ghisalberti, "Paolo di Perugia," pp. 535ff. Boccaccio copied a "Geonologie tam hominum quam deorum secundum Paulum de Perusio" into his
early commonplace book, the Zibaldone Magliabechiano (Florence, Biblioteca Nazionale, MS II, II, 327 [now Banco Rari, 50], fols. 110r–114v),
published by Attilio Hortis, *Studi sulle opere latine del Boccaccio* (Trieste:
1879), pp. 525–536. See also Aldo Maria Costantini, "Studi sullo Zibaldone Magliabechiano," *Studi sul Boccaccio* 7 (1973): esp. 53, who suggests that the pages containing the "Geonologie" were copied in Naples
and later inserted into the Zibaldone Magliabechiano.

22. Vittore Branca, *Tradizione delle opere di Giovanni Boccaccio,* vol. 1, *Un
Primo Elenco dei codici e tre studi* (Rome: Edizioni di Storia e Letteratura,
1958), pp. 3–7 and 66–69, lists fifty-three copies of the *Teseida* and fifty-
eight copies of the *Decameron* from the fourteenth and fifteenth centuries.
Branca's three additions to *Tradizione,* published in *Studi sul Boccaccio* 1,
4, and 9, add three fifteenth-century copies of the *Teseida* and two (fragmentary) copies of the *Decameron,* giving totals of fifty-six and sixty. The
numbers change dramatically if we include manuscripts copied in the sixteenth to eighteenth centuries; more than thirty copies of the *Decameron*
have come down to us from these later centuries, fewer than ten of the
Teseida. The fourteenth- and fifteenth-century copies of the *Teseida* are:
Ai, Ar, Bg, CaM, Ch, Cn, L-5, L-2, L-1, L-3, L-4, Aut.Laur., L-8, L-6, A,
L-7, S, M-1, M-2, M-3, M-4, M-5, M-7, M-6, F, P-1, P-2, P-3, Pn, R-1,
R-2, R-3, R-4, R-5, G, Lo, Ma, MA, MA-1, MT, NO, Pr-1, Pr-2, Pr-3, Ph,
RL, RL-1, RN, Si, T, V-3, V-1, V-2, V-4, Vz, VzQ. For descriptions see
now Agostinelli, "The Manuscripts of *Il Teseida.*"

23. Eighty-four copies of the *Canterbury Tales* are known to survive; only
twenty manuscripts of the *Troilus* (and of these, four are short fragments):
Geoffrey Chaucer, *Works,* ed. F. N. Robinson, 2d ed. (Boston: Houghton
Mifflin, 1957), pp. 886–887, 905–906.

24. On French translations of the *Teseida,* see Carla Bozzolo, *Manuscrits des
traductions françaises d'oeuvres de Boccace, XVe siècle* (Padua: Antenore,
1973), esp. pp. 33–37; on the Greek translation, see Enrica Follieri, "La
Versione in greco volgare del *Teseida* del Boccaccio," in *Atti dell'VIII Con-
gresso internazionale di studi bizantini e neoellenici,* (ed. Silvio Giuseppe

Mercati, vol. 7 (Rome: 1953), pt. 1, pp. 66–77, and the note by Charles Astrue, "La *Théséide* de Boccace adaptée en grec vulgaire," *Scriptorium* 5 (1951): 303–304. For the editio princeps (Ferrara, 1475) see below, note 51; the Neapolitan edition (del Tuppo, ca. 1490) is described in *Mostra di manoscritti*, vol. 2, pp. 42–43.

25. Paul F. Watson, "Apollonio di Giovanni and Ancient Athens," *Bulletin of the Allen Memorial Art Museum* 37 (1979–1980): 3–25. The formal tray or salver was painted about 1420 by Mariotto di Nardo and shows Palamon and Arcite in prison looking through a barred window at Emilia (see also Guy de Tervarent, *Les Énigmes de l'art au Moyen Age* [Paris: Editions d'art et d'histoire 1938], pp. 51–53). The same scene appears in the series of beautiful miniatures accompanying a translation of the *Teseida* in French prose that was copied in Anjou about 1460, now in Vienna: Österreichische Nationalbibliothek, Cod. 2617. See Otto Pächt and Dagmar Thoss, *Die illuminierten Handschriften und Inkunabeln der Österreichischen Nationalbibliothek*: Französische Schule I (Vienna: OAW, 1974), pp. 32–37. Other examples appear in the preliminary index for "Boccaccio visualizzato," by Vittore Branca, Victoria Kirkham, and Paul Watson, in *Studi sul Boccaccio* 15 (1985–1986): 121–166.

26. David Anderson, "An Early Reference to Boccaccio's *Teseida*," *Studi sul Boccaccio* 16 (1987), forthcoming.

27. The standard survey by Robert Pratt, "Chaucer's Use of the *Teseida*," *PMLA* 62 (1947): 598–621, has been augmented by Piero Boitani, *Chaucer and Boccaccio*, Medium Aevum Monographs n.s. 8 (Oxford: Society for the Study of Medieval Languages and Literature, 1977) and by Russell A. Peck, *Chaucer's Lyrics and "Anelida and Arcite": An Annotated Bibliography* (Toronto: University of Toronto Press, 1983), pp. 103ff. See below, Chapter 4.

28. Boitani, *Chaucer and Boccaccio*, pp. 50ff.

29. Georges Mounin, *Teoria e storia della traduzione* (Turin: Enaudi, 1965), traces the characteristic distaste for paraphrase and the corresponding exaltation of "integral" translations that reproduce both the sense and the rhetorical features of an original, to Goethe in the *Westöstlicher Diwan* (see pp. 54–56). On experiments with archaism and anachronism in nineteenth-century translation, which reflect the same desire to reproduce the original effects of a literary work, see George Steiner, *After Babel: Aspects of Language and Translation* (London and New York: Oxford University Press, 1975), pp. 341ff. On the exaltation of Greek "originality" over Roman imitation, of Homer over Vergil, in nineteenth-century classical scholarship, see Landau's reference to the Homeric poems as examples of epic par excellence here below (and note 31), and the remarks of Georg N. Knauer, "Vergil's *Aeneid* and Homer," *Greek, Roman and Byzantine Studies* 5 (1964): 61–62.

30. The essay was published in 1896. I quote from a reprint of the 1905 edition, Matthew Arnold, *On Translating Homer*, with introduction and notes by W. H. D. Rouse (London: Murray, 1905; repr. New York: AMS, 1971), pp. 35–36.

31. Marcus Landau, *Giovanni Boccaccio: Sein Leben und seine Werke*, 2d

printing (Stuttgart: J. G. Cotta, 1877), pp. 75–76; translated (with extensive additional notes) by Camillo Antona-Traversi, *Giovanni Boccaccio: Sua Vita e sue opere* (Naples: Del Vaglio, 1881), p. 236. "Noch sonderbarer, als die Helden des Epos, ist seine Maschinerie. Boccaccio, der hier ein antikes Sujet in romantischem Costüm darstellte, benusste nur die olympische Göttermaschinerie. Er verschmähte die Feen und Zwerge, die bezauberten Lanzen und undurchdringlichen Rüstungen der Ritterromane, und fesste nur die Götter der Griechen und Römer in Bewegung. Aber so wie seine Emilie keine Helena, sein Palemon kein Achill ist, so sind auch seine Götter nicht die Homers."

. Bibliographies of the early modern scholarship may be found in Guido Traversari, *Bibliografia boccaccesca* (Città di Castello: Lapi, 1907); and Enzo Esposito, *Boccacciana: bibliografia delle edizioni e degli scritti critici (1939–1974)* (Ravenna: Longo, 1976).

32. See, for example, Landau's attacks on the thesis that the Zibaldone Magliabechiano was written by Boccaccio, as described by Francesco Macrì-Leone, "Il Zibaldone Boccaccesco della Magliabechiana," *Giornale storico della letteratura italiana* 10 (1887): 2–4.

33. Trans. Osgood, in *Boccaccio on Poetry*, p. 65.

34. Francesco DeSanctis, "Il Boccaccio e le sue opere minori," *Nuova Antologia di scienze, lettere ed arti* 14 (1870): 234–235:

> Il successo del Filocolo alzò l'animo del giovane a più alto volo. Pensò qualche cosa, come l'Eneide, e scrisse la Teseide. Ma niente era più alieno della sua natura, che il genere eroico, niente più lontano dal secolo che il suono della tromba. Qui hai assedii, battaglie, congiure di Dei e di uomini, pompose descrizioni, artificiosi discorsi, tutto lo scheletro e l'apparenza di un poema eroico; ma nel suo spirito borghese non entra alcun sentimento di vera grandezza, e Teseo, e Arcita, e Palemone e Ippolita ed Emilia non hanno di epico che il manto.

The metaphors of clothing and of skeletal outlines were to reappear in the writings of Crescini, where they are applied a little differently (see below, note 38).

35. Gustav Koerting, *Boccaccio's Leben und Werke* (Leipzig: Fues, 1880); Vincenzo Crescini, *Contributo agli studi sul Boccaccio, con documenti inediti* (Turin: Loescher, 1887).

36. Crescini, *Contributo*, p. 220.

37. Paolo Savj-Lopez, "Sulle Fonti della *Teseide*," *Giornale storico della letteratura italiana* 36 (1900): 57–78; see also Crescini's later remarks in *Kritischer Jahresbericht über die Fortschritte der romanischen Philologie* 3 (1897): 395 and *Atti del Reale istituto veneto* 60 (1900–1901): 449–457; and Savj-Lopez's *Storie tebane in Italia* (Bergamo: Instituto italiano d'arti grafiche, 1905).

It has since been suggested that the Byzantine epic *Digenis Akritas* may have been an indirect source for the name of Boccaccio's hero and for certain narrative motifs in the *Teseida*: Henry Kahane and Renée Kahane, "Akritas and Arcita: A Byzantine Source of Boccaccio's *Teseida*," *Specu-*

lum 20 (1945): 415–425; and Salvatori Impellizzeri, *Il "Digenis Akritas," l'epopea di Bisanzio,* Studi di lettere, storia e filosofia . . . Scuola Normale superiore di Pisa, 18 (Florence: Sansoni, 1940).

38. Crescini, *Contributo,* pp. 246–247: "Resta invece ben chiaro, mi sembra . . . che il Boccaccio abbia rimaneggiato, se non inventato, un racconto cavalleresco con superba intenzione letteraria, tentando di fare, sull'orme di Vergilio e di Stazio, un poema epico. Così vediamo che domina pur nella *Teseide,* come in altre opere del nostro, la tendenza a vestire di forme classiche, che'egli traeva da' suoi diletti scrittori latini, un contenuto moderno. Per questo abbiamo nella storia di Arcita e Palemone il meccanismo dell'antica epopea: intervento di numi, sacrifizi a' celesti, rassegna di eroi, battaglie, come nella *Eneide* e nella *Tebaide.* Ma, poiché nel Boccaccio era imperfetta la conoscenza e non pieno il senso della antichità, poiché, d'altra parte, lo sforzavano . . . le disposizioni e il gusto del pubblico per il quale scriveva, avveniva che nell'opera sua si producesse un conflitto strano fra i due elementi, che non gli riusciva di comporre, il classico, e, direi quasi, il romantico."

39. For a survey of the literature concerned with reconstruction of the classical past in nineteenth-century Italy, see Piero Treves, *Lo Studio dell'antichità classica nell'Ottocento* (Milan and Naples: Ricciardi, 1962), esp. pp. vii–xlvi.

40. I give the text edited by Alberto Limentani, *Teseida delle nozze di Emilia,* in *Tutte le opere,* vol. 2. Guglielmo Volpi quotes the passage from an unspecified edition, with no significant variants from the modern edition. For my English translation, see p. 17.

41. Guglielmo Volpi, *Il Trecento,* 2d ed. (Milan: Vallardi, 1912), pp. 185–186:

> Il Boccaccio ebbe l'idea di dare colla Teseide all'Italia un poema volgare che fosse quello che era per i Romani l'Eneide e la Tebaide. La divisione in dodici libri, la solennità dell'invocazione, la rassegna degli eroi, l'intervento degli dei pagani, le descrizioni di battaglie e di feste lo proverebbero chiaramente, anche se non ce lo dicesse l'autore stesso in questi versi dell'ultimo libro: [quotes 12.84]. In queste parole si sente l'eco d'un passo del De vulgari eloquentia. Dante nel libro II (cap. 2°) del suo trattato dice che tre cose principalmente erano da celebrarsi dai cultori del volgare illustre: le armi, gli amori e la rettitudine; e dopo aver citato Cino da Pistoia come poeta dell'amore e se stesso come poeta della rettitudine, aggiunge "Arma vero nullum latium adhuc invenio poetasse = Non trovo che alcun italiano abbia finora cantato le armi". Il Boccaccio accenna coll'onesto parlare al cantore della rettitudine e coll'amoroso a quello dell'amore; e quindi conclude che primo affida al "volgar lazio" (non è inutile il ricorrere di questa parola usata da Dante per latinum nel senso di Italiano) le fatiche di Marte. E le armi, mentre gli davan novità, davan anche carattere di poesia epica al suo lavoro.
>
> Inutile dire che egli s'illuse, se credè di aver raggiunto lo scopo. La sua cultura non valse a fargli comporre un poema vero secondo gli

esempj classici. Come già nella letteratura francese, la materia antica
veniva travestita e trasfigurata; anzi quel tanto che il Boccaccio potè
derivare dalla cognizione diretta di alcuni scrittori latini servì solo a
rendere più stridente il contrasto tra i vecchi e i nuovi elementi. . . .
Una storia d'amore è dunque la sostanza del poema (I. stanza 5): Due
amici divengon rivali per amore: si azzuffano, ma la lotta vien tron-
cata e rimandata, e il duello convertito in una giostra. . . . Questo è lo
scheletro, da novella anzi che da poema, che il Boccaccio rivestì più
che potè di polpe, per dargli la figura maestosa dell'epopea.

42. "Circa que sola, si bene recolimus, illustres viros invenimus vulgariter poe-
tasse, scilicet Bertramum de Bornio arma, Arnaldum Danielem amorem,
Gerardum de Bornello rectitudinem. . . . Bertramus etenim ait 'Non posc
mudar c'un cantar non exparia'" (Dante Alighieri, *De vulgari eloquentia,*
ed. P. V. Mengaldo, in *Opere minori,* 2 vols. [Milan and Naples: Ricciardi,
1979], vol. 2, p. 152).

43. G. M. Mazzuchelli, *Gli Scrittori d'Italia,* pt. 3 (Brescia, 1762), repr. in
La Teseide di Giovanni Boccaccio, tratta dal manoscritto del conte Guglielmo Camposampiero, 2 vols. (Venice: Francesco Andreola, 1821), vol. 2,
pp. 329–330.

44. *La Teseide* (1821), vol. 1, p. iv. This publisher's note shows no particular
concern with "tension" between form and content: "Del metro però
adoprato in questo, inventore non fu il Boccaccio, ma quello si fu non-
dimeno, che si servì il primo in componimenti di lunga estensione, e che
diede la prima idea del poema eroico."

45. Giovanni Battista Baldelli, *Vita di Giovanni Boccaccio* (Florence: Ciardetti,
1806), pp. 31–33. His assessment of the poem's place in epic tradition can
be traced to Trissino: "Egli colla Teseide aperse la nobile carriera de' ro-
manzeschi poemi, degli epici, per cui posteriormente tanto sopravanzò l'Italiana ogni altra straniera letteratura" (p. 33 and n. 1). The critical topos
asserting the "sorry state of the text" first appears in the introduction to the
edition of 1528, by Tizzone Gaetano da Pofi, an ally of Trissino in the debates over the regularization of Italian grammar. He had published a "corrected" edition of Boccaccio's *Fiammetta* in 1524. See Ghino Ghinassi,
"Correzioni editoriali di un grammatico cinquecentesco," *Studi di filologia
italiana* 19 (1961): 33–93.

46. "Ma perché fino a l'età sua non furono scritte in questa lingua cose d'arme,
come [Dante] dice nel suo libro de la Volgare Eloquenzia, parve a Giovanni
Boccaccio trattare ancora questa parte, e trovò l'ottava rima, ne la quale
scrisse il suo Arcita e Palemone, le quali ottave rime, senz'alcun dubbio . . .
sono state poi usate da quasi tutti coloro, che hanno scritte in materia
d'arme, cioè dal Pulci, dal Bojardo, da l'Ariosto, e simili" (Giovanni
Giorgio Trissino, *Poetica,* pt. 6, in *Tutte le opere,* vol. 2 [Verona: Vallarsi,
1729], p. 114). Trissino (1478–1550) published four *Discorsi* on poetry in
1529; the fifth and sixth parts, from which I quote, were published posthu-
mously in 1563. Tasso's references to the *Teseida* in his *Discorsi del poema
eroico* (1594) also associate it with the romance epics and defend "love" as
one of the themes appropriate to poetry written in the high style: "In somma,

l'amore e l'amicizia sono convenevolissimo soggetto del poema eroico. . . .
Concedasi dunque che 'l poema epico si possa formar di soggetto amoroso,
com[e] quelli . . . d'Arcita e di Palemone" (Torquato Tasso, *Prose*, ed. Et-
tore Mazzali [Milan and Naples: Ricciardi, 1959], pp. 550–551).

47. Paris, Bibliothèque Nationale, Cod. ital. 581 (*olim* 7758 bis); anonymous,
but once in the possession of Angilberto Del Balzo, a nobleman of the
Regno who was executed in Naples in 1490. On the books of Del Balzo,
including this commentary, see Tammaro de Marinis, *La Biblioteca napole-
tana dei re d'Aragona*, suppl. (Verona: Stamperia Valdonega, 1969), vol. 1,
p. 82. Watermarks suggest a date for the codex of ca. 1450: see Agostinelli,
"The Manuscripts of *Il Teseida*," pp. 49–50. The lexical and phonologi-
cal characteristics of the commentary also suggest a date of composition
ca. 1450, in or near Naples.

48. On the topics in academic prologues of the later Middle Ages, see now A. J.
Minnis, *Medieval Theory of Authorship* (London: Scolar, 1984), chap. 1,
and below, Appendixes 1 and 2.

49. In the following transcription, I have normalized punctuation and capitalization, expanded abbreviations, and supplied accents, leaving the orthography in other respects as it appears in the manuscript.

> El titulo del libro è questo, Comedia Johan Boccaczo et cet. Onde
> quactro sono li stili de lu parlare poetico, czio è, tragedici, comedici,
> satiri, et legici. Onde tragetici è lo stilo chi tracta Locano et Virgilio
> nelle Eneydes, che comintia de felicitate et finisse in miseria. Comedici
> è uno stilo de tractare continuamente de cose basse menczane et altre
> ove chi incomintia de miseria et termina ad felicitate come Ovidio allo
> Methamorfoseos. Satira è uno stilo de tractare con repetisione sì
> como Oratiu oy Juvenale. Eligici è uno stilo de tractare cose di miseria
> sì come fa Boetiu. Onde puotese dire che questa opera tracta de questi
> tucti quactro stili in alcuni parti de questo libro se bene li mercaray.
> (fol. 1r)

Boccaccio's mixed style was to be noted as late as G. M. Crescimbeni,
Comentarj . . . intorno alla sua istoria della volgar poesia, vol. 1 (Rome:
Rossi, 1702), p. 31: "Nel medesimo secolo del Petrarca il Boccaccio diede
principio all'Epica colla sua Teseida, e col Filostrato, ma nello stile non ec-
cede la mediocrità, anzi sovente cadde nell'umile." On the same page of his
commentary, Crescimbene remarks that for Dante, the term "tragic poet"
meant a poet writing in the high style (see note 50, below).

50. On theories of "tragedy" and "comedy" in the fourteenth century, see
Robert Hollander, *Il Virgilio dantesco: Tragedia nella "Commedia"* (Flor-
ence: Olschki, 1983), chap. 3.; on Chaucer's use of the term in the *Troilus*,
A. J. Minnis, "The Influence of Academic Prologues on the Prologues and
Literary Attitudes of Late-Medieval English Writers," *Medieval Studies* 43
(1981): 375ff.; in commentaries on Aristotle, H. A. Kelly, "Aristotle–
Averroes–Alemannus on Tragedy: The Influence of the *Poetics* on the
Latin Middle Ages," *Viator* 10 (1979): 161–209.

51. De' Bassi's commentary survives in five manuscripts as well as the editio

princeps of the *Teseida* (Ferrara, 1475) (Hain, 3308), from which I quote below. For a description of the edition, see the catalog of *Books Printed in the XVth Century Now in the British Museum*, vol. 6 (London: British Museum, 1930), pp. 606–607; and for the manuscripts, Agostinelli, "Manuscripts," p. 73.

> Circa a la expositione del presente libro si come nel principio de li altri libri è costume de fare se de volere sapere cinque cosse. La prima chi fo lo auctore. La seconda qual'è il titulo del libro. La terza quale è la materia de che vole tractare. La quarta a quale fine lo auctore lo ha compilato. La quinta a quale parte de philosophia la opera del presente libro è sottoposta. . . . Quanto ala terza parte cognoscemo lui auctore volere tractare, et essere la materia el suo subiecto de bataglie, de la possanza de amore, de li effecti de venere, le quale cosse con abondante copia de polito parlare inscerto [sic] a infinite poetice fictione e historie, lui elegantissimamente proferisse. (fol. 2v)

I have expanded abbreviations and normalized punctuation silently, and have distinguished between vocalic and consonantal *u*.

52. Paris, Bibliothèque Nationale, Cod. ital. 581, "Declaratio 131": "In questi versi et fine de la sua opera, lu auctore vuole fare sua conclusione, la quale la fay in questi vintiquactro versi sopradicti, ove alli primi ipso dice: che da poi chelle muse, scilicet le scientie, incomentiaro ad conversare colli gienti, videlicet, che per li mondani se incomentiaro ad trovare le dicte scientie" (fol. 118r).

53. Ibid.: "Onde lasciamo li facti del savio, et tornimo ad quello chi lu auctore dice al dicti versi sopra, alli quali dice al dicti versi, che può chelle scientie in tucto se demostraro et diedero ad cognoscere nelli conspecti de li homini, fuoruno de quelli chi le exercitaro con bella philosophia, et altri fuoruno chi con bello stilo exercitaro la dicta scientia e dolce parole, et altri che tucto se dedero et fecero libri de amore" (fol. 120r).

54. Ibid.: "vi ha piazuto commandare a mi pieroanndrea de ibassi vostro antico e fidele famiglio de chiarì lo obscuro texto del detto theseo facendo a quello giose, per le quale li lecturi possano cavare sugo del la loro lectura, el quale texto per la obscurità de le fictione poetice è difficile ad intendere" (fol. 2r).

55. The Neapolitan commentary is almost exclusively mythographical. Although the prologue does not use the term "poetic fictions," its references to the "obscurity" of the *Teseida* seem in context to refer specifically to Boccaccio's learned allusions, especially to classical legend:

> La natura delle cose aromathiche è questa, che multo maiormente peste che integre rendeno odore, onde el grano del senapo entegro pare lieve cosa, ma trito in tra li denti mordica e l gusto sa più forte. Et così la scriptura è molte volte, quando non è intesa però ca la scorsa de fuore sola non ave sapore; ma veramente quando averà dispositione, czio è che serà marinato, spanderà de la sua suavitate l'odore che è dentro. . . . Addumque cum socia causa che questo libro in al-

cuna parte sia obscuro, digna causa è che'lla intelligencia de questa opera spanda el sua odore. (fol. 1r)

56. Salvatore Battaglia, *Le Epoche della letteratura italiana* (Naples: Liguori, 1965), p. 342: "Più promiscua risulta la struttura del Teseida (1340), un poema in ottave, tratto dalle letture della Tebaide di Stazio. . . . Sebbene l'opera aspiri a dare all'Italia un campione di poesia eroica e marziale (la guerra di Teseo contro le Amazzoni), si tramuta per via in una storia di amore e di cavalleria (la competizione tra Arcita e Palemone per Emilia)." Three recent formulations of this critical commonplace read as follows: (1) ". . . l'anno prima (1475), era stata pubblicata in Ferrara la *Teseida* di Boccaccio, un poemetto in ottave di impianto virgiliano di cui il nucleo sentimentale finisce per prevalere sul desiderio di rinnovare l'epica antica" (Giuseppe Anceschi, *Boiardo: Orlando innamorato* [Milan: Garzanti, 1978], vol. 1, p. viii). (2) "[Boccaccio,] anche nel concepire il nuovo lavoro [il *Teseida*], proprio mentre lo viene plasmando sopra il modello classico, egli si mostra interessato e proteso a un'opera di conciliazione, di contaminazione e di intarsio dell'esemplare latino con le predilezioni della sua sensibilità per le storie d'amore" (Alberto Limentani, introduction to the *Teseida*, in *Tutte le Opere*, vol. 2, p. 233). (3) "Ma la contraddizione immanente nel nuovo genere epico-cavalleresco tentato da Boccaccio poteva essere risolta solo esteriormente [that is, by mixing classical and medieval names and phrases, costumes, and scenes]? In realtà questo nuovo genere comportava la trasformazione di entrambe le componenti, classica e romanza" (Carlo Muscetta, *Giovanni Boccaccio*, Letteratura Laterza 8 [Bari: Laterza, 1972], 78). One notes the tendency, most prominent in Muscetta, to view the "contradiction" between epic form and romance subject in a more positive light, as something that "transforms both components, classical and romance."

57. A landmark among recent studies of classical sources in Boccaccio's earlier vernacular works is E. A. Quaglio, "Tra Fonti e testo del *Filocolo*," *Giornale storico della letteratura italiana* 139 (1962): 321–369 and 513–540, where Boccaccio's close imitation of passages from classical authors, especially Lucan and Ovid, is examined as an aid to textual criticism. The long essay continues in *Giornale storico della letteratura italiana* 140 (1963): 321–363 and 489–551, with notes on medieval sources. On the method, see also Quaglio's "Parola del Boccaccio," *Lingua nostra* 20 (1959), as well as his study of the *Filocolo*'s textual tradition in the first number of *Studi sul Boccaccio* (1963). With the focus exclusively on Boccaccio's method as translator: "Boccaccio e Lucano: Una Concordanza e una fonte dal *Filocolo* all'*Amorosa visione*," *Cultura neolatina* 23 (1963): 153–171; and with the focus on Boccaccio's literary milieu in Naples and the characteristics of his copy of a classical text: "Valerio Massimo e il *Filocolo* di Giovanni Boccaccio," *Cultura neolatina* 20 (1960): 45–77. Quaglio provides a list of such earlier work as concerned imitation in the *Filocolo* (e.g., Vincenzo Ussani, Jr., "Alcune Imitazioni ovidiane del Boccaccio," *Maia* 1 [1948]), and he in turn inspired the sophisticated studies of Giuseppe Velli, "Cultura e *imitatio* nel primo Boccaccio," *Annali della*

Scuola normale superiore di Pisa 2.37 (1968): 65–93; and "Sulla Similitudine dotta del Boccaccio," *Studi linguistici in onore di Tristano Bolelli*
(Pisa: Pacini, 1974), both now reprinted in Velli, *Petrarca e Boccaccio: Tradizione, memoria, scrittura* (Padua: Antenore, 1979).

Quaglio's studies are not directly concerned with the sources of the *Teseida*. This subject was taken up at about the same time by Alberto Limentani: "Boccaccio traduttore di Stazio," *Rassegna italiana di letteratura* 64
(1960): 231–242, which offers several examples of Boccaccio's tendency to
gloss as he translates; and "Tendenze della prosa del Boccaccio ai margini
della *Teseide*," *Giornale storico della letteratura italiana* 135 (1958): 524–
551, which takes up the suggestion of Vandelli that Lactantius provided
Boccaccio with a stylistic model for the glosses. Limentani's edition of the
Teseida for *Tutte le Opere*, vol. 2, includes notes on Boccaccio's sources,
especially thorough in regard to Boccaccio's echoes of Dante. That Limentani's notes on classical sources are not exhaustive became apparent shortly
after publication of the edition: Giuseppe Velli, "L'Apoteosi di Arcita: Ideologia e coscienza storica nel *Teseida*," *Studi e problemi di critica testuale* 5
(1972): 33–66 (and reprinted in *Petrarca e Boccaccio*), demonstrated the
range of Boccaccio's classical sources in a single episode of the poem and
the sophistication with which they are combined and adapted. See also
Bruno Porcelli, "Il *Teseida* del Boccaccio fra la *Tebaide* e *The Knight's
Tale*," *Studi e problemi di critica testuale* 32 (1986): 57–80. Piero Boitani
includes a "Table of the Sources, Influences, and Reminiscences in the
Teseida" in his *Chaucer and Boccaccio*, Medium Aevum Monographs,
new series 8 (Oxford: Society for the Study of Medieval Languages and
Literature, 1977), pp. 61–71.

Running parallel to these studies of Boccaccio's use of the classics in
the *Teseida* are the investigations of his nonclassical sources, especially
Branca's monograph on the popular cantari traditions, a little book still influential today: *Il Cantare trecentesco e il Boccaccio del Filostrato e del
Teseida* (Florence: Sansoni, 1936); and Quaglio's essays on Boccaccio's
astrological and astronomical learning, collected as *Scienza e mito nel Boccaccio* (Padova: Liviana, 1967), which is concerned with Boccaccio's Neapolitan period. Among the shorter studies: Kahane and Kahane, "Akritas
and Arcita"; Daniela Branca, "La Morte di Tristano e la morte di Arcita,"
Studi sul Boccaccio 4 (1967): 255–264; Ernesto Travi, "L'Introduzione al
Teseida e l'epistologia del '500," *Studi sul Boccaccio* 10 (1977–1978):
307–314.

Several American scholars have considered Boccaccio's sources in the
effort to identify medieval traditions that are useful in interpreting the
poem "as a literary work." This approach leads to different emphases than
the studies mentioned above, which developed out of concern with establishing a text, but the two schools—if they may be so called—converge
around the topics of Boccaccio's library and Boccaccio's known sources:
Robert Hollander, "The Validity of Boccaccio's Self-Exegesis in His *Teseida*," *Medievalia et humanistica* n.s. 8 (1977): 163–183, an important
essay, inspired in part by the discussion of Chaucer's figurative gods in
D. W. Robertson, *A Preface to Chaucer* (Princeton: Princeton University

Press, 1962), with observations on Boccaccio's mythographical material in the glosses to the temples of Mars and Venus (see especially n. 14 for Boccaccio's use of Ovid's *Metamorphoses*); Janet Levarie Smarr, "Boccaccio and the Stars: Astrology in the *Teseida,*" *Traditio* 35 (1979): 303–332; Victoria Kirkham, "*Chiuso parlare* in Boccaccio's *Teseida,*" in *Dante, Petrarch, Boccaccio: Studies in the Italian Trecento in Honor of Charles S. Singleton,* ed. Aldo S. Bernardo and Anthony Pellegrini (Binghamton, N.Y.: MRTS, 1983), pp. 305–351. One of this author's several essays on Boccaccio's numerology, "*Chiuso parlare*" also opens the question of his sources for the philosophical terms in the glosses on the temples (n. 37); James McGregor, "Boccaccio's Athenian Theater," which proposes the chronicle of Martinus Polonus among other sources for Boccaccio's elaborate theater.

Identifying echoes of contemporary events that may have added resonance to Boccaccio's narrative is Rita Librandi, "Corte e cavalleria della Napoli Angioina nel *Teseida* del Boccaccio," *Medioevo romanzo* 4 (1977): 53–72. Among the many works treating the common sources of Chaucer's Knight's Tale and the *Teseida,* two in particular deserve mention here: Boyd A. Wise, *The Influence of Statius upon Chaucer* (Baltimore: Furst, 1911); Robert Haller, "The *Knight's Tale* and the Epic Tradition," *Chaucer Review* 1 (1966): 67–84. Haller and, more recently, Porcelli (see above) have observed the general similarity of the main action in the *Thebaid* to that of the *Teseida.*

58. The terms are those of Vittore Branca, "Giovanni Boccaccio, rinnovatore dei generi letterari," in *Atti del convegno di Nimegia sul Boccaccio (28–29–30 Ottobre 1975),* ed. C. Ballerini (Bologna: 1976), pp. 13–35. The essay is reprinted under the title "Boccaccio e le tradizioni letterarie," in *Il Boccaccio nelle culture e letterature nazionali,* ed. Francesco Mazzoni (Florence: Olschki, 1978), pp. 473–496.

Alstair Fowler has proposed the same terms, with broad reference to genre theory in the Middle Ages, in his book *Kinds of Literature: An Introduction to the Theory of Genres and Modes* (Cambridge, Mass.: Harvard University Press, 1982), pp. 142–148. Noting that "it is commonly agreed that medieval writers felt a supreme indifference toward the traditional genres: even got on pretty well without any genre theory at all. Their few generic terms are supposed to be casual and chaotic," Fowler argues cogently that medieval response to genre might better be characterized as "conscious transformation" of recognized traditions. "Such generic transformations make up [a large] part of medieval and later literature. . . . Here it may be enough to recall the transformations of epithalamium that began with Martianus Capella's enormously influential *De Nuptiis Philologiae et Mercurii.* Generic transformations and innovations became so frequent that we find Matthew of Vendome having to argue the advantages of old subjects and genres against new" (pp. 142–144).

CHAPTER 1

Imitation of the Main Action

Two similes

The twelfth-century *Thebaid* now in Florence (Biblioteca Medicea-Laurenziana, MS Plut. 38.6) was long in Boccaccio's personal library. It passed with most of that library to the Augustinian convent of Santo Spirito, Florence, after Boccaccio's death in 1375 and from there went to the Laurenziana in the later eighteenth century. An old shelfmark, VIII 9, is still visible in the codex. It corresponds to the shelfmark of one of the two *Thebaid*s in a fifteenth-century inventory of the "Parva Libraria" at Santo Spirito, which contained Boccaccio's books.[1] The manuscript was first identified as Boccaccio's by Oscar Hecker in *Boccaccio-Funde* (1902), and Hecker also left a note with the manuscript, now fixed inside its back cover, in which he records that folios 43, 100, 111, and 169 are copied in Boccaccio's own hand.[2]

This handsome manuscript was made in the early twelfth century. It has the small dimensions (23.5 × 16.5 cm) characteristic of twelfth-century copies of classical Latin verse and a format somewhat more squarish than the norm for that period.[3] Its pages are wide relative to their height because the book was designed to contain the Lactantius commentary beside the text of the *Thebaid*. Its makers ruled the outer margins for the commentary at the same time that they ruled for the single column of text, and they copied the commentary in a smaller, denser script with lighter brown ink than the poetic text. Red ink was used to highlight the small capitals at the beginning of each verse of the poem.

The book must have been damaged at some early date, because leaves in two gatherings near the end have been copied in a thirteenth-century hand (folios 163–164, 173–178). Then four more leaves must have fallen out before the manuscript reached Boccaccio, around 1340. Like the previous restorer, he maintained the colors and the proportions of the original when he inserted four replacement leaves, copying the text in his neat book hand. He did not, however, rule the margins, and the glosses he wrote between the lines and in the margins do not derive from Lactantius.

Boccaccio's four leaves are of singular importance. That they are in his hand confirms that the manuscript was in the Parva Libraria, so strongly suggested by the old shelfmark and the fifteenth-century inventory. Because the script on the four leaves has all of the characteristic features of Boccaccio's writing early in his career, they indicate that the manuscript came into his possession at an early date, certainly before 1345.[4] And because Plut. 38.6 contains a copy of Lactantius's commentary on the *Thebaid* as well as a good text of the *Thebaid* itself, the date at which he came into possession of the manuscript must correspond to the date at which he first came to know this commentary, which was apparently rare in Italy in the fourteenth century. Boccaccio draws on it, though only sparingly, in the *Teseida,* and extensively in later works such as the *Genealogie.*[5] Finally, the four leaves contain interlinear and marginal glosses that do not derive from Lactantius; the copyist, Boccaccio himself, probably composed them.

What does Boccaccio's manuscript tell us about his knowledge of the *Thebaid*? As Giuseppe Billanovich has pointed out, Boccaccio's reference to studying the *Thebaid,* made near the end of the letter "Sacre famis" of 1339, cannot be taken to mean that he was reading the work for the first time.[6] He had drawn from it in his earlier writings, including the *Filocolo* (ca. 1336), and he must have encountered it earlier still, in his formal schooling and through his reading of Dante. In the letter, Boccaccio says that he has been studying, laboriously, a new copy of the *Thebaid* without the guidance of glosses, and he goes on to request a copy of Lactantius's commentary. This request might be nothing more than a literary topos in a letter never sent, an exercise in composition: it is certainly close to a Dantean model, and the only surviving copy appears in one of Boccaccio's commonplace books with no name given for the addressee. But even if we are cautious in evaluating autobiography in the letter, Boccaccio's request makes it clear that in 1339 he was aware of the tradition of commentaries on the *Thebaid,* including Lactantius's, and that he had special esteem for the latter, which was difficult if not impossible to find in Naples.[7] Plut. 38.6 fills out the picture. When Boccaccio came into possession of it, he apparently had access to another copy of the poem, a copy without glosses or in any case without Lactantius's commentary.[8] Had he had easy access to that commentary, he surely would have included the apposite glosses in the margins of the four new folios he added not too long before or after the very year 1339. He knew the *Thebaid* before this time but now took it up again, obtaining for himself, either by letter or by some other means, a copy of Lactantius to guide his studies.

It is particularly impressive that his ability to supply the text of the *Thebaid* was not matched by an ability to add the marginal commentary as it appears in the rest of the manuscript. The situation corresponds to that sketched in "Sacre famis" in 1339: whether in response to that letter or not, we shall probably never know, but certainly during the same period, ca. 1339–1340, Boccaccio had a *Thebaid* without Lactantius and probably without any glosses at all; and then came into possession of the old book now Plut. 38.6, with Lactantius but lacking four leaves, which he replaced with a text carefully copied in his own hand, supplying glosses of his own.

These glosses represent Boccaccio's interpretation of four passages in the *Thebaid* at the time Plut. 38.6 came into his possession. They are accompanied by other signs of Boccaccio's studies, such as paragraph marks blocking out sections of the text and small superscript letters, used to mark grammatical relations. The letters ·a· and ·b· regularly show the agreement of a verb with its subject or a noun with its modifying adjective, as for example in *Thebaid* 7.670 (fol. 100r), where Boccaccio has placed an ·a· over the adjective *primam* and then in the next line a ·b· over *rabiem*, the noun with which it agrees (see plate 1).[9]

Miraculously, it is possible to turn directly from Boccaccio's study of the *Thebaid* to its imitation in the *Teseida*. This glossed passage at *Thebaid* 7.666ff. can now be identified as the source of a formal simile at *Teseida* 7.115, which describes Arcite entering the amphitheater at the head of his group of knights. I italicize words and phrases that have close verbal similarity to the source passage in the *Thebaid:*

> tale a veder *qual tra giovenchi giunge*
> *non armati di corna il fier leone*
> libico, e affamato i denti munge
> con la sua lingua e aguzza l'unghione,
> e *col capo alto,* qual innanzi punge,
> *l'occhio girando,* fa dilibrazione;
> e sì negli atti si mostra *rabbioso*
> che ogni *giovenco* fa di sé dottoso.   (7.115)

> [such to see as a fierce Libyan lion when it gets among the
> hornless bullocks and famished presses its tongue on its teeth
> and sharpens its claw, and with raised head thrust forward and
> eye roving deliberates, and by its actions shows itself so furious
> that every bullock makes itself submissive.][10]

The principal model for the simile is *Thebaid* 7.670–674, where in the midst of the first battle of the Theban War, Capaneus confronts an insig-

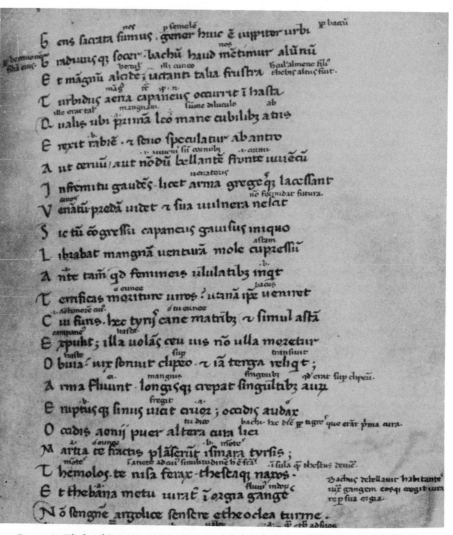

PLATE 1. *Thebaid* 7.666–688, in Boccaccio's hand. Florence, Biblioteca Medicea-Laurenziana, MS Plut. 38.6, fol. 100r

nificant Theban braggart. Statius's formal simile refers to the first rousing of Capaneus's martial anger, and the effect of his verbal retort:

> qualis ubi primam leo mane cubilibus atris
> erexit rabiem et saevo speculatur ab antro
> aut cervum aut nondum bellantem fronte iuvencum,

it fremitu gaudens, licet arma gregesque lacessant
venatum, praedam videt et sua volnera nescit.   (7.670–674)

[As a lion when it stirs its newly awakened rage in its dark lair
at daybreak and watches from the grim cave a deer or a young
bull with forehead yet unarmed, leaps forward exulting in its
roar, though spears of hunters and their flocks assail, it looks at
its prey and does not feel its wounds.]

The simile of the hunting lion is not especially prominent among the
scores of extended comparisons in Statius's epic, but it happens to fall on
folio 100r of Boccaccio's manuscript, one of the four leaves with text and
gloss copied in his own hand. Because the glosses here do not come from
the Lactantius's commentary, they must reflect Boccaccio's interpretation
of the passage at the time he copied folio 100, and the paleographical
evidence suggests that he did the copying during the same period in which
he composed the *Teseida*, the early 1340s. To be sure, there is some possibility that this is not the actual book from which Boccaccio worked. He
might well have copied this text and these glosses from another *Thebaid*
in his possession. But whether we have the book itself or Boccaccio's own
copy of part of the book, we are in the presence of the poet's classical
source in the form in which he knew it. Text and gloss on 100r represent
the state of *Thebaid* 7.666ff. from which Boccaccio worked when he
composed *Teseida* 8.115.

In adopting Statius's simile, Boccaccio has left some details out and he
has added some new ones. The changes show him translating from the
interpretive gloss and modifying the simile to suit its new context in the
Teseida. He makes the lion a Libyan, a conventional epithet, to be found
elsewhere in the *Thebaid* itself and not very noteworthy here unless it
foreshadows the association of Arcite with "Libyan Antaeus," also made
in a formal simile, in the next book.[11] More remarkable is Boccaccio's
rendering of Statius's "nondum bellantem fronte iuvencum" (bullock not
yet warlike of forehead) as "giovenchi . . . non armati di corna." Here he
is translating from his gloss as well as from Statius's text, rendering the
mannered language of his source in somewhat more familiar terms. In his
manuscript, Boccaccio glossed "nondum bellantem fronte" with "id est
iuvenis sine cornubus" and "fronte" again with "id est cornu." The verbal similarity of Boccaccio's version and its model appears much more
clearly in light of this gloss, and the strategy of translating from both the
gloss and the text reflects a general tendency to step down from the uniformly high style of the *Thebaid* to a mixed level of diction, containing
both elevated and more familiar words and phrases.

Like some other medieval copies of the *Thebaid*, Boccaccio's manuscript reads "in fremitu gaudens" at the beginning of line 673 rather than "it fremitu gaudens," as it does in modern editions. The Loeb translation exaggerates the verb of the modern edition somewhat, giving: "He leaps forth with a joyous roar," but Boccaccio would not have known even a plainer "he goes forth." The lion in Boccaccio's text remains stationary, delighting *in* his roar. This textual variant certainly has something to do with the way the lion in the *Teseida* remains stationary, but that aspect of the simile in the *Teseida* also reflects a more programmatic change that Boccaccio works on his source as he applies it in a different context (of which more shortly).

Other points of verbal and semantic contact in the two versions show through the systematic changes. Boccaccio's stationary lion licks its chops and sharpens its claws in anticipation of a kill, perhaps an elaboration of "in fremitu *gaudens*" (*delighting* in his roar). Boccaccio's "capo alto" recalls Statius's rather abstract "primam rabiem . . . *erexit*," while "l'occhio girando" and "fa dilibrazione" elaborate denotation and connotation, respectively, of Statius's "speculatur." "Primam . . . rabiem" is also echoed in Boccaccio's seventh line, "rabbioso." The bullock from the third line of Statius's simile, which attracted Boccaccio's attention in the gloss and which appears in the first line of his simile, reappears in the eighth verse. In all, Boccaccio's simile is a little longer than its source, even though various features of Statius's complex vehicle are omitted: the elements that Boccaccio does employ are concerned with the visual appearance of the lion, and in describing them, Boccaccio amplifies the words of his source with doubling, such as "l'occhio girando . . . fa dilibrazione" and with repetition, such as "giovenco . . . giovenchi."

There is one other point of verbal similarity between the metaphorical vehicle here and its classical model, and it begins to explain the systematic differences as well. Among the various conventional words for introducing his simile, Statius uses *qualis* here, and Boccaccio has glossed it in his copy with the words "ille erat talis." The simile in the *Teseida* begins with a modified version of *qualis*: "tale a veder qual. . . ."[12] Now, as Boccaccio's gloss indicates, Statius designs the vehicle of his extended simile to describe Capaneus speaking and acting ("He was such") and the lion in Statius's rather complicated vehicle matches Capaneus in several ways, including his sound: the lion's first rage is expressed in a roar; it attacks clearly inferior, indeed unarmed, prey in the midst of a pack (of dogs) and the weapons of hunters, which it scarcely notices. Boccaccio, however, applies his lion simile to the appearance of Arcite at the head of his troops as they enter the theater, before the battle begins. Arcite does not speak, and he does not act with battle raging around him. Thus the aspects of Statius's vehicle adopted and augmented by Boccaccio are only those concerning the visual appearance of the lion, and Boccaccio signals this governing characteristic of his simile at the introduction: "tale a *veder* qual" (Such to *see* [was Arcite] as is a lion). Boccaccio's system of employing or redeploying the verbal material in Statius's simile reflects his analysis of the original context and its new application. Gone is the roar, gone are the hunters around the lion, while its appearance is described to the fullest, by a process augmenting the visual connotations of several of Statius's terms.

Boccaccio's glosses on *Thebaid* 7.666ff. and their reappearance in the *Teseida* confirm in the most vivid way that he worked closely from the Latin text of Statius's poem, as we have assumed to be the case since the discoveries of Crescini a century ago. But the identification of the source for *Teseida* 7.115 does more than add another pair of numbers to the already lengthy list of corresponding passages in the Latin and Italian works, for it confirms what E. A. Quaglio, Alberto Limentani, and Giuseppe Velli have taught us about Boccaccio's practice in imitating a verse or passage: that he glossed as he translated, explaining his source and often transforming it to suit the new narrative context.[13] Indeed, we can now say that Boccaccio's "glossing" in the vernacular sometimes meant translating from glosses on the Latin original. The two operations are so closely related that we may well imagine a glossed copy of passages such as Lucan's description of the aftermath of battle (*De bello civili* 7.834ff.) that Boccaccio translated in the *Filocolo* and then reworked in the *Amorosa visione,* or Ovid's ekphrasis on the cave of Sleep (*Metamorphoses* 11.592ff.) imitated in the *Filocolo,* where the practice of "glossing" is so evident and for which Boccaccio's glossed copies of the classical sources have not survived or have not been identified.[14]

Folio 100r of Plut. 38.6 also offers a slight, but nonetheless interesting, contrast with Boccaccio's glosses in the *Teseida.* The latter are exclusively lexical and mythographical. The glosses in the *Thebaid* may be characterized as primarily lexical, concerned to give a more direct expression beside Statius's rarefied usage or circumlocution. They are occasionally mythographical, but they also show concern with grammatical construction, a feature absent in the glosses to the *Teseida.*[15]

Finally, the classical passage behind *Teseida* 7.115 serves well to introduce the subject of Boccaccio's imitative design in the main action of his poem, where the traces of Statius's narrative are seen in Boccaccio's systematic borrowings for the "romance" of Palamon and Arcite. In keeping with the general pattern that associates the main action of the *Teseida*

with that of the *Thebaid*, Boccaccio employs a number of similes for Palamon and Arcite in the grove (5) and the amphitheater (8–9) that have as
models the similes Statius applies to principals of the Theban War, when
they are in competition during the funeral games of Opheltes (*Thebaid* 6)
and during the siege of Thebes (*Thebaid* 7–11). In general, what Statius
says of the princes involved in the Theban War Boccaccio redeploys for
his "Tebani nobilissimi" and their companions in the smaller "giuoco a
Marte" of the *Teseida*. Among these borrowings are the formal comparisons with wild animals that later reappear in an often-noted sequence
in Chaucer's Knight's Tale.[16] Boccaccio also draws from analogous scenes
in the *Aeneid*, notably Vergil's simile describing the speed of Camilla in
the catalog of *Aeneid* 7, which he translates closely and employs in a
nearly identical context to describe the speed of Idas Piseus, one of the
Greek princes who have come to participate in the "giuoco a Marte."

Mosaic-like patterns of borrowed passages are more or less obvious to
the reader in relation to the reader's knowledge of the work from which
the pieces are borrowed. But Boccaccio's imitation of Statius's main action also finds open expression, as is evident in his handling of the vehicle
in another formal simile, this one appearing at the point in Boccaccio's
"romance" at which the personal rivalry turns violent: *Teseida* 5.13.

With the care so evident in his transformation of the hunting lion simile,
Boccaccio now matches his main action to that of the *Thebaid*, proposing
as vehicle the entire episode with which Statius begins his narrative. The
eight lines of Boccaccio's stanza summarize *Thebaid* 1.46–130, moving
from the curse of Oedipus (46–87) to the rising of Tisiphone from Avernus and her passage over the earth (88–122) and arrival at Thebes,
where she inspires jealousy and the "fierce love" of undivided power in
Oedipus's two sons. The Statian episode is itself woven of Vergilian motifs, recalling the description of Allecto at the beginning of the Italian civil
war (*Aeneid* 7), and the flight of Mercury to Carthage (*Aeneid* 4), and
with thematic words from the *Aeneid* deployed in a pattern of inversion
("impius Oedipus," 46; "adsueta infecit nube penates," 124). Boccaccio's summary focuses on the climactic moment to which Statius builds
over so many lines, the conception of jealous rivalry by the brothers and
the consequences of that fierce passion:

> E sì come Tesifone, chiamata
> dal cieco Edippo nella oscura parte
> dov'elli lunga notte avea menata,
> a' due fratei del regno con su' arte
> mise l'arsura, così a lui 'ntrata

con quel velen che 'l suo valor comparte,
d'Emilia aver, dicendo: —Signoria
né amore stan ben con compagnia.—   (5.13)

[And just as Tisiphone, called by blind Oedipus in the dark place
where he had passed a long night, set afire the two brothers of
the kingdom with her art, just so she had entered him (Palamon)
with the poison that her power imparts, of possessing Emilia,
saying, "Neither kingship nor love goes well in company."]

The proverbial ring of Boccaccio's concluding phrase does, in fact, owe
something to a traditional sententia, but he has employed it to tie vehicle
and tenor more closely together.[17] In his gloss on the simile, Boccaccio
restates the terms of comparison in even plainer language:

[Edipo] essendo pessimamente trattato da' figliuoli, cominciò
a pregare Tesifone, che è l'una delle tre Furie infernali, che tra
loro mettesse scandalo e briga, e così fu fatto: e come ella entrata nel petto de' due fratelli vi mise briga, così entrata nel petto
di Palemone vi generò la discordia che seguita, che fu tra lui e
Arcita.   (in 5.13)

[Oedipus, as he was being so badly treated by his children, began to pray to Tisiphone, who is one of the three infernal Furies,
that she stir up quarrels and contention between them; and this
was done. And just as she entered the breasts of the two brothers and stirred up a quarrel, she entered the breast of Palamon
and planted there the discord that followed between him and
Arcite.]

In the simile, Boccaccio has focused on the nature of Tisiphone's "venom"
and its consequences, as they are stated at the conclusion of Statius's episode. Boccaccio's conclusion, "dicendo: 'Signoria / né amor stan ben con
compagnia,'" reduces the list of effects in Statius's version to which Boccaccio's may be compared:[18]

protinus adtoniti fratrum sub pectore motus,
gentilisque animos subiit furor aegraque laetis
invidia atque parens odii metus, inde regendi
saevus amor, ruptaeque vices iurisque secundi
ambitus impatiens, et summo dulcius unum
stare loco, sociisque comes discordia regnis.   (1.125–130)

[Immediately there were stunning commotions in the brothers' hearts, the insanity of their kinfolk overcame their minds, with bitter envy of others' happiness and suspicion the parent of hate and thence the fierce love of ruling, broken reciprocity, ambition bridling at the second place and the thought that it is sweeter to stand alone in the highest, and discord the companion in partnered kingship.]

Statius's breathtaking series, with its constant ironic play on words for "kinsman" and "companion" ("gentilis furor," "parens odii metus," "ruptae vices," "comes discordia"), progresses from the motivating "furor" itself to its ethical and then political consequences in the acts of Polynices and Eteocles.

Although Boccaccio draws the vehicle from the entire opening scene of the *Thebaid*, this climactic passage provides its focus and its only verbal echoes; they are "velen" (from 1.106), "a lui 'ntrata" ("sub pectore motus") and, in the gloss, "discordia." Statius's concluding line, "summo dulcius unum / stare loco, sociisque comes discordia regnis," seems to have suggested Boccaccio's unusual phrase "fratei del regno [brothers of the kingdom]" and especially the wording of his concluding *sententia*, "signoria / né amore stan ben con compagnia," which uses the same verb in a negative construction to express the same sentiment (cf. "dulcius unum stare"). The whole simile in the *Teseida* might be said to elaborate Statius's characterization of the "furor" as "saevus *amor* regendi," the fierce *love* of ruling, with its implicit likening of the desire for power to erotic desire, a comparison that reappears elsewhere in the *Thebaid* as well.

In this simile Boccaccio matches the onset of rivalry between Palamon and Arcite against that between Eteocles and Polynices. That is, the simile compares a significant episode in Boccaccio's narrative with another in the *Thebaid*. It appears in the *Teseida* during the scene in which Palamon, in prison in Theseus's tower (recalling perhaps the "Cadmean towers" over which Tisiphone hovers in *Thebaid* 1.123ff.), first conceives a passionate envy of his cousin, Arcite, and a consuming jealousy over possession of Emilia ("d'Emilia aver"). Arcite soon reciprocates ("Solo d'amarla fia in possessione": 5.53), and the personal rivalry between these Theban kinsmen quickly expands to include representatives of various provinces of Greece, much as the rivalry of Eteocles and Polynices is magnified in the course of *Thebaid* 1–4. The situation is analogous, however, not identical. Palamon and Arcite are at once younger and much less powerful than their elder relatives Eteocles and Polynices had been; the violence of their conflict will be controlled to some extent by Theseus;

and they are rivals not for power and a throne but for love and a beautiful young Amazon, to whom they have little claim beyond that provided by the intensity of their desire. Much in the narrative design and the verbal texture of the *Teseida* develops regularly and decorously from this analogy, in its similarity and differences, with the main action of the *Thebaid*.

The analogy is anticipated in the invocation to book 3, where Boccaccio announces that he will turn from the wars of Mars to those of Cupid. The first stanza recalls the end of the civil war at Thebes:

> Poi che alquanto il furor di Iunone
> fu per Tebe distrutta temperato,
> Marte nella sua fredda regione
> con le sue Furie insieme s'è tornato;

> [When the furor of Juno was somewhat abated by the destruction of Thebes, Mars and his Furies returned together to his cold lands]

and Boccaccio hopes to be inspired by Cupid to recount his battles:

> per che omai con più pio sermone
> sarà da me di Cupido cantato
> e delle sue battaglie, il quale io priego
> che sia presente a ciò che di lui spiego.

> [thus of Cupid and of his battles I shall sing now, with more pious speech; to whom I pray, that he be present for that which I set down about him.]

That the change from the *impius* battles of Mars at Thebes to the less *impius* battles of Cupid between Palamon and Arcite will develop a systematic analogy between the former and the latter is adumbrated in the following stanza, where the "power of Cupid" enters the "hearts of the Thebans" just as the power of Tisiphone enters the hearts of Eteocles and Polynices at *Thebaid* 1.127ff.:

> Ponga ne' versi miei la sua potenza
> quale e' la pose ne' cuor de' Tebani
> imprigionati, sì che differenza
> non sia da essi alli loro atti insani;

> [May he fill my verses with the power that he put in the hearts of the imprisoned Thebans, so that there be no difference between these and their mad acts.]

The analogy between the two "battles," those of Mars and of Venus, is underscored by the paired references to Thebes and by the reference to Cupid's power entering the "hearts of the Thebans," to inspire their madness. At 5.13, that inspiration is likened explicitly to the "venom of Tisiphone" that set afire the passions of Eteocles and Polynices. Then at the end of his invocation in *Teseida* 3, Boccaccio suggests the analogy again by describing the fraternal strife that will result from this cupiditous "venom":

> . . . li loro atti insani;
> li qua', lontani a degna sofferenza,
> venir li fero a l'ultimo a le mani,
> in guisa che a ciascun fu discaro,
> e a l'un fu di morte caso amaro.

> [their mad acts; which led them in the end, far from worthy
> forebearance, into battle, in a way that was displeasing to both
> of them, and the cause of the bitter death of one.]

The reference to this battle of Cupid as "more *pius*" than the Theban civil war ("omai con più pio sermone / sarà da me di Cupido cantato") anticipates the different ending that this case of Theban fraternal strife will have, a difference also anticipated in Boccaccio's concluding reference to the "death of one."

Because the simile of Tisiphone takes part in a larger design of open imitation of the *Thebaid*, Boccaccio's handling of his source passage presents certain distinctive features not present in an essentially closed act of imitation like the simile of the Libyan lion. In the first place, there is the matter of alterations. The lion simile does not try to point us to its source by preserving the characteristic features of that source. It simply employs a poetic framework and some verbal material from a passage in the *Thebaid,* augmenting and modifying it to suit a new context. If Boccaccio's lion does not recall Statius's lion, it is no matter. Boccaccio is free to silence the roar and make of the fierce appearance what he will. But the job of the second simile is not simply to describe Palamon's "furor"; it also invites us to match that furor against the example of Polynices and Eteocles in the *Thebaid*. The vehicle in this metaphor must reflect its source accurately. And indeed, even though there is no more verbal resemblance here, with regard to the source passage in the *Thebaid,* than there is in the case of the Libyan lion, this simile stays very close to the sense of Statius's episode. The vehicle of Boccaccio's simile accurately recalls the episode, and with it the main action of the *Thebaid*. Boccaccio

provides an explanatory gloss as well, to encourage further the identification of that source and all it implies. In the second place, the strategy of
open imitation influences the application of vehicle to tenor. To be sure,
Boccaccio modifies his source in doing this. He shortens the "chain of
consequences" passage, which in the *Thebaid* sketches the larger narrative pattern that will follow from Tisiphone's "furor," so that Tisiphone's "venom" in the *Teseida* merely says that "neither kingship nor
love will satisfy if shared." But the new conclusion ties the *Thebaid* the
more closely and explicitly to the *Teseida*. Although Boccaccio's source
is concerned with rivalry over a throne while the *Teseida* is concerned
with rivalry over a beautiful young woman, Boccaccio has the venom of
Tisiphone inspire both at once, recalling the *Thebaid* (where *signoria* is
not shared) and matching it to the *Teseida* (where *amore* is not shared) in
a simple equation. His use of verbal materials from his source cannot well
be defined as a borrowing of convenient motifs or of stylistic felicities. It is
designed to recall that source and to develop an extended pattern of correspondence between the main action of the *Thebaid* and that of the *Teseida*.

Speciem refert . . .

Boccaccio built his "romance" in the *Teseida* by way of an analogy. He
substituted rivalry in love for rivalry in political affairs, with the distant
image of Emilia standing in place of the throne of Thebes as the object
disputed by the two Theban kinsmen. Boccaccio then developed his narrative, scene by scene, in open imitation of the main action of Statius's
Thebaid. I have arrived at this hypothesis after examining two learned
similes, the first having a place in a pattern of borrowing from the *Thebaid*,
the second explicitly likening the onset of strife between royal brothers in
the *Thebaid* to the onset of strife between royal cousins in the *Teseida*. It
is a hypothesis that has been proposed, if not pursued, before,[19] which
urges examination of the mosaic of motifs and scenes that recall the
Thebaid in the *Teseida*. And while it raises questions about Boccaccio's
pattern of borrowings from his literary source, it also gives a particular
direction to the search for critical terms adequate to describe this kind of
imitation. What examples of allusive narrative structure might have influenced his imitative strategy? To approach this question systematically, we
must begin by distinguishing the rhetorical tradition that defines *imitatio*
as an aspect of style and diction only, from another tradition, characteristic of commentary on the classical epics, that defines it with reference to
narrative structure.

Petrarch's remarks on imitation in his letters, including *Familiares* 23.19, addressed to Boccaccio, all refer to imitation as a means by which a writer may acquire mastery of literary style. In this context it is not surprising that he favors a dissimulative strategy, in which the writer's verses "appear similar to no one and will seem to have brought, from the old, something new to Latium": *ars est celare artem*. But as G. W. Pigman has noted of Petrarch's undogmatic statements distinguishing concealed from open imitation, "one notices the combination of concealing and transforming: making something new from a variety of sources and then disguising the process that has produced it. . . . The relation between text and model is not necessarily to be obliterated or completely disguised; the possibility of alluding in order to be recognized is left open." And Petrarch himself alludes to a verse in one of Horace's *Epistles* in the clause cited here.[20] Now, imitative passages in Boccaccio's works show a greater enthusiasm for the unconcealed repetition of source material than Petrarch's statements would seem to approve,[21] and in *De mulieribus claris*, Boccaccio offers quite detailed and apparently sincere praise of the *Centos* of Proba, where the artistry consists entirely of redeploying Vergilian verses in a paraphrase of biblical narrative:

> She searched here and there through the *Bucolics,* the *Georgics,* and the *Aeneid,* sometimes taking entire lines from one place or another and at times parts of lines. She connected them for her purpose with such great skill, aptly placing the entire lines, joining the fragments, observing the metrical rules and preserving the dignity of the verses, that no one except an expert could detect the connections.[22]

As the context here is very different from that of Petrarch's remarks in praise of dissimulation in *Familiares* 23.19, where the aging poet reflects paternally on the compositional exercises of a young versifier, it would be hazardous to draw a straight comparison. Boccaccio, in his short biography of the early Christian poet, simply approves a different imitative strategy. But it is noteworthy that these remarks on the art of Proba concur with the evidence of his own practice in "vernacularizing" classical authors to suggest that Boccaccio favored open, or allusive, imitation, which acknowledges at the verbal level its sources, inviting reflection on the way they have been transformed.

It is important to bear in mind that Boccaccio's praise of the skillful cento, like Petrarch's praise of artful dissimulation, refers to imitation as a feature of style and to the act of imitation as a means for creating phrase, verse, or paragraph. Neither addresses the question of imitation of poetic form, be it a generic model such as epic or its minor forms such as invocation, speech, simile, ekphrasis. And their remarks do not concern the aspect of epic form that is the design of a principal action.

The same is not the case with Boccaccio's own term for the composition of the *Teseida,* which appears first in the introductory epistle in the context of a summary of the poem's narrative structure. Boccaccio twice uses the term "compilation" to describe the *Teseida.* In the concluding sonnet of the poem, he says in the first person that he has "compiled" the work:

> io ho ricolte della vostra mensa
> alcune miche da quella cadute,
> e come seppi qui l'ho compilate

> [I have collected some crumbs that had fallen from your (the Muses') table and, as best I could, I have put them together here.]

The word also appears in the introductory epistle, right after Boccaccio alludes to the "ancient source" of his main action. He tells Fiammetta: "E che ella da me per voi sia compilata, due cose fra l'altre il manifestano" (and two things in particular demonstrate that it [the *Teseida*] has been compiled for you).[23] The word connotes openness and allusion rather than dissimulation of sources, and especially in this context it would seem to describe narrative shape as well as verbal texture, the "plundering" of a main action as well as a style.

The verb *compilare* is an Old Latin formation, but its use in fourteenth-century Italian reflects semantic developments in Medieval Latin. Its basic elements *com-pīlo,* "to pile together" apparently took on the connotation of "piling up plunder" at an early time, so that it emerged from preclassical Latin with the meaning "to steal." In classical times it is not a term used for literary compositions: it does not appear in Quintilian, for example, and its two occurrences in Horace's first satire may be translated "to plunder" and—by an obvious metaphorical extension of meaning—"to beat soundly."[24] Although *compilare* and its derivatives do not appear in the Vulgate translation of the Bible, they were common in Medieval Latin, where they conserved the old meanings "to steal" and "to pile/pack together" and where they developed new ones regarding literary composition.[25] In the Scholastic writings of the thirteenth century, *compilare* was assigned a specific place in the group of terms describing the ways a written text comes into existence. St. Bonaventura distinguished the works of a compiler from those of scribe and author: unlike the copyist, he creates something new and useful, but he does it without adding new words of his own. That is the work of the author or the commentator. Instead, the compiler rearranges and collects passages from various sources, giving them a convenient new order.[26] Richard de Bury's *Philobiblon*, which Boccaccio most probably knew, continues in this tradition, dividing the semantic territory between author and copyist into four parts: correction, exposition, tabulation, and compilation.[27] And it is in this sense of "composing a literary work by giving order to materials taken from various sources" that the verb makes its appearance in the Italian of Dante's *Convivio* (2.13.12),[28] though it clearly has lost the strict definition of Bonaventura in Giovanni Villani's references to "compiling" a historical narrative from other historical accounts. Here the meaning extends from "collect and reorder" to include "recast, rewrite," and this broader sense is clearly intended by Dante in *De vulgari eloquentia* (1.10.2), also with reference to historical narrative.[29]

This use of "compile" in reference to historical narrative provides the best context in which to take Boccaccio's statements that he "compiled" the *Teseida*. For one, the setting of the narrative has much in common with those legendary histories of Troy and Rome that Dante refers to as "compilations" in *De vulgari eloquentia*. Even more impressive is the appearance of the word in Isidore's *Etymologiae*—another prominent element of Boccaccio's personal library—to refer to Vergil: he is a *compilator veterum*, a plunderer of the ancients (10.44). Significantly, Boccaccio also uses the verb *compilare* in reference to Petrarch's composition of the *Africa*, as if the term had special pertinence to literature in the epic tradition.[30]

The open and allusive imitation suggested by Boccaccio's use of the verb *compilare* in preference to the more general *comporre* or *scrivere* is characteristic of classical epic. Statius imitates Vergil's *Aeneid* in every major aspect of the *Thebaid*, beginning with style and diction but including the design of whole episodes, which Statius builds on Vergilian models, substituting characters of different name in the familiar Vergilian roles. The best example is the episode of Hopleus and Dymas in *Thebaid* 10, modeled on the nocturnal raid of the companions Nisus and Euryalus in *Aeneid* 10. Here Statius not only draws attention to his source with verbal reminiscence and a strict correspondence in character and action, but also with explicit reference to the Vergilian episode itself, made in the concluding verses (*Thebaid* 10.447–448).[31] And again in his envoy to the *Thebaid,* which Boccaccio later echoes in the envoy to the *Teseida,* Statius makes the most explicit of references to his literary model, adapting a common metaphor for the process of imitation to pay homage to the *Aeneid* by name.

Statius's open imitation of the *Aeneid* was noted as a matter of course by his medieval commentators. It is not uncommon to find references to the author of the *Thebaid* as "simia Maronis" in glosses that can be traced to Italy in the fourteenth century. The phrase is not necessarily disparaging.[32] The older academic prologue to the *Thebaid* beginning "In principio uniuscuiusque auctoris," which was probably composed in northern France in the twelfth century, and which circulated widely—copies of English and north Italian provenance survive along with those from northern continental Europe—notes that Statius "imitates Vergil" and cites the envoy. A later prologue, north Italian, from the late fourteenth or early fifteenth century, says much the same thing: "Note that in Statius's *Achilleid* [the author] imitates Homer, but in this work he imitates Vergil, following the treatise *Aeneid.*"[33] Along with these we may place the extensively glossed *Thebaid* described by De Angelis, probably Bolognese, from about 1350, the marginal commentary of which seems to reflect the schools of Giovanni del Virgilio and Pietro da Moglio. "In the manuscript, great attention is given to the *auctores* whose verses find echoes in Statius (Lucan and Vergil most prominently, then Ovid and Cicero, *Rhetoric*), with the Statian *imitatio* occasionally declared explicitly."[34] Especially remarkable is that the glosses point in the other direction as well, to Cassiodorus and the *Alexandreis* of Walter of Châtillon, showing how Statius in turn was a model for imitation.

Both of these academic prologues follow the late classical example of Servius's prologue to the *Aeneid,* which declares that Vergil intended "to imitate Homer and to praise Augustus,"[35] and like Servius they imply that the imitation was to some extent open and evident. That Boccaccio knew Statius as imitator of Vergil seems to be beyond question. He knew Statius and Statius's great model too well. The matter of Vergil's imitation of Homer presents a different aspect, for Boccaccio, at least during the years he worked on the *Teseida,* did not know Greek or have access to the Homeric poems in the original language. It seems likely, nevertheless, that he knew that the main action of Vergil's epic in its first six books repeats in broad but recognizable outline the action of Homer's *Odyssey,* while the last six books reflect the action of the *Iliad.*[36] He certainly knew Servius's commentary on the *Aeneid;*[37] he was well acquainted with the narrative content of the two poems by way of other classical authors, including Valerius Maximus, whom Boccaccio studied with the commentary of his "father and teacher" Dionigi da Borgo;[38] and then through medieval Latin traditions, including the encyclopedists and perhaps the *Ilias latina*.[39] The absence of the Homeric texts would place limits on the understanding of Servius's statement with regard to imitated diction and echoed verses, but not with regard to the imitation of narrative structure.

Moreover, Vergil's open imitation of the Homeric narratives is described in some detail in the *Saturnalia* of Macrobius, a work that Boccaccio came to know well, probably early in his career, though the certain indications are later: He cites the *Saturnalia* in the *Genealogie;* Coluccio Salutati writes to him in 1372 requesting a copy; Boccaccio's manuscript, apparently bound with a copy of Macrobius's commentary on the *Dream of Scipio,* is listed among the books in the Parva Libraria at Santo Spirito.[40]

The second chapter of the *Saturnalia*'s fifth book begins an extended discussion of Vergil as an imitative poet and especially of the *Aeneid* as an imitative poem, which fills the subsequent chapters of the book with notes on parallel passages. Chapter 2 sets out a general theory of imitation by summarizing certain pedagogical commonplaces of late classical rhetorical education. It holds that Vergil has drawn from many Greek sources, which are, however, subordinate to a broad structure of narrative borrowings from the Homeric poems. These analogies among characters and the sequence of events form as it were an Arch of Titus under which the other butterflies are gathered. The pattern is easily recognized in the reappearing scenes and motifs, even before the verbal echoes, of the Homeric model. In this way, Vergil's poem holds a mirror (*speculum*) to Homer.

In the person of Eustacius, Macrobius recalls the pedagogical commonplace that identifies the Odyssean and Iliadic portions of the *Aeneid:*

> I pass over in silence these things and others as well, which are things recited to schoolboys. Furthermore, the *Aeneid* itself— did it not borrow from Homer first the wanderings from the Odyssey and then the battles from the *Iliad*? Only that the order of events had to change in this work: for while in Homer the Ilian war is fought first and afterward he deals with the wanderings of Ulysses on the return from Troy, in Vergil Aeneas's journey after the war precedes the wars he fought in Italy.[41]

Within this broad mirroring of Homer's narrative, Vergil arranges scenes and motifs of Homeric inspiration. Although they are modified, their origin is easily recognized. Vergil's art is to be admired in part for its skillful transformations within these familiar structures *speciem refert mira imi-*

tatione. He composes his scenes by the "admirable imitation" that arranges characters and actions by analogy to their well-known models:

> What can I say? Vergil's entire work was made as if it were a
> faithful reflection [*speculum*] of the works of Homer. Indeed,
> the tempest is described by wonderful imitation [*mira imita-
> tione*] . . . Venus takes up the role of Nausicaa, daughter of King
> Alcinous, Dido herself in hosting the banquet recalls the image
> [*refert speciem*] of King Alcinous. Scylla, Charybdis, and Circe
> are elegantly touched upon. And in place of the Oxen of the
> Sun, the isles of the Strophades are created [*finguntur*] . . . Pali-
> nurus corresponds to Elpenor, the councils of Anchises to those
> of Tiresias.[42]

Here is a critical terminology perfectly suited to Boccaccio's imitation of
narrative action, with its sequence of scenes and characters and the associated themes. Whether it is attributed to Macrobius's description of
Vergil, the kind of imitation we see in the *Teseida*, with its fictional characters and action created by analogy with those in the *Thebaid*, clearly
has its roots in the epic poems themselves and in critical traditions associated with them, rather than in the rhetorical tradition, where imitation is
discussed primarily as a way to master literary style. The latter, recently
described by G. W. Pigman and Thomas Greene, clearly lie behind Petrarch's comments on dissimulation.[43] Boccaccio's imitation of the *Thebaid* in the *Teseida* begins in the epic strategies of open analogies in a
familiar narrative sequence.

   If we turn to Boccaccio's vernacular poetry from the late 1330s and
early 1340s, the works closest to the *Teseida* in time of composition show
us this kind of allusive imitation. In the *Filostrato*, the course of events
leading to the fall of Troilo parallel the historical course of the fall of the
city of Troy: in microcosm, his passion for Criseida recalls the desire of
his brother Paris—and then Troy, acting in Paris's behalf—for Helen.
The name Troilo underscores the analogy, as does the identical role of
Cassandra in both narratives. And Boccaccio has Cassandra identify the
central terms of analogy when she says that Troilo suffers from the "love
that will ruin us all."[44] The narrative model in this case is the most famous chapter in the legendary history of the gentile empires; the opening
narrative of the *Amorosa visione* recalls the shape of a specific literary
work: as Vittore Branca's notes on that poem suggest, and as Carlo
Paolazzi has recently argued in detail, Boccaccio's use of a familiar poetic
form introduces an equally familiar literary situation. The terza rima of

the *Amorosa visione,* along with its frame as an allegorical vision, introduce a series of motifs and scenes that repeat the pattern of action at the
beginning of the *Commedia.* Verbal echoes mark the reader's way: the
protagonist goes to sleep in a state of confusion ("smarrimento"); a noble-
woman ("donna gentil, piacente e bella," 1.26) appears before him, inviting him to travel with her toward the greatest good ("somma felicità,"
1.29). He follows her up a hill, arriving quickly at the entrance to a castle,
where after an invocation to the angelic intelligence of the third sphere
woven entirely from Dantean verses, he faces the choice of entering the
castle through a narrow gate or one that is wide open. As Paolazzi observes, this is a variation on the pattern of the *Commedia,* but it is one
suggested by the *Commedia* itself, for it has the look of a "literary variant
of the *corto andar* and of the *altro viaggio* that appear before Dante at
the beginning of the *Inferno.*"[45] The "obvious symmetry with the narrative line" of the literary model then takes Boccaccio's dreamer to a gate
with an inscription above it (3.10–11) and finally to a catalog of philosophers (4.40–88). "The second part of canto 4 is built on the foundation
of a passage in *Inferno* 4 (130–147), from which Boccaccio draws his
catalog . . . amplifying it with illustrative or descriptive notes and adding
a series of other figures, for the most part minor."[46] Boccaccio recalls the
narrative pattern and then varies it: *speciem refert mira imitatione.* He
does much the same thing in the *Teseida,* where as we shall see, the strict
symmetry with action in the *Thebaid* is finally altered, but altered according to a pattern suggested by the *Thebaid* itself; and where catalogs are
borrowed and amplified with illustrative and descriptive notes.[47]

Allusive narrative and learned similes

When Boccaccio likens the rivalry of Palamon and Arcite to that of
Eteocles and Polynices by means of a formal simile, it is clear that his use
of narrative motifs from the *Thebaid* is not simply imitation but also allusion. Literary reminiscences may be unintentional. A poet can hope his
imitations escape the notice of his public. But allusions do not produce
the intended effect unless the reader remembers the text or the historical
event to which they refer.[48] Both in the simile and in the reflection of
Statius's main action throughout the narrative of the *Teseida,* the sophisticated artistry depends on the reader's ability to recognize the legendary
events of the Theban civil war—especially as they are recounted by Statius—and to match them to the characters and their situation in the foreground of the "romance." The importance of this legendary background

to the similes and the allusive narrative of the *Teseida* finds its most direct expression in the authorial glosses on the poem, which include an extended summary of the *Thebaid* at *Teseida* 3.5, and in the massive apparatus of mythographical and historical commentary that characterizes the two fifteenth-century commentaries on the poem.

Because Boccaccio drew on the *cantari* traditions in composing the *Teseida* and because he wrote in Florentine Italian, it has sometimes been assumed that his primary audience was the group of Florentine merchants and bankers in Naples. This audience, "unlearned" in the sense that it was more comfortable with the vernacular than with Latin, would seem to preclude the possibility of an allusive narrative constructed as open imitation of the Latin *Thebaid*. There is, however, no external evidence at all to support this assumption, while the internal evidence suggests a more ambitious and a broader conception of the implied audience.

The problems posed by allusive poetry are essentially problems of information. And on the one hand, the information necessary to recognize Boccaccio's allusions to the *Thebaid*'s main action was partly available in French and Italian sources, notably the chapters on Thebes in the vernacular compilations of ancient history. It was also summarized in Boccaccio's own glosses to the poem, and it was available in simpler Latin in some universal chronicles, notably the *Chronologia tripartita* compiled by Paolino Veneto, present at Robert's court during the 1330s, and the chronicle of Benzo d'Alessandria, who had been a chancellor to Can Grande early in the century. Paolino gives an unusually long description of Theban history, apparently based on the vernacular compilations; Benzo actually recast the *Thebaid* in prose.[49] But on the other hand, there is no reason to imagine "vernacular" culture in isolation from the study of classical Latin authors, or to assume that Boccaccio was unable to write with a miscellaneous audience in mind. The *Teseida* is broad and deep, a river where the lamb and elephant both can swim. At least in its conception, the *Teseida* was a product of Boccaccio's Neapolitan period, and in his autobiographical references to his life in Naples, he usually presents himself in association with the court. If we focus on this environment for a moment, we are struck by the fact that Robert's court was a center of Latin learning, learning that included the classical poets. Petrarch was to go there for his examination before the crowning with laurel, in 1341. There is no a priori reason to exclude the learned members of court, Boccaccio's revered teacher Dionigi, the elderly court librarian Paolo di Perugia, the other noted correspondents of Petrarch, the young Luca da Penne, from Boccaccio's actual or implied audience. The provenance of manuscript copies of the *Teseida* proves nothing with regard to the original audience, for they are almost all from the fifteenth century, but they do show a marked number of courtly, as well as mercantile, owners. This fact is not very surprising, if we remember the courtly setting and themes of the narrative. To give just two examples: the de' Bassi commentary was dedicated to Ercole d'Este, and de' Bassi recommends the figure of Theseus to his noble patron as a model of princely behavior;[50] and there was a copy of the *Teseida* in the Visconti library at Pavia in the fourteenth century. Moreover, the literary koine of Florentine Italian was certainly not incomprehensible to the members of the Neapolitan court. During Robert's reign, daily business was apparently conducted in both French and Italian. Robert wrote his sermons in Latin, and it is not clear in what language he delivered them, but many were directed to predominantly Italian-speaking groups, in convents, at the Studio.[51] Robert's son Charles of Calabria was podestà of Florence for more than a year, and he spent much of 1328 in that city. Broadening our conception of Boccaccio's first audience in yet another direction is the Latin gloss summarizing *Teseida* 1–2.40, from the Franciscan convent of Santa Croce, Florence.[52]

The internal evidence of the *Teseida* clearly suggests a "learned" audience, at least in the sense that the rhetorical mechanisms of the poem require the reader to have a good deal of information from classical literature. To the extent that we argue for an audience more comfortable with the vernacular than with Latin, it must be subjoined that the poem's allusive style and its scholarly apparatus propose to that audience a vernacular experience of poetry in the classical tradition. But the more reasonable conclusion would be to assume that some members of that audience had direct access to the classical tradition itself.

In an important essay dedicated to Boccaccio's similes in the *Comedia delle ninfe fiorentine,* Giuseppe Velli has shown the markedly literary nature of Boccaccio's metaphorical vehicles. Here and in other vernacular works before the *Decameron,* the poet draws his terms of comparison "from a world that has no immediate correspondence to the common experience of living, practical or affective."[53] Boccaccio's learned similes require readers to move through the distant and bookish world of classical legend and example, essentially that of the "Latin" Boccaccio, if they are to place the terms of comparison in relation to the larger design of his work. The literary vehicles generally come from Roman poetry through Dante: Amphiaraus disappearing into the earth at Thebes (from *Thebaid* 7.818–820, by way of *Inferno* 20.31–36) at *Comedia ninfe* 18.30; the appearance of Venus to Anchises (from *Aeneid* 2.692–697) at *Comedia ninfe* 21.14; the appearance of Eriton to the sons of Pompey (from *De bello civili* 6.755 by way of *Inferno* 9.23–24) at *Comedia ninfe* 23.15; the awakening of Achilles (from *Achilleid* 1.247–249, by way of *Purgatorio* 9.34–35) at *Comedia ninfe* 28.10. Faced with some vehicles of considerable obscurity, we can do no less than reach for a copy of the *Genealogie* or *De casibus* and in doing so overturn the artificial distinction between Boccaccio the erudite encyclopedist and Boccaccio the vernacular poet.

What Velli remarks in the similes holds true of the narrative structure as well. The simile of Tisiphone, with which I began tracing the imitative pattern of action in the *Teseida*, invites comparison of one point in Boccaccio's narrative with a similar point in the *Thebaid*. A series of these points will then suggest the outline of Boccaccio's analogy, so that the main action of the poem is constructed as an extended comparison: his allusive narrative constantly invites the reader to recall the classical model and to match it against the new imitation. Thus the "romance" of Palamon and Arcite has a quality that Thomas Greene would call "transitive," meaning that it invites reflection on the way the model is transformed (the Theban civil war is like a fight over a beautiful woman); but it is preeminently metaphorical, meaning that the *Thebaid* serves as the vehicle of a metaphor defining the characters and main action of the *Teseida* (the rivalry of Palamon and Arcite is like the fight for the throne of Oedipus).

It is not a flattering comparison. The terms of Boccaccio's analogy align the desire of Palamon and Arcite "to possess Emilia alone" with that of Eteocles and Polynices to possess the throne of Thebes; to possess it whatever the consequences. The metaphorical aspect of this narrative thus characterizes the motivating passions behind the armed rivalry of Palamon and Arcite by reference to a larger, "political" conflict, which suggests the more serious implications of their essentially private, if not entirely harmless, acts. The same analogy, in its transitive aspect, comments on the *Thebaid,* for it presents anew the theme and pattern of action in Statius's work with various elements—notably the role of the pagan gods—modified, and with a focus on the personal origins rather than the public consequences of the conflict. To use the Aristotelian terms so common in the philosophy of Boccaccio's culture, and which Renaissance critics used so often to describe epic, the *Teseida* recasts the *Thebaid* with its focus on the sphere of ethics instead of politics.

Throughout the poem, Boccaccio employs formal similes to define the motivating passions and the ensuing acts of his contentious Theban kinsmen. These similes present in a smaller rhetorical form the same technique of the allusive narrative, so that careful attention to their sophisticated match between background and foreground provides the best introduction to the art of Boccaccio's allusive main action. There is also a marked similarity in the subjects chosen as vehicles, all negative exempla from the repertoire of classical myth and legend. One instance is the simile at *Teseida* 4.54 describing Arcite's joy on his return to Athens after a year or more in exile. When he is accepted into Theseus's services, the disguised Arcite delights in admiring Emilia and is noticed by none save Emilia herself. He thanks Fortune for leading him "into this port" (4.53). Boccaccio suggests the potentially violent force of Arcite's passion by means of a formal comparison to Tereus shortly after he had sailed into the port of Athens to fetch Philomena:

> Maggior letizia non credo sentisse
> allor Tereo quando li fu concesso
> per Pandion che Filomena en gisse
> alla sua suora in Trazia con esso,
> che or Penteo   (4.54)

> [No greater joy, I believe, did Tereus feel when he was permitted by Pandion to carry Philomena with him to her sister in Thrace, than Pentheus (i.e., Arcite) now]

To understand the comparison, we need to recall the story of Pandion, a ruler of Athens before the time of Theseus, the marriage of his daughter Procne to Tereus, king of Thrace, and Tereus's later return to Athens to bring Procne's sister Philomena to Thrace for a visit. The vehicle of Boccaccio's simile specifies a particular moment in the story as it appears in Ovid's *Metamorphoses*,[54] with King Tereus newly arrived in Athens, already infatuated by the rediscovered beauty of his sister-in-law, and now prevailing on an apprehensive Pandion to let him carry her away to Thrace. It is a learned simile built on the analogous moments of pleasure at a concession by a king of Athens. But its extended application is highly unflattering to Arcite. And as if to underscore the implications of this particular vehicle in its extended form, Boccaccio refers later in *Teseida* 4 to a later episode in the myth of Tereus, there likening Arcite's "joy" at the thought of Emilia to the "joy" of Philomena when she contemplated the revenge she would take on her violator (4.73).

That Boccaccio leaves the full implications of his similes to the learned application of his reader is nicely mirrored in the way his speaking characters sometimes fail to perceive the full implications of their own metaphorical expressions, while these are suggested by the poem's gloss. At 5.32, for example, Palamon asks the moon to guide his steps "like those of Leander in the sea." Now, the moon did guide Leander across the Hellespont for a while, but as the gloss quietly reminds us (at 5.32 and 1.40), he was soon to drown.[55] Likewise in the narrator's two references to the "joy" of Tereus, the full significance of a match between the gaze of the King of Thrace and that of Arcite is left to the glossing reader. How does this legendary vehicle apply to the little picture of Arcite looking devotedly at Emilía? To be sure, the *tertium comparationis* is easily grasped. In both parts of the comparison a man overwhelmed by the attractive appearance of a young woman happily contemplates the "concession" that will put him in her company. But the extended application of this vehicle also leads us to compare the violence of Tereus in his broken pledge to Pandion and his rape and disfiguring of Philomena.

Like the events of the *Thebaid*, the rape of Philomena represents an extreme form of human *furor*. When it is employed as an extended analogy to this part of the main action, it constitutes a forceful suggestion of the extent to which Arcite's passion has overcome his better nature. Although the intended tone of this comparison may well be one of comic exaggeration, the serious implications of Arcite's lusty stare—which, after all, will lead him to break pledges and to enter the arena against his closest kin—emerge quickly when the reader recalls the nature and consequences of Tereus's "joy." And Boccaccio's gloss is there to help our recollection.

Yet another formal simile offers an example of Boccaccio's technique at its best. Like the simile of Tisiphone's venom at *Teseida* 5.13 and that of the hunting lion at *Teseida* 7.115, this simile was drawn from the *Thebaid* and employed to characterize the passions motivating Palamon and Arcite in their fierce rivalry. The elaborate match between vehicle and tenor requires us to look back at what led the cousins into the arena and also forward to their reconciliation and Arcite's apotheosis.

Well along in the "giuoco a Marte" of the *Teseida*, with the outcome still in doubt, Arcite is so fatigued by the battle that he takes a moment to catch his breath and regain his confidence. He glances at his beloved Emilia as she sits watching the great events, and the sight of her gives him new vigor. At first, Boccaccio uses the figure of flowers lifting their heads in the spring sunshine (8.79) to describe the effects of her beauty, perhaps alluding to *Inferno* 2.127 where a similar figure appears. This brief simile is followed by an extended comparison of one full stanza, based on two similes from *Thebaid* 6, which Statius uses in close succession to describe the inspiration of the contestants in the wrestling match.[56] Boccaccio's sophisticated handling of the simile reflects his knowledge of Statius's antecedents in the epic tradition as well as the immediate context of the similes in *Thebaid* 6.

In the fifth game of *Thebaid* 6, *uncta pale*, Tydeus competes with the very large but awkward Agylleus. Agylleus himself, as will be seen below, makes a brief appearance in Boccaccio's tournament along with other defeated contestants in the games of *Thebaid* 6.[57] Statius builds his narrative of the wrestling match on the general outline of the contest between Hercules and Achelous (*Metamorphoses* 9.27ff.), and he alludes to the literary antecedent by genealogy and epithet: here a descendant of Hercules (Agylleus) fights with a disciple of Achelous (Tydeus).[58] But the roles are exchanged. Hercules defeated Achelous, but here Tydeus will defeat Agylleus.

The first of Statius's two reinvigoration similes anticipates Arcite's situation in the tournament directly, for in it Agylleus and Tydeus are likened to bulls fighting over a desirable heifer. The same vehicle had been used by Ovid in *Metamorphoses* to describe Hercules and Achelous in their fight over Deianira:[59]

> non aliter vidi fortes concurrere tauros,
> cum, pretium pugnae, toto nitidissima saltu
> expetitur coniunx   (9.46–48)

> [In the same way I have seen powerful bulls rush at each other,
> when the most beautiful heifer in the meadows is desired, the
> prize of the battle]

Statius's simile has another important antecedent in *Aeneid* 12.715ff., where it is used to describe the combat of Turnus and Aeneas for Lavinia. Statius employs the Vergilian words *coniunx* (for the heifer) and *obnixus* (to describe the bulls) in homage to his source, but proposes a new point of comparison when he adds that the appearance of the *coniunx* makes the bulls forget their wounds and redouble their efforts. In doing this, Statius may well be recalling Vergil's earlier bull simile at *Aeneid* 12.101ff., which describes the effects that the sight of Lavinia has on Turnus.[60] Statius's simile concludes:

> . . . medio coniunx stat candida prato
> victorem exspectans, rumpunt obnixa furentes
> pectora, subdit amor stimulos et volnera sanat.   (6.865–867)

[in the middle of the meadow stands the white heifer waiting for
the victor, while (the bulls) burst their straining chests in a rage,
and love plies the goad and heals their wounds.]

One notes with interest the thematic words *furor* and *amor* recurring
here in the microcosm of Statius's games, the Vergilian simile describing
the cause of a war reappearing in the context of a wrestling match. It is,
on the one hand, an interesting example of Statius's frequent use of literary formulas associated with erotic love in his description of other passionate desires that lead men to fight (for Tydeus and Agylleus it is the
love of glory: *animosa citavit/gloria;* for Eteocles and Polynices it is love
of ruling: *amor regendi*). On the other hand, it is a good example of the
way Boccaccio returns Statius's formulas to a context in which the *casus
belli* is again a beautiful woman. He will adopt the last line of Statius's
simile for the purpose of describing Arcite as he is involved in a martial
"game" for the hand of Emilia.

The second reinvigoration simile in Statius's fifth game provides the
main vehicle for Boccaccio's extended comparison. In the *Thebaid,* the
two competing strongmen do not remain on even terms, and as soon as
Tydeus gains the upper hand, Statius follows the short simile of the bulls
with a longer, mythological comparison in which the motif of reinvigoration appears again, only to be negated. The vehicle here involves Hercules
himself and another of his legendary contests, but ironically Agylleus's
powerful ancestor is matched with Tydeus, while Hercules' victim is likened to Agylleus:

> . . . Herculeis pressum sic fama lacertis
> terrigenam sudasse Libyn, cum fraude reperta
> raptus in excelsum, nec iam spes ulla cadendi
> nec licet extrema matrem contingere planta.   (6.893–896)

[So, fame tells, did Hercules hold fast in his arms the sweating,
earth-born Libyan, when he discovered the trick and snatched
him up on high and left him no hope of falling nor suffered him
to touch even with the tip of his foot his mother earth.]

Tydeus, in triumphing over Agylleus, is likened—implicitly in the action
of the poem, for he crushes his opponent in his arms, and explicitly in the
simile—to Hercules. Agylleus corresponds to Antaeus, the "earth-born
Libyan" who has been found out and held in the air away from the invig-

orating touch of the earth. Statius plays masterfully on the irony of defeat in exaltation ("raptus in excelsum") and the frustrated desire of Antaeus that he might fall ("nec iam spes ulla cadendi").

The formal simile at *Teseida* 8.80 describes the return of Arcite's strength at the sight of Emilia:

> E qual Anteo, quando molto affannato
> era da Ercul con cui combattea,
> *come a la terra sua madre* accostato
> s'era, tutte le forze riprendea,
> cotale Arcita, molto faticato,
> mirando Emilia forte si facea;
> e vie più fiero tornò al ferire
> che prima, *sì lo spronò il disire*.   (8.80)

> [And just as Antaeus, when he was exhausted by Hercules, with
> whom he was fighting, regained all his strength as soon as he
> was brought to the earth his mother, just so Arcite, very tired,
> made himself strong looking at Emilia; he returned to the fray
> much more fierce than before, desire spurred him so.]

Arcite's desire spurs him on and heals his wounds, with an echo of Statius's "subdit amor stimulos" in "sì lo spronò il disire." This single phrase from the first reinvigoration simile appears in the *Teseida* as part of a new construction involving Antaeus and Hercules. Boccaccio's simile contains several verbal echoes of its model in *Thebaid* 6, including one in Boccaccio's gloss, which specifies that Antaeus was a giant "in Libya" much as Statius does at 6.894. But the remarkable thing about *Teseida* 8.80 is not how it joins two related similes from the same passage in the *Thebaid,* but how it employs the vehicle of Hercules and Antaeus to describe reinvigoration. Statius had used it to describe reinvigoration that fails, a trick that was discovered ("fraude reperta") and an answering contrast to the earlier simile of the two passionate bulls. Statius uses the simile to say that, like Hercules, Tydeus did not let his opponent regain his strength, and that Agylleus, like Antaeus, was defeated. By matching vehicle to tenor in this way, Boccaccio suggests that the reinvigorating force that animates Arcite will not sustain him and that he will be kept from the worldly beauty that offers it. It anticipates Arcite's Boethian perspective in his apotheosis, when he, like Antaeus, will be "raptus in excelsum."[61]

Rivals and exiles: *Thebaid* 1–4 and *Teseida* 3–6

Statius's list of the consequences of Tisiphone's venom, adopted or better adapted by Boccaccio at the end of his simile at *Teseida* 5.13, defines the general pattern of action in his narrative ("broken reciprocity, the discord of shared rule") with an echo of the proemium to Vergil's *Aeneid:* "dum conderet urbem / inferretque deos Latio; genus unde Latinum / Albanique patres atque altae moenia Romae" (until he could found a city / and carry his gods into Latium, whence rose the Latin race, / the royal line of Alba and the high walls of Rome). Similar in rhetorical form, the two passages both sketch an outline of the main action, but that of the *Thebaid* recalls the *Aeneid* by inverse analogy: Statius's principal characters are *impius* in direct contrast to Vergil's *pius* Aeneas. The narrative begins (1.46) with the negated form of the Vergilian word, and with an act exemplifying the negation of the Vergilian concept. Also in direct contrast to the *Aeneid,* which recounts the founding of Rome and *gens Julia,* the main action of the *Thebaid* concerns the destruction of a city and its ruling family. While Aeneas exemplifies the self-sacrificing devotion of a leader to the future peace and prosperity of his city, the contentious sons of Oedipus exemplify by their selfish disregard for the common good, and even for the claims of duty to one's family, the kind of misgovernment whereby established cities and their ruling families are confounded. It is emblematic in the *Thebaid* that the walls of Thebes are not high but old and in need of repair: "vetusto / moenia lapsa situ" (4.356; cf. 2.700). Statius's inversion of Vergilian motifs includes the key word *furor* as well: While the first scene in the *Aeneid* gives us "furor" calmed as a synecdoche for the main action of the epic, the first scene of the *Thebaid* shows "furor" entering the breasts of the major characters, and then sketches the consequences (compare *Aeneid* 1.150 and *Thebaid* 1.126).[62]

Medieval discussions of the aim or "intention" of the two epics point to this perfect contrast with reference to Roman history. Thus the *Aeneid,* as it is introduced in the commentary of Servius and its later derivatives, identifies Aeneus as a positive exemplum of the prince, intended by Vergil as praise and also instruction for Emperor Augustus. One of the oldest and most widely known prologues to the *Thebaid,* itself modeled on the Servian prologue, defines Statius's probable aim in writing the *Thebaid:* to warn, with a negative exemplum, two prospective rivals for the *imperium* at Rome, Titus and Domitian:

> Intentio Statii in hoc opere est Thebanam describere hystoriam, cuius intentionis diverse a diversis assignantur cause. Quidam

dicunt quod mortuo Vaspasiano filii eius Titus et Domicianus in
tantam cupiditatem regni exarserunt, ut fraternale odium incur-
rerent. Ad quorum dehortationem actor iste Thebanam proponit
hystoriam. Et secundum hanc causam talis huius intentionis utilitas est, ut viso quid contingerit illis duobus fratribus qui tanta
imperii exarserunt cupiditate quod sese mutuis interfecerunt vulneribus, isti a consimili scelere desistant.[63]

[Statius's intention in this work is to describe Theban history,
concerning which intention different people identify different
motives. Some say that when Vespasian died his sons Titus and
Domitian burned with such desire for power, they risked fraternal conflict; to discourage them, the author offered Theban history. And according to this motive, the utility of his intention is
such that, having seen what happened to those two brothers who
burned with such desire for rule that they killed each other in
battle, these two would desist from a similar misdeed.]

I shall return to this passage when examining some of the mediating factors in Boccaccio's literary culture that influenced his views of classical
epic; but it may serve here as a clear statement of the singular features in
the theme and main action of the *Thebaid*.

Boccaccio had an intimate familiarity with both the *Aeneid* and the
Thebaid when he composed the *Teseida*, and he imitated both in his
formal structure and in single passages and motifs. But the main action
of the *Teseida* is modeled directly on the *Thebaid*, to which it stands in
a relation of direct analogy. The nature of Boccaccio's open imitation
in his main action is determined by the main action of the *Thebaid*.
This is perhaps the most distinctive feature of Boccaccio's use of epic
tradition in his poem. The foreground does not develop against a background that establishes a positive norm. The "heroic" proportions and
high solemn style that characterize epic do not in the case of Statius's
Thebaid magnify the virtues of an epic hero; rather they magnify the *impietas* of Eteocles and Polynices, and the grim political consequences of
that *impietas*.

The main action of the *Teseida* begins near the end of the second book,
where Palamon and Arcite are introduced for the first time. Boccaccio
then develops it in books 3–6 as an analogy to the action of *Thebaid*
1–4, that portion of Statius's narrative which takes the rivalry between
Eteocles and Polynices from their agreement to share power and Polynices' year-long exile (1) to the beginning of armed conflict on a small
scale when the exile, represented by another person, makes his bid to return (2), followed by the decision of both rivals to make war, news of

which spreads across Greece and attracts many sympathetic allies (3), described in the formal catalog of the troops who will take part in the larger conflict (4). Boccaccio defines the terms of the analogy in the simile at *Teseida* 5.13, where he asks us to observe how this rivalry between these Theban kinsmen for possession of Emilia ("d'Emilia aver") is like that rivalry between those Theban kinsmen for the lordship of Thebes (the "due fratei del regno"); and he repeats the terms of the analogy in the final line of the simile, remarking that *amore,* like *signoria,* will not be shared. This comparison of desire for Emilia to desire for a "regno" recurs explicitly in the speeches of the *Teseida,* as for example when Arcite in exile complains of being "povero e pellegrino / del regno mio cacciato" (4.84) [poor and a pilgrim, thrown out of my kingdom (i.e. Athens)] or when Arcite on his sick bed asks to hear Emilia's voice "a me più cara ch'alcuno altro regno" (9.25) [dearer to me than any other kingdom], while it recurs implicitly through the narrative structure. Boccaccio's use of narrative motifs from *Thebaid* 1–4 is strictly governed by this pattern of analogy: from the pact of shared suffering and desire (3), the exile of Arcite and his return under another name (4), which leads to armed conflict on a small scale (5), and then the catalog of troops who will take part in the larger conflict, involving representatives of all the provinces in Greece (6).

But what has Boccaccio done in the introductory books, *Teseida* 1 and 2? Why has he begun the pattern of analogy only with book 3? A general answer is that he uses these two books to introduce his positive exemplum, Theseus, often *pio Teseo* (pious) or *buon Teseo* (good), in allusion to Vergil's Aeneas. Because Theseus's moderating influence on the *Thebaid*-like manifestations of *furor* in Palamon and Arcite will contribute to the ending in Boccaccio's poem, which is not *Thebaid*-like, we might want to identify Theseus's role in *Teseida* 1–2 and 7–12 as a kind of Aeneidic frame around the Thebaidic main action of personal rivalry and civil war. This is a rather schematic view, however, and as a close analysis of Boccaccio's alternate ending shows, the figure of Theseus has more than one classical model. It is more important to recognize how Boccaccio's redeployment of the last half of *Thebaid* 12, as a frame for the action in *Teseida* 1–2, sets up his main action as a continuation of the *Thebaid* itself. Boccaccio's imitative strategy in *Teseida* 1–2 is to offer an expanded version of the events sketched by Statius in the last three hundred lines of his epic. This narrative continuity introduces not only Theseus but the "open" or allusive use of Statius's narrative structures in the rest of the *Teseida.*

Boccaccio's imitation of the narrative at the end of the *Thebaid* also draws on a long digression in *Thebaid* 5. His redeployment of these two books seems to reflect a careful assessment of Statius's narrative structure, especially its punctuation of the main action by unrelated events. Statius's subject, announced in the proemium to the *Thebaid,* is fraternal strife ("fraterna acies") and the Theban misdeeds that lead to civil war ("sontes Thebas"). The first six books are concerned with the events before the war and the last six with the war itself,[64] but two of Statius's books are not directly concerned with either phase of this main action: the fifth, a long digression in which Hypsipyle tells the story of the Lemnian women and the expedition of the Argonauts against them; and the twelfth, an epilogue to the Theban War, concerned with Creon's tyranny and Theseus's expedition against Creon. These books are the ones that Boccaccio adapts in books 1 and 2 of the *Teseida.* Book 1 tells of Theseus's expedition against the Amazons in Scythia (briefly referred to in *Thebaid* 12), drawing on Hypsipyle's story of the Argonauts and the Lemnian women; and book 2 is adapted directly from the account in *Thebaid* 12 of Theseus's expedition against Creon. To be more precise, the passage in *Thebaid* 12 describing Theseus's return to Athens from Scythia (12.519ff.; cf. *Teseida* 2.10ff.) refers only briefly to that campaign, but Boccaccio expands on the narrative frame in the *Thebaid,* offering a full account in *Teseida* 1. Thus the narrative in the first two books of the *Teseida* overlaps Statius's narration at the end of the *Thebaid,* greatly expanding on *Thebaid* 12 with the help of *Thebaid* 5. This aspect of Boccaccio's design in *Teseida* 1–2 was acknowledged by an early reader of the *Thebaid.* As I have already noted in another context, the manuscript now Plut. 18 sin. 4 in the Laurenziana, which once belonged to Tedaldo della Casa, contains a long gloss opposite *Thebaid* 12.529ff., indicating that Boccaccio's *Teseida* (or as the glossator calls it, "lu Theseo") contains information about Theseus's expedition in Scythia and providing a summary of *Teseida* 1–2.40.[65]

Two significant consequences of this imitative design in *Teseida* 1–2 are that Boccaccio specifies the "Theseus" of his title to be Statius's Theseus of *Thebaid* 12 and that Boccaccio will introduce his own main action in the *Teseida* as a continuation of Statius's narrative. Points of similarity in later scenes become the more striking for this introductory frame and narrative continuity. Palamon and Arcite appear first among the wounded after Theseus's capture of Thebes, emerging as it were from the last chapter in the legendary history of the Theban civil war. They, like the principal characters of the *Thebaid,* prove to be Thebans of no-

ble birth, indeed members of the royal house, descendants of Cadmus
(2.86–88): "In casa sua nati e cresciuti / fummo, e de' suo' nepoti semo"
(We were born and raised in his house and we are among his descendants). But as their story of fraternal strife takes its course, the figure of
Theseus will be present at every turn, influencing it with a moderating
justice that appears only at the very end of Statius's darker poem.

As Boccaccio develops the general pattern of action in *Teseida* 3–6 according to the model of *Thebaid* 1–4, he invites us to watch the translation of Statius's principal characters into a different scale and perspective.
This play of smaller events in the imitation against the solemn grandeur
of its epic subtext does not take the parodic extreme of mock epic; the
somewhat smaller scale of characters and events is matched by Boccaccio's mixture of high and middle styles. There is no marked violence to
Horatian decorum, no bucket described in Vergilian hexameters. But the
constant shadow of the *Thebaid* in the poem does provide Boccaccio
with occasion for a gentle comedy of scale, even as the similarity of his
characters to Eteocles and Polynices suggests the ultimately serious implications of their acts.

The rather delicate blending of comic and serious effects can be seen
immediately in the "tower and garden" scene at the beginning of *Teseida*
3, when Palamon and Arcite are struck by the arrow of Emilia's beauty.
In the long opening scene of *Thebaid* 1, Statius had remarked on the
bitter irony of a Theban civil war fought over an impoverished and unattractive kingdom. Shortly after Tisiphone visits Thebes and inspires the
mistrust and rivalry between Polynices and Eteocles, the author describes
the primitive conditions at Thebes: "yet then no ceilings glittered with
gold, nor did Grecian pillars bear aloft vast halls," concluding, "sed nuda
potestas / armavit fratres, pugna est de paupere regno" (1.150–151). In
context, *nuda potestas* means "power itself" or "power unadorned," in
that it is power that brings little else with it. It is clearly no promise of
material gain or other comprehensible motive for this intense desire to
possess that has "inspired" Polynices and Eteocles, and which will cost
their allies so dearly: "naked power it was that armed the brothers; the
contest is for a poor kingdom."

In the analogy of Boccaccio's *Teseida*, the two Theban kinsmen also
desire *possessione*, and they desire it with an intensity equally disproportionate to the promise of any reward. The sentiment of Statius's "nuda
potestas armavit fratres" thus finds a similar place in Boccaccio's poem,
where it is usually expressed by the narrator or by Theseus. The bluntest
formulation is in Theseus's astonished remark to the armies assembled in
Athens that "sì poca di cosa" (such a small thing) as desire for Emilia

should have brought about such violent passions and should have led so many allies to join in the rivals' bitter dispute (7.5); but it appears frequently in more muted tones and by implication,[66] and it is anticipated as early as the scene beginning the main action, in which Boccaccio establishes the conditions for the coming rivalry. As he describes the effects of Emilia's beauty on the imprisoned cousins, the narrator pauses over the disproportion between the intensity of their newly conceived desire and Emilia's response to the ardent glances she has noticed coming from their prison window. What they desire, and what she is pleased to have them desire, is "sì poca di cosa":

> Né la recava a ciò pensier d'amore
> che ella avesse, ma la vanitate
> che innata han le femine nel core,
> di fare altrui veder la lor biltate;
> *e quasi nude d'ogni altro valore*
> contente son di quella esser lodate (3.30)

[She was not brought to that (pleasure at being admired) by any thought of love that she might have, but by the vanity that is born in the hearts of women, to have someone admire their beauty; and as if naked of other merits they are satisfied to be praised for this (alone).]

The unadorned power that "armed" Eteocles and Polynices against each other corresponds in Boccaccio's analogy to the unadorned beauty of Emilia, which alone has caused the *innamoramento* of Palamon and Arcite. As the aside on feminine vanity suggests, Emilia is content to be admired for her beauty alone, "as if naked of other merits." The transformation of Statius's bitter disapproval into the lighter satire of Boccaccio's aside, which incidentally touches Emilia as well as her admirers, is in keeping with the terms of Boccaccio's analogy and may be seen to follow naturally from his change in the scale of this Theban rivalry. At the same time, the verbal reminiscence of "nuda potestas" in Boccaccio's beauty "nud[a] d'altro valore" underscores the broad correspondence in situation and sentiment, which here, too, matches the main action of the vernacular to that of the classical Latin poem.

The terms of Boccaccio's analogy may themselves be traced to the *Thebaid*, which had replaced Vergil's "coniunx" with "nuda potestas" as the cause of civil war, and where Statius repeatedly describes the motivating passions of Polynices and Eteocles with the language of erotic desire. Theirs is a "fierce love of ruling" (regendi saevus amor) in the proemium, and the desire that overcomes Polynices, to return to Thebes and claim his part of the city's government, is described first as a lovesickness. Argia notices the signs of a secret longing in her husband at the end of his year of exile, and she interprets them to mean that he longs for some woman at Thebes: "I know your wakeful complainings and your bitter sighs, your ever-troubled slumber" (2.336–337), she says to him, asking, "Where does your journey lead you unless it be a secret, cherished passion that draws you back to Thebes?" (2.351–352). Polynices assures her that it is desire to possess his kingdom that keeps him awake, like a lover, all night.

These wakeful nights and lover's sighs reappear in the *Teseida* along with the narrative pattern of exile and return that Statius establishes in *Thebaid* 1–2. On leaving Athens, Boccaccio's exile seems to enjoy the favor of Emilia (*Teseida* 3.83) much as Polynices enjoys the favoring glances and hushed comments of the citizens of Thebes as he leaves that city (*Thebaid* 1.168); Arcite wanders through the provinces of Greece (*Teseida* 4.1–39) following the pattern of Statius's narrative, in which Polynices wanders, newly exiled from Thebes (*Thebaid* 1.312–335); and Arcite's exile begins on a stormy night (4.2), like the night of Polynices' arrival in Argos (*Thebaid* 1.346). Arcite looks longingly back toward Athens (4.4) as Polynices had looked back to Thebes (*Thebaid* 1.312), and both lament their bad fortune and contemplate the object of their desires: "iam iamque animis male debita regna / concipit" (already now he is longing for the kingdom that is unfortunately due to him), while jealousy stirs at the thought that someone else possesses it:

> . . . tenet una dies noctesque recursans
> cura virum, si quando humilem decedere regno
> germanum et semet Thebis opibusque potitum
> cerneret   (1.316–319)

> [One thought recurring night and day torments him: if he could only see his brother, humbled, give up the throne and see himself reigning over Thebes and its dominion]

with the difference that Arcite has not yet identified his cousin as his rival. For now he fears Emilia's betrothed, Acate:

> . . . e ciò che mi dà duol maggiore
> e con asprezza più il cor m'asale,
> è che mi par vederti maritata
> ad uom che mai non t'avrà più amata.   (4.8)

[and the thing that makes me suffer most and assails my heart most fiercely is imagining you married to a man who will not then love you.]

Also modeled on Polynices is the way Arcite's health and appearance change during his exile: he cannot rest, he sighs day and night (*Thebaid* 2.330ff., 3.678; *Teseida* 4.26ff.).

As he does at the beginning of his main action, here too Boccaccio makes explicit reference to the events of the *Thebaid*, against which the pattern of his own narrative should appear. Arcite passes by the site of Thebes, recently destroyed in the wars of the *Thebaid* and of *Teseida* 2. He recalls the sons of Oedipus in his lament for his ancestors and royal house, of which he and Palamon are the last survivors:

> Ov'è lo spesso popolo, ove Laio,
> ove Edippo dolente, ove i figliuoli? (4.16)

> [Where is the teeming populace, where is Laius, where is sorrowing Oedipus, where his sons?]

The passage is one of many explicit references to the Theban War that appear in *Teseida* 3–6, drawing attention back to the legendary history that constitutes the main action of the *Thebaid* as the pattern of that action is itself echoed in the rivalry between Palamon and Arcite. Already in *Teseida* 3, Arcite had recalled the Theban War, its place in the very near past, and the blame his royal house bears for its sad consequences:

> E' ti de' ricordare
> ch'ancor non son trapassati due anni
> che sei gran re per lo nostro operare
> fur morti a Tebe, e gravissimi danni
> n'ebber gli Argivi e popoli altri assai,
> per che odiati sarén sempre mai. (3.65)

> [You must remember that two years have not yet gone by since six great kings were killed at Thebes on our account, and the Argives took heavy losses in it, as did many other peoples, for which we will always be hated.]

Here Arcite is speaking to Pirithous as his exile begins, and before the pattern of his own actions has progressed far enough to show its similarity to that of the exile in the *Thebaid* and his rivalry with his Theban kinsman. But the lament for Theban misfortunes and misdeeds is a leitmotif recurring after that pattern develops as well, and in *Teseida* 5, after the strife has begun, Arcite recalls the long series of his ancestors (5.57–60), concluding with Eteocles and Polynices:

> Quai fosser poi fra loro i due fratelli
> d'Edippo nati, non cal raccontare:
> il fuoco fé testimonianza d'elli,
> nel qual fur messi dopo il lor mal fare.   (5.59)

> [There is no use in recounting what happened then between the two brothers, sons of Oedipus; the fire gives witness to them, in which they were put after their evil deeds.]

Like the description of Emilia's vain pleasure in her beauty, the tone of this passage and its comic ironies depend on the play between foreground and background; but here the background is explicitly recalled for us. In an analogy to Polynices and Eteocles that Arcite all but recognizes for himself, the young Theban kinsmen will also rush into battle with one another: "E e' mi piace, poi che t'è in piacere / che pure infra noi due battaglia sia" (And it pleases me, as it is pleasing to you, that there should be a battle between us as well).

Arcite's return to Athens (*Teseida* 4.40) and the beginning of armed conflict between the cousins (*Teseida* 5) are modeled on the long episode in Statius's epic that describes the beginning of the struggle between Polynices and Eteocles. Both the pattern of action and the setting of *Thebaid* 2.370–744 reappear, with adjustments of scale and tone, in *Teseida* 5. Consider first the two principal characters: Statius has the exiled Polynices return to Thebes by proxy, in the person of his brother-in-law Tydeus. After he makes claim to the throne on Polynices' behalf and is denied, Tydeus leaves Thebes, and Eteocles sends fifty men to ambush him. Thus the first battle of the Theban War, the battle involving a few that would lead to the war involving many, occurs between representatives of Polynices and those of Eteocles, not the brothers themselves. Boccaccio summarizes these events in a gloss at *Teseida* 1.14, which explains an allusion to Mars, said in the text to have come

> dal bosco dentro al qual guidati avea,
> con tristo augurio del re furioso
> di Tebe, l'aspra schiera   (1.14)

> [from the wood into which he had led, with the dark wishes of the furibund king of Thebes, the harsh flock.]

The terms of the circumlocution in the text as well as its explanatory gloss are shaped to anticipate the similar pattern in the *boschetto* of *Teseida* 5:

> E essendo finito l'anno che Etiocles dovea avere regnato venne a Tebe Tideo, a richiedere il regno per Polinice; il quale non sola-mente non gli fu renduto, ma fu di notte in uno bosco assalito da cinquanta cavalieri, li quali Etiocle avea mandati a stare in guato, perché l'uccidessero; li quali Tideo, fieramente combat-tendo, tutti uccise. (in 1.14)

> [And because the year in which Eteocles was supposed to reign had ended, Tydeus came to Thebes to request the reign for Poly-nices; not only was it not turned over to him, but he was at-tacked at night in a wood (*bosco*) by fifty knights, which Eteo-cles had sent to lay an ambush, so that they might kill him; but Tydeus, fighting fiercely, killed all of them.][67]

The sequence of events leading to the first armed conflict between Pala-mon and Arcite develops on a smaller scale, with each principal acting on his own behalf, but the echoes of Statius's action are clear, and the scene in the *boschetto* contains some close verbal imitation of the correspond-ing scene of the *Thebaid*.

The identity of Polynices with Tydeus, who goes to Thebes on his be-half, is emphasized by Statius, both at the time of Tydeus's embassy itself and in *Thebaid* 9, where Polynices recalls the embassy to Thebes in his lament over Tydeus's dead body:

> . . . Thebas me propter et impia fratris
> tecta libens, unde haud alius remeasset, adisti,
> ceu tibimet sceptra et proprios laturus honores. (9.65–67)

> [On my account you went to Thebes and willingly entered my brother's impious palace, whence no other would have returned, as if to carry away power for yourself and your personal honors.]

In the *Teseida*, Arcite's appearance has been so transformed by love-sickness that he is like another person, and when he returns to Athens under an assumed name, only Emilia (and later, with the help of the moon, Palamon) is able to recognize him (cf. *Teseida* 4.57, 5.35). As Ar-cite weighs his desire to return to Athens against the risk of transgressing Theseus's edict of banishment, his altered appearance encourages him to take the risk:

fra sé dicendo: "Io son sì trasmutato
da quel ch'esser solea, che conosciuto
io non sarò, e vivrò consolato,
me ristorando del mal c'ho avuto,
vedendo il bello aspetto ove fu nato
il disio che mi tene e ha tenuto.   (4.38)

[saying to himself: "I am so changed from what I used to be,
that I will not be recognized, and I will live consoled, having
corrected that was done me, and seeing the lovely face where the
desire was born that holds, and has held me.]

The language in this passage nicely suggests other aspects of Tydeus's embassy as well. Tydeus, too, had undertaken a dangerous mission ("audax
ea munera Tydeus / sponte subit" [2.370]) to press Polynices' claim, and
Statius has Jove refer to the failed ambush of Tydeus as the beginning of
the Theban war (3.235). Boccaccio's transformed Arcite goes to "correct
a wrong" and to "restore" himself to what he believes is his rightful
place. Then after Arcite's arrival in Athens, Palamon will intercept him in
a grove outside the city, and there they will begin the armed conflict that
will lead to the great military tournament.

    If we look from the characters to the setting here, the echo of Tydeus's
embassy to Thebes is present again. Palamon will intercept Arcite in a
boschetto or little wood. Tydeus, as Boccaccio recalls in the gloss to 1.14,
"was assailed at night in a grove [bosco]." Palamon and Arcite also meet
in the boschetto at night, though close comparison of Statius's scene in
the Thebaid and the corresponding passages of the Teseida reveals a difference in the time of night: Tydeus approaches the grove (silva and
nemus) at nightfall, while Boccaccio has Palamon find Arcite near dawn.
In both cases, however, the darkness, the shadowy trees that obscure the
vision, and revealing beams of moonlight all play a role. Palamon prays
to the moon to guide his search (5.30), and it is moonlight falling across
the face of Arcite as he sleeps in the grove that reveals his identity to Palamon. The motifs all appear at the beginning of the corresponding scene in
the Thebaid, where Tydeus approaches the wood of the ambush:[68]

Coeperat umenti Phoebum subtexere palla
nox et caeruleam terris infuderat umbram.
ille propinquabat silvis et ab aggere celso
scuta virum galeasque videt rutilare comantes,
qua laxant rami nemus adversaque sub umbra
flammeus aeratis lunae tremor errat in armis.   (2.527–532)

[Night had begun to shroud Phoebus in her wet mantle, and had cast her dark shadow on the earth. The hero approached the woods and from a high ridge saw the red gleam of warriors' shields and crested helmets where the forest boughs left an open space, and through opposing shadows the flame-like flickering of the moon played across the bronze weapons.]

Boccaccio's version of this scene divides between Palamon and Arcite motifs that Statius uses for Tydeus alone, which suggests perhaps that the particular association of Arcite with Tydeus and Polynices, or of Palamon with Eteocles, is less important to Boccaccio's design than the general pattern associating Statius's brothers with his cousins. It is Palamon who approaches the *boschetto* by moonlight and peers into the shadows:

giunse nel bosco per gli albori ombroso
e con intento sguardo in quel cercava
acciò ch'Arcita trovasse   (5.33)

[he arrived in the wood through the shadowy trees and searched in it to find Arcite, with an intent gaze.]

When he climbs a small rise ("di sopra la rivera" 5.34, compare "[Tydeus] ab aggere celso"), he sees Arcite asleep among the greenery and recognizes him by the light of the moon:

Ma Febea, che chiara ancor lucea,
co' raggi suoi il viso li scopria   (5.35)

[But Phoebe, who was still shining, showed his face to him with her rays.]

Boccaccio combines the elements on a smaller scale; we are at closer range here than in the *Thebaid,* and the light (perhaps "Phoebe" in place of Statius's *luna* for the influence of "Phoebus" in line 527?), instead of quivering across distant armor ("errat in armis"), falls on a sleeping face and stirs Palamon's feelings of old friendship, so that he hesitates to awaken Arcite (5.36). But the pattern of action will be the same, as are the first words spoken: when Tydeus approaches the ambush, he shouts "Unde, viri, quidve occultatis in armis?" (Where do you come from, men, and what do you mean lurking thus armed?), echoed by Arcite as he wakes to see Palamon: "Cavalier, che vai cercando / per questo bosco, sì armato andando?" (Knight, what are you looking for in this wood, armed in this manner?).[69]

Because I have begun by examining the simile of Tisiphone, the correspondence of scenes and motifs in *Thebaid* 1–4 and *Teseida* 3–6 may appear less systematic than it is. Boccaccio has placed the simile here in *Teseida* 5, yet it refers to a scene at the beginning of *Thebaid* 1. Note, however, that the introductory scene in the *Thebaid* (1.46ff.) anticipates the action of the entire epic and does not announce the beginning of strife between Eteocles and Polynices in the narrative sequence. In Statius's narrative, the mistrust and discord figured by Tisiphone actually manifest themselves only in the events of *Thebaid* 2–3, with Tydeus's return to Thebes on Polynices' behalf, his ambush, and his report back to Polynices in Argos. Before Eteocles denies Tydeus's request and orders him ambushed, the Theban brothers abide peacefully by their agreement for alternating rule, Eteocles in Thebes and Polynices in Argos.

When Boccaccio places the important simile of Tisiphone in *Teseida* 5, he is using it to mark the beginning of strife in close accord with the sequence of Statius's narrative.[70] It makes explicit the similitude of action that has been developing since Arcite's exile began (*Teseida* 3, *Thebaid* 1), and which will now be reflected more openly in Boccaccio's allusive language. In the next stanza, for example, Palamon asserts that he will "conquistar per arme Emilia" (win Emilia in war or "by arms") before he goes to search for Arcite in the grove. After the small battle in the grove, the pattern of action in Statius's *Thebaid* suggests that we should hear an account of it from each party: Tydeus returns to Argos to recount his tale to Polynices and Adrastus, while Maeon, the only Theban to survive the failed ambush, returns to Thebes with words for Eteocles (*Thebaid* 3); then preparations begin for the larger battle, culminating in the arrival of allies and the formal catalog of troops (*Thebaid* 4). The shape of *Teseida* 5–6 is precisely the same. At the end of *Teseida* 5, Theseus interrupts the fight in the grove and asks Palamon and Arcite for accounts of themselves. The book concludes with Theseus's decision to settle their dispute in a tournament, and *Teseida* 6 then describes the "kings and barons" arriving in Athens to take the sides of Palamon and Arcite.

The catalog of *Teseida* 6 represents Boccaccio's most elaborate imitation of any of the minor forms of classical epic, and it is placed so that it will mark a significant point in the correspondence between his main action and that of the *Thebaid*. Like the catalog in *Thebaid* 4, it marks the expansion of personal rivalry into a conflict involving the entire Greek countryside. Moreover, in the *Thebaid*, two books now intervene before that war actually begins: *Thebaid* 5 is entirely given over to the digression of Hypsipyle, and *Thebaid* 6 to the funeral and games in honor of Opheltes, both of which occur during the progress of Polynices' army to-

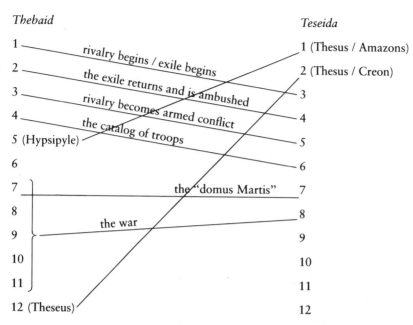

Thebaid   Teseida

FIGURE 1. The analogies of the *Teseida:* Palamon and Arcite to Eteocles and Polynices. Books in the *Thebaid* that are not directly concerned with the strife of Polynices and Eteocles (5 Hypsipyle and 12 Theseus) form the models for *Teseida* 1
and 2. The action of *Thebaid* 1–4, from the onset of rivalry to the catalog of
troops, is repeated in *Teseida* 3–6.

ward Thebes. Thus Boccaccio's design for the main action of the *Teseida*
has tidily matched the corresponding sequence of events in the *Thebaid*
by the midpoint of the narrative. The second half will in both cases be
concerned with the larger armed conflict, and in both poems book 7 begins with a description of the "house of Mars." In the *Thebaid*, this figurative representation of the spirit of martial wrath appears at 7.35–63;
Boccaccio translates it closely, with some additions and an extensive
gloss, at *Teseida* 7.24–41. (This pattern of correspondences is summed
up in Figure 1.)

One other scene from *Thebaid* 4 reappears in the elaborate preparations for Theseus's "giuoco a Marte" and introduces the broadly Statian
pattern of action in the second half of the poem. The long scene of Emilia's sacrifice at the temple of Diana is based on *Thebaid* 4.443ff., Manto's rites in honor of Hecate and other infernal gods. In both poems, these
rites involve forecasting the outcome of the approaching conflict and the
end of the rivalry between the principal characters, and in both they follow a formal catalog of troops mustering for war. *Thebaid* 4 opens with

the catalog of Polynices' allies arriving in Argos; it is shorter than Boccaccio's catalog in *Teseida* 6, leaving room in the book for the contemporary events at Thebes, where Eteocles has heard rumors of his brother's army and has ordered the seer Tiresias and his daughter Manto to perform the rites of augury. Boccaccio uses several details from Manto's ceremony when he describes Emilia in the temple of Diana (*Teseida* 7.70ff.).[71] Emilia, like Manto, would prefer to learn that there will be no conflict at all, but if there must be one, she wants to know which of the Theban cousins will triumph. Like Manto, Emilia is *virgo,* and like Manto she offers wine, milk, and blood (*Teseida* 7.75, *Thebaid* 4.449–454). The change in tone could not be sharper, however, as Manto and her father pour the offerings on the ground beside an infamous dark wood and pray over roaring flames to the goddess in her aspect as Hecate, while Emilia, in the refined temple in Athens, prays to her in her aspect as Diana. Manto builds her fires to Hecate, to the infernal furies, to Pluto and Persephone, while Emilia in her brighter surroundings simply builds two fires on an altar and addresses Diana as goddess of earth, sky, sea, and the realms of Pluto (*Teseida* 7.72, 77; *Thebaid* 4.456). Both supplicants offer up the entrails of sacrificed animals still pulsing with life (*Teseida* 7.76; *Thebaid* 4.466), but Manto herself catches the blood in bowls as cattle are butchered and quickly carries the *spirantia viscera* to the flames, while Emilia has them brought from smaller lambs by her servants.

The similarity in design and contrast in tone also appear in the prophetic signs that conclude the two scenes. At *Thebaid* 4.461ff., the long series of Theban ancestors has appeared in Avernus, standing in a lake of blood, and Laius gives an ambiguous prophecy: victory is sure for one side, and the other rival will not have the throne, but furies will possess it and by the brothers' swords the cruel father will triumph. The meaning of the prophecy is clear in *Thebaid* 11, when Eteocles and Polynices kill each other. Boccaccio borrows the striking motif of struggling flames over their funeral pyre (*Thebaid* 12.429–466) for the ambiguous response given to Emilia in the temple of Diana, changing it somewhat to suggest the outcome of the rivalry between Palamon and Arcite: Emilia sees two flames on the altar, one dying down and then flaring up again, the other flaring first but then extinguished. In the clearest echo of the *Thebaid* in this highly imitative scene, both flames seem to moan, and they strike each other with their points (7.91–93).[72]

Other minor characters in the *Teseida* also appear in roles that develop either the main action or its themes according to the model of Statius's *Thebaid*. Notable examples are the friends to Palamon and Arcite who frame the acts of fraternal conflict in book 5. In the early books of the

Thebaid, a contrast of the same sort appears in the friendship of Tydeus and Polynices. Their initial mutual mistrust and hostility turn to reconciliation under the controlling influences of Adrastus (1.390ff.), soon becoming affection and finally kinship, as Tydeus and Polynices marry Adrastus's daughters (2.134ff.). The breaking of fraternal bonds in the *Teseida* is also anticipated by a period of friendship, here between the Theban kinsmen themselves (*Teseida* 3–4). Palamon and Arcite begin as comrades in arms (2.85–88) and misfortune; like Polynices and Tydeus they are away from their home city, living at the mercy of a foreign ruler. They are friends ("caro amico" at 3.39 and again at 3.74–75) as well as kinsmen. When their rivalry for "possession" of Emilia leads them to break these bonds, Boccaccio frames the scene with contrasting examples of more enduring friendship, highlighted with the thematic phrase "caro amico": Arcite is freed by Theseus because of intercession by a mutual friend, none less than Pirithous, whose legendary friendship with Theseus survived even a journey to the underworld.[73] Palamon escapes later with the help of a friend and faithful servant, Panfilus, who is willing to take his master's place in prison (5.25) and whose name, if not rich with legendary associations like that of Pirithous, would seem nevertheless to carry the same connotations of affection and loyalty.

Buttressed as it is by minor characters and by the correspondence of minor forms in the catalogs and description of the temple of Mars, the *Thebaid*-like pattern is well established in the main action of the *Teseida* before the tournament begins. Then it will change somewhat in and after the tournament, but the variation itself may be traced to the *Thebaid.* Boccaccio's expansion of the first game in the *Thebaid* 6 as the general frame for the narrative in the second half of the *Teseida* calls for a separate discussion, which will occupy the following chapter. But even at this point in our comparison of the two works, the systematic relations in their narrative structures indicate that Boccaccio's imitative strategy has everything to do with epic tradition even while it does not represent an attempt to recreate the epic genre in the style and tone of the august Latin models. The medieval poet has not aimed to recreate the abstract model that nineteenth-century critics identified as epic, he has transformed a single, recognizable epic action. "Mirroring" a pattern of action, with analogies among characters, Boccaccio works out an imitative structure in the tradition of Macrobius's description of Vergil's art and of the other literary criticism, late classical and medieval, associated particularly with epic poetry. At the heart of this open imitation, an analogy places the beauty of a young woman in a position corresponding to the throne of Thebes in Statius's *Thebaid.* This substitution itself has important antecedents: Vergil had made his second *Iliad* a war over Lavinia, recalling more or less explicitly the Homeric war: *causa mali tanti coniunx iterum.* Statius in turn had deployed the language of erotic desire in his portraits of Polynices and Eteocles and the *amor regendi,* the love of ruling. In a sense then Boccaccio has only reversed Statius's substitution and returned to the old epic subject of a wife as the cause of war. This observation does not make the *Teseida* an epic in the sense intended by the nineteenth-century critics, but it points up once again the extent to which the *Teseida* is written in the epic tradition, its narrative action like its extended similes designed to take on meaning as it is matched against a particular classical background.

Notes to Chapter 1

1. Oscar Hecker, *Boccaccio-Funde* (Brunswick: Westermann, 1902), pp. 33–34; Antonia Mazza, "L'Inventario dell 'Parva Libraria' di Santo Spirito e la biblioteca del Boccaccio," *Italia medioevale e umanistica* 9 (1966): 57–58.
2. Although Robert D. Sweeney's catalog of glossed *Thebaid* manuscripts, in his *Prolegomena to an Edition of the Scholia to Statius,* Mnemosyne, supplementum octavum (Leiden: Brill, 1969), p. 12, states that folios 43, 100, 111, 165, 166, and 171 are all in Boccaccio's hand, and Mazza, "L'Inventario," leaves the question open, the careful descriptions by Casamassima in *Mostra di manoscritti, documenti e edizioni, Sesto Centenario della morte di Giovanni Boccaccio* (Certaldo: 1975), vol. 1, pp. 155–156, and Birger Munk Olsen, *L'Étude des auteurs classiques latins aux XIe et XIIe siècles,* vol. 2 (Paris: Editions CNRS, 1985), p. 535, reconfirm Hecker's judgment. My own brief examination of the manuscript and longer study of a microfilm copy confirm Hecker's judgment again, as regards whole pages copied entirely by Boccaccio. In addition to these four folios (eight pages) copied entirely by Boccaccio, there are some scattered glosses in his hand elsewhere in the manuscript.
3. On the narrow, one-column format characteristic of twelfth-century copies of Vergil's works, see Birger Munk Olsen, "Virgile et la Renaissance du XIIe siècle," in *Lectures médiévales de Virgile,* Actes du Colloque organisé par l'École française de Rome (25–28 October 1982), Collection de l'École française de Rome, 80 (Rome: 1985), esp. pp. 38–42.
4. Boccaccio's script in this *Thebaid* is very similar to that of his copy of the comedies of Terence, now Florence, Biblioteca Medicea-Laurenziana Plut. 68.17, a manuscript that bears his signature in the colophon. See *Mostra di manoscritti,* vol. 1, pp. 145–147, with bibliography; Claudia Villa, *La "Lectura Terentii": Da Ildemaro a Francesco Petrarca* (Padua: Antenore, 1984), vol. 1, pp. 173–176. On Boccaccio's handwriting see above, Introduction, note 11, especially Pier Giorgio Ricci, "Studi sulle opere latine e volgari del Boccaccio," *Rinascimento* 10 (1959): 3–21.
5. I am rather surprised that an unsystematic collation of the text in Plut. 38.6 with Boccaccio's citations of Lactantius in the Romano edition of the *Ge-*

nealogie indicates that Boccaccio did not copy directly from this manuscript. I have not determined whether the variants can be traced to another recension of Lactantius.

6. Giuseppe Billanovich, *Restauri boccacceschi*, 2d printing (Rome: Edizioni di Storia e Letteratura, 1947), pp. 69–78.

7. The provenance of Boccaccio's manuscript is at the present time as mysterious as the identity of the correspondent—if there was a real correspondent—to whom Boccaccio addressed his request for a copy of Lactantius in the letter "Sacre famis." Whence and from whom did he get this manuscript? The paleographical and textual evidence in Plut. 38.6 may eventually provide some answers. We can be fairly certain that the manuscript had its origin on the German side of the Alps. The recension of Lactantius in this codex (manuscript *m* in Sweeney's stemma) is not part of the "Italian vulgate" which circulated widely in Italy in the fifteenth century and appeared in early printed editions. Sweeney has identified one fifteenth-century Italian copy made from Plut. 38.6 itself (Rome: Biblioteca Vallicelliana C. 60; see *Prolegomena*, pp. 71 and 85) but no other Italian offspring of the "northern" recension of Lactantius. The closest relation to Plut. 38.6 in the northern branch of the stemma of Lactantius is E^1, part of a later tenth-century manuscript (now Paris: Bibliothèque Nationale, lat. 10317) that was apparently written at Echternach (Sweeney, p. 16, Munk Olsen, *L'Étude*, vol. 2, p. 552). And the two subgroups of manuscripts in the northern recension that are closest to Plut. 38.6 came from Bavaria—Scheftlarn (S), Freisingen (f), and Tegernsee (M)—and from central Germany (BHKW). The script of the twelfth-century portion of Plut. 38.6 has usually been attributed in a general way to "northern Europe" but this has been questioned by Munk Olsen, who has cautiously suggested "Italy (?)," noting especially that the script is not French (vol. 2, p. 536, and letter to the author, 28 September 1987). My comparison of the script with that of Bibliothèque Nationale, lat. 10317, and related early copies of Lactantius leads me to assign the twelfth-century portion of Boccaccio's manuscript to southern Germany, in agreement with the evidence of its textual relations. The provenance of the thirteenth-century portion may be the same. I hope to offer a thorough discussion of this question in the near future.

8. The text of the *Thebaid* that Boccaccio copied onto these four leaves does not derive from the same family of manuscripts as that of the rest of Plut. 38.6, another detail that supports the assumption that Boccaccio obtained the book when these leaves were already lost, and that he supplied them with a text copied from another manuscript. Plut. 38.6 contains an authoritative text of Statius's epic. It appears in the sigla codicum of Hill's critical edition as "M: codex Mediceus Plut. 38.6 saec XI" [*sic*]: D. E. Hill, *Thebaidos libri XII* (Leiden: Brill, 1983), p. xxi. Surprisingly, Hill records variants from the manuscript even for those four folios copied by Boccaccio from another source.

The text of the Lactantius commentary is also very good, slightly fuller than the version published by Richard Jahnke (Leipzig: Teubner, 1898). Jahnke did not use the manuscript in preparing that (very unsatisfactory) edition. See Sweeney, *Prolegomena*, pp. 12–13.

9. For a description of the codex and a transcription of Boccaccio's glosses on *Thebaid* 7.666ff. see below, Appendix 3.
10. I have used the *Thebaid* in the edition of Hill (1983), the *Teseida* in the edition of Alberto Limentani (1964), in Giovanni Boccaccio, *Tutte le Opere*, ed. Vittore Branca, 12 vols. (Milan: Mondadori, 1964–), vol. 2. Numerical references to the *Thebaid* are by book and line; those to the *Teseida* by book and stanza. The translations are my own. For the *Thebaid* I have consulted the translation by J. H. Mozley in the Loeb Library, *Statius*, 2 vols. (London: Heinemann, and Cambridge, Mass.: Harvard University Press, 1928; rep. 1967) and the Italian version by Antonio Traglia and Giuseppe Aricò in their useful edition, *Opere di Publio Papinio Stazio* (Turin: UTET, 1980). On the shortcomings of Mozley's translation, see Lennart Håkanson, *Statius' Thebaid: Critical and Exegetical Remarks*, *Scripta Minora 1972–1973* (Lund: Gleerup, 1973), especially pp. 79–85. Currently, the only complete English translation of the *Teseida* is Bernadette M. McCoy, *The Book of Theseus* (New York: Medieval Text Association, 1974), which contains many errors. See, for example, McCoy's misconstruing of *Teseida* 5.34 and 6.56, discussed here, pp. 77, 112.
11. For the simile likening Arcite to "Libyan Antaeus" (*Teseida* 8.80), see pp. 62–65 and note 61 of this chapter.
12. The function words governing Boccaccio's formal comparisons are those used by Dante, and they conserve much of their classical models. Here "tale . . . quale" corresponds to the classical "talis . . . qualis"; elsewhere "non altrimenti" derives from the classical "non / haud secus." See Giuseppe Velli, "Sulla Similitudine dotta del Boccaccio," in his *Petrarca e Boccaccio: Tradizione, memoria, scrittura* (Padua: Antenore, 1979), pp. 156–171.
13. E. A. Quaglio, "Tra Fonti e testo del *Filocolo*," *Giornale storico della letteratura italiana* 139 (1962): esp. 332–333; Alberto Limentani, "Boccaccio traduttore di stazio," *Rassegna italiana di letteratura* 64 (1960): 231–242; Giuseppe Velli, "Cultura e *imitatio* nel primo Boccaccio," in *Petrarca e Boccaccio*, esp. pp. 62–66.
14. E. A. Quaglio, "Boccaccio e Lucano: Una Concordanza e una fonte dal *Filocolo* all'*Amorosa visione*," *Cultura neolatina* 23 (1963): 45–77. Velli notes the use of Lucan in the *Teseida*, "Cultura e *imitatio*," pp. 66ff. On Boccaccio's imitation of *Metamorphoses* 11.592ff., see Quaglio, "Tra Fonti e testo," pp. 344ff.
15. Alberto Limentani, "Tendenze della prosa del Boccaccio ai margini della *Teseide*," *Giornale storico della letteratura italiana*, 135 (1958): 524–551, takes up the suggestion of Vandelli (in "Un autografo della *Teseide*," *Studi di filologia italiana* 2 [1929]: 5–76), that Boccaccio's model for the glosses might have been Lactantius's commentary on the *Thebaid*, noting the imperfect correspondence between Boccaccio's subjects and those of Lactantius. The question of literary style in the chiose is also examined by Robert Hollander, "The Validity of Boccaccio's Self-Exegesis in His *Teseida*," *Medievalia et humanistica* n.s. 8 (1977): 163–183; and by Piero Boitani, *Chaucer and Boccaccio* (Oxford: Society for the Study of Medieval Languages and Literature, 1977), pp. 45ff.
16. The anonymous commentator on the *Teseida* takes special note of the sim-

iles that liken Palamon and Arcite to animals, interpreting them in the conventional manner as figurative statements that the two rivals, overcome by their passionate desire and jealousy, have lost the good of their reason (Paris: Bibliothèque Nationale, Cod. ital 581, fol. 20r).

17. Limentani suggests in his notes to the *Teseida* that Ovid, *Metamorphoses* 2.846–847 is a source for the concluding verses of Boccaccio's simile: "non bene conveniunt nec in una sede morantur / maiestas et amor" (Majesty and love go ill together, nor can they long share one abode), adding that this sententia may have been familiar to Boccaccio in other contexts as well (see Cesare Segre, ed., *Li Bestiaires d'amours di maistre Richart de Fornival e Li response du bestiaire* [Milan and Naples: Ricciardi, 1957], pp. x–xi). But the sense is different from that of the *Teseida*, the Ovidian sententia saying that love is unbecoming of regal majesty (the passage quoted above refers to the indecorous transformation of Jove into a bull, so that he might carry off Europa), and the sententia of the *Teseida* saying that neither rival lovers nor rivals for a throne will stand for sharing the object of their desires. The distinction has been drawn before by Richard L. Hoffman, *Ovid and the "Canterbury Tales"* (Philadelphia: University of Pennsylvania Press, 1966), pp. 63–67. In this regard a gloss on *Thebaid* 1.130 in Wolfenbüttel, Herzog-August Bibliothek, MS 52 Gud. lat. is especially suggestive. The manuscript is of Italian origin and dates to the fourteenth century. A gloss in the same hand as the text notes "*Discordia.* iuxta illud. non bene cum sociis regna venusque manent" (*Discordia:* as it is said: "kingship and Venus do not endure well with company"). The verse, from Ovid's *Ars amatoria* (3.564), is much closer than *Metamorphoses* 2.846–847 to Boccaccio's verses, and it may well have been his source. Moreover, the appearance of this Ovidian verse in a gloss on the very passage that Boccaccio will transform into "signoria / ne amore stan bene con compagnia" suggests that at least one contemporary reader also saw in Statius's main action a theme analogous to rivalry in love. The association is encouraged by Ovid's implicit allusion to the Trojan War, and by the fact that Statius in this episode is himself imitating the scene of Allecto in *Aeneid* 7, where the nominal cause for civil war is rivalry over the hand of Lavinia.

18. Statius's episode of Tisiphone itself imitates *Aeneid* 7.343–561, the scene describing the origins of civil war in Latium. In several respects, Boccaccio's scene of the beginning of discord in *Teseida* 5 resembles the corresponding scene in the *Aeneid* more than that in the *Thebaid*. Boccaccio clearly recognized the imitative relations between Statius's Tisiphone and Vergil's Allecto and wanted in his version to allude to both. Allecto infects Turnus alone, away from Aeneas, and she finds him in a "high place" ("tectis hic Turnus in altis," 7.413). Tisiphone enters Palamon's breast first in the *Teseida*, while he is in the prison tower. Moreover, Allecto appears to Turnus in the figure of an old priestess, who rouses his jealousy with the news of Aeneas's arrival from far away (7.421–434), just as Panfilus reports to Palamon about the arrival of Arcite in the *Teseida* (5.5–8). Like Turnus, Palamon is not initially roused by what he hears. Then, in the *Aeneid*, the fury reveals herself in her terrifying, unanthropomorphic es-

sence and hurls her brand into Turnus's heart (7.457); Boccaccio describes the process whereby Palamon reaches a pitch of fury in less figurative language ("Poi cominciò a pensar fortemente / sopra l'affar d'Arcite innamorato," 5.9).

19. By Robert Haller, "The *Knight's Tale* and the Epic Tradition," *Chaucer Review* 1 (1966): 67–84, who identifies the analogy to the *Thebaid* in the narrative of the Knight's Tale but limits his discussion to the simile of Tisiphone as amplified by Chaucer; and recently by Bruno Porcelli, "Il *Teseida* del Boccaccio fra la *Tebaide* e *The Knight's Tale*," *Studi e problemi di critica testuale* 32–33 (1986): 57–80, who notes the general correspondence in the pattern of action leading to the armed conflict (*Teseida* 8 / *Thebaid* 7–11).

20. G. W. Pigman, "Versions of Imitation in the Renaissance," *Renaissance Quarterly* 33 (1980): 10–11.

21. At least in his Italian works. He even names his source on one notable occasion in the *Teseida*: 6.53, where the gloss reads: "della leggereza che qui pone l'autore che avea questo Ida, scrive Virgilio di Camilla, e quinde fu tolto ciò che qui se ne scrive." Boccaccio's tendency to lift verbal elements more or less intact from his sources is noted throughout the literature on his "translations" of classical sources (see notes 12–14, above).

22. Trans. Guido Guarino, *Boccaccio: Concerning Famous Women* (New Brunswick, N.J.: Rutgers University Press, 1963), p. 219. The original passage appears as follows in the edition of Vittorio Zaccaria, *De mulieribus claris*, in *Tutte le Opere*, vol. 10, pp. 392–393:

> Operam igitur pio conceptui prestans, nunc huc nunc illuc per buccolicum georgicumque atque eneidum saltim discurrendo carmen, nunc hac ex parte versus integros, nunc ex illa metrorum particulas carpens, miro artificio in suum redegit propositum, adeo apte integros collocans et fragmenta connectens, servata lege pedum et carminis dignitate, ut, nisi expertissimus, compages possit advertere.

The connections are artfully disguised, but the source of the lines and phrases is readily evident. Indeed, Proba is praised especially for the way she forms the Vergilian elements into a dramatically different narrative (miro artificio in suum redegit propositum).

23. Ed. Limentani, *Tutte le Opere*, vol. 2, p. 246. On this passage see also below, Chapter 3, pp. 152–153.

24. Horace, *Sermones* 1.1.78 and 1.1.121.

25. The semantic range even generalized to mean simply "carry away." Francesco Arnaldi, *Latinitas italicae medii aevi*, in Archivium latinitas medii aevi (Brussels: Bulletin Du Cange, 1939), cites Paulus Diaconus: "nec vis ventorum nubis compilare cessabat."

26. On the uses of the term *compilatio* in reference to written compositions, see Malcolm B. Parkes, "The Influence of the Concepts of *Ordinatio* and *Compilatio* on the Development of the Book," *Medieval Scribes, Manuscripts and Libraries: Essays Presented to N. R. Ker*, ed. M. B. Parkes and A. G. Watson (London: Scolar, 1978), pp. 115–144. Parkes quotes the

passage from Bonaventura's fourth quaestio on the first book of the *Sentences* distinguishing a compiler (*compilator*) from a scribe (*scriptor*), an exegete (*commentator*), and an author (*auctor*), pp. 126–131. See also Alastair J. Minnis, *Medieval Theory of Authorship* (London: Scolar, 1984), pp. 190ff.

27. *Philobiblon* 8.138: "viros . . . qui diversorum librorum correccionibus, exposicionibus, tabulacionibus ac compilacionibus . . . incumbebant" (men who [occupied themselves with] the correction, exposition, tabulation, and compilation of books). These categories are all subdivisions of the semantic territory between *auctor* and *scriba*. On Boccaccio and the *Philobiblon*, Vittore Branca, *Boccaccio Medievale* (Florence: Sansoni, 1970), p. 288. Petrarch met Richard DeBury in Avignon, probably in 1333 (*Fam.* 3.1).

28. Ed. Maria Simonelli (Bologna: Patron, 1966), p. 60.

29. Giovanni writes, with reference to the composition of his *Chronicle:* "Non sanza grande fatica mi travaglierò di ritrarre e di ritrovare di più antichi e diversi libri . . . le geste . . . compilando in questo." It is the standard term for "historical narration" also in Matteo Villani: "E massimamente nel cominciamento dell'undecimo libro della nostra compilazione" (6.47). Compare Dante's use in *De vulgari eloquentia* 1.10.2: "biblia cum Troianorum Romanorumque gestibus compilata."

30. In "De vita et moribus domini Francisci Petracchi de Florentia" (ca. 1348): "et inter alia memoratu dignissima, opus suum illud magnum et mirabile cui Affrica nomen imposuit, eo quod maioris Affricani gesta in eodem heoryco metro monstrentur, ingenio divino potius quam humano creditur compilasse" (ed. A. F. Massèra, *Opere latine minori* [Bari: Laterza, 1928], p. 240). Along with the chronicle, Justinian's *Corpus iuris civilis* could be defined as a "compilation." It is interesting to note the use of terms like those in the *Philobiblon* when the *Ottimo Commento* describes Justinian: "Giustiniano fu correttore, o vero compilatore, delle leggi civili" (in *Paradiso* 3.110 and again at 3.119). Boccaccio uses the term for Dante's *Vita nuova* (*Esposizioni* 8.1.49), in keeping with Dante's references to it as a selection from the book of his memory.

31. R. D. Williams, ed., *P. Papini Stati Thebaidos liber decimus* (Leiden: Brill, 1972), pp. 76–86, remarks in detail on the parallel passages. The literature on Statius's imitation of Vergil is extensive. See Paola Venini, "Studi sulla Tebaide di Stazio," in *Rendiconti, Istituto Lombardo, Accademia di Scienze e Lettere*, 95 (1961): 55–88 and 371–400, especially the bibliographical excursus on 371–373; and Bernhard Kytzler, "*Imitatio* und *aemulatio* in der *Thebais* des Statius," *Hermes* 97 (1969): 209–232, especially pp. 209–219, on the episode of Hopleus and Dymas in *Thebaid* 10. Venini remarks: "l'imitazione si manifesta nella *Tebaide* in misura assai cospicua, sopratutto, com'è noto, l'imitazione virgiliana che lungi dal dissimulare Stazio stesso riafferma orgogliosamente a più riprese," citing *Thebaid* 10.445ff., 12.816ff., and *Silvae* 4.54ff., 7.25ff. (p. 374).

32. In the compendium "Hoc ex ordine," which circulated with the *Achilleid* from the early part of the fourteenth century, Statius is said to imitate Vergil so openly "ut aliqui eum Virgilii simiam figurale appellent." See Violetta

de Angelis, "Magna Questio preposita coram Dante et Domino Francisco Petrarca et Virgiliano," *Studi petrarcheschi*, n.s. 1 (1984): 165, who notes that the phrase "simia Maronis" is quoted by commentators in the later fourteenth century in such a way as to suggest that it had only recently been applied to Statius. It is used by Francesco Nelli in a letter to Petrarch in 1355, which indicates that it circulated in Florence at that time: "Nelli quindi che poco si mosse da Firenze . . . e la cui cultura trovava alimento e centro di discussione nel circolo fiorentino di Forese Donati, Lapo di Castiglionchio, Zanobi da Strada, Boccaccio, e che aveva solo cinque anni prima iniziato i suoi rapporti epistolari con Petrarca, in Firenze sapeva che Stazio era detto 'simia Maronis,' ed era qui che probabilmente la definizione circolava" (p. 168). The term *simia* need not be interpreted as disparaging in this context (p. 167, n. 119). Salutati refers to Statius frequently as "Maronis imitator" and "maximus imitator Maronis" (cf. *De laboribus Herculis*, ed. Berthold L. Ullman [Zurich: Thesaurus Mundi, 1951] pp. 468, 457).

33. I give the text of both *accessus* in the Appendixes, below.
34. De Angelis, "Magna Questio," pp. 187–189.
35. I have used Servius, in the edition of Georg Christian Thilo and Hermann Hagen, *Servii Grammatici qui feruntur in Vergilii carmina commentarii*, vol. 1 (Leipzig: Teubner, 1881; repr. 1923), p. 4.
36. The influential discussion in English is that of Brooks Otis, *Vergil: A Study in Civilized Poetry* (Oxford: Clarendon, 1964), chaps. 6 ("The Odyssean *Aeneid*") and 7 ("The Iliadic *Aeneid*"). More detailed mapping of the Homeric scenes and verses imitated by Vergil appeared the same year in Georg Nikolaus Knauer, *Die Aeneis und Homer*, Hypomnemata 7 (Gottingen: Vandenhoeck and Ruprecht, 1964). Knauer also offered a concise statement of his views in English: "Vergil's *Aeneid* and Homer," *Greek, Roman and Byzantine Studies*, 5 (1964): 61–84. Although the greater detail offered by *Die Aeneis und Homer* shows Vergil using the Homeric poems in a less schematic fashion than is suggested by Otis, with more mixing and "contaminating" of several characters and episodes, both scholars share the central assumption that Vergil's imitation is allusive, that the poet expected his audience to recognize his transformation of a particular source. Such recognition is prompted by verbal echoes and allusive narrative structures (see "Vergil's *Aeneid* and Homer," pp. 66–67).
37. That Boccaccio read the *Aeneid* with the gloss of Servius is evident as early as the *Filocolo:* see A. E. Quaglio, "Tra Fonti e testo," p. 329. See also Mazza, "L'Inventario," pp. 58–59; James McGregor, "Boccaccio's Athenian Theater: Form and Function of an Ancient Monument in *Teseida*," *Modern Language Notes* 99 (1984): 18–19.
38. See especially Valerius Maximus 8.8, "De otio"; also 9.128.
39. On Boccaccio's early knowledge of the Homeric poems through medieval Latin sources, see Manlio Pastore Stocchi, "Il Primo Omero di Boccaccio," *Studi sul Boccaccio* 5 (1969): esp. 110–119. The discussion of Homer and Vergil in the *Esposizioni,* though it dates to the end of Boccaccio's career, is also suggestive. Commenting on Dante's description of the encounter be-

tween Vergil and the "quattro grand'ombre"—Homer, Horace, Lucan, and Ovid—Boccaccio notes again that Vergil imitated Homer: "Né si sono vergognati i nostri poeti di seguire in molte cose le sue [i.e., di Omero] vestigie, e massimamente Virgilio," but distinguishes their subjects, even as his summaries suggest their similarities: Homer, Horace, Lucan, and Ovid have in common with Vergil only the name "poet," for "in altro con lui non si convengono; percioché le materie, delle quali ciascun di loro parlò, non furono uniformi con quella di che scrisse Virgilio: in quanto Omero scrisse delle battaglie fatte a Troia e degli errori d'Ulisse, Orazio scrisse ode e satire, Ovidio epistole e trasformazioni, Lucano le guerre cittadine di Cesare e di Pompeo, e Virgilio scrisse la venuta d'Enea in Italia e le guerre quivi fatte da lui con Turno re de'Rutoli." The distinctions here involve a curious mixture of criteria, however, which tend to associate Vergil and Homer. Vergil is not "uniform" with Horace and Ovid because of genre. The latter wrote in different forms: odes and satires, "epistles" and "metamorphoses." The distinctions among Lucan, Homer, and Vergil, by contrast, involve the "materia" rather than the poetic form: the battles at Troy and the wanderings of Ulysses; the civil wars of Caesar and Pompey; the journey of Aeneas to Italy and the wars there with Turnus. Boccaccio has already established that Vergil and Homer wrote in the same poetic form ("lo stilo eroico d'Omero o di Virgilio"), and here he distinguishes their subjects ("materia") only as different. But even in doing so, he suggests a similarity by dividing Vergil's narrative into two parts, "the journey to Italy" and "the wars fought there," which echoes his description of the two Homeric subjects, "the battles at Troy . . . the wanderings of Ulysses" (quotations from the edition of Domenico Guerri, *Il Comento alla Divina Commedia* [Bari: Laterza, 1918], vol. 2, pp. 28, 33, 34).

40. Mazza, "L'Inventario," p. 19. It is not clear when Boccaccio came into possession of the *Saturnalia*, and it is not yet possible to establish without doubt that the work was present in Naples in the 1330s, even though one of the most precious early copies is now conserved in that city (Biblioteca Nazionale, MS V B 10, a ninth-century codex). See Antonio LaPenna, "Studi sulla tradizione dei *Saturnali* di Macrobio," *Annali della Scuola normale superiore di Pisa* 22 (1953): 225–249; James Willis, "De Codicibus aliquot manuscriptis Macrobii Saturnalia continentibus," *Rheinisches Museum für Philologie* n.s. 100 (1957): 152–164, on the *stemma codicum*. Rudolf Arbesmann, "Der Augustinereremitenorden und der Beginn der humanistischen Bewegung," *Augustiniana* 14 (1964): 269, notes only that Dionigi da Borgo cites Macrobius's commentary on the *Dream of Scipio*.

41. I have used the edition of James Willis (Leipzig: Teubner, 1970), pp. 244–245:

> sed et haec et talia pueris decantata praetereo. iam vero Aeneis ipsa nonne ab Homero sibi mutuata est errorem primum ex Odyssea, deinde ex Iliade pugnas? quia operis ordinem necessario rerum ordo mutavit, cum apud Homerum prius Iliacum bellum gestum sit, deinde

revertenti de Troia error contigerit Vlixi, apud Maronem vero Aeneae
navigatio bella quae postea in Italia sunt gesta praecesserit.

42. Ibid., p. 246: "quid quod et omne opus Vergilianum velut de quodam Ho-
merici operis speculo formatum est? nam et tempestas mira imitatione
descripta est—versus utriusque qui volet conferat—ut Venus in Nausicaae
locum Alcinoi filiae successit, ipsa autem Dido refert speciem regis Alcinoi
convivium celebrantis [etc.]."

43. Pigman, "Versions of Imitation," esp. p. 10; Thomas M. Greene, *The Light
in Troy: Imitation and Discovery in Renaissance Poetry* (New Haven: Yale
University Press, 1982), esp. chap. 5. Pigman finds evidence in the rhetorical tradition for both "transformative" and "dissimulative" strategies, the
first a variety of stylistic imitation that invites the reader to recognize a
source and its transformation, the second, one that seeks to hide verbal
reminiscence of the source in the imitative passage. Greene suggests "tran-
sitivity" as a critical term to describe transformative imitation; he develops
the concept with special reference to Petrarch's vernacular lyric poetry.

44. Parallels between the story of Troilo and the legendary history of Troy have
been noted in several studies of Chaucer's *Troilus*. See especially John P.
McCall, "The Trojan Scene in Chaucer's *Troilus*," *ELH* 29 (1962): 263–
275; Chauncey Wood, *The Elements of Chaucer's "Troilus"* (Durham,
N.C.: Duke University Press, 1984), chap. 1; David Anderson, "Cassandra's Analogy (*Troilus* V. 1450–1521)," *Hebrew University Studies in
Literature and the Arts* 13 (1985): 1–17.

45. Carlo Paolazzi, "Dall'Epitafio dantesco di Giovanni del Virgilio all'elogio
dell *Amorosa visione*, in *Vestigia: Studi in onore di Giuseppe Billanovich*,
ed. Rino Avesani, Mirella Ferrari, et al. (Rome: Edizioni di Storia e Letteratura, 1984), pp. 485–502; citation from p. 490.

46. Paolazzi, "Dall'Epitafio," p. 491. Boccaccio's major alteration in the Dantean pattern involves including Dante himself in the catalog; Paolazzi
identifies the source of Boccaccio's elegy (*Amorosa visione*, canto 5) in the
epitaph by Giovanni del Virgilio (pp. 494–499).

47. See below, Chapter 2.

48. This distinction between source and allusion is inspired by Giorgio Pasquali, "Arte allusiva," *L'Italia che scrive* 25 (1942): 185–187; repr. in
Stravaganze quarte e supreme (Venice: Pozza, 1951), pp. 11–20. It is made
nicely by Pigman, "Versions of Imitation," pp. 13ff. Richard F. Thomas, in
"Virgil's *Georgics* and the Art of Reference," *Harvard Studies in Classical
Philology* 90 (1986): 171–198, responds vigorously to Pasquali's call for
study of "allusive art" in Roman poetry and proposes several categories of
"reference" with examples from the *Georgics*. For fraternal studies of Alex-
andrian imitation of Homer, see Thomas, p. 171, nn. 3–4.

49. On Benzo d'Alessandria, see Giuseppe Billanovich, "I Primi Umanisti e
l'antichità classica," in *Classical Influences on European Culture, A.D.
500–1500*, ed. R. R. Bolgar (Cambridge: Cambridge University Press,
1971), pp. 61–62; J. R. Berrigan, "The *Achilleid* of Statius in the *Chronicon* of Benzo d'Alessandria," *Manuscripta* 16 (1972): 177–184; idem,
"Benzo d'Alessandria and the Cities of Northern Italy," *Studies in Medi-*

eval and Renaissance History 4 (1967): 125–192; idem, "The Prehumanism of Benzo d'Alessandria," *Traditio* 25 (1969): 249–263; E. Ragni, "Benzo d'Alessandria," in *Dizionario biografico degli Italiani* 8 (1966), pp. 723–726; de Angelis, "Magna Questio," pp. 143–145; I have seen the *Chronicon* in Milan: Biblioteca Ambrosiana, MS B. 24 inf., where the introduction to the paraphrased *Thebaid* appears on fol. 212v. Benzo remarks that he has translated Statius's work because of the difficulty moderns encounter in reading the poetic text: "Ego autem considerans quod modernis temporibus sic ars metrica in dissuetudinem venit, ut nec eam moderni fere amplectentur, immo paucissimi . . . possunt, absque multis commentis et glossis ad intellectum, conprehendere. . . ."

On Paolino's universal chronicle see Francesco Sabatini, *Napoli angioina: Cultura e società* (Naples: Edizioni Scientifiche Italiane, 1975), p. 77; Vittore Branca, "Boccaccio e i veneziani 'bergoli,'" *Lingua nostra* 3 (1941): 49–52; Giuseppe Billanovich, "Autografi del Boccaccio nella Biblioteca Nazionale di Parigi (Parigini Lat. 4939 e 6802)," *Accademia nazionale dei lincei, Rendiconti,* Classe di scienze morali, storiche e filologiche, 8th ser., 7 (1952): 378–388. Aldo Maria Costantini, "La Polemica con Fra Paolino da Venezia," in *Boccaccio, Venezia e il Veneto,* ed. Vittore Branca e Giorgio Padoan (Florence: Olschki, 1979), pp. 101–121. In the fuller version of Paolino's chronicle, entitled *Chronologia magna* in Biblioteca Apostolica Vaticana, MS Vat. lat. 1960, the ample summary of Theban history extends from the birth of Oedipus to the deaths of Polynices and Eteocles, following, that is, the outline of the *Roman de Thèbes.* See Vat. lat. 1960, fol. 56r–v, "De Tebarum descritione." Boccaccio's notes appear in the margins of a different redaction, in Paris, Bibliothèque Nationale, MS lat. 6802, which I have not seen. The chapter on Thebes does not appear in the three Florentine manuscripts of Paolino's chronicle, which also represent a shorter redaction: Biblioteca Medicea-Laurenziana, MS Plut. 21 sin. 9 and Plut. 21 sin. 4; Biblioteca Riccardiana, MS 3033/3034 (*olim* 3204/3205).

On the prose *Roman de Thèbes* in Naples in the early fourteenth century, see Bernhard Degenhart and Annegrit Schmitt, "Frühe angiovinische Buchkunst in Neapel: Die Illustrierung französischer Unterhaltungsprosa in neapolitanischen Scriptorien zwischen 1290 und 1320," in *Festschrift Wolfgang Braunfels,* ed. Friedrich Piel and Jörg Traeger (Tübingen: Wasmuth, 1977), pp. 71–92; Clem C. Williams, "A Case of Mistaken Identity: Still Another Trojan Narrative in Old French Prose," *Medium Aevum* 53 (1984): 59–72. On the place of the prose *Roman de Thèbes* in compilations of ancient history, see Paul Meyer, "Les Premières Compilations françaises d'histoire ancienne," *Romania* 14 (1885): 1–81; David Anderson, "Theban History in Chaucer's Troilus," *Studies in the Age of Chaucer* 4 (1982): esp. 110–115.

50. The relatively large number of manuscript copies of the *Teseida* with courtly provenance has been noted by Edvige Agostinelli in the introduction to her catalog, "The Manuscripts of Boccaccio's *Teseida*," *Studi sul Boccaccio* 15 (1986): 4–5, 77–81. On the Visconti manuscripts, see Elisabeth Pellegrin, *La Bibliothèque des Visconti et des Sforza* (Paris: Publications de Recherche et d'Histoire des Textes, 1955); and William Coleman, "Chaucer,

the *Teseida*, and the Visconti Library at Pavia: A Hypothesis," *Medium Aevum* 51 (1982): 92–101.

51. Carlo DeFrede maintains that the spoken languages at Robert's court would have been Italian (Tuscan, not Neapolitan) and French. He notes visits of Tuscan "giullari" to entertain. See *Storia di Napoli* (Naples: Società Editrice Storia di Napoli, 1967–1972), vol. 3, p. 213.

No thorough investigation of Robert's sermons has been made, but it is generally true of late-medieval sermons that the language in which the text is written down offers no sure indication of the language in which it was delivered. See the remarks of Siegfried Wenzel, *Preachers, Poets, and the Early English Lyric* (Princeton: Princeton University Press, 1986), p. 19. Robert was a layman, often addressing lay audiences, yet even clerics addressing clerics sometimes used the vernacular. Thus in 1273 Thomas Aquinas gave a series of doctrinal addresses before supper ("collationes") at the convent of San Domenico, Naples, speaking in Neapolitan. Pietro de Andria took down the words and transmitted them to posterity in Latin. See Domenico Ambrasi, *Storia di Napoli* (Naples: Società Editrice Storia di Napoli, 1967–1972), vol. 3, p. 494.

52. On Charles of Calabria in Florence, see Introduction, note 17; on the gloss in Tedaldo's *Thebaid*, ibid., note 26. David Wallace has recently revived the hypothesis that the *Filostrato* and the *Teseida* "could not have pleased Robert the Wise" because "they draw inspiration from the *cantare*, a Tuscan tradition of popular narrative composed and performed by street-singers or *cantarini*," *Chaucer and the Early Writings of Boccaccio* (Woodbridge, Suffolk: Boydell and Brewer, 1985), p. 32. Several specific objections can be raised to his argument: the audience of the *canterini* was neither exclusively Florentine nor exclusively "popular"; the presence of the *cantari* among the sources of Boccaccio's works does not make them *cantari* in turn; what Wallace calls "Robert's deep distaste for the practice and influence of popular verse" as expressed in the Angevin statutes is clearly a "distaste" for disturbers of the public peace, who sing songs at strange hours for illicit purposes, not a "distaste" for vernacular poetry as a whole. There is ample evidence of vernacular poetic entertainments at the Neapolitan court (see Sabatini, *Napoli angioina*, pp. 84–85). And finally, even if we agree with Wallace that Robert probably would have disapproved of certain frivolities represented by Palamon and Arcite, we need not conclude as well that Robert therefore disapproved of the *Teseida*. Rita Librandi, "Corte e cavalleria della Napoli angioina nel *Teseida*," *Medioevo romanzo* 4 (1977): 53–72, has collected the abundant evidence that Robert enjoyed, promoted, and regularly attended tournaments.

53. Giuseppe Velli, "Sulla Similitudine dotta del Boccaccio," in his *Petrarca e Boccaccio*, pp. 156–171. For Boccaccio's models, see especially Richard Lansing, *Similes in the "Divine Comedy"* (Cambridge, Mass.: Harvard University Press, 1978).

54. *Metamorphoses* 6.424ff. Ovid uses the form "Philomela." The story of Procne and Philomena appears as the vehicle of a simile at *Thebaid* 12.478–480 that should probably be included among the sources for Boccaccio's

similes in *Teseida* 4. Statius likens the Greeks' lamentations against Creon to the perpetual lamenting of the nightingales:

> Geticae non plura queruntur
> hospitibus tectis trunco sermone volucres,
> cum duplices thalamos et iniquum Terea clamant.

[The Getic birds make no greater complaint on the foreign housetops, in their mutilated speech, when they cry out against the treachery of the double wedding bed and Tereus's wicked act.]

Statius applies the same figure in much the same way at 8.616.

55. Leander is mentioned in the catalog of *Teseida* 6, where his drowning is recalled once again and where the gloss sends us back to 1.40. On Boccaccio's probable sources see here below, Chapter 2, esp. note 22.

56. The classical source for Boccaccio's simile has not been noted before.

57. See below, Chapter 2, p. 105, on Boccaccio's systematic use of competitors from Statius's games in his "giuoco a Marte."

58. Håkanson, *Statius' Thebaid,* pp. 46–48, and Gisela Gräfin von Stosch, *Untersuchungen zu den Leichenspielen in der Thebais des P. Papinius Statius* (Diss. Tübingen: 1968), pp. 75–85.

59. *P. Ovidii Nasonis Metamorphoseon,* ed. B. A. Van Proosidij (Leiden: Brill, 1959), p. 246 and n. 46.

60. The descriptions of fighting bulls in *Georgics* 3 would seem to stand behind Statius's simile along with the similes of *Aeneid* 12, for it is in the *Georgics* that Vergil follows his description of the fights with a peroration on the power of love (3.242–244). On this example of Vergil's using narrative material from the *Georgics* for similes in the *Aeneid,* see Georg Nicolaus Knauer, "Vergil and Homer," in *Aufsteig und Niedergang der Römischen Welt,* eds. Hildegard Temporini and Wolfgang Haase, vol. 2 (Berlin and New York: De Gruyter, 1981), pp. 914–918; and Ward W. Briggs, Jr., *Narrative and Simile from the Georgics in the Aeneid,* Mnemosyne, supplementum quinquages imum octavum (Leiden: Brill, 1980), pp. 46–50. For *coniunx,* see also the prophecy of the Sibyl in *Aeneid* 6.93–94, "causa mali tanti coniunx iterum hospita Teucris / externique iterum thalami," the cause of such evils (i.e., wars) will again be "a wife."

61. Conventional figurative interpretations of the myth of Antaeus and Hercules may well come into play here also. Hercules' victory was often glossed as the victory of reason over *luxuria,* as it is in Boethius, *De consolatione philosophiae* 4 meter 7. The *Consolation* is an important source for Boccaccio in the section of the *Teseida* concerning Arcite's death and celestial apotheosis: see Giuseppe Velli, "L'Apoteosi di Arcita: Ideologia e coscienza storica nel *Teseida,*" *Studi e problemi di critica testuale* 5 (1972): 33–66. The interpretation is elaborated by Coluccio Salutati, *De laboribus Herculis* 3, chapter 27 (ed. B. L. Ullman, pp. 319–326), who quotes Statius's simile and Lactantius's gloss, turning then to Fulgentius's allegory: "Antheus . . . autore Fulgentio 'in modum libidinis ponitur'" (p. 322). Salutati

devotes special attention to Lucan's description of Hercules and Antaeus (*De bello civili*, 4.600ff.), for which see also Frederick M. Ahl, *Lucan: An Introduction* (Ithaca and London: Cornell University Press, 1976), p. 95. For Statius's phrase *cum fraude reperta*, "when the trick was discovered," compare *Thebaid* 4.170–171, *pars arte reperta/conditur*, and the annotation by Lennart Håkanson, *Statius' Thebaid*, p. 22.

62. On the opposition of *furor* and *pietas* as the central theme of Vergil's *Aeneid*, see Otis, *Virgil*, chaps. 6 and 7, esp. pp. 215–250. For remarks on Statius's imitation of Vergil, see the edition of Williams cited above, note 31, and Frederick M. Ahl, "Lucan and Statius," in *Ancient Writers*, ed. T. J. Luce (New York: Scribner's, 1982); on the theme of *impietas* in later Roman literature, Richard A. Bauman, *Impietas in principem* (Munich: Beck, 1974).

63. From the *accessus* "In principio uniuscuiusque actoris," here following the Berlin manuscript. See Appendix 1, p. 231.

64. Venini notes that Statius's bipartite structure is imitated from Vergil and Homer: 1–6 before the arrival, 7–12 after the arrival at Thebes, reproducing the structure of the *Aeneid* (1–6 before the arrival and 7–12 after the arrival in Latium) as well as that of the *Odyssey* (1–12 before the arrival, 13–24 after the arrival in Ithaca) ("L'Imitazione," p. 374). In the *Aeneid* and *Thebaid*, this division also marks off the events leading up to civil war (1–6) and civil war (7–12), the pattern imitated by Boccaccio in the *Teseida*.

65. Introduction, note 26.

66. Emilia is present when Theseus comes upon Palamon and Arcite fighting in the grove, and his comments after they have told him their story courteously suggest that she is worth fighting for. But his speech is keyed to the word "folly" as he notes the disproportion between their zeal for killing each other (and for risking death by staying in Athenian territory) and the unlikely possibility that either one might gain by it:

> . . . ben che meritato
> l'aggiate per la vostra gran follia;
> ché l'un contra 'l mandato è ritornato
> e l'altro ha rotta la mia prigionia
>
> . . .
>
> Ma però ch'io già innamorato fui
> e per amor sovente folleggiai,
> m'è caro molto il perdonare altrui   (5.91–92)

[Although you deserve (death) for your great folly, because one has returned against my decree and the other has escaped from prison . . . it pleases me well to pardon others, for I was once in love myself and often committed folly for love.]

Chaucer's Theseus remarks the same "folly." It is the central theme of his speech at the Knight's Tale, lines 1785–1825:

And yet hath love, maugree hir eyen two,
Broght hem hyder bothe for to dye.
Now looketh, is nat that an heigh folye?   (1796–1798)

67. All but one, that is. Tydeus spares Maeon and sends him back to Eteocles
     with threats of war (*Thebaid* 2.690–703). Boccaccio's omission does not
     reflect inattention so much as the requirements of this particular gloss. He
     uses the speech of Maeon (*Thebaid* 3.59–87), along with several other
     sources, when he composes Arcite's prayer to Mercury (*Teseida* 10); see
     Velli, "L'Apoteosi d'Arcita," pp. 56–59. And note that Tydeus later boasts
     that he slew all fifty at the ambush (*Thebaid* 8.666).

68. There are several "dark woods" in the *Thebaid*. Boccaccio's description of
     the beginning of strife between Palamon and Arcite may also allude to the
     silva capax aevi of *Thebaid* 4.419ff. because of its associations with the
     first instance of fraternal strife at Thebes. It is on the edge of this famous
     wood ("notae in limite silvae," 4.450) that Tiresias and Manto perform
     their rites, recalled by Boccaccio in the rites of Emilia at the temple of
     Diana (see above, p. 79). During these rites, Manto enters a trance and de-
     scribes for Tiresias the familiar shades of the Theban race as they gather in
     Avernus in a bloody lake (4.549ff.), a catalog echoed in Arcite's disquisi-
     tion in the *boschetto* on his Theban ancestors (*Teseida* 5.56–59; compare
     especially the sequence in *Thebaid* 4.553–578). Moreover, Statius com-
     ments that the old wood itself is the very place in which the first of those
     Theban ancestors, Cadmus, slew the serpent of Mars, and that on the
     "Martian plains" next to the wood, the serpent's teeth were sown from
     which the *terrigenae* sprang to life and to battle with one another (*Thebaid*
     4.435–441). Statius concludes his account of the *terrigenae* with a descrip-
     tion of their spirits still haunting the *silva* and plain. The irony of Statius's
     elaborate references to this example of fraternal strife in Theban history
     derives from the fact that the war between Polynices and Eteocles will soon
     repeat the ancient pattern, and will do so on that same plain. Boccaccio's
     "grove" and catalog of Theban ancestors has much the same ironic burden
     in *Teseida* 5, where strife between Palamon and Arcite begins.

69. The parallel passages in these scenes are not noted by Limentani.

70. The tantalizing association of numbers with subjects in the *Teseida* has
     been analyzed by Victoria Kirkham, "*Chiuso parlare* in Boccaccio's *Te-
     seida*," in *Dante, Petrarch, Boccaccio: Studies in the Italian Trecento in
     Honor of Charles S. Singleton*, ed. Aldo S. Bernardo and Anthony Pel-
     legrini (Binghamton, N.Y.: MRTS, 1983), who points out that five is gener-
     ally associated with Mars and strife, especially Theban internecine strife
     (see pp. 312–314, 319–320). Reserving the simile of Tisiphone and the
     onset of strife between Palamon and Arcite for book 5 has the effect of rein-
     forcing this number symbolism, or to put the same case a little differently,
     the figurative associations of the number five underscore the theme of this
     book, much as the simile of Tisiphone does.

71. Parallels noted by Boyd A. Wise, *The Influence of Statius upon Chaucer*

(Baltimore: Furst, 1911), pp. 28–29. But see also *Thebaid* 10.597ff., another passage that certainly influenced the design of Boccaccio's scene.

72.   Arcite has mentioned the flames at *Teseida* 5.59. The motif was known to Boccaccio in Dante (*Inferno* 26.52–54) as well as in Statius, and he alludes to it frequently. See *Amorosa visione* 34.28–34; *Comedia ninfe* 33; and the *Trattatello in laude di Dante,* where he mentions the flames as a type of Florentine factionalism.

73.   Pirithous is a prominent minor character in the *Teseida* whose friendship with Theseus is mentioned first at *Teseida* 1.130. Statius had cited Theseus and Pirithous as examples of enduring friendship, comparing them to Polynices and Tydeus (1.473). Boccaccio would tell the story of their friendship again in his commentary on *Inferno* 9, where their positive example is cast against conventional figures for discord: when the three Furies appear in the tower of Dis, recalling the towers where Allecto appeared before Turnus and Tisiphone infected Polynices and Eteocles, Dante has them mention their antagonism for Theseus, who risked descent to the underworld for Pirithous (9.54). And Chaucer, who reduced the number of minor characters in the Knight's Tale, nevertheless preserved "Perotheus, / That fellawe was unto duc Theseus / Syn thilke day that they were children lite" (1191–1193), with the implicit contrast of this "felawshipe" and that of Palamon and Arcite.

CHAPTER 2

The Alternate Ending

In the second half of his poem Boccaccio varies the pattern of close imitation that has, through books 3–6, aligned his main action with that of *Thebaid* 1–4. The books of war in his new account of Theban fraternal strife will allude to the corresponding section of the *Thebaid* in their general outline but without the repetition of narrative sequences and the verbal reminiscences that have characterized events leading up to the war, and Boccaccio's noble kinsmen will in the end come to be reconciled with each other and to denounce the "crime" (10.98) and "injustice" (11.34) of their acts. He varies but does not abandon it: the framing of the second half of the *Teseida* at the beginning of book 7 and the end of book 12 tells us just where we are in the old pattern. *Teseida* 7 opens with a description of Mars, taken directly from the beginning of *Thebaid* 7, where it stands as a figurative prologue to Statius's five books of war. Boccaccio then places a martial tournament or "giuoco a Marte" opposite Statius's account of the siege of Thebes. With its preliminary ceremonies and ensuing funerals, the tournament occupies a similar reach of books, 7–11, and leads to a similar book in epilogue: as in the *Thebaid*, the last book of Boccaccio's poem is dominated by the figure of Theseus and as in the *Thebaid* it is concerned with the reestablishment of social harmony. Boccaccio's books of war, however, develop no systematic pattern of correspondence to those of the *Thebaid*. The "Game to Mars" that is caused by the rivalry of Palamon and Arcite does not reproduce the scale of Statius's great war or its sequence of battles. The smaller armed conflict occupies only one book, *Teseida* 8, which does not reflect the events of the Theban War in its details. What Boccaccio has done with his main action is nevertheless very Statian, in the sense that it derives from the *Thebaid* and it serves to maintain the focus of action on Statius's theme of fraternal strife. In fact, it maintains this focus more consistently than does the *Thebaid*. In his second six books, instead of imitating Statius's Iliadic narrative with its multiple foci of action, Boccaccio expands on the pattern of a long episode involving Polynices in the funeral games of *Thebaid* 6. Both the setting and the event reappear in the *Teseida*. By adopting games as his setting, Boccaccio effectively steps down from the epic scale of warfare to a kind of middle range that is characteristic of both the action and the diction in the *Teseida*. And with this reduction in the scale and complexity of the battles, Boccaccio's narrative action also serves to keep the focus of his poem on the personal rivalry between Palamon and Arcite, its motivating passions and their consequences. The Mars who presides over the second half of the *Teseida* is a figure both of war and of personal wrath.

As regards its "sources," Boccaccio's narrative mirrors *Thebaid* 1–6 rather than the entire epic, yet its structure alludes to the action of *Thebaid* 7–12 nonetheless because it presents the "giuoco a Marte," modeled on *Thebaid* 6, as simulated war, or war on a smaller scale. This treatment of the games owes something to the conventions of the medieval tournament, which are ever present in Boccaccio's description,[1] but it also has a literary antecedent in *Thebaid* 6, where Statius announces the funeral games as "a foretaste of the sweat of war," and designs the sequence of six ludic victories as a foreshadowing of the defeat and death of six Greek leaders during the siege of Thebes. The paralleling of victories in the games with defeats in the war is quite explicit.[2] During the first game, Apollo looks down to find with surprise two of his favored servants competing against one another, and comes quickly to the decision that he will favor Amphiaraus over Admetus because Amphiaraus does not have long to live. He will win the chariot race, because he is about to disappear from the Theban plains in the first battle of the war, driving the same chariot: "Thebes is near, and the abyss" (6.382). Adrastus is asked to participate in a concluding exhibition, "lest one victory alone be lacking to the number of leaders" (6.926–927), and the prodigy that ends this game (and the book) foretells Adrastus's role as the only one of the seven leaders who will return from the war. Throughout *Thebaid* 6, the games themselves are said to be like battles: *pugnae inermes* (6.249) and *certaminis instar* (6.369; cf. 456–459).[3]

With the kind of programmatic irony that is so characteristic of his art, Statius anticipates the series of dramatic deaths in battle that will punctuate *Thebaid* 7–11 by means of a series of victories in the athletic contests of *Thebaid* 6.[4] In the first game, Amphiaraus wins a chariot race because of the intercession of Apollo on his behalf; then Parthenopaeus wins the second event, Hippomedon the third, Capaneus the fourth, and Tydeus the fifth. Each of these victories foreshadows the role the leader will have in the ensuing war and especially his final act: *Thebaid* 7, will conclude with the disappearance, by intercession of the gods, of Amphiaraus, before whom the earth gapes open taking in the seer and his chariot alike; *Thebaid* 8 ends with the death of Tydeus, whose dying act of vengeance on his slayer Melanippus provided Dante with the most vivid of emblematic acts in the *Inferno,* that of Ugolino. *Thebaid* 9 recounts the falls of Hippomedon and Parthenopaeus, the second coming at the end of the book; and *Thebaid* 10 ends with the death of Capaneus, who taunts the gods to stop him as he mounts the walls of Thebes—yet another scene recalled for its emblematic force in the *Inferno.* In the sixth and last game of *Thebaid* 6, Polynices is restrained from a duel with Agreus, which looks forward to the fatal duel with his brother Eteocles, from which nothing will dissuade Polynices, at the conclusion of the Theban War in *Thebaid* 11.

As even so brief a summary suggests, the action of *Thebaid* 7−11, complicated by many characters and many battles, is given a structure by the sequence of dramatic deaths that mark off its major divisions. These events are especially vivid to a reader like Boccaccio, who at the time he composed the *Teseida* had an intimate familiarity with Dante's *Commedia.* But this sequence of "sei gran re . . . morti a Tebe" (*Teseida* 3.65) is not the narrative structure Boccaccio imitates in *Teseida* 7−11. In its place, he adopts the scale and setting of the games themselves and the action of Statius's chariot race.

The name Theseus gives to the tournament in the *Teseida* points in the direction of the *Thebaid,* his "giuoco a Marte" recalling the "Martial games" announced in the proemium to book 6:

> ludum . . . quo Martia bellis
> praesudare paret seseque accendere virtus.   (6.3−4)

> [games by which martial spirits may prepare to catch fire and may have a foretaste of the sweat of war.]

The role of Theseus in organizing, controlling, and judging the tournament is modeled on that of Adrastus in *Thebaid* 6, and the "giuoco a Marte" takes place in a *teatro* more elaborate than, but recalling the essential features of, the *theatrum* of Statius's games. This similar setting introduces a similar action. Boccaccio's contest between Palamon and Arcite develops on the model of Statius's account of Polynices in the first funeral game: the divine intervention that summons a snake-haired phan-

tom to frighten Arcite's horse, his backward fall, his injury, and its consequences all imitate Statius's account of Polynices in the chariot race.
Moreover, Statius's apostrophe at *Thebaid* 6.513–517, just after Polynices' fall, sketches an alternate ending to the *Thebaid* that effectively describes the new course of action taken by Boccaccio's narrative in *Teseida*
7–11. Statius's apostrophe serves to recall the major theme of fraternal
strife in a book that is otherwise not directly concerned with that theme,
and by adopting it as the model for his main action in *Teseida* 7–11,
Boccaccio is able to focus more steadily on that theme than does Statius
in the complex narrative of *Thebaid* 7–11.

That important apostrophe will be discussed in due course. Because
Boccaccio draws on *Thebaid* 6 more extensively than on any other book
in the *Thebaid*, analysis of his imitative strategy often requires close attention to the order of its constituent scenes. For this reason, the following commentary is organized according to the sequence of events in
Thebaid 6, with the single exception of the funeral rites of Opheltes,
which are described at the beginning of *Thebaid* 6 but reappear only at
the end of the "giuoco a Marte," in *Teseida* 11.

Starting with Statius's description of the games, the pattern of correspondence to *Teseida* 7–11 may be summarized as follows: the setting
for and the rules governing the "giuoco a Marte" are modeled on those of
the martial competitions in *Thebaid* 6 (see sections 1–6, below); one important group of participants in the "giuoco a Marte," introduced by the
catalog of *Teseida* 6 and then reappearing in the tournament itself, is
drawn systematically from the contestants in Statius's games (see para-
graphs 5 and 7–13); and another contestant, who does not himself reappear in the *Teseida*, provides the model for Arcite, his fall at the end of
the tournament, and the conclusion of Boccaccio's main action as the rivalry comes to an end in *Teseida* 9–11.

The expansion of the games: *Thebaid* 6 and *Teseida* 6–11

(1) The nature of the games (*Teseida* 7.7–15)

Theseus at first had imagined the contest to be a kind of wrestling
match ("palestral giuoco," 7.4; cf. 11.62, "l'unta palestra" from *Thebaid*
6.826ff.), but because so many have come in arms, to participate, it will
take the form of Martial games ("Questo sarà come un giuoco a Marte, /
li sacrifici del qual celebriamo / il giorno dato"), in which "we exercise
the arts of bearing arms" (e vederassi l'arte / di menar l'armi in che c'eser-
citiamo: 7.13).

In the proemium to *Thebaid* 6, Statius announces the "games" that will be his subject for most of the book (lines 249–946):

> et nunc eximii regum . . .
> concurrunt nudasque movent in proelia vires   (6.15–18)

> [and now the distinguished princes . . . gather together and rouse their unarmed strength in battles.]

These games are like the Greeks' customary festivals (*Thebaid* 6.5ff.), in which princes "meet in rivalry and arouse their naked [i.e., unarmed] force in battle" (*Thebaid* 6.18), just as Theseus's "giuoco" will be "like a game of Mars, whose sacrifices we celebrate on a particular day" (*Teseida* 7.13).

(2) The theater (*Teseida* 7.108–110)[5]

Both Statius and Boccaccio refer to the site of the martial games as a theater (*Thebaid* 6.714: "opaca theatri / culmina"), outside a city, surrounded by woods. Statius suggests a natural amphitheater; Boccaccio describes an elaborate construction, for the details of which he has drawn on other sources; but Statius's theater occasionally suggests a kind of colosseum as well: it is circular (255), with seats (262; called *sedilia* at 449).

(3) The judge of the games: Theseus and Adrastus (*Teseida* 5.83–86; 7.7–13; 12.3–19)

Adrastus arranges and judges the contests, assigns rewards, and has to command restraint on two occasions: once during the fourth game, when an enraged Capaneus is ordered not to kill his opponent, a "brother in arms and one of us" (6.816–817), and again in the sixth game, when Adrastus will not allow combat with swords (6.911ff.). In Theseus, Boccaccio recreates the role of patriarchal judge and even has him set the terms of combat with an allusion to the Theban War:

> E come poria io mai sofferire
> vedere il sangue larisseo versare
> e l'un pe' colpi dell'altro morire
> come al seme di Cadmo piacque fare?   (7.9)

> [And how could I ever stand to see Greek blood spilled and one dying by the hand of another as the children of Cadmus liked to do?]

Adrastus forbids bloodshed in the games preceding that war: "manet ingens copia leti, / o iuvenes. servate animos avidumque furorem / sanguinis adversi" (A great abundance of death is in store, young men; preserve your warlike spirits and wild desire for an opponent's blood: 6.914–916).

Adrastus's son-in-law Polynices competes before him in the first game, just as Palamon and Arcite compete before Theseus, the guardian and brother-in-law of Emilia, and in effect the future father-in-law to one of them.

Boccaccio uses Adrastus as a model for Theseus in two other scenes as well: the peacemaker in the grove (*Teseida* 5.83ff.) and master of the funeral rites after Arcite's death (12.3ff.). The scene in the grove, which foreshadows Theseus's role as judge in the "giuoco a Marte," is built on the model of Statius's scene at *Thebaid* 1.401ff., in which Adrastus makes peace between Tydeus and Polynices.[6] Statius introduced Adrastus as a good king of a prosperous realm, aging and without a male heir: "Rex ibi . . . dives avis . . . inops sed prole" (1.390–394). The poet then introduces his theme of brotherhood and brotherly strife by means of Polynices and Tydeus, both in exile because of their own brothers, quickly in conflict with each other as well, but soon reconciled and then made brothers-in-law under the governance of Adrastus. The two exiles happen to arrive in Argos on the same inclement night and come to blows over their claims to take shelter. Adrastus is awakened by the noise of their fighting, appears before them, orders the quarrel stopped, demands who they are and where they come from. Theseus comes upon Palamon and Arcite in the same way. He does not recognize the bloodied young men whose single combat he has interrupted, and he demands to know who they are: "mi dite chi voi sete e chi in tal parte / a battaglia v'induce tanto ria" (tell me who you are and who brought you to this place for such a grim battle: 5.83). Here is Adrastus: "quae causa furoris, / externi iuvenes" (whence this fury, young strangers: 1.438–439). In both scenes the answers to these questions, given reluctantly and with reference to noble lineages, are followed by the king's provisions for resolving the dispute. In Argos, these provisions will soon include marriages to Adrastus's two daughters; in Athens, a marriage to Emilia.

The role of Adrastus as judge of the games in *Thebaid* 6 is itself modeled on the role of *pater* Aeneas in the games of *Aeneid* 5, so that Boccaccio's imitation of Statius recalls the venerable series of epic figures representing a good governor, at once just and merciful, who oversees civic customs. The associations of Theseus with Aeneas are set up right at the beginning of the *Teseida*, with its *Aeneid*-like motifs of a sea voyage, a marriage to a foreign queen, the hero's lingering among the comforts of that alien city, and his eventual decision to depart, which occurs in a scene modeled directly on the visit of Mercury to Aeneas in *Aeneid* 4.[7] Boccaccio's parallels are underscored by his use of the epithet *pius* for Theseus, as clear a reference to Vergil's *pius* Aeneas as is Statius's inverted *impius* Oedipus at the beginning of the *Thebaid*. The word is first applied to Theseus in the scene before the temple of Clemency (2.43 and 46) and repeated during the tournament (e.g. 7.3 and 9.16).

(4) The audience (*Teseida* 6.13)

The announcement of the games brings people from "every city and field" (cunctis arvis ac moenibus adsunt / exciti: *Thebaid* 6.250–251), echoed in Boccaccio's description of the crowds coming to Athens: "per che ad Attene assai gente abbondava: / d'ogni paese, per tutti i sentieri" (for this reason many people flocked to Athens, from every city, along every road) (*Teseida* 6.13).

(5) The procession (*Teseida* 6.14–64)

The games are preceded by a procession of images showing the Greek "founding fathers" (magnanimum series antiqua parentum: *Thebaid* 6.268), one of the models for the historiated shields carried in the procession of *Teseida* 6: scenes of Io and Argus appear in both (*Thebaid* 6.276–279; *Teseida* 6.38, with no verbal resemblance). The procession in *Teseida* 6 has as its primary model the catalog of troops (especially that of *Thebaid* 4) rather than the funeral procession and represents Boccaccio's formal imitation of this epic convention. To a surprising extent, however, Boccaccio has drawn the names of the kings in his catalog from the games of *Thebaid* 6, and he has begun the catalog with one of his few open references in the later books of the *Teseida* to the events of the *Thebaid*:

> Il primo venne, ancora lagrimoso
> per la morte d'Ofelte, a ner vestito
> il re Ligurgo . . .   (*Teseida* 6.14)

> [The first came, King Lycurgus, still weeping for the death of Opheltes, dressed in black.]

Book 6 of the *Thebaid* begins with the weeping of Lycurgus, and the funeral games are held in honor of his infant son Opheltes. The games are announced as a "foretaste" of the war to come; in time we see with what systematic and bitter irony, for the winners of the five competitions are the five princes whose dramatic deaths will mark the end of each of the subsequent books. Boccaccio's steady attention to the relations between his main action in the *Teseida* and that of the *Thebaid* shows itself again in the systematic use he makes of the contestants in book 6, for he brings forward only those contestants—indeed, virtually all of those contestants—who do not die at the Theban War. The pattern in Boccaccio's appropriation of names from *Thebaid* 6 appears clearly when the participants in Statius's games are arranged into a table (see Table 1). The names of Boccaccio's Greek princes draw attention to two other "sources" as well, the Trojan War (Agamemnon, Menelaus, Ulysses, Diomede, Nestor) and the war between Athens and Crete (Nisus, Minos), with some echoes of other legendary conflicts; but the most prominent series derives from *Thebaid* 6.

(6) The beginning of the contest (*Teseida* 8.1)

The funeral games of Opheltes open with the sounding of a "Tyrrhenian trumpet" (*Thebaid* 6.404), and it is "il terzo cenno del sonar tireno" that opens the "giuoco a Marte" in the *Teseida* (8.1). Boccaccio probably recognized that Statius in turn was repeating a detail from his great model, the *Aeneid,* where Tyrrhenian (Etruscan) trumpets announce the vision of battle in the sky (*Aeneid* 8.526).

(7) Polynices and Arcite

As has been mentioned, the larger analogy that Boccaccio develops between the rivalry of Polynices and Eteocles and that of Palamon and Arcite aligns Arcite specifically with Polynices. He is the one exiled (*Teseida* 3–4), who returns with the name Penteo, recalling the exile of Polynices and the return to Thebes, on his behalf, of Tydeus. That Boccaccio built the role of Arcite on the model of Polynices is especially evident in a comparison of *Thebaid* 6 with the later books of the *Teseida*. Polynices competes in the first game, the chariot race; it is by far the longest of Statius's games, its description occupying lines 296–549 of the book. Significantly, it is one game that Boccaccio omits entirely from his short catalog of the games honoring Arcite's funeral in *Teseida* 11.59–67, which mentions four of the games in *Thebaid* 6: Boccaccio had other uses for the material in Statius's extensive *primus ludus,* uses that reflect a design

TABLE 1. Participants in the games of *Thebaid* 6 who reappear in the "giuoco a Marte"

Thebaid	*Teseida*
Primus ludus (296–549)	
Polynices—dies at Thebes (*Thebaid* 11)	
Amphiaraus—dies at Thebes (*Thebaid* 7)	
Admetus of Thessaly	"Ameto" (*Teseida* 6.55)
Thoas and Euneos, sons of Hypsipyle	"Toàs col suo frate Eunео" (*Teseida* 8.24)
Chromis, son of Hercules	"Cromis" (*Teseida* 6.27)
Hippodamus, son of Oenomaus	"Ippodomo" (*Teseida* 6.29)
Secundus ludus (550–645)	
Parthenopaeus—dies at Thebes (*Thebaid* 9)	
Dymas—dies at Thebes (*Thebaid* 10)	
Idas of Pisa	"Ida pisano" (*Teseida* 6.52)
Alcon of Sicyon	"sicionio Alcone" (*Teseida* 6.19)
Phaedimus—dies at Thebes (*Thebaid* 8)	
Tertius ludus (646–728)	
Hippomedon—dies at Thebes (*Thebaid* 9)	
Phlegyas of Pisa	"Flegiàs" (*Teseida* 6.19)
Menestheus—bears the same name as Creon's son, who dies at Thebes	
Quartus ludus (729–825)	
Capaneus—dies at Thebes (*Thebaid* 10)	
Alcidamas	"Alcidamàs" (*Teseida* 8.28)
Pollux	"Polluce" (*Teseida* 6.25)
Quintus ludus (826–910)	
Tydeus—dies at Thebes (*Thebaid* 8)	
Agylleus	"Agilleo" (*Teseida* 8.24)
Sextus ludus (911–923)	
Agreus from Epidaurus	"Agreo epidaurio" (*Teseida* 6.19)

for the last six books of the *Teseida* not based on the design of *Thebaid* 7–12 (Statius's account of the siege of Thebes and its aftermath) but on the alternate ending to the Theban civil war, projected by Statius in *Thebaid* 6.513–517.

(A) POLYNICES IN THE CHARIOT RACE (*Teseida* 9.4–9; 11.18, 91)

Statius begins his account of the first game ("sudor equis": *Thebaid* 6.296; the line is marked in many late medieval *Thebaid*s as the beginning of the third chapter of the book or the "primus ludus") with a brief invocation, asking for inspiration to "name" both the drivers and their horses. Boccaccio borrows three pairs of names for *Teseida* 6 but he does not, of course, use Polynices in that catalog. In the *Thebaid*, Adrastus turns over his own chariot, with its magical horse Arion in its team, to his son-in-law Polynices. He instructs Polynices in the arts that "would soothe the horse when enraged" and warns him "not to let him gallop free of the rein" (317–319). The situation is immediately compared in a formal simile to Apollo and Phaeton:[8]

> . . . sic ignea lora
> cum daret et rapido Sol natum imponeret axi,
> gaudentem lacrimans astra insidiosa docebat.   (*Thebaid* 6.320ff.)

[even so, when the sun granted the fiery reins and set his son
upon the whirling chariot, with tears did he warn the rejoicing
youth of the treacherous stars.]

Boccaccio uses a simile to liken Arcite to Phaeton at *Teseida* 9.31, where Arcite's chariot in the triumphal procession is said to surpass that of the sun itself:

> . . . né di splendore
> passato fu da quello il qual Fetone
> abbandonò per soverchio tremore,
> quando Libra si cosse e Iscorpione,
> e e' da Giove nel Po fulminato
> cadde, e li l'ha l'epitafio mostrato.   (*Teseida* 9.31)

[nor was it surpassed in splendor by the one that Phaeton abandoned for overpowering terror, when Libra was buffeted, and Scorpio, and he fell into the Po, blasted by Jove, and there his epitaph reveals it.]

Boccaccio draws on Ovid's description as well as Statius's (see especially *Metamorphoses* 2.80ff.), with only an echo of Statius's "astra insidiosa" (322) in "quando Libra si cosse e Iscorpione." Indeed, Boccaccio does not imitate Statius at the verbal level as much as he competes with him in reducing the famous Ovidian episode into a formal simile. But he follows Statius closely in associating his unfortunate Theban horseman with Phaeton and Phaeton's fall,[9] and repeats the association in Arcite's epitaph, which, as this simile in book 9 has already suggested, will be modeled on that of Phaeton (*Teseida* 11.91; *Metamorphoses* 2.327–328).

Like Phaeton and like Polynices in *Thebaid* 6, Arcite falls from his horse. Boccaccio models the scene in which this happens (*Teseida* 9.4–9) closely on *Thebaid* 6.492–512, where once again Statius likens the event to the fall of Phaeton (*Thebaid* 6.500–501).

Statius's description of the first game is longer than any of the others because it involves an intercession by one of the gods.[10] Apollo has determined to give the race to his prophet Amphiaraus, and to assure his victory, Apollo summons from hell a snake-crested monster to frighten the horses drawing Polynices' chariot. In Statius's words, Apollo "visits the grim spaces of the dusty racecourse" near the end of the race, when "for the last time victory hovers doubtful," and raises to the world above ("tollit in astra") a phantom:

> anguicomam monstri effigiem, saevissima visu
> ora, movet sive ille Erebo seu finxit in astus
> temporis, innumera certe formidine cultum. (6.495–497)

> [a snake-haired image of a monster, its face most fierce to look on, whether he moved it from Erebus or wrought it for the cunning purpose of the moment, certainly endowed with countless terrors.]

Surprisingly, the passage has not before been identified as the source of Boccaccio's description of the fury raised by Mars to frighten Arcite's horse, despite the close similarity at the verbal level and in the general design of the scene.[11] Boccaccio's description also begins with reference to the snakes in its hair: "Venne costei di ceraste crinita," a dauntingly learned construction, which the gloss translates for us as "[ceraste]: serpenti; [crinita] capelluta." Boccaccio's rendering of *anguicoma*, and in fact much of the passage at *Teseida* 9.5 in which he elaborates Statius's description of the phantom, derives from *Thebaid* 1.100ff., the awful picture of Tisiphone inspiring "furor" in Polynices and Eteocles to which Boccaccio has alluded once before in his crucial simile at *Teseida* 5.13. Tisiphone has "a hundred horned snakes, erect" around its face: "centum illi stantes umbrabant ora *cerastae*" (1.103). Fiery vapor issues from its foul mouth: "*igneus atro / ore vapor*" (1.107–108), and it carries a water-snake in one hand and a funeral torch in the other: "haec igne rogali / fulgurat, haec *vivo manus aera verberat hydro*" (1.112–113), which Boccaccio integrates at *Teseida* 9.5 as follows:

> Venne costei di *ceraste crinita*
> e di verdi *idre* li suoi ornamenti
> erano . . . le quai *lambenti*
> *le sulfuree fiamme, che uscita*
> *di bocca le facevan puzzolenti,*
> più fiera la faceano; e questa Dea
> *di serpi scuriata in man tenea.*

> [She of the serpent hair came, and her ornaments were of green hydras . . . with tongues of sulfurous flames that made them smell foul when they came out of the mouth, making her more terrifying; and this goddess held a whip of snakes in her hand.]

This description of the snake-crested fury continues with *Thebaid* 6.498ff. as its base. Statius, having described the appearance of the phantom, sketches its effect on those who see it; Boccaccio imitates this short passage in *Teseida* 9.6, with echoes of *Inferno* 3.133–134. Then the fury appears before Arcite's horse (*Teseida* 9.7), which rears in fright, just as Arion rears in the traces of Polynice's chariot (*Thebaid* 6.501–504). Both riders fall off backward (*Thebaid* 6.504–506; *Teseida* 9.7.8).[12] Polynices is briefly entangled by, and then frees himself from the reins of his chariot, which careers off without him, while Arcite falls under his horse. In both cases, however, helpers run to pick up the injured body and carry it to the judge of the tournament, who fears the accident has been fatal (*Thebaid* 6.510–512; *Teseida* 9.8 and 16). Statius's *alter Phaeton* is dizzy from the blow to his head (6.511); Boccaccio's *alter Phaeton* is wounded more seriously in the chest (9.8).[13]

(B) STATIUS'S APOSTROPHE ON THE DEATH *MANQUÉ* OF POLYNICES

Boccaccio's conclusion to the "giuoco a Marte" and to the personal rivalry that brought about the tournament differs notably from the corresponding parts of Statius's main action in the *Thebaid*, but they reflect the influence of the *Thebaid* nonetheless. In shaping the larger pattern of action in *Teseida* 9–11 from Arcite's fall to his funeral, Boccaccio imitates an action sketched by Statius in an apostrophe at *Thebaid* 6.513–517. After Polynices has been carried from the racecourse to Adrastus and is found to be still alive, Statius calls attention back to the main action and theme of his poem by projecting all that might have come to pass had Polynices not survived:

> Quis mortis, Thebane, locus, nisi dura negasset
> Tisiphone, quantum poteras dimittere bellum!
> te Thebe fraterque palam, te plangeret Argos
> te Nemea, tibi Lerna comas Larissaque supplex
> poneret, Archemori maior colerere sepulchro.

> [How timely then, O Theban, your death would have been, if only cruel Tisiphone had not forbidden it! What a terrible war you could have prevented! Thebes and your brother would have cried openly for you, and Argos and Nemea; Lerna and Larissa would have shorn their hair in supplication for you, and you would have excelled Archemorus in funeral pomp.]

This apostrophe on the death *manqué* of Polynices recalls the list of consequences defining the general pattern of action in the *Thebaid* after Tisiphone's arrival at Thebes (*Thebaid* 1.125–130). But here Statius sketches an alternate sequence: the terrible war prevented, the surviving brother reconciled and grieving, the wider circle of Greek provinces that suffered in the Theban War—Argos, Nemea, Lerna, Larissa—all joining with Thebes in public lamentation. Like the earlier list, this passage focuses attention on the theme as it is reflected in a larger pattern of action, and it does so again with characteristically bitter irony: only the death of one brother could have put an end to the "furor" instigating this conflict.[14] And although the apostrophe seems to open at least the promise of reconciliation, even if only in the most extreme circumstance, this too will be denied in the final scene of *Thebaid* 11, when the strife between Polynices and Eteocles seems to continue even after their deaths.

Boccaccio imitates Statius's hypothetical action not once but twice in the *Teseida*, using it as Statius does to focus attention on the theme of fraternal strife, but dramatizing what Statius merely describes in apostrophe. The first imitation occurs at *Teseida* 5.64–76, when Arcite knocks out Palamon and believes for a time that he has killed him. The second provides the frame for *Teseida* 9–11, from Arcite's fall to his funeral.

Personal rivalry turns to armed conflict in *Teseida* 5. The book has opened with the simile of Tisiphone (5.13) and progressed through Palamon's escape, his search for Arcite whom he finds asleep in the grove, and their ensuing debate over "possession" of Emilia. Statius's theme of fraternal strife and Boccaccio's analogy between his Theban cousins and Statius's Theban brothers are reflected throughout the language of the debate preceding the first armed conflict. Palamon will not leave, he says, until their dispute (*quistione*) is settled:

> . . . sì che l'un de' due amanti
> solo d'amarla fia in possessione   (5.53)

[so that one of the two lovers alone will have possession . . .],

and Arcite reflects on their situation with reference to the pattern of fraternal conflict in Theban history:

> . . . che moiamo
> per le man nostre, come noi sogliamo   (5.55)

[. . . that we die by our own hands, as we are wont
to do]

and to the example of the sons of Oedipus (5.59). The new example of strife has barely begun when Arcite knocks Palamon off his horse:

> Ma non pertanto il valoroso Arcita
> su l'elmo con la spada a Palemone
> diede un tal colpo, ch'appena la vita
> li rimanesse fu sua oppinione.   (5.66)

[And meanwhile the capable Arcite delivered such a blow with
his sword to Palamon's helmet, that he thought his life was
barely maintained.]

There is a little echo here of the fall in *Thebaid* 6, which will be so prominent when the pattern of this scene is repeated and Arcite falls from his horse after the "giuoco a Marte." After Arcite lands his blow, Palamon falls under his horse, striking the ground with his head. As Arcite dismounts to aid his cousin, the Statian pattern becomes more evident: he thinks he has killed Palamon and in his sorrow forgets their rivalry and his anger, regretting the desire for *possessione* that has brought him to take arms against his cousin and companion:

. . . mai battaglia con lui disiai;
O me dolente, perché mai amai?   (5.70)

[Never did I desire a battle with him; O my sorrow! Why did I
ever love?]

In this first dramatization of Statius's apostrophe, Boccaccio uses the narrative motif to underscore the obduracy of the cousins' mutual jealousy:
it is soon apparent that Palamon has not died, and as he returns to his
senses, the "venom" of Tisiphone returns to inspire him and Arcite as
well. Their fight begins anew, and the narrative motif returns again to
frame the cousins' eventual reconciliation in *Teseida* 9, 10, and 11.

The pattern of action suggested by Statius's apostrophe, with all of its
predicted consequences, is carried through in the second imitation of the
scene. Arcite's injury at the end of the "giuoco a Marte" and his subsequent reconciliation with Palamon respond to Statius's rhetorical wishes
in every detail: it is the exiled rival who falls from his horse and receives a
mortal wound (*Teseida* 11.1–3). Before the specter of his passing, the
passions animating the rivalry dissolve and bonds of affection return between the two kinsmen. Palamon cries openly for Arcite (10.30, 36–51;
11.6), along with representatives of the provinces of Greece (11.7–21),
as Statius foresees happening in the event of Polynices' death. Statius's list
of the happy consequences that wait on such an event ends in the suggestion that Polynices would be honored with funeral rites even more
magnificent than those accorded Opheltes/Archemorus, and Boccaccio
expands on his own analogy between Polynices and Arcite by giving Arcite those very rites. They represent Boccaccio's most sustained passage of
close translation from the *Thebaid* in the *Teseida,* and they include an
open acknowledgment of his source. Statius's apostrophe concludes with
these words: "Archemori maior colerere sepulchro" ([for you, Polynices]
they would observe rites greater than for Archemorus's tomb: 6.517).
And in his description of the funeral rites accorded to Arcite, Boccaccio
again echoes Statius's verse as he answers its promise:

. . . la selva vecchia,
la qual Teseo comandò a tagliare
s'andasse, *acciò ch'una pirra parecchia*
alla stata d'Ofelte possan fare
o se si puote, ancor la vuol *maggiore.*   (11.18)

[the old wood that Theseus had ordered be cut down, so that
they might make a pyre similar to the estate of Opheltes or, if
possible, he wants it even greater.]

By modeling his action on the frame suggested by Statius's apostrophe, Boccaccio is able to use the description of Opheltes' funeral as an allusion to Polynices as well, once again associating his theme and principal characters with those of the *Thebaid*. But adopting Statius's alternate ending has also brought Boccaccio's action to a very different point of conclusion, as is underscored by the contrast between this funeral pyre in *Teseida* 11 and the other one, burning angrily at the end of the *Thebaid*.

(8) Other contestants in the first game (*Thebaid* 6.296–549; *Teseida* 6–8)

Having modeled Arcite's fall on that of Polynices, Boccaccio surrounds him with royal competition drawn in part from the games of *Thebaid* 6. Statius describes seven games, but only the first five involve competition: the sixth, fighting with swords, is banned by Adrastus as too dangerous, and the seventh, archery, is stopped by an omen. Boccaccio draws names for the catalog of *Teseida* 6 and the tournament of *Teseida* 8 from the contestants of all five of the principal games, and one more name mentioned by Statius as a prospective contestant in the sixth game. Boccaccio's most striking imitation of his source concerns contestants in the first two games, whose actions in Adrastus's *ludus* reappear, somewhat transformed, in Theseus's "giuoco a Marte."

(A) ADMETUS AND HIS HORSES (*Teseida* 6.55–56)

Admetus of Thessaly (Boccaccio's Ameto), who takes such a prominent role among the champions of Palamon in *Teseida* 8 and whose legendary past Boccaccio mentions frequently in text and gloss, is Polynices' chief rival in the chariot race of *Thebaid* 6. He drives a team of horses that includes two descendants of the centaurs (*Thebaid* 6.333) "worthy to be deemed of the Castalian herd" (from *Thebaid* 6.338: "de grege Castalio" in most medieval copies of the *Thebaid*, including Plut. 38.6, owned by Boccaccio; modern editions read "de grege, Castaliae"). Boccaccio repeats the phrase in text (*Teseida* 6.56: "da il castalio somigliando / gregge") and gloss (*Teseida* 6.56.1, gloss, p. 437). Statius later names them as "Iris" and "Pholoe" (6.461), as does Boccaccio: "Foloèn" and "Irim" (*Teseida* 6.56 and gloss; 8.51, 119). In Boccaccio's procession, Ameto rides Foloèn, while a groom leads Irim beside him "to his right."

(B) CHROMIS AND HIS HORSE (*Teseida* 6.27–28; 8.120–123)[15]

Minor roles in the chariot race are played by Thoas and Euneos, sons of Hypsipyle and Jason (*Thebaid* 6.342–343), for whom Boccaccio finds a minor role in the "giuoco a Marte" (*Teseida* 8.24). Of greater prominence (and more remarkable circumstance) is Chromis, with his team of carnivorous horses, and his companion Hippodamus (*Thebaid* 6.346–353). Chromis is described at length in *Teseida* 6.27–28, where he rides with "Ippodomo" (6.29). Boccaccio's rubric "Viene Cromis, figliuol d'Ercule" recalls Statius's language ("it Chromis . . . satus Hercule magno" [6.346], a verse that Boccaccio quotes in *Genealogie* 13.4) while his description of Chromis's attire, inherited, like the horses, from his father, Hercules, draws on *Thebaid* 2.618–619, where a (perhaps different) Chromis has "a hide of captured lion and a stout club of knotted pine wood." Statius first refers to Chromis's horses without proper names, as those "bred by Getic Diomede" (*Thebaid* 6.348), but later (6.464) identifies one of them as Strymon. Boccaccio names the horse his Chromis rides at its first appearance: "Strimon, caval di Diomede, / d'uomini mangiator, sì com si crede," and adds a gloss on Hercules' expedition to the Getic stables. During the tournament Palamon is taken by Chromis's biting horse (*Teseida* 8.120–123), a memorable scene the poet has borrowed from *Thebaid* 6.485–490. Here, when Hippodamus is thrown from his chariot, Chromis's horses see him and revert to their old customs, or as Statius puts it, "their old hunger returns." Boccaccio works a mildly comic variation on the scene by having the horse bite Palamon, pull him out of the saddle, and then shake him vigorously; he adds a formal simile at *Teseida* 8.121 to describe the shaking and then concludes precisely along the lines of his model: in the *Thebaid,* Hippodamus is saved by Chromis, his rival in the race (6.487–488), while Palamon is saved "by his enemies" (da' suoi avversi: 8.122).

Boccaccio apparently lingered over *Thebaid* 6.479–512, the episodes of Chromis and Hippodamus (479–490) and Polynices (491–512) in the long first game, because he later closely modeled the falls of Palamon and Arcite on their patterns of action. The consecutive episodes in *Thebaid* 6 are recast in the same order as the climax of the tournament and the sudden reversal of fortunes in Arcite's fall just after the tournament. A comparison of the models, their place in Statius's narrative and in his thematic program, with their likenesses in the *Teseida* provides a remarkably clear view of Boccaccio's imitative strategy in the main action of his poem. As a systematic imitation of the action in the *Thebaid,* the *Teseida* is built around the first six books only. These episodes from *Thebaid* 6 are taken as the frame on which to build all of the *Teseida*'s second half.

The sudden reversal of fortune at the end of Boccaccio's tournament also reflects the model of Statius's games. The characteristically bitter and relentlessly emphasized irony of *Thebaid* 6 is that each of the winners in the games will lose in the subsequent battles, their deaths marking out the structure of the epic's next five books. In Boccaccio's game there is only one winner—Arcite—and he too will soon be the loser, as fortune turns suddenly on him after the tournament is completed. Boccaccio's imitation of this narrative pattern can be diagrammed as seen in Table 2.

The previous chapter concluded with a map of the narratives in the *Teseida* and *Thebaid*, the pattern of correspondences represented by lines

TABLE 2.   The chariot race of *Thebaid* 6 reflected in *Teseida* 6–11

Thebaid 6.296–549			*Teseida* 6–11
301–354	names of men and horses		6
355–388	Apollo takes note	Mars and Venus hear the prayers	7
389–468	the race begins		8
469–490	Chromis and the hunger of the Thracian horses	Palamon unhorsed by Chromis	8.120–123
491–494	Apollo's intercession	intercession of Venus	9.2–4
495–500	the Fury		9.5–6
501–512	Arion rears; Polynices falls	Arcite falls	9.7–9
513–517	Statius's apostrophe		10
513	quis mortis?	Arcite's wound is fatal	10.10–35
514	quantum poteras dimittere bellum?		10.36–51
515–516	te Thebe fraterque . . . te plangeret Argos	Palamon and Arcite reconciled	10.52–53; 86–88
517	Archemori maior . . . sepulcro (from 54–248, ritus Archemori)	funeral of Arcite	11.18–91

from book to book (Figure 1). That map is much more orderly at the top than at the bottom, with the sequence of events in *Teseida* 3–6 corresponding regularly to that in *Thebaid* 1–4. But the armed conflicts in the second six books offer no such symmetry. Now, however, we are in a position to see that the second half of the *Teseida*—Boccaccio's alternate ending—is built around the pattern of action in Statius's long first game, *Thebaid* 6.269–549. The bottom of the map does not show parallel but radiating lines, like the expanding image thrown by a slide projector, as the events of the chariot race fan out to corresponding points in the main action of *Teseida* 7–11. The map of correspondences in narrative structure may now be redrawn as in Figure 2.

(9) Idas Pisaeus in the second game (*Teseida* 6.52; 8.58–64)

The second game in *Thebaid* 6 is the footrace (550–645). The favorite is Parthenopaeus, who wins the race. His youth, beardless face, and physical beauty (571), which distinguish him in Statius's formal catalog of troops as well (*Thebaid* 4.251–252), find correspondence in Boccaccio's description of Nestor (*Teseida* 6.30) and especially Pirithous (6.41), though the motif is common enough in epic catalogs and need not be ex-

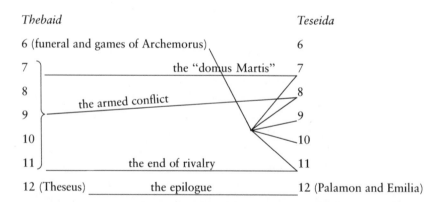

FIGURE 2. The books of war in the *Thebaid* and *Teseida*. The books of war in the *Thebaid* (7–11) are introduced by Statius's description of the "house of Mars" (7.34–89) repeated (as the first of the three temples) in *Teseida* 7 before the battle of *Teseida* 8. Books 9–11 of the *Teseida*, which do not correspond to the action in *Thebaid* 9–11, carry out the program suggested by Statius at *Thebaid* 6.513–517; this correspondence is underscored by a simile at *Teseida* 11.18. Like the *Thebaid*, the *Teseida* ends with a book in epilogue concerning the events, after the death and funeral pyre, that put an end to the rivalry between two kinsmen.

plained with reference to a particular source (cf. *Aeneid* 7.761ff.). Next to him in beauty and speed, and not much older, is Idas ("proximus et forma nec multum segnior Idas / cursibus atque aevo iuxta prior": 6.583–584), from Pisa in the province of Elis (6.555–556). Idas's quickness afoot also takes prominence in Boccaccio's description (*Teseida* 6.52–54), which incorporates a close translation of Vergil's verses on the ethereal speed of Camilla (*Aeneid* 7.803–811). Statius's Idas steals the race from Parthenopaeus when, close behind him near the finish line, he pulls backward on Parthenopaeus's long hair (*Thebaid* 6.614–617); then in the corresponding scene of the tournament, Boccaccio has Ida grab Arcite from behind, in an effort to pull him from his horse (8.58–59). In the *Thebaid*, a furor erupts between the followers of Idas and those of Parthenopaeus until Adrastus intervenes, giving the race to Parthenopaeus; in the *Teseida*, "Pisans" and "Thebans" are soon involved in Idas's unsuccessful effort to bring down Arcite (8.62–64).

(10) The third game: Phlegyas (*Teseida* 6.19)

Another contestant in the second game, "Sicyonius Alcon" (*Thebaid* 6.556), also appears in Boccaccio's catalog ("sicionio Alcone": *Teseida* 6.19)[16] along with "Flegiàs di Pisa." Phlegyas competes in Statius's third game, where he is specified as "Pisaeus Phlegyas" (*Thebaid* 6.668).

(11) The fourth game: Pollux and Alcidamas (*Teseida* 6.25, 8.28)

In the fourth game, boxing, Pollux is the trainer of Alcidamas, the huge but slow-moving opponent of Capaneus. Pollux, with his brother Castor, appears first at *Teseida* 6.25, while Alcidamas makes a brief entrance onto the scene of the "giuoco a Marte" in *Teseida* 8.28. The uncontrolled rage of Capaneus after Alcidamas humiliates him ("furit": *Thebaid* 6.812), which threatens to turn the game into deadly battle and which makes necessary a swift intervention by Adrastus, may well have served as a model for the episodes in the tournament in which the contestants become enraged, break Theseus's rules, and begin to kill (see, for example, *Teseida* 8.112–114).

(12) The fifth game: Agylleus (*Teseida* 8.24, 31, and 80)

In the wrestling match, Tydeus competes with Agylleus, who later passes into the "giuoco a Marte" at *Teseida* 8.24 and 31. Boccaccio also draws on two of the similes in this episode, the first comparing Agylleus and Tydeus to fighting bulls who are invigorated by the sight of the object they are fighting for (*Thebaid* 6.867), the second comparing them to Hercules and Antaeus (6.893–897). The formal simile at *Teseida* 8.80 combines these two metaphors on the basis of their common theme of revitalization. Comparison of Boccaccio's stanza at *Teseida* 8.80 and its sources appears above and need not be repeated here.[17]

(13) The sixth game: Agreus of Epidaurus (*Teseida* 6.19; 8.27)

Before Adrastus forbids fighting with swords as a sixth game, two contestants have already risen to compete, Agreus of Epidaurus and Polynices (6.912: "Epidaurius Agreus"). Boccaccio brings forward Agreus and applies the same epithet to him, in *Teseida* 6.19 ("Agreo epidaurio") and in the "giuoco a Marte" (8.27).

(14) The funeral rites for Opheltes (*Teseida* 11)

Again, Boccaccio's broad imitation of the games in *Thebaid* 6 develops the figure of Arcite on the model of Polynices, and the pattern of events centered on him in *Teseida* 9–11 follows the outline suggested by Statius in an apostrophe at *Thebaid* 6.513–517. These would be the consequences should Polynices have died falling from the chariot. Among these consequences would be funeral rites more magnificent than those of Opheltes, and it is, in fact, Statius's account of the funeral of Opheltes that Boccaccio imitates in the elaborate ceremonies after Arcite's death in *Teseida* 11. More than any other book of the *Teseida*, this one translates closely and systematically from a single section of the *Thebaid* (6.25–248).[18] Table 3 gives corresponding lines and passages.

Boccaccio's expansion of the games in *Thebaid* 6 as a "giuoco a Marte" is nicely characterized by his second, more concentrated use of the same material in Arcite's funeral games. Although the ceremonies described in *Teseida* 11 are in other respects equal to "or if possible greater" than those of Opheltes (11.18), the funeral procession is followed by games described in only seven octaves. Considering the use to which he had put the fall of Polynices in Statius's first game, along with certain motifs in other competitions, it is not surprising that Boccaccio gives only the name of the events and some of the contestants when he reuses them in *Teseida* 11. He omits the first and the last two of Statius's seven games, changing also the order of the four he does adopt (see Table 4).

TABLE 3.   Funeral rites in *Thebaid* 6 and *Teseida* 11

Thebaid 6		*Teseida* 11
1–24,	Proemium	
	5–14 "customary among the Greeks is such a festival"	11.68
25–248		
	28–44 mourners	11.30–32
	45–53 Adrastus's speech of consolation	11.33, also 11, 12
	54–83 the pyre is prepared	11.15, 27–29, 35–36
	96–107 the old wood is cut down	11.21–25
	128–130 the bier is carried on shoulders	11.38
	130–132 the principal mourners walk surrounded	11.40
	138–185 Euridice speaks and puts fire to the pyre	11.41–44
	193–196 Lycurgus cuts his beard in offering	11.48
	202–212 the pyre burns, silver and gold melt	11.49–51
	213–237 seven squadrons of one hundred men each	11.52–57 (ten men each)
	242–248 the historiated temple	11.69–91

TABLE 4.   The games of *Thebaid* 6 and Arcite's funeral games

Thebaid 6	*Teseida* 11
296–549 "sudor equis"	none
550–645 "cursus"	11.59 "il corso"
553–555 "Idas Piseus"	59.5 "Ida pisano"
646–728 "discus"	11.66 "il desco"
729–825 "caestus"	11.64 "il cesto"
741 "Pollux"	64.2 "Polluce"
826–910 "uncta pale"	11.62 "l'unta palestra"

Abbreviated though this imitation may be, it points up the contrast between Boccaccio's "giuoco a Marte" and the athletic games that provided the model for it. As Theseus remarks at the beginning of *Teseida* 7, before the tournament begins, the contestants have come armed for battle and their contest will not take the form of athletic competition, or "palestral giuoco." The tournament resembles the wars of epic tradition more closely than an athletic contest. But the scale of the tournament, if too large for epic games, is also too small for epic warfare. Closest in scale to a medieval tournament, what Boccaccio describes is a little war fought under strict rules that limit but do not eliminate casualties. Boccaccio has evidently not sought to emulate the scale of the games in *Thebaid* 6 nor the battles of *Thebaid* 7–11. He has set his books of war in the middle of the scale. This middle scale in the second half of the *Teseida*, like the poet's middle diction, violates epic decorum, and if the reader begins with the assumption that Boccaccio was attempting to reproduce an abstract idea of the epic genre, it will be hard to avoid concluding that "imperfect knowledge of antiquity" or perhaps love of medieval tournaments overcame his powers of imitation. "His wars are not the wars of Homer!" But Boccaccio's imitative strategy involved open transformation of a single epic rather than emulation of a generic model. Considering his systematic allusions to the main action of the *Thebaid,* and the terms of his governing analogy likening love for Emilia with love for the throne of Thebes, the middle scale of his wars appears much more consistent and artful. The new ending keeps a focus on the motivating passions that cause civic division. It also underscores the political consequences of that division by alluding to the wars of the *Thebaid.* In fact, the tournament recalls both the Theban and the Trojan wars, for most of its participants have just taken part in the former or will soon be engaged in the latter, and their names, along with the martial character of the games, weave a dense pattern of allusion throughout the central books of the *Teseida,* beginning in the formal catalog of book 6.

The expansion of the catalog: *Teseida* 6

In *Teseida* 6, the focus of narrative shifts from Palamon and Arcite to the Greek heroes arriving in Athens to take up their cause. Their arrival marks the transition from an essentially private rivalry to a public conflict involving several provinces and cities. The transition is accomplished by means of a formal catalog, just as it is in *Thebaid* 4, where Statius describes the gathering of Polynices' allies before the Theban War. In the *Teseida* as in the *Thebaid*, the second half of the narrative is concerned with the events of this wider, public conflict. However, while Boccaccio's war is diminished, his formal catalog extends over a much larger number of verses than do those in his classical models, occupying almost an entire book of the poem in contrast to the three hundred or so lines in Statius's catalog in *Thebaid* 4 and the two hundred lines of Vergil's in *Aeneid* 7. Such a long interruption of the main action gives *Teseida* 6 a static and pictorial quality, which Boccaccio establishes in the first ten stanzas with his authorial reflections on Fortune and the several turnings of her wheel in the events touching Palamon and Arcite in *Teseida* 1–5.

Following this invitation to reflect, the long catalog at once shows the political implications of its central theme. The legendary figures, taken singly and in association with others, compose a kind of tapestry of historical examples that matches different aspects of the Theban cousins' rivalry, its motivating passions and unhappy consequences. Boccaccio's systematic redeployment of names from *Thebaid* 6 to the catalog, noted above, establishes one of the more prominent threads of allusion. This sequence is woven together with other names and portraits, which expand the range of allusion and with it the suggestion of meaningful analogies elsewhere in legendary history.

The "Theban" portraits in Boccaccio's catalog reflect on the *Teseida*'s theme and action in the familiar way, associating the rivalry of Palamon and Arcite with that of Polynices and Eteocles. Because it is a muster of troops placed a few years after the Theban War, the seven leaders of that siege, who appear in the catalog of *Thebaid* 4, do not reappear. The Theban War, however, is recalled by a contingent of surviving veterans that Boccaccio builds from the ranks of defeated opponents in the athletic contests of *Thebaid* 6: Chromis and Agylleus are here, and the catalog concludes with portraits of Idas Piseus and Admetus, who also have some prominence in the battles of *Teseida* 8. Boccaccio begins his catalog with a portrait recalling the events of the *Thebaid*, for the first to arrive in Athens is Lycurgus, king of Nemea, whose infant son was honored in the games of *Thebaid* 6, and who is said now to be dressed in black, "still weeping for the death of Opheltes" (*Teseida* 6.14). Boccaccio adds a gloss to the portrait of Lycurgus, making the reference even more clear.

The presence of these figures in the tournament of Palamon and Arcite anticipates an explicit comparison of the two conflicts at the very end of *Teseida* 6. The significance of the passage is obscured somewhat by the anonymity Boccaccio grants to its authors, but its humorous implications clearly depend on the reader's knowledge of the Theban War to which they refer. As the catalog ends, Boccaccio invites us to overhear certain "visitors" to Athens, who allow that the motives in this dispute between Palamon and Arcite justify their actions as well as or better than those of Eteocles and Polynices:

> E ben fu giudicato che 'l suo amore
> fosse troppo più caro da comprare,
> che pria non fu di Tebe esser signore
> o di quantunque cinge il verde mare (6.68)

[And it was judged well that love of her was much more precious to obtain (*comprare*) than, before, to be ruler of Thebes, or of any place surrounded by the green sea.]

The similitude is less flattering to Palamon and Arcite than the anonymous visitors seem to intend. Even if the force of *ben* in the first line quoted here appears slightly ambiguous (is Boccaccio saying that the judgment is a good one, or that they judged the contest to be good?), its meaning is made clear by the lines that follow:

> e che bene investito era 'l valore
> di tanti probi quanti ivi adunare
> avea fatti fortuna.

[and that the valor of as many heroes as fortune had brought together there was well spent.]

The visitors, presumably including the veterans of the Theban War itself, approve of the motives for this conflict as much as, or rather even more than they approved of the motives for the Theban civil war.

In the catalog, references to the Theban War are combined with those to several other legendary events, most prominent among which is the war at Troy. Boccaccio is careful with his chronology and reminds us frequently that we stand in time somewhere between the two great conflicts. And he invites the reader to note the likeness between the "giuoco a Marte" and the Trojan War to come, which will also begin with a dispute over "possession" of a beautiful woman. After the Theban veterans, the future leaders of the Greek forces at Troy are the most conspicuous figures in Athens: Achilles' father Peleus, at whose wedding the Trojan War began, is following Lycurgus. Agamemnon appears fourth in the catalog and is followed by Menelaus, Castor, and Pollux. Ulysses and Diomede come later. In the portrait of Agamemnon, we are told that he already shows the ability that will make him famous as a commander:

sé già degno mostrando degli onori
ch'ebbe da' Greci nella ossidione
a Troia fatta . . .   (6.21)

[showing himself already worthy of the honors that the Greeks
offered him during the siege made at Troy.]

And the allusion is developed in the following portrait of Menelaus,
which combines several playful references to his future role as rival:

. . . se Venere fosse sanza amante,
ch'ella prendesse lui credean coloro
che lui vedean   (6.24)

[those who saw him believed that, if Venus were without a lover,
she would choose him.]

The reference to Venus choosing lovers precedes the first mention of
Helen, which comes in the double portrait of Castor and Pollux. Helen's
brothers follow Menelaus in Boccaccio's procession, carrying shields
with a representation of Leda and the Swan (6.25). The gloss patiently
explains the association, in case some of us have not perceived it for our-
selves: Helen, born with Castor and Pollux to these parents, "poi fu
moglie di Menelao e rapita da Paris" (later [Helen] was Menelaus's wife
and was abducted by Paris).[19]

   As he does with the series of portraits recalling the Theban War, Boccaccio brings these references delicately to rest against his own theme and
main action. In Theseus's speech to the assembled victors, which opens
Teseida 7, the "giuoco a Marte" is compared implicitly to the Trojan
War. Theseus is surprised by the multitude of armed troops assembled to
fight in this cause, and he insists that it not be allowed to reach the dimensions of a general war:

non mi credetti che lance né spiedi
né troppi ferri chiari o rugginosi
né gran cavai né grandi uomini a piedi
dovesser terminar cotanto foco   (7.4)

[I did not imagine that so many lances and pikes and swords,
both shining and rusty, and great horses and troops of foot-
soldiers should have to put an end to such a fire.]

The cause, he goes on, is such a small one, "sì poca di cosa" (7.5), yet to his surprise all of Greece has arrived, ready for battle.

Theseus's surprised "sì poca di cosa" echoes in a lighter key the bitterly ironic comments of Statius on the cause of the Theban War and also the common motif in reflections on the cause of the war at Troy. "Ilias ipsa quid est, nisi turpis adultera de qua / inter amatorem pugna virumque fuit" (What is the Iliad itself but an adulteress over whom her lover and her husband fought?) as Ovid puts it in *Tristia* 2.371–372, a work Boccaccio borrows from in *Teseida* 10.[20]

In arguing his case that the tournament concerns "sì poca di cosa," Theseus hopes to draw a contrast with other armed conflicts, but he suggests the points of similarity even as he insists on the differences:[21]

> qui non ha zuffa per acquistar regno
> o per pigliar perduto ereditaggio,
> qui non è tra costor mortal sdegno,
> qui non si cerca di commesso oltraggio
> vendetta, ma amore è la cagione
> com'ho già detto, di cotal quistione.   (7.7)

> [Here is no fight to win a kingdom or regain a lost inheritance, here is no mortal hate between them, here is no desire for revenge for an outrage committed; but love is the reason for all this dispute, as I have already said.]

Theseus is comparing the tournament of Palamon and Arcite to wars for which he believes so many troops and so much equipment, swords and pikes and lances, might be better suited, and of course Theseus is in a position to command that the tournament have smaller and less dangerous proportions. But the context and the terms of Theseus's argument effectively establish as well that this conflict is analogous to the wars at Thebes and Troy. He recalls the Theban (to win a kingdom and regain a lost inheritance, with mortal hate between them) and, anachronistically, the Trojan (to take vengeance for an outrage) wars. The prominence of Menelaus and others soon to fight at Troy among the heroes in Boccaccio's catalog tends to qualify Theseus's confident assertion that a *zuffa* over *amore* is necessarily a small affair. Even in defining the tournament and its rules, Theseus suggests an analogical relation with Thebes and Troy: "Questo sarà come un giuoco a Marte" (This will be like games in honor of Mars), not athletic games but martial games, a little war.

The double analogy is elaborated by the catalog of *Teseida* 6, more than half of which is devoted to figures associated with either the Theban or the Trojan wars or the personal rivalries that gave rise to them.[22] In the sequence of portraits in the catalog, Boccaccio juxtaposes one with the other and introduces yet other examples of fraternal strife and violent rivalry, to suggest various aspects of his principal action. The melee of the "giuoco a Marte" itself continues to cross and recross the strands of allusion in these figures associated with one legendary war or the other, not without some comic effect.

The first portrait is the first in the "Theban" sequence, King Lycurgus of Nemea. The allusions to Troy begin with the second portrait, describing Peleus and his followers from Aegina. Peleus has already appeared in *Teseida* 5 as one of Arcite's hosts during his exile, and Peleus's friendship with Arcite will be mentioned again at 10.106–109. His portrait in the catalog begins with reference to the legendary origins of his people, the Myrmidons, in the time of Peleus's father; Peleus's association with the Trojan War is not stated explicitly until book 7, where the story of his wedding with Thetis and the ensuing discord among the goddesses Juno, Minerva, and Venus appears in explanation of the golden apple held by Venus in her temple (7.66, p. 472). But the Trojan War is recalled indirectly by Peleus's armor: "e 'n mano avea, quale a lui si convenne, / una termodontiaca bipenne" (and in his hand, as was suitable for him, he carried a *thermodontiaca bipennis*: 6.17). The two-edged axe of Thermodon is conventionally associated with the Amazons, not with Peleus or Aegina, but it is suitable here because Ovid had used the phrase in describing the death of Peleus's son Achilles. The passage at the end of *Metamorphoses* 12 was apparently dear to Boccaccio, for he borrows from it at *Teseida* 2.83.[23] It is distinguished by the same sentiment of "sì poca di cosa" noted in the *Tristia,* as Ovid reflects on the disgrace of Achilles' death at the hands of Paris:

> . . . ille igitur tantorum victor, Achille,
> victus es a timido Graiae raptore maritae.
> at si femineo fuerat tibi Marte cadendum,
> Thermodontiaca malles cecidisse bipenni   (12.608–611)

> [And so you the great Achilles, victor over so many heroes, were defeated by a cowardly thief of a Greek man's wife. If you had to die in women's war, you would far rather have fallen beneath a double-edged axe of Thermodon (i.e., of an Amazon).]

It is, of course, possible that Boccaccio has simply borrowed a Latinate phrase at random for the arms of Peleus, but the context in which Ovid uses the phrase "Thermodontiaca . . . bipennis" suggests a more sophisticated choice. The axe is suitable for Peleus to carry just as it would be suitable in the hands of an adversary of Achilles. The Ovidian phrase points in the direction of Peleus's son as Ovid describes him.

Peleus's companions include his two brothers, Phocus and Telamon, along with Cephalus. The presence of Telamon and Phocus in the catalog reintroduces the motif of fraternal strife: when Boccaccio records the story in his *Genealogie* he follows Ovid's account in the *Metamorphoses* (*Genealogie* 12.46, 47), and that work is probably the source of his arrangement of names here as well. In *Metamorphoses* 7.471ff., we read that Aeacus, king of Aegina, had three sons, Telamon, Phocus, and Peleus; and later, that Peleus and Telamon killed Phocus and were subsequently exiled for the crime. Peleus took refuge with King Ceyx of Trachis: "fraterno sanguine sontem / expulsumque domo patria Trachinia tellus / accepit" (the land of Trachis took him in, expelled from his homeland, guilty of shedding a brother's blood: 11.268–270). The association of Cephalus with this group provides a nice contrast to the fratricide, for Ovid portrays him as a friend to the younger Phocus, who instructs and looks after him like an elder brother (*Metamorphoses* 7.470ff.). The other followers of Peleus in Boccaccio's catalog are Phlegyas, Agreus, and Alcon, all from the games of *Thebaid* 6.

The legendary events mentioned in Boccaccio's brief portrait of Nisus reappear later in his description of Minos (6.46–50) and constitute a third strand in the pattern of allusions worked through the catalog. Of Nisus we learn first that he still wears the magical lock of purple hair on which depended the safety of his kingdom:

> . . . quel capel dal qual tenea
> la signoria delle terre ch'avea. (6.20)

[that lock of hair, by which he held the lordship of the lands he possessed.]

Because the story of Nisus appears in *Metamorphoses* 8 immediately following the story that associates Cephalus with Peleus and his brothers, we have further reason to suspect that Ovid was Boccaccio's primary source. His summary of the story in the gloss to 6.50 also resembles Ovid's version. As the gloss explains, Minos of Crete attacked Athens to avenge the death there of his son Androgeus. Boccaccio is careful to note that the expedition took place after the events of the *Teseida*, though he strains the implicit Ovidian chronology to do so. In any case, what happens is that Minos also besieges Nisus's city of Alcathous because it is allied with Athens, and during the siege Nisus's daughter Scylla conceives an overwhelming passion for the besieging king. The impious act that follows is described in Boccaccio's gloss:

> [Silla] si pensò di trarre al padre uno capello porporino, il quale mentre egli l'aveva non poteva perdere la terra; e così fece, e trattogliele, il portò a Minos, laonde Minos prese la città e uccise Niso; e dispiacendogli ciò che Silla aveva fatto, la fece gittare della nave.   (in 6.50)

> [Scylla decided to take from her father that lock of purple hair by which he could not lose his lands (as long as he possessed it). And she did this, and having taken it from him, she carried it to Minos, whence Minos seized the city and killed Nisus. And because what Scylla had done displeased Minos, he had her thrown from his ship.]

The voice of Boccaccio's patient commentator is almost comically matter-of-fact. In Ovid's version, Scylla presents the lock to Minos with a more dramatic assessment of her act:

> suasit amor facinus. proles ego regia Nisi
> Scylla tibi trado patriaeque meosque penates.
> praemia nulla peto, nisi te. cape pignus amoris
> purpureum crinem nec me nunc tradere crinem,
> sed patrium tibi crede caput.   (8.90–94)

> [Love compelled the crime. I, Scylla, daughter of King Nisus hand over to you the gods of my country and my home. I ask for no reward but you. Take this pledge of love this lock of purple hair, and know it is not my father's hair but his head that I deliver up to you.]

The purple lock itself, which appears in the portrait of Nisus, anticipates Boccaccio's fuller reference to Scylla's treachery at the end of his description of Minos. Some of the onlookers in Athens are so taken by his youthful beauty that they will remember it later, and pardon Scylla:

> e furvi assai che poi non disser rea
> né biasimarono il focoso amore
> di Silla, allor ch'ogni altro la dicea

degna di morte per lo padre ucciso,
sé remembrando qual e' l'avean viso. (6.50)

[Many there were who later, remembering what they had seen,
would not censure nor speak ill of Scylla's fiery love, nor call her
guilty, when everyone else said she deserved death for her slain
father.]

We are further here from the pattern of Boccaccio's main action than in
the surrounding allusions to the wars in Thebes and Troy; further, too,
in the allusive background itself, for Scylla does not herself appear in
Athens, and the story of her *impietas* emerges only as the common theme
in two of Boccaccio's portraits, Nisus and Minos. But the allusions to her
act and her motive for it call forth echoes in the main action of the
Teseida in much the same way as do the more persistent references to
Thebes and Troy: the fall of a city because of uncontrolled desires to possess something, and at any cost, even the death of kin.

Following Nisus are Agamemnon, Menelaus, Castor, and Pollux, who
are followed in turn by Chromis and Hippodamus. These figures from
Thebaid 6 cede to Nestor, characterized by his age and wisdom in the
Troy books of Boccaccio's time as well as in classical tradition, but here
still in his youth, just as Ovid describes him in the catalog of heroes come
to hunt the Calydonian boar: "et primis etiamnum Nestor in annis" (and
Nestor still in his early years: 8.313), a phrase Boccaccio seems to be amplifying in the open lines of his portrait:[24]

Di Pilos venne il giovane Nestore,
di Neleo figliuol, la cui etate
nelle vermiglie guancie il primo fiore
mostrava . . . (6.30)

[The young Nestor came from Pilos, the son of Neleus, who
showed the first flower of his age in his red cheeks.]

And following Nestor is Evander, whose presence also anticipates a more
familiar role in the Italian civil wars of *Aeneid* 7–12, which begin as a
dispute over the hand of Lavinia.

The "Trojan" sequence comes to an end with Ulysses and Diomede,
who in addition to recalling the circumstances of that war recall the
theme of friendship as well, and it is this theme that unites the series of
portraits around them. Pirithous comes first, after Evander, who goes immediately to greet his friend Theseus (6.43); Ulysses follows, "e con seco

menò Diomede, / cui sempre amò con amichevol fede" (and brought Diomede with him, whom he always loved in faithful friendship: 6.44).
After these two examples of sterling friendship, however, come Pygmalion and Sychaeus. The latter, we are told, has not yet married Dido.
Although Boccaccio offers no gloss to the passage in the *Teseida*, he later
described the relations between Sychaeus and his brother-in-law Pygmalion as follows in the *Genealogie:*

> . . . Belo mortuo, Elyssam filiam eius [Sychaeus] accepit uxorem,
> que postea Dydo vocata est, quam precipue dilexit. Verum cum
> Pygmalion, Beli filius, patri successisset in regno, auri avidus,
> eius desideratis divitiis, clam illi tetendit insidias et incautum in-
> teremit.   (2.57)[25]

> [When Belus died, Sychaeus married his daughter Elyssa, who
> was later called Dido, whom he greatly enjoyed. To be sure,
> when Pygmalion, Belus's son, succeeded his father to the throne,
> Sychaeus, who was greedy for gold, desired his wealth. He se-
> cretly arranged a conspiracy and murdered the incautious
> Pygmalion.]

Like the main action of the *Teseida* in book 5, this section of the catalog
juxtaposes examples of enduring friendship with examples of kinsmen
who turn against their kin. The pattern continues in the next rubric,
which describes Minos and his brothers Radamanthus and Sarpedon.

Boccaccio's catalog concludes with portraits of Idas and Admetus, both
from *Thebaid* 6 and both to play significant roles in the "giuoco a Marte"
between Palamon and Arcite. He then adds a short list of figures not
present, in which Boccaccio seems to have elaborated on a passage in
Statius's second, and shorter, catalog of troops in *Thebaid* 7. Among the
allies of Thebes, one absence is noted:

> tu quoque praeclarum forma, Cephise, dedisses
> Narcissum, sed Thespiacis iam pallet in agris
> trux puer; orbata florem, pater, adluis unda.   (7.340–342)

> [Cephisus, you too would have sent Narcissus, preeminent in
> beauty, but already that stubborn-hearted boy is a pale flower in
> a Thespian field. You, his father, wash it with a childless wave.]

Boccaccio translates the passage closely at *Teseida* 6.61 and appends to it
two other figures, Leander and Erisychthon. The exemplary legends al-

luded to in these stanzas have as a common feature the self-destructive potential of immoderate desire: Narcissus dies enamored of his own image in the fountain, "per troppa bellezza" (for too much beauty) as Boccaccio delicately puts it; Erisychthon, whose sacrilege is punished by insatiable hunger, dies by consuming himself after he has exhausted his wealth and the resources of his daughter (Boccaccio imagines him still alive at the time of the tournament, but "già magro e sanza forza" [already thin and weak]); and Leander, who drowns while imprudently swimming the Hellespont at night, spurred by desire for Hero. All three portraits might be called Ovidian, though Boccaccio's immediate source for the stanza on Narcissus is the *Thebaid,* and the *Thebaid* may also have contributed something to the representation of Leander;[26] and all three are described as part of the procession at Athens but for the chance of their misfortunes occurring before the tournament. In them, the exemplary force that has united groups of portraits throughout the catalog has become extremely blunt, even as the language of Boccaccio's allusions remains comically euphemistic.

The contrapuntal arrangement of exemplary portraits in the catalog of *Teseida* 6 is one rather intricate variation on a technique that Boccaccio uses elsewhere in the poem and in other works of the same period. It is related to the nonrepresentational "triumph" as conceived by Petrarch, whose *Triumphus cupidinis* probably dates to the late 1330s and may have been the specific inspiration for Boccaccio,[27] though the influence may also have gone in the other direction. The *Amorosa visione* was later to influence Petrarch's *Trionfi,* though here too the give and take was apparently reciprocal.[28] And as has been noted before, the exemplary figures in Dante's *Commedia,* grouped by terrace according to their similar vices, also contributed to the development of this literary form.

It is interesting to note that in the static ekphrasis of the temples in *Teseida* 7, where the portraits adorning the walls are described as "istorie dipinte" (painted histories), Boccaccio again associates his exempla by common theme. In one series from the temple of Venus, he identifies the theme as young women once dedicated to anything but erotic love, who are eventually won over by the goddess of embraces:

Quivi molti archi a' cori di Diana
vide appiccati e rotti . . .   (7.61)

[There I saw many bows from the followers of Diana hanging broken (on the wall)], followed by the examples of Calisto and Atalanta. In the next stanza, the theme changes to famous couples, the sequence of painted histories containing "la sposa di Nin" (i.e., Semiramis); "Piramo e Tisbe"; Ercul . . . in grembo a Iole"; and "Biblis . . . pregando Cauno." Here the first and fourth involve incest, and they frame two "histories" in which the passionate attachment brought harm on one or both of the lovers. In the biblical exemplum, Semiramis married her son Ninus; in the Ovidian counterpart, Biblis was the twin sister of Caunus, and in Ovid's phrase, she loved him "not as a sister loves a brother." A similar sequence of Semiramis, Biblis, and Myrrha appears in the *Triumphus cupidinis* (3.76–77).

Minor sequences like these form the threads of Boccaccio's tapestry in *Teseida* 6. As the gathering of heroes in Athens expands the conflict between Palamon and Arcite to the dimensions of a small civil war, the sequence of portraits in the catalog suggests analogies to different aspects of the theme represented in the story of their rivalry. The procession is somewhat reminiscent of a triumph, but unlike the legendary figures in the Petrarchan visions, here the troops follow the banners of two mortals rather than a personified abstraction, and they have no single common experience to unite them. By weaving together several minor sequences of exempla in the description of their parade, Boccaccio shows various aspects of the theme he has been concerned to develop in the main action of his poem. References to wars caused by personal rivalries (Thebes, Troy, the coming war in Latium, perhaps a hint of the rivalry during the boar hunt at Calydon) run together with examples of friendship and of friendship betrayed despite the bonds of kinship (Sychaeus and Pygmalion, Peleus and Phocus, perhaps Minos and his brothers as well), and the whole comes to rest on a bald and vicious little sequence saying that immoderate passion can be destructive of self and kin.

The critical consensus that developed in the later nineteenth century around the question of the *Teseida*'s epic form encouraged a search for a "medieval source" because Boccaccio's main action was perceived to fit ill and awkwardly into the rhetorical clothing of classical epic. As we have seen, this search was productive, but its most significant contribution to the study of Boccaccio's sources was Crescini's demonstration that long passages in the poem derived not from a medieval but from a classical source, the *Thebaid*. And Crescini left in the air the question of Boccaccio's source for Palamon and Arcite: "this . . . could be his own invention and with greater likelihood, it could be the reflection of some medieval novella. Doubtless, because of the influence that Latin poetry had over him, he attempted to elevate a simple fable almost to the level of epic dignity."[29] These chapters have approached the old question somewhat indirectly, arguing that Boccaccio composed the story of Palamon and Arcite on the model of the *Thebaid* itself, not in an act of reconstructive imitation with the aim, assumed for Boccaccio by his nineteenth-century critics, of reproducing the "spirit" of classical epic poetry, but as an extended simile wherein his main action develops an analogy to the main action of the *Thebaid*. In this way, the "romance" presents again the themes of *impietas* and *fraterna acies* that are represented in Statius's main action.

From the old question about Boccaccio's failure to reproduce "epic" we have come to the more engaging issue of his strategy in transforming the main action of Statius's *Thebaid*. Given the multitudinous additions to this long narrative—that is, the materials not borrowed from or spun out of the *Thebaid* by analogy, those from other classical sources, those from postclassical literary traditions such as the *cantari,* and even the significant portion of scenes and descriptions that seem to be modeled on institutions and events in Boccaccio's own time—we may ask how these are arranged under the great arch of this *Thebaid*-like narrative structure. This seems to be the most promising direction for critical investigation. The poem in its main action and major themes recalls and openly transforms the *Thebaid;* let us then examine the mediating factors that influenced Boccaccio's interpretation of this source and his strategy for re-presenting it to his fourteenth-century audience.

These questions immediately suggest the need for a sophistication of historical method, for it is dangerous to focus on questions of imitative procedure without taking into account the history of the model imitated. One of the most striking aspects of the nineteenth-century consensus is the hauteur with which the critics refer to Boccaccio's "imperfect knowledge" of classical antiquity and their own superior situation. Perhaps they did have some advantage. But let us not blame Boccaccio for failing to make a poem like the classical epics that only nineteenth-century critics can see. To do so is like blaming a translator for work done with an edition different from one's own. His may be an interesting interpretation or a faithful reproduction, but of a different text.[30] To appreciate the work, one really needs to compare it with the text it translates. The similar problem of Boccaccio's model of epic identifies itself the moment we open a fourteenth-century copy of the *Thebaid*.

Notes to Chapter 2

1. Rita Librandi, "Corte e cavalleria della Napoli Angioina nel *Teseida* del Boccaccio," *Medioevo romanzo* 4 (1977): 53–72. On the development of

the tournament, see Maurice Keen, *Chivalry* (New Haven: Yale University Press, 1984).

2. Paola Venini, "Studi sulla *Tebaide* di Stazio: L'Imitazione," *Rendiconti Istituto Lombardo, Accademia di Scienze e Lettere*, 95 (1961): 375–384, discusses parallelism in Statius's organization of scenes at Thebes and Argos (*Thebaid* 2–4) and in the games of book 6. More detailed discussions of the games are: David Vessey, "The Games in *Thebaid* VI," *Latomus* 29 (1970): 426–441; idem, *Statius and the Thebaid* (Cambridge: Cambridge University Press, 1973), pp. 209–229; and Bernhard Kytzler, "Beobachtungen zu den Wettspielen in der *Thebais* des Statius," *Traditio* 24 (1968): 1–15.

3. Lactantius's gloss on certaminis instar is "speciem enim belli" (in the image of a war): *Lactantii Placidi commentarios in Statii Thebaida . . .* , ed. R. Jahnke (Leipzig: Teubner, 1898), p. 317. The gloss is the same in Boccaccio's copy of Lactantius, where it appears in interlinear position.

4. On the relation of Vergil's book of games and the larger design of the *Aeneid*, see Michael Putnam, "Unity and Design in *Aeneid* V," *Harvard Studies in Classical Philology* 66 (1962): 203–239; idem, *The Poetry of the "Aeneid"* (Cambridge, Mass.: Harvard University Press, 1965); R. A. Hornsby, *Patterns of Action in the "Aeneid"* (Iowa City: University of Iowa Press, 1970); and Gordon Williams, *Technique and Ideas in the "Aeneid"* (New Haven: Yale University Press, 1983).

5. Compare *Aeneid* 5.286, certainly Statius's source, just as Vergil's Aeneas of book 5 is the model for Statius's Adrastus in *Thebaid* 6. James McGregor, "Boccaccio's Athenian Theater: Form and Function of an Ancient Monument in *Teseida*," *Modern Language Notes* 99 (1984): 1–42, does not consider Statius's influence in this section of the *Teseida* to be significant: "While the *Thebaid* . . . mentions a theater, it is a natural amphitheater like the one described in *Aeneid* V. Thus it is no precedent for Boccaccio's urban and monumental theater" (p. 18). McGregor's discussion of Boccaccio's other sources for the Athenian theater demonstrates the extent to which Boccaccio elaborated and transformed his model, to be sure. But a focus on the sources for the description of the theater without reference to the narrative context obscures the meaningful pattern of borrowing from *Thebaid*, apparent throughout the "giuoco a Marte" and to which the description of the theater contributes.

6. Adrastus is associated with the calm after the storm at *Thebaid* 1.390ff. like the statesman, the *vir pietate gravis*, of Vergil's simile at *Aeneid* 1.148ff. Statius models the storm itself on that of *Aeneid* 1. See Venini, "L'Imitazione," p. 378, and Vessey, *Statius and the Thebaid*, pp. 94–95.

7. On Boccaccio's imitation of *Aeneid* 4.238ff. in his scene of Theseus in the garden of Hippolyta, see here below, Chapter 3, pp. 150–152. Transformations of the narrative topos in epic tradition have been discussed by Thomas M. Greene, *The Descent from Heaven* (New Haven: Yale University Press, 1965).

8. Gisela Gräfin von Stosch, *Untersuchungen zu den Leichenspielen in der Thebais des P. Papinius Statius* (Diss. Tübingen: 1968), pp. 16–25, points out that each of the doomed winners in games 1–5 is likened to a single

mythological type by means of an extended simile, and that each mythological type foreshadows the dramatic death of the leader in the Theban war: 1) Polynices/Phaeton; 2) Parthenopaeus/Hesperos; 3) Hippomedon/Polyphemus; 4) Capaneus/Tityos; 5) Tydeus/Hercules. Absent from the list are Amphiaraus (from the first game) and Adrastus (from the last game). The sequence of mythological similes is even more remarkable because there is nothing similar in Vergil's games in *Aeneid 5*. Boccaccio uses the mythological simile from the fifth game, Hercules and Antaeus, and applies it to Arcite at *Teseida* 8.80, but likens Arcite to Hercules' defeated adversary. Here Boccaccio borrows the mythological simile of the first game, likening Arcite to Phaeton. The figure of Phaeton also appears in Vergil's book of games (though not in a simile) and has been discussed by William Nethercut, "*Aeneid V.105*: The Horses of Phaeton," *American Journal of Philology* 107 (1986): 102–108, where the thematic force of the story of Phaeton, his loss of control and his failure to take over the role of his father, serves to highlight the *contrasting* figure of Aeneas. As used by Statius and Boccaccio, the figure appears in a direct comparison in which conventional figurative meanings for "losing the reins" and "failing to control the fire of heaven" would seem to apply.

9. On Statius's use of the (Ovidian) narrative of Phaeton as a model for the role of Polynices in the chariot race, see von Stosch, pp. 17–18.

10. McGregor is wrong to assert that classical tradition did not allow the intervention of the gods in the funeral games: "What is unprecedented in Boccaccio's treatment, however, is the intervention of these deities in the *ludus*. The gods' partisan intervention in the theater . . . is not part of the epic tradition" ("Boccaccio's Athenian Theater," p. 39). Not only does Apollo intervene on behalf of Amphiaraus in *Thebaid 6*, but the intervention itself is imitated by Boccaccio in the *Teseida*.

11. Alberto Limentani's notes to his edition of the *Teseida* (Boccaccio, *Tutte le Opere*, ed. Vittore Branca [Milan: Mondadori, 1964], vol. 2) refer us to the scene of Tisiphone at the end of *Thebaid 8*, yet another appearance of Statius's snake-haired monster. The figure of the infernal fury had been used by Dante as well, and his influence may also be noted in Boccaccio's portrait; compare *Inferno 9* and perhaps *Inferno 7.85* as well, where Fortune is likened to a snake in the grass. See also *Aeneid 12.843–868*. As the present work goes to press, I find that John K. Newman has noted Boccaccio's use of the scene of the fury and the fall in *Thebaid 6* as a model for the fall of Arcite: *The Classical Epic Tradition* (Madison: University of Wisconsin Press, 1986), pp. 296–297 and 357–360.

12. Statius's description of the fall involves the obscure expression *per terga*: ". . . Ruit ilicet exsul / Aonius nexusque diu per terga volutus / exuit" (6.504–506) (Immediately the Theban exile is thrown; rolling on his back, finally he frees himself from the knots [in the reins]). Håkanson, however, argues that *per terga* means supine, and therefore Polynices is "sprawling on his back" (*Statius' Thebaid*, pp. 44–45); however, he notes that *per terga* is used only one other time by Statius (*Thebaid 9.334*) and there to describe Europa sitting "on the back" of the Jovian bull. Boccaccio seems to have taken *per terga* in 6.505 as the equivalent of the more common *in*

terga, "backwards," for he has the rearing horse of Arcite fall backwards on top of the rider: "il qual (destrier) . . . indietro cader tutto lasciossi" (9.7).

13. Arcite's chest is struck by the saddle-bow of the horse that has fallen on top of him ("'l forte arcione li premette 'l petto"). Boccaccio may have changed the location of the wound to make use of the figurative associations of the chest with the passion of wrath. In the *Secretum,* Petrarch notes the traditional associations of certain passions with parts of the body: "I believe that wrath has the first place among these motions (of the soul), so that those who divide the soul into three parts with good cause place reason in the head, as in a fortress, wrath in the chest, and concupiscence under the diaphragm. This way it (reason) is ever ready to put down the violent motions of the lower-standing diseases" (Francesco Petrarca, *Prose,* ed. G. Martellotti, et al. [Milan and Naples: Ricciardi, 1955], pp. 122–124). Petrarch is following Cicero, *Tusculan Disputations* 1.10.20. Although Palamon and Arcite are both "full of love and wrath" when they enter the tournament, it is Arcite especially that Boccaccio has associated with wrath by means of the figurative temple of Mars.

14. The apostrophe actually occurs twice, the first time in the scene of Polynices' fight with Tydeus, just before the intervention of Adrastus in *Thebaid* 1:

> forsan et accinctos lateri—sic ira ferebat—
> nudassent enses, meliusque hostilibus armis
> lugendus fratri, iuuenis Thebane, iaceres,
> ni rex, insolitum clamorem et pectore ab alto
> stridentes gemitus noctis miratus in umbris,
> movisset gressus . . .   (1.428–433)

> [Perhaps compelled by their wrath, they would have drawn the swords girt to their sides and then you would have lain dead, O young Theban, a victim of enemy arms, and earned the tears of your brother: far better so, had not the king wondering at the unusual clamor in the night . . . advanced.]

15. Because the echoes of Lactantius in the *Teseida* are so rare, it is worth noting that Boccaccio's gloss on Chromis (Tes. 8.120) and the man-eating horses seems to be drawn from the corresponding gloss in the commentary on *Thebaid* 6.486 (ed. Richard Jahnke [Leipzig: Teubner, 1898], p. 321).

16. With regard to the source of Boccaccio's Alcon, Giorgio Padoan, "Boccaccio e la rinascita dello stile bucolico," in *Giovanni Boccaccio: Editore e interprete di Dante,* ed. Società dantesca italiana (Florence: Olschki, 1979), n. 24 (pp. 30–31), has proposed Vergil's *Eclogue* 5.11 and its posterity, noting that the name is rare: "difficilmente derivera dalle *Metamorfosi* (13.683–684) . . . o dal *Culex* (v. 67)." Boccaccio transcribed Servius's note on Alcon (in *Eclogue* 5.11) for *Culex* 67 in his commonplace book, the Miscellanea Laurenziana 33.31; and Giovanni del Virgilio mentions an Alcon in his eclogue to Mussato, "dove a quel nome (ripreso certamente da *Buc.* 5.11, egloga che ha offerto al Del Virgilio anche altri sicuri

spunti) è apposta la seguente chiosa: 'probus grecus fuit . . . Alcon dicitur, quia viri probissimi nomen habet'. Nel *Teseida* Alcone è appunto tra i più fedeli compagni del re Peleo." The possible influence of this tradition is well noted, but the immediate source of the name in the *Teseida* would seem nevertheless to be the sixth book of the *Thebaid*, where the epithet "sicionius Alcon" appears as it does in the *Teseida* and where Alcon is accompanied by the same "Phlegyas" and "Agreus." See especially *Thebaid* 6.556.

17. See Chapter 1, pp. 62–65.

18. Boccaccio's close imitation of extensive passages from *Thebaid* 6 in his description of Arcite's funeral was first noted by Vincenzo Crescini, *Contributo agli studi sul Boccaccio, con documenti inediti* (Turin: Loescher, 1887), pp. 238ff. For the place of this discovery in the nineteenth-century arguments about the presumed "medieval" and "Greek" sources of Boccaccio's narrative, see above, Introduction, pp. 12–13.

19. Such references to the Trojan War continue in Boccaccio's tournament, or small civil war, itself. At 8.25, the narrator describes Pollux's brave deeds in arms with the comment that he would certainly have caused a great deal of trouble for Hector at Troy, had Jove not stellified him first: "Polluce . . . fece assai chiaro sapere / che sed e' non l'avesse fatto andare / Giove sì tosto il cielo a possedere, / che elli avrebbe per Elena a Troia / al grande Ettor donato molta noia." The glossator patiently explains that Castor and Pollux set sail for Troy with the Greek allies but were lost at sea, and that the Greek poets pretended (*finsero*) that Jove transformed them into the constellation Gemini (p. 508, in 8.25). (On the tradition of the term *fingere* as applied to fictions about the gods, see pp. 152–153, 167–168, 182–183.) See also the language of *Teseida* 11.7, where the similes refer to the death of Hector. In this context of continuous allusion to the Trojan War, it seems especially appropriate that both Palamon and Arcite fall because of horses, and that Agamemnon and Menelaus take control of the field of battle on Arcite's behalf (9.14).

20. On Boccaccio's use of the *Tristia*, see Giuseppe Velli, "L'Apoteosi di Arcita: Ideologia e coscienza storica nel *Teseida*," *Studi e problemi di critica testuale* 5 (1972): 33–66, who also suggests the general relevance of this Ovidian verse to the battle in Theseus's amphitheater (pp. 58–65).

21. Bruno Porcelli has noted the passage in Theseus's speech as a statement of the analogy governing relations between the *Teseida* and the *Thebaid*: "quella rivalità . . . che è irriducibile odio originale in Eteocle e Polinice, si sviluppa in Arcita e Palemone sul terreno di un solido affetto, da cui non può perciò prescindere, si che alla feroce e costante guerra di Stazio si sostituisce nel *Teseida* una alternanza di momenti contrapposti: amore e avversione . . . collaborazione e scontro armato. Un collegamento di questo tipo con le vicende di Eteocle e Polinice è stabilito a chiare note dal Teseo boccacciano" ("Il *Teseida* del Boccaccio fra la *Tebaide* e *The Knight's Tale*," *Studi e problemi di critica testuale* 32 [1986]: 58). Porcelli sees the difference in scale between the war of the *Thebaid* and the *giuoco* of the *Teseida* as an extension of the more moderate passions animating Palamon and Arcite ("that rivalry, which is implacable hate from the beginning in Eteocles and Polynices, develops in Arcite and Palamon on the

grounds of a solid affection"), and there can be no doubt that we see Palamon and Arcite as friends and companions before the arrival of Tisiphone,
in contrast to the situation in the *Thebaid*. But Boccaccio also suggests that
the quality of their motivating passions is the same as those in the *Thebaid*.
"Wrath" (*ira*) is the thematic word applied to them by Theseus ("when I
came upon them in the wood, full of love and wrath") in reference to their
rivalry, and it is Theseus himself, in this speech of *Teseida* 7, who imposes
the humane limits on the little civil war they have brought about.

22. Boccaccio's models for the catalog include, with the epic catalogs of *Thebaid* 4 and *Aeneid* 7, the shorter list of allies to Thebes at *Thebaid* 7, the
Minyae of *Thebaid* 5.431–444, and the list of heroes in Ovid's account of
the Calydonian boar hunt in *Metamorphoses* 8. Although Boccaccio draws
from each of these classical sources in *Teseida* 6, Ovid's list of the heroes at
Calydon corresponds the most closely to the group of heroes Boccaccio
brings to Athens. Ovid's list is as follows (see *Metamorphoses* 8.310ff.),
with those names marked that reappear in the *Teseida*'s catalog: "Sons
of Tyndareus" (*Castor and Pollux*); Jason; *Theseus and Pirithous*, "insepa-
rable companions"; "Sons of Thestius" (and uncles of Meleager); Meleager;
Atalanta; Aphareus's sons, *Lynceus and "swift Idas"*; Caeneus; Leucippus;
Acastus; Hippothous, *Dryas, and Phoenix*; Phyleus; *Telamon and Peleus*;
Admetus "son of Pheres"; Iolaus of Boeotia; *Nestor*, "then still in the prime
of life"; Mopsus, "Ampycus's son"; Amphiaraus, "not yet fallen victim to
his wife's treachery."

   The general design of *Teseida* 6—wherein the heroes are described in
procession, each followed by warriors from his province, the historiated
shields with episodes of legendary history represented on them, the lineage
of warhorses, and the concluding references to heroes who could not appear at the muster—derives from the epic catalogs the *Thebaid* and the
Aeneid. Even Boccaccio's references to the physical beauty of the younger
heroes, reminiscent though they may be in language to the popular *cantari,*
have precedent in the epic tradition (compare, for example, Vergil's description of Aventinus or Statius's description of Parthenopaeus).

23. On Ovidian materials in the *glosses,* see Robert Hollander, "The Validity
of Boccaccio's Self-Exegesis in His *Teseida,*" *Medievalia et humanistica* n.s.
8 (1977): 163–183, who believes they may have come from mythographical compilations as well as from the *Metamorphoses* (see esp. n. 14); but
see also Giuseppe Velli, "Cultura e *imitatio* nel primo Boccaccio," *Annali
della Scuola normale superiore di Pisa* 2d ser. 37 (1968): 60–75; and on
the *Tristia* in the *Teseida,* idem, "L'Apoteosi di Arcita," pp. 62–65. On the
termodontiaca bipenne of *Teseida* 6.17 and echo from the same passage
of *Metamorphoses* at *Teseida* 2.83, see idem, "L'Apoteosi d'Arcita,"
pp. 63–64, n. 52.

24. Like Boccaccio after him, Ovid places an episode in time by referring to
events in which his heroes will later take part. In the catalog before the Calydonian boar hunt, Ovid establishes the historical moment as being before
both the Theban and Trojan wars with his description of Amphiaraus, "not
yet fallen victim to his wife's treachery," and Nestor, "still then in the prime
of life."

25. *Genealogie deorum gentilium libri,* ed. Vincenzo Romano (Bari: Laterza, 1951), p. 105.

26. *Heroides,* 18–19; *Thebaid* 6.540–547, where the representation of Leander swimming the Hellespont appears on one of the ceremonial prizes of the funeral games. Compare *Teseida* 5.32, and the discussion here above, Chapter 1, p. 62.

27. E. H. Wilkins, *Life of Petrarch* (Chicago and London: University of Chicago Press, 1963), p. 22. But Wilkins's theses have been challenged, and the chronology of the *Trionfi*'s composition remains a vexed problem. For bibliography, see the works of Branca cited in the next note.

28. On the literary models of Boccaccio's *Amorosa visione,* see the introduction to Vittore Branca's edition, in *Tutte le Opere,* vol. 3, esp. pp. 6–13; and for the relation of *Amorosa visione* and *Trionfi,* see idem, "Petrarch and Boccaccio," in *Francesco Petrarca, Citizen of the World,* ed. Aldo S. Bernardo (Padua: Antenore, 1980), esp. pp. 203–206. Also Giuseppe Frasso, *Studi sui "Trionfi"* (Padua: Antenore, 1983).

29. Crescini, *Contributo,* p. 220.

30. The comparison is suggested to me by the case of Ezra Pound's Cavalcanti translations, which were made for the most part in 1911 from the edition of Zanzotto, but reprinted in 1953 facing Italian texts from a very different edition, containing substantially different readings for about one poem in four. I give examples in *Pound's Cavalcanti: An Edition of the Translations, Notes, and Essays* (Princeton: Princeton University Press, 1983) and in "The Techniques of Critical Translation: Ezra Pound's Guido Cavalcanti, 1912," *Paideuma* 8 (1979), pp. 224–225.

CHAPTER 3

Boccaccio's Model of Epic Narrative

If we retrace the steps of an argument like Guglielmo Volpi's, we will begin with the observation that the *Teseida*'s title and its twelve book divisions invite comparison with a classical model even before the reader encounters its opening verses. But we may note as well that the physical layout of the *Teseida* presents us with a good deal more than book divisions, and that the examining of even such gross features in Boccaccio's design quickly involves us with one of the problems fundamental to the study of any literary imitation, namely our understanding of the model imitated. In this particular case, it is significant that an *Aeneid* or a *Thebaid* in the fourteenth century usually contained subdivisions and other features in the text's physical layout that were not made by the author and that are, for that reason, absent from the pages of modern critical editions. These features include summaries in verse (less often, in prose) prefixed to each of the twelve books and a general verse argument summarizing the action of the whole poem, placed at the beginning or the end.[1] Along with the twelve book divisions, the fourteenth-century copy often contained subdivisions, identified as *capitula*, and sometimes further subdivisions as well, or *partes*. Now, the form of the *Teseida* reflects these medieval features of "epic" along with the classical divisions into twelve books. This revised observation has only slightly different implications from Volpi's, but it has the distinct virtue of establishing both that Boccaccio imitated classical epic and that classical epic was not in every way the same for Boccaccio as it is for us.

From the Scholastic period on, the technical term most often employed in reference to the formal divisions of a text was *forma tractatus* or the form of the writing. The topic had a stable place in the traditional series of questions or "circumstances" discussed in academic prologues to authoritative texts of every kind.[2] In the prologues to classical epic poems, it is generally the case that the *forma tractatus* did not occasion elaborate

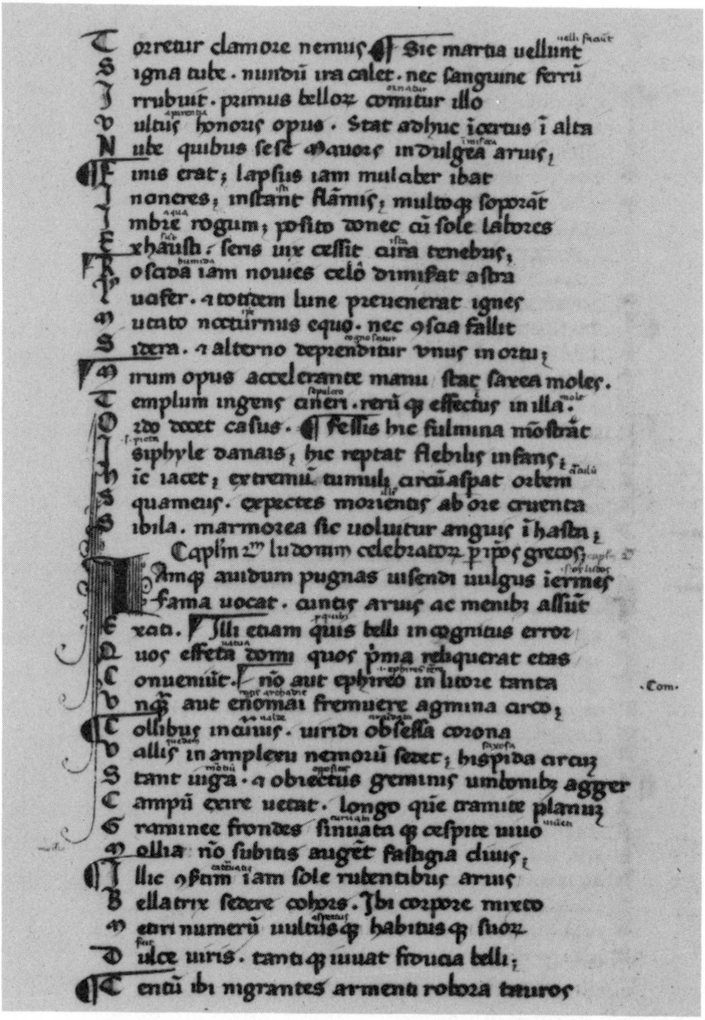

PLATE 2. *Thebaid* 6.229–265, with a chapter rubric at 249: "Capitulum 2ᵐ ludorum celebratorum per ipsos grecos" and a marginal notation "com[paratio]" opposite 253. Vatican City, Biblioteca Apostolica Vaticana, MS Chigi H.VI.210, fol. 55r

comment, being defined there simply as a division into twelve books. A rather dismissive tone had been established in late antiquity by Servius, who says of the "numerus librorum" in his prologue to the *Aeneid* that the topic should be investigated in detail when dealing with other literary works, but not here. He implies that in Latin epic, or at least in the *Aeneid*, the twelve divisions are well known and conventional.[3] Medieval commentaries on the *Aeneid* and the *Thebaid* as well tend to follow suit and do not mention subdivisions of the twelve books in their prologues; but such subdivisions appear in the texts of the epics themselves, and they are sometimes discussed in the marginal commentary. Even in the case of Statius's *Achilleid,* where the number of major divisions in the text had become, by the later fourteenth century, a significant part of a debate over whether the poem was fragmentary or complete, the commentator's discussion appears in the margins rather than in the prologue.[4] Subdivisions of the *Thebaid*'s twelve books into chapters sometimes take the form of numbered *capitula* noted in the margin and sometimes that of rubrics placed in the text itself (see Plate 2).[5] Rubrics, in the margin or in the text, varied widely, and one occasionally finds mention in them of disagreement about the proper place for dividing the text.[6] In many codices, there is further subdivision of the *capitula* into *partes.* Subdivisions of the text are also marked by a large capital letter at the beginning of a chapter or part.

Turning to the *Teseida,* we can easily see the influence of this medieval tradition. In the surviving autograph copy of the poem, Boccaccio has divided the twelve books further by means of rubrics, and a large capital letter follows each rubric at the beginning of the first stanza of each chapter (see Plate 3). The rubric scheme appears in many other copies as well, and although Boccaccio does not refer to his rubrics with the term *capitoli,* at least one scribe referred to them as such.[7] Boccaccio's rubrics appear about twice as frequently as do chapter divisions in contemporary *Thebaid*s, but this difference need not obscure the relation between model and imitation, because when subdivided into *partes*—usually two per chapter—a contemporary *Thebaid* would have approximately the same number of divisions. Moreover, there is some correspondence at the verbal level between Boccaccio's rubric texts and those in contemporary copies of the classical epics.[8]

As the plain example of medieval chapter formation suggests, there is reason to doubt any critical procedure that examines imitative poetry with reference to the history of ideas about imitation yet ignores the history of the texts imitated. Nor is it sufficient to assume that generic models change slowly, glacially, over time as new literary works add to the sum of a tradition.[9] We must also consider the shifts in the old models themselves, shifts brought about by changing modes of interpretation and even by developments in the material disposition of the texts. We have already noted the importance of investigating the particular state of Boccaccio's text of the *Thebaid* in connection with *Teseida* 6.56, where the poet translates from the manuscript reading "de grege Castalio" at

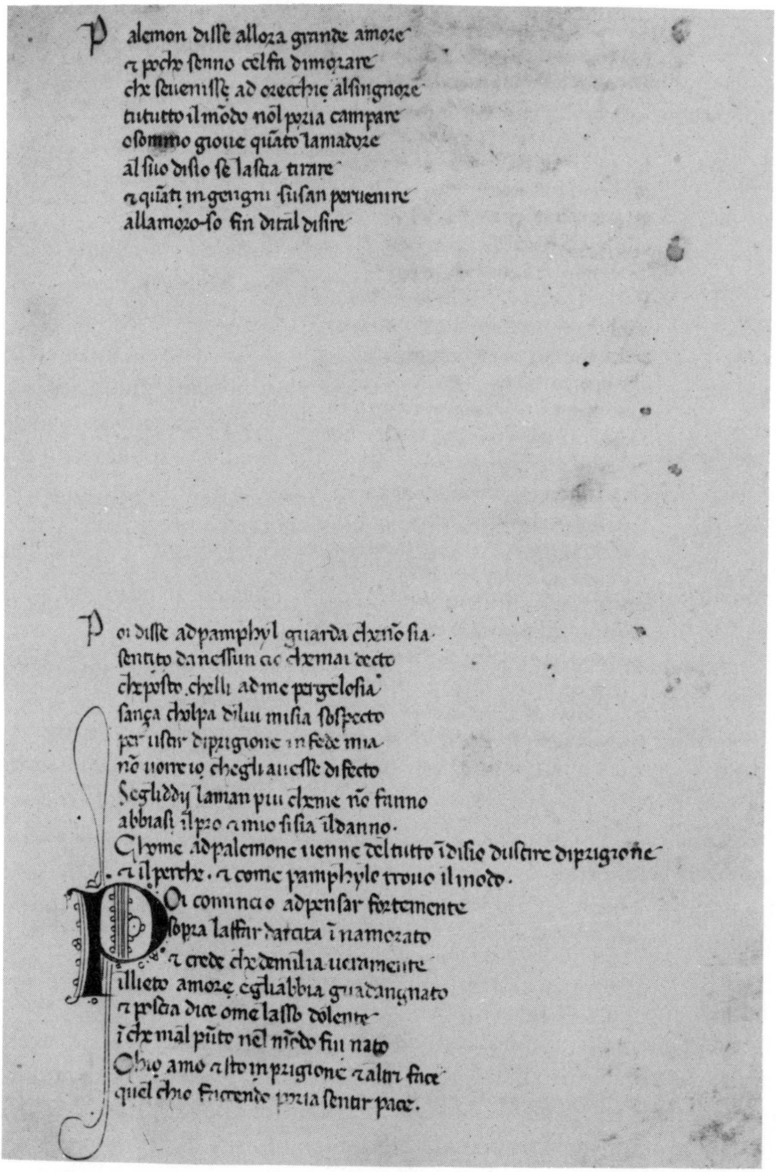

PLATE 3. Boccaccio's autograph copy of the *Teseida* (ca. 1350). Chapter rubric (in red) before 5.9: "Chome ad palemone uenne del tutto *in* disio d uscire di prigione . *e* il perche. *e* come pamphyle trovo il modo." Large capital at the beginning of 9; space left for illustration after 7. Florence, Biblioteca Medicea-Laurenziana, MS Acq. e Doni 325, fol. 51r

Thebaid 6.338 rather than from the reading "de grege, Castaliae," now standard in critical editions (see Chapter 2, p. 112). But the methodological challenge does not end with textual variants. Consider the apparently simple matter of the number of lines in the *Teseida*. It has become something of a commonplace to say that Boccaccio designed the poem to have the same number of lines—9,896—as Vergil's *Aeneid*.[10] The assumption here is that our poet thought the *Aeneid* had 9,896 lines, and perhaps that his implied audience thought the same. This assumption about the model, however, is difficult to sustain with any rigor. Boccaccio himself never drew such a sum in his own writings, and the evidence of medieval codices of the *Aeneid* is highly variable. Even without exploring the medieval recensions of the text, the situation appears muddled because Servius had preserved two passages that he says Vergil wrote and then deleted from the *Aeneid*. If we include the twenty-two lines said to have been deleted from *Aeneid* 2, as most modern editors do, and we exclude the four prefatory lines that Servius says once preceded "Arma virumque cano" in *Aeneid* 1, the total number of lines is 9,896. But if we include the four prefatory lines, which were often present in late medieval copies and often imitated in renaissance epics (such as the *Faerie Queene*, I.1.1), and which probably appeared authoritative in Boccaccio's eyes as well, the total is a more rounded 9,900. By my count there are 1,238 octaves or 9.904 lines of verse in modern editions of the *Teseida*, editions based on Boccaccio's late autograph manuscript. This number does not match either of the provisional totals for the *Aeneid*, but my interest is not with the calculation itself. Indeed, some manuscripts of the *Teseida* contain one octave less, or 9,896 lines, and these manuscripts may well bear witness to an earlier authorized version of the *Teseida*. The interesting point concerns methodology, for a method that takes account of the history of the model must qualify the statement that "Boccaccio imitated the number of lines in the *Aeneid*." The qualification is the more emphatic if we also take account of the fact that, at least in my experience, late medieval copies of classical epics never contain remarks on the total number of lines in a single book or in the whole poem, even though scribes often note the number of some minor forms appearing in the poem, especially of similes.

Another small and simple example of the way a historical investigation of Boccaccio's model can sharpen our critical understanding of his imitative strategy concerns the title of the poem. According to the failed epic hypothesis, the long title "Teseida delle nozze di Emilia" may be thought to announce the heterogeneous components of Boccaccio's narrative: the "Thesiad" or epic of Theseus points to the decorous representation of martial events in the episodes (especially in books 1 and 2) involving duke Theseus, while the subtitle "Marriage of Emilia" refers to the less decorous "romance" of Palamon and Arcite, the main action that would seem to betray Boccaccio's grand epic designs. Both parts of the title, however, appear to be open and unexceptional references to epic poetry when they are viewed against the conventions of titling in medieval codices. Prologues to the *Thebaid* discuss Statius's title, and one of the earliest and most widely diffused of them discusses it in a passage that also mentions a *Theseid:*

> Est autem Thebais femininum patronomicum,
> sicut Eneis et Theseis.[11]

> [for Thebais is a feminine patronymic, like Aeneis and Theseis.]

The only surviving copy of Statius's *Thebaid* that was certainly in Boccaccio's possession does not contain this prologue, but there is good reason to believe that he was familiar with this conventional discussion of the poem's title. The medieval prologues to the *Thebaid* incorporated, with additions and modifications, the series of topics that Servius had employed in his introduction to the *Aeneid*, recasting their discussion of each topic to suit the particular case of the *Thebaid*. "Title" is one of these topics, and its definition varies little from prologue to prologue. It is fair to assume that Boccaccio encountered some version of a prologue to the *Thebaid*, either during his early schooling or during that period of informal and impassioned study in Naples, which was nurtured by the fine Neapolitan libraries and Boccaccio's many learned acquaintances. But even if he did not encounter such a prologue, he certainly knew Servius's prologue to the *Aeneid* by the time he set about writing the *Teseida*, and the same discussion of epic titles appears there:

> Titulus est Aeneis, derivativum nomen ab Aenea,
> ut a Theseo Theseis; sic Iuvenalis vexatus totiens
> rauci Theseide Codri.[12]

> [The title is Aeneis, a derivative noun from Aeneas, as is Theseis
> from Theseus; thus Juvenal (*Satires* I.2): "(I) . . . so often bored
> by the Theseid of ranting Codrus."]

Little else is known of the (apparently) unsuccessful *Theseid* of Codrus, but Juvenal has assured it a small place in literary history as the name of an epic, and Servius has increased its fame by adopting it as an example of the way an epic poem may take its title from the name of a legendary character. Moreover, the reflections of Statius's Theseus throughout the early books of Boccaccio's narrative suggest further that his title *Teseida* alludes to a specific epic as well as to the generalized literary form: Theseus dominates the last book of Statius's *Thebaid*, and Boccaccio adopts Statius's narrative at *Thebaid* 12.519ff. as a frame for the beginning of his narrative in the *Teseida*. As it were, Boccaccio's narrative picks up where the *Thebaid* leaves off and the conclusion of the *Thebaid* is built around the figure of Theseus and the theme of clementia he represents.

Boccaccio actually gives us two titles for the poem, the short *Teseida* and a longer version with a qualifying phrase, *Teseida delle nozze di Emilia*. It is the short form that he adopts regularly in the titles and colophons of his twelve books (for example, "Qui finisce il libro sesto del Teseida" [Here ends the sixth book of the *Teseida*]), and the copyists responsible for the many surviving manuscripts of Boccaccio's poem generally gave it the title *Teseida* or even *Il Teseo* in preference to *Teseida delle nozze di Emilia*. But in the introductory epistle and again in the sonnet that concludes the poem, Boccaccio employs the longer title. Late medieval copies of the classical epics offer some precedent for augmenting a title in this manner, though none for this particular modifying phrase. One example is the copy of Statius's *Thebaid* surviving from Boccaccio's library, Plut. 38.6, in which the text is headed *Statius Thebaydos ystoria destructionis thebarum*.[13]

Finally, we might note the presence and disposition of Boccaccio's commentary on the poem, which also points to the epic model as Boccaccio knew it. These *chiòse* or glosses address lexical and mythographical matters, and on occasion they also offer allegorical interpretations of the poem's "poetic fictions." Because they appear in every branch of the *stemma codicum*, they must have been part of Boccaccio's design from the earliest publication of the *Teseida*.[14] He revised them at least twice, adding new glosses and expanding old ones, with the final revision represented by the extensive commentary in the autograph. To be sure, glosses are common features in late medieval copies of every variety of authoritative text, and they do not by themselves point specifically to epic tradition. But in the *Teseida*, where they appear with other features so clearly modeled on the Latin epics, these glosses complete a most suggestive design: with longer notes in the margins and short glosses between the lines of the text, Boccaccio has effectively reproduced the appearance of the Latin epics in their full regalia of arguments, divisions, subdivisions, and learned commentary. The content and the style of his prose in the glosses recalls that of Servius on the *Aeneid* or Lactantius on the *Thebaid*. Like these commentaries, the lexical, mythographical, and other interpretive materials are offered in succinct, summary form and plain terms.[15] Although they are certainly the products of Boccaccio's own pen, the glosses are presented as the work of an anonymous scholar, who always refers to "the author" of the poem in the third person; and their straightforward, schoolmasterly style contrasts, sometimes to amusing effect, with the challenging, allusive style of the poetic text.

The examples of Boccaccio's model given so far have involved gross features in medieval copies of epics, features that are quite simple to identify and recover, such as divisions and subdivisions, the number of lines in the text, conventions for composing titles, and the history of textual variants—material artifacts in an archaeology of the book. The important conclusion is that Boccaccio imitated Statius's *Thebaid* as it appeared in medieval codices. But the method of analysis these examples illustrate may also be applied to more abstract matters. The present chapter proposes to extend the investigation of Boccaccio's model to those definitions of epic narrative that influenced his imitation of the pagan gods, human characters, and the main action of the *Thebaid*. The subject involves a tradition of critical generalizations by late classical and medieval commentators on the nature of epic narrative. These critical definitions are more abstract than the features considered heretofore, but their significance for our understanding of Boccaccio's imitation of classical epic is finally no less plain and convincing.

The argument here is not only that Boccaccio intended to reproduce an epic narrative and that his understanding of the rules for that literary form determined the nature of his narrative in the *Teseida*. To be sure, a clearer view of this aspect of Boccaccio's model does lead one to see new resemblance to it in the *Teseida*, but as a comparison with the main action of the *Thebaid* has shown, Boccaccio's imitative design does not preserve or reproduce as much as it recalls and transforms. For this reason the reconstruction of a medieval definition of epic narrative proves most useful as a means for characterizing Boccaccio's transformative design. It provides a critical vocabulary in which to describe his changes in the patterns of his source as well as his repetition of them. In the same way, though on a smaller scale, Boccaccio's glosses on Statius's simile of the roaring lion did not show us a model that Boccaccio reproduced in the *Teseida* but an interpretive approach to the model that mediated his transformation of it.

The *metrum heroicum*

In the dramatic scene that concludes *Purgatorio* 21, Dante reveals to an awed and grateful Statius that the shade standing beside him is Vergil. In making his careful explanation, Dante uses a succinct definition of epic narrative to recall the poetic form that associates famous disciple and famous master: [16]

> He who is guide, who leads my eyes on high,
> is that same Vergil from whom you derived
> the power to sing of men and of the gods.   (21.124–126)

As Statius's shorter poems were unknown to the fourteenth century, this characterization of his song "of men and of the gods" refers exclusively to epic poetry. The phrase itself may be traced to Servius's commentary on the *Aeneid,* and from Servius to the tradition of academic prologues on the *Thebaid.*

Servius established a series of topics to be considered in academic prologues that was adopted for prologues to every sort of authoritative text during the Middle Ages.[17] As a general type for prologues, the Servian topics came to have less and less influence after the twelfth century, as rival Scholastic terms were adopted in their place; but the Servian topics continued to enjoy prestige in the special case of prologues to the classical epics. Servius's commentary itself circulated widely, and the late medieval prologues to the *Aeneid* and the *Thebaid* generally adopted his topics and definitions as a base, to which several other terms might be added.[18]

One of Servius's topics introduces a definition of epic narrative. The general topic is *qualitas carminis* or the quality of the poem, which Servius defines in the case of the *Aeneid* as follows: [19]

> The quality of the poem is evident, for it is heroic verse and
> mixed action [metrum heroicum et actus mixtus] in which the
> poet speaks and also presents others speaking; it is "heroic" in
> that it consists of both human and divine characters, containing
> the true with the false. For it is evident that Aeneas did come to
> Italy, but Venus speaking with Jove or Mercury dispatched con-
> sist of fictions.

Of the two specific terms employed here, one refers to rhetorical procedure only: *actus mixtus* identifies the *Aeneid* as a poem incorporating narrative voice and speaking characters as well. Servius's next topic is "style," and there he will pursue this aspect of his definition: An epic has mixed action with high or formal diction in the case of the speaking characters and narrator alike. Medieval commentators sometimes added *ordo artificialis* to this group of terms, to specify that an epic tells its story out of chronological order, beginning in medias res.[20] Further rhetorical conventions, such as those of the characteristic minor forms of epic, may well appear in the commentary proper following the prologue.

The second term in Servius's discussion of the *qualitas carminis* stands somewhat apart, for it refers not to the rhetorical features of the *Aeneid* but to its subject and its dramatis personae. In this regard, an epic may be defined as a *metrum heroicum* because it contains both "true" and "false" or fictional elements ("est autem heroicum quod constat ex divinis humanisque personis, continens vera cum fictis"). Later prologues attest to the importance of this definition, which provided a clear distinction between two features in epic narrative that medieval commentators, including Boccaccio, were especially interested to distinguish. On the one hand, the human characters and the main action of the *Aeneid* and the other classical epics were *historia* and *vera* not only in the sense that they were credible but in the sense that they represented events that actually occurred. Medieval histories of the ancient world, such as the universal chronicles that appear so prominently in Boccaccio's commonplace books and his *Genealogie*, followed their patristic and classical sources in giving the wars of Thebes and Troy great prominence among the events of the old gentile kingdoms.[21] Troy and Aeneas's wanderings after Troy had a singular importance, because so many civic and national histories followed the model of Rome and traced their origins to the Trojan exiles. On the other hand, the commentator's view of these episodes in ancient history had no place in it for the pagan gods as actors in human affairs. The gods had been worshiped by the erring citizens of the old gentile kingdoms, but they had not existed in fact. Thus the intervention of the pagan gods in epic narrative, so characteristic a feature of the epic tradition, must be defined as "false," and the literary mode of "poetic fiction" concerning acts by the pagan gods must represent something else, something "true." That is, these fictions must be allegories.

Descriptions of the Latin epics from the twelfth century on draw this distinction between "human" and "divine" characters with some variation in terminology. An especially instructive example is the *Dialogus super auctores* of Conrad of Hirsau, in which the writings of historians and poets alike are characterized. Conrad defines the historian as one who writes of "things seen," in contrast to the poet or "maker" who will substitute the "false" for the "true" and "mix the false in with the true."

In the specific cases of the *Aeneid* and the *Thebaid,* he identifies the narrative as involving a "mixture" of history and fiction: the subjects are historical, Vergil and Statius (in the *Achilleid*) deal with persons and events related to the Trojan War and the founding of Rome, while Statius (in the *Thebaid*) deals with the siege and destruction of Thebes. The epic poet is, like the authors of other kinds of poem, a trafficker in falsehoods, but his work is distinguished by the nature of his historical main action and principal characters.[22] Thus the twelfth-century schoolmaster Alexander Neckham directs his students to read, among other classical authors, the "historians" (*ystoriographi*) Vergil, Statius, and Lucan, arguing that their epics provide examples of virtuous behavior to be imitated and vicious behavior to be shunned, examples the more forceful for their status as history.[23] In the next century, Guido delle Colonne asserts in his prologue to the *Historia troiana* that his narrative will include only the factual history of the Trojan War, which he will piece together from the evidence of the poets who "dealt with the truth lightly, as poets do." Homer, he believes, invented "many things which did not happen and altered those which did happen. For he maintained that the gods the ancient pagans worshipped fought against the Trojans and were vanquished with them just like mortal men." Guido goes on to explain that many poets followed Homer in this error. And although Vergil was more careful than Homer, "even [he] in his work the *Aeneid,* though for the most part he related in the light of truth the deeds of the Trojans when he touched upon them, was nevertheless in some things unwilling to depart from the fictions of Homer." Guido sees his own task, in the phrase of his modern translator, as "that of removing what was actually history from the mode of poetry and restoring it to the mode of history."[24]

In light of the Servian definition of a *metrum heroicum,* Lucan's epic presented something of an exception, but it was an exception that proved a rule. It contained none of the "deorum ministeria" and even placed the human events in chronological order, beginning at the beginning as historians do. A commonplace in medieval descriptions of *De bello civili* has it that Lucan composed "in the manner of the historians" rather than in the manner of the epic poets.[25] Application of the Servian definition to the *Thebaid* was a more direct process. An especially dramatic instance in a medieval commentary on the *Thebaid* is to be found in the elaborate set of chapter rubrics, probably composed in fourteenth-century Italy, that systematically distinguish between the "true" or historical and "false" or fictional elements in Statius's narrative.[26] Beginning with the council of the gods at *Thebaid* 1.197, each appearance of the divine characters is noted and characterized as a "transgression" from the main, historical subject of the epic.

The term *historia* as used by these medieval authors reflects a conception of historical narrative that is exemplary rather than documentary, a narrative that may involve fictional elaboration of historical figures that heightens their exemplary value. As such, it differs markedly from the modern English term "history"; it means, in modern terms, something like "credible action involving persons who lived in the past" rather than "history." Any more specific definition would have to be developed with reference to late medieval conventions of historiography, a task well beyond the scope of the present study. It is very clear, however, within the limited context of these remarks on classical epic, that *historia* is defined in opposition to *fabula* and that the mode of representation of the pagan gods stands in opposition to that involving "human characters."

In Servius's definition of the *metrum heroicum,* the two clauses "divinis humanisque" and "vera cum fictis" appear to be strictly parallel, the "human characters" corresponding to the "true" and the "divine characters" to the "false." Confirming this impression, Servius goes on to elaborate his general observation with examples from the text: "for it is evident that Aeneas came to Italy, but Venus speaking with Jove and Mercury dispatched are invention." Medieval prologues to the *Thebaid* repeated and varied this rather simple equation, as the following passages clearly show. The first is from a prologue that circulated from the twelfth century until the fifteenth, and seems to have originated on the Continent north of Italy. The second dates from the late fourteenth or early fifteenth century, and survives in a single copy probably made in Padua:[27]

(1) . . . *metrum heroicum,* and this is the verse (*metrum*) containing divine as well as also human characters, mixing the false with the true.

(2) . . . he employs heroic verse (*carmen heroicum*), the high style and artificial order. "Heroic verse" is made up of divine and human characters, containing the false with the true. For it is true that Polynices, coming from Thebes, and Tydeus, coming from Calydon, took refuge with Adrastus, because the histories declare all of this. But Mercury sent to the lower world, and Laius recalled to earth, constitute fictions.

Servius had written that it was "well known Aeneas came to Italy," but that Venus certainly never spoke with Jove. The latter prologue to the

Thebaid adapts the formula to the "divine and human" characters of that epic, saying that Polynices was indeed exiled from Thebes, as was Tydeus from Calydon, and that they came to the court of Adrastus; but that Mercury was not sent to the infernal regions (*Thebaid* 1) and that Laius was never called up to earth after his death by will of the gods (*Thebaid* 4).

The tidy division of an epic narrative into "fictional" and "historical" elements, fabulous gods to be interpreted figuratively and historical men to be understood as exempla, presents some problems of definition only with reference to the parallel terms *historia* and *vera*. Do not the human characters of epics also bear the clear imprint of the poet's imagination? Medieval criticism showed an awareness of this difficulty, which apparently was not resolved entirely by the broader medieval definition of "historical narrative." Servius himself had set the pattern, in his exposition of *Aeneid* 1.235, where he introduced a third term, "argument": "It must be understood that the difference between fable and argument—that is, history—is that fable is a said thing contrary to nature, whether it happened or not, such as the story of Pasiphae; history is anything according to nature whether it happened or not, such as the story of Phaedra."[28] Although Servius equates *historia* and *argumentum,* Isidore was to use the second term for distinguishing between events in poetic narratives that are true in the sense that they are credible (in other words, they do not involve the fictitious pagan gods), and others that are true in the sense that they actually took place. In Isidore's scheme, both of them stand in contrast to "fables" about the pagan gods, which are neither credible nor historical.[29]

Boccaccio's discussion of "poetic fiction" in *Genealogie* 14 presents a somewhat more complex scheme, involving four categories of fiction as well as "history." There is, however, a point of direct correspondence in his treatment of fables about the pagan gods. In his commentary on the affair of Aeneas and Dido, Boccaccio indicates that the descent of Mercury in *Aeneid* 4.238ff. is a poetic fiction, its meaning "concealed within the poetic veil," to be interpreted as follows: "By Mercury, Vergil means either remorse, or the reproof of some outspoken friend, either of which rouses us from slumber in the mire of turpitude and calls us back unto the fair and even path to glory."[30] Although this passage in the *Genealogie* was almost certainly written many years after the *Teseida,* this interpretation of the "fiction" of Mercury also seems to have been present in Boccaccio's mind when he imitated the Vergilian scene in *Teseida* 2.2–7. There is a large measure of general correspondence between the two scenes, with Boccaccio's Theseus taking the role of Aeneas and his Pirithous that of Mercury. The correspondences in theme and action are underscored by one verbal reminiscence in particular, for Mercury says to Aeneas:

> . . . aut qua spe Libycis teris otia terris?
> si te nulla movet tantarum gloria rerum . . .   (4.271–272)

[or with what expectation do you waste your leisure in the Libyan lands? If no glory of such great things moves you . . . (consider Ascanius)],

words as well as sentiments echoed by Pirithous in his speech to Theseus:

> —Che fai tu ozioso
> con Ipolita in Scizia dimorando,
> sotto amore offuscando il tuo famoso
> nome? Perché in Grecia oramai
> non torni, ove più gloria avrai assai?   (2.4)

[What are you doing, staying leisurely with Hippolyta in Scythia, clouding your famous name with love? Why don't you return to Greece now, where you will have much more glory?]

In the *Genealogie,* Boccaccio argues that Mercury either represents Aeneas's own remorse or "the reproof of some outspoken friend, either of which rouses us from slumber in the mire of turpitude." The imitation at *Teseida* 2.2–7 reflects this interpretation, for it is Theseus's friend Pirithous who reproves his idleness and recalls him to the fair and even path of glory.[31]

Boccaccio's discussion of the encounter between Aeneas and Dido also offers a specific application of the general concepts of *historia* and *argumentum* in epic narrative. He notes that Vergil brings together the historical Aeneas with the historical Dido in a fictional encounter. Dido, "to be sure, is supposed to have dwelt [in Carthage] not then, but many generations later; yet Dido he presents as already living and makes her the hostess of Aeneas; and we read how at her command he told the story of his own troubles and those of his friends."[32] These characters are human and their actions credible, though not strictly speaking historical. Boccaccio explains that this fiction allowed Vergil to adopt an artificial order for his narrative, "for poets are not like historians, who begin their account at some convenient beginning and describe events in unbroken order of their occurrence to the end. [Vergil] . . . desired to bring his hero to somebody worthy of regard who might receive him and urge him to tell of his own fate and that of the Trojans." Boccaccio goes on to suggest that the encounter, though fictional, also serves to dramatize the moral rectitude of Aeneas, which is proper to his reputation in history:

> Vergil's second purpose, concealed within the poetic veil, was to show with what passions human frailty is infested and the strength with which a steady man subdues them. Having illustrated some of these, he wished particularly to demonstrate the reasons why we are carried away into wanton behavior by the passion of concupiscence; so he introduces Dido. . . . he represents in Dido the attracting power of the passion of love, prepared for every opportunity.[33]

Here Boccaccio has made of the traditional division of literary modes— those proper to "fiction" and to "history"—something more subtle, for the "human characters" may be involved in actions that also have figurative significance: Dido represents the attracting power of the passion of love much as Mercury represents the remorse of conscience. He had suggested much the same possibility of actions by "human characters" in classical epic, when he had defined the "third kind" of fiction as "more like history than fiction" but then specifying that "famous poets have employed it in a variety of ways. For however much the heroic poets seem to be writing history—as Vergil in his description of Aeneas tossed by the storm, or Homer in his account of Ulysses bound to the mast to escape the lure of the Sirens' song—yet their hidden meaning is far other than appears on the surface."[34] The simple scheme of "true" history and "false" gods is greatly sophisticated here, but it is nevertheless apparent in the background of Boccaccio's terms and his analysis of *Aeneid* 1–4. Although we have "human characters" whose exemplary significance may be elaborated by figurative details such as a storm or a siren's song, their actions are "more like history than fiction" in contrast to the fictions of the gods, which "superficially lack all appearance of truth."

The major distinction between "fabulous" and "historical" elements in epic narrative also appears in Boccaccio's comments on the *Teseida*, both in his glosses on the poetic text and in his introductory epistle. In the latter, he compliments the lady "Fiammetta" by declaring that one of the ways in which his poem will reveal itself to be addressed specifically to her is its difficulty: Fiammetta, he suggests, unlike many other women, has the learning to recognize different literary modes and master his meaning. The author of the *Teseida* has not spared to use "history or fable, or concealed speech of another sort":

il non avere cessata né *storia* né *favola* né chiuso parlare in altra
guisa, con ciò sia cosa che le donne sì come poco intelligenti ne
sogliano essere schife, ma però che per intelletto e notizia delle
cose predette voi della turba dell'altre separata conosco, libero
mi concessi il porle a mio piacere.   (p. 247)

[not having spared to use history or fable or figurative speech in
another guise. For women, who lack understanding, usually
avoid these things; but since I know you to stand far from the
herd of the others for your understanding and your knowledge
of the aforesaid things, I allowed myself free rein to use them as
I wished.]

Boccaccio does not refer to his *Teseida* as a *metrum heroicum*,[35] but he
defines it in Servian terms as a work including both *storia* and *favola*,
adding that *favola* is one of the kinds of "chiuso parlare" or figurative
representation that he has employed.

If we view Boccaccio's imitation of the *Thebaid* against this definition
of epic narrative, several features come prominently to light. The most
evident, perhaps, is the blunt, systematic presentation of the gods as poetic fictions requiring allegorical interpretation. It is apparent in Boccaccio's references to the "Mercury" of Vergil that he was inclined to believe
that this feature was present in the classical model itself, and that his use
of the gods as figurative representations of human "appetites" imitated
that classical model fairly closely. Statius's handling of the gods, and especially his descriptions of temples in the *Thebaid,* must have encouraged
Boccaccio in this belief as well. Somewhat less evident are the relations
between Palamon and Arcite and the Servian concept of *historia*. Like the
principal characters in classical epics, they are high-ranking noblemen in
an ancient gentile kingdom; and as has been noted, the definition of *historia* as Servius used the term might well include fictional elements in the
portrayal of historical characters. But Palamon and Arcite are not historical characters in the same sense that Aeneas or Polynices were considered
to be historical characters. They do not appear in any classical literary
works or later romances before the *Teseida;* they have no place in the
chronicles of ancient Greek history, ancient or medieval. Working at approximately the same time as Boccaccio, Petrarch chose the very historical Scipio Africanus as the leading character of his *Africa,* and Boccaccio
was certainly aware of Petrarch's efforts to compose a poem on the model
of Latin epic, even if he, along with so many others, was long denied passages from the *Africa* itself.[36] In contrast, Boccaccio's characters are distinctly fictional. Their story does, however, present a fictional analogue

to a noted historical action, namely, the rivalry between Eteocles and Polynices that led to the Theban civil war. By means of this analogy, Boccaccio at once acknowledges the Servian model of a *metrum heroicum* and transforms it. He presents a main action that is not historical, but which presents anew the historical pattern of the *Thebaid*.

Cum fictis: Boccaccio's gods

The traditional definition of "divine characters" in epic narrative is clearly reflected in the gods of the *Teseida,* which are introduced as figurative representations of the desires animating the human characters. The first appearance of Mars, in *Teseida* 1.14–15, sets the pattern. Boccaccio describes Theseus's preparations for war with the Amazons and interposes an extended reference to Mars "returning from the Theban wood" to which he had "led the harsh flock" of Eteocles' soldiers, who had attempted to ambush Tydeus:

> E 'n cotal guisa, in Trazia ritornando,
> si fé sentire al crucciato Teseo
> in lui di sé un fier caldo lasciando.   (1.15)

> [And in the same way, returning to Thrace, he made himself felt
> to the angry Theseus leaving a fierce warmth of himself in him.]

Very much as Statius's personified *furor* enters the thoughts and feelings of Eteocles and Polynices, Boccaccio's Mars figures a series of thoughts and their accompanying passions in Theseus. Their nature is made explicit in two glosses, the first on 1.14 and the second on the following stanza:

> "Marte tornava, etc." Vuole in questa parte l'autore mostrare,
> poeticamente fingendo, qual fosse la cagione che movesse Teseo
> contra le donne amazone a fare guerra; e a mostrar questo,
> pone due cose: l'una è i ramaricamenti fatti da'suoi degli oltraggi
> ricevuti ne' porti d'Ipolita, e questa è posta nella stanza che è
> dinanzi a questa [i.e., 1.13]; l'altra è l'animoso sdegno che di ciò
> gli nacque, il quale vuole mostrare gli nascesse per una valorosa
> cosa fatta, in quegli tempi, magnificamente da uno valente
> uomo, chiamato Tideo . . .   (in 1.14)

> ["Mars was returning, etc." The author in this place wants to
> show, by means of a poetic fiction, what the cause was that

moved Theseus to make war against the Amazon women; and
to show this, he offers two things: the first is the displeasure of
(Theseus's) people at the outrages endured in Hippolyta's har-
bor, and this appears in the preceding stanza; the other is the
spirited indignation that this gave birth to in him, which he
wants to show to have been inspired by a valorous deed splen-
didly carried off in those days by a great man named Tydeus.]

"Mars" represents Theseus's sense of indignation at this particular moment; that Mars is said in the poetic fiction to be "returning from the
Theban wood" means that Theseus's desire for battle has been encouraged further by thoughts of Tydeus's heroic exploits.

This figurative Mars returns again at the beginning of the "giuoco a
Marte," in a long descriptive passage modeled closely on *Thebaid* 7.34ff.
Boccaccio was also to use this passage in his description of Mars in the
Genealogie, which offers an unusual opportunity for comparing the classical source together with Boccaccio's commentary on it against his imitation of that source in the *Teseida*. His comments in the *Genealogie*
leave little room for doubt that he understood Statius's description as figurative and that he composed the corresponding section of his *Teseida*
according to this understanding of the classical model.[37] But he also
adapts the model to the different scale of the *Teseida* and its characteristic
emphasis on the moral rather than political aspects of fraternal strife. In
both commentaries, "Mars" and the house of Mars are taken to represent
"wrath," "furor," and other passions that lead to armed conflict; but the
commentary on the *Teseida* focuses on these aspects of the moral allegory, while the commentary on the *Thebaid* gives equal attention to the
motivating passions and their political effects.

The long third chapter of *Genealogie* 9 is structured as a text with
gloss, with the text a compilation from various sources. It begins with
accounts of the birth of Mars, Ovid's version in the *Fasti* being favored
over the others; it then moves to a description of the "fierce god" and his
"house" (*domus*). Here Boccaccio shifts from paraphrase and summary,
his usual mode in the *Genealogie,* to direct quotation. He cites the entire
passage from *Thebaid* 7.34−63 in which Statius describes the appearance of Mars as he returns to Thrace, and the "domus Martis" with its
personifications of Recklessness, Misdeeds, Fear, Treachery, Discord,
Threats, Furor, and Death. Boccaccio adds to this passage the shorter description of Mars on his chariot at *Thebaid* 7.70−74 and that of Bellona
at *Thebaid* 3.424−431. The end of the "text" is Boccaccio's summary of

the story of Mars's adultery with Venus. Next, the commentary proposes
an exposition of the text following the order in which it has just appeared, so that the exposition of the passage in *Thebaid* 7 begins after it
has been established that the poetic fiction of "Mars" represents war, in
both its moral and its political manifestations. In his Latin gloss on "tri-
stissimus Virtus," one of the personifications in the "domus Martis," Boccaccio refers to Statius's complex figurative description as "this man of
wars" (homo bellorum),[38] a phrase that recalls the oft-repeated "l'uomo
adirato" of the corresponding gloss in the *Teseida,* and with it provides a
succinct definition of the difference in model and imitation, for Boccaccio's glosses on the "domus Martis" refer the poetic fiction to the subject
of war and of man at war, while the poetic text and its gloss in the
Teseida represent the passion of wrath and its effects. The difference is
one of emphasis rather than kind. Moral personifications such as *furor*
and *ira* have a place in the broader description of the "homo bellorum,"
and when, at *Thebaid* 7.70–74, Statius says that *furor* and *ira* adorn
Mars's helmet as he arrives in Thrace on his chariot, Boccaccio's commentary concludes that "little remains to be said of the arrival of Mars,
whose beginning is in furor and in wrath."[39] His commentary on the
Thebaid includes these moral causes for armed conflict while emphasizing their political manifestations, the spectacle of armed conflict itself;
in contrast, text and gloss in the *Teseida* focus on wrath and its moral
effects, with the political effects mentioned only in summary fashion.

At the beginning of his exposition in the *Teseida,* Boccaccio notes the
four divisions in his poetic description of the "casa di Marte," its location, construction, inhabitants, and ornaments, all of which he says represent the "irascibile appetite" ("il tempio di Marte, cioè questo appetito
irascibile"). This figurative description of man overcome by wrath differs
from the "homo bellorum" that Boccaccio finds in the corresponding
passage in the *Thebaid* largely in its emphasis on cause rather than effect.
For example, in the text of both *Thebaid* and *Teseida,* the house of Mars
is in the north, blasted by storms, under a cloudy sky, surrounded by ice
and snow and a barren forest. Both commentaries take the references to
the north to mean that the appetite for battle is greatest in those men who
have an "excess of blood, as is often the case in cold climates." Boccaccio's comic exuberance in describing this warlike nature is more evident
in the Latin commentary on the *Thebaid* than in the vernacular glosses of
the *Teseida,* but it may be noted in both: constitutions up north, he says,
tend to be excessively sanguine and therefore rambunctious. "Sunt hi
sanguine abundantes, obtruncatores ciborum, vini ingurgitatores immo-
derati, consilio segnes" (these men of abundant blood, gobblers of food,

immoderate guzzlers of wine, refractory to counsel).[40] Such natures are quick to anger and to take up arms; hence the association of the "domus Martis" and the "homo bellorum" with the north. In the *Teseida*, a distinctly moral allegory now comes to the fore, as several details in the location and description of the "casa di Marte" are said to represent the operation and effects of the "irascible appetite" in man. The cloudy sky is a figure for the way wrath obstructs the counsel of reason ("nebuloso dice che è a dimostrare che l'ira offuschi il consiglio della ragione"); and the barren wood around the house indicates the general effects of this appetite, for wrath destroys the fruits of man's labors. In like manner, the iron roof of the house, which reflects the rays of the sun, figures the obduracy of the wrathful man, whose governing passion keeps away the light of reason. In his commentary on the corresponding passage in the *Thebaid*, Boccaccio describes not wrath but war. The raging storms and the clouds represent the rage and fury of combatants and the roar of battle; the shiny iron of the house of Mars represents the weapons of the armed men in battle, weapons that shine with a livid gleam that appears to darken and cloud the rays of sunlight. These two contrasting passages may be translated as follows:

> Appropriately the region is described as enclosed by storms and a mass of clouds and of howling north winds and hail, so that we might recognize the violence, the fury, the anger, and the noise and confusion of those rushing around in wars. Thereafter, the house is described as being of iron, so that we might recognize the fortifications of the places around which war is fought, for these are of iron; that is, they are full of armed men, of spears and shields. These indeed darken the sun when, as is usually the case, they are used for the bad, because light was created for the good. Moreover, the gleam of the sun's rays reflected from the weapons turns color a little, and for this coloring the golden light of the sun seems to darken and cloud over. (*Genealogie* 9.3; commentary on *Thebaid* 7.36–46)

> [The poet] says that it is cloudy, to show that wrath obscures the counsel of reason, which he will refer to further down as the rays of the sun, which he says the house of Mars throws off from itself. By the ice, he means the coldness of the soul of the wrathful man, who, conquered by this fit of wrath, becomes cruel and stiff and pitiless. By the rains he means the tears that the wrathful often shed out of disdain. . . . And he says that [the house] is all of shining steel, and has doors of adamant and columns of

iron: by the steel he means the hardness of the obstinacy of a
wrathful person, and shows that it is the covering of the house,
because he says that the columns are of iron; and this steel, he
says, throws off the light of the sun by reflecting it—justly, for if
this steel should soften so that it let the light of the sun pass
through, that is the sound counsel of reason in the mind of the
wrathful man, it would no longer be the house of Mars, that
is of war and tribulation, but of peace. (*Teseida,* from the gloss
on 7.30)[41]

Boccaccio adopts the series of personified inhabitants of the "domus
Martis" more or less directly from *Thebaid* 7, and his glosses on the
Teseida are similar to his exposition of the *Thebaid*. With "Discord" he
comes closest to a direct reference to the theme of Statius's epic, and his
remarks at the corresponding point in his gloss on *Teseida* 7.30 are essentially the same:

> Dicit et inter Martis ministros esse Discordiam duplici gladio
> accinctam, ut sentiamus cum in hoc veniunt homines, ut non
> eque sentiant, sed in diversas tendant sententias, ab hac ani-
> morum diversitate unicuique parti arma suaderi et bellum in
> reliquam.[42]
>
> [He says that Discord is among the attendants of Mars, girded
> with a double sword, so that we understand that when men
> come to it, because they do not see matters in the same way, but
> diverge in their views, each side is urged by this divergence of
> opinion to arm and to make war against the other side.]

The shorter gloss on Discord in the "casa di Marte" remarks:

> E èvvi la Discordia co' ferri sanguinosi, la quale similmente è
> degli effetti dell'ira, come che molti dicano l'ira nascere dalla
> discordia.
>
> [And Discord is there, with bloody swords; she is similar to the
> effect of Wrath, for many say that Wrath is born of Discord.]

The allegory is again referred explicitly to wrath and its effects, but, as
in the Latin commentary, discord is identified as a cause rather than
an effect.

The description of another personification, "Armed Death," near the
end of the sequence in the vernacular commentary, also refers to the

nize Boccaccio's imitative strategy in the *Teseida,* where the moral principle represented by the temple is dramatized in the acts of Theseus.

The concluding episode of the *Thebaid* describes the Argive widows going to Athens after the death of Polynices and Eteocles and after the failure of the siege of Thebes. They are in need of a protector who will recover the bodies of their dead husbands, which lie exposed outside the walls of Thebes by order of the tyrant Creon. The women take refuge in Athens at the only temple not consecrated to force but reserved for compassion. Statius's description begins: "In the midst of the city was an Altar, belonging not to Power nor the gods thereof, but to gentle Clemency. There Clemency has fixed her seat, and misery has made it holy" (12.481–483). In the Roman world, the virtue of clemency denoted that variety of mercy which people with great power showed to those without it. It was associated especially with the emperor: the goddess Clementia reminded the emperor of his absolute power and also of his kindness in not using it.[45] Boccaccio probably had some knowledge of this association from Seneca's epistle on Clemency, which is addressed to Emperor Nero and which defines the virtue largely in terms of imperial actions. Such late medieval commentaries on the *Thebaid* as survive from the fourteenth century in Italy, however, tend to gloss *clementia* with the more familiar and somewhat more general term *misericordia,* translating Statius's term into the common vocabulary of the virtues. When Boccaccio mentions the temple of *Teseida* 2.25ff., he calls it the temple of pity, "[i]l pietoso tempio"; and Theseus before the temple is moved by "intima pietà nel cor" (2.25, 43).

Statius's sharp distinction in the opening verses of the ekphrasis between the old gods of power and this Athenian goddess of Clemency may reflect an interest in Stoic doctrine and may even allude to popular religious movements of the first century. It may also reflect his reading of Euripides, who, if he did not invent, at least established the version of the Theban War in which the Athenians intervene on behalf of the Argive dead.[46] But to the late medieval reader of the *Thebaid* this distinction carried somewhat different connotations. The gods of power are the pagan gods, "fictions" who were nevertheless worshiped by the ancient gentiles; the goddess-personification Clementia, by contrast, is an imperfect perception of the true God, and Clementia's temple a dim type of the church. This interpretation of Statius's description of the temple is widely attested in late medieval commentaries and may even have influenced Dante's assertion that Statius had been a "concealed Christian," for which there is little other precedent.[47] The glossators did not identify the temple as a veiled statement of Christian beliefs, but they frequently identified it as a historical building and institution that foreshadowed Christianity, much as certain aspects of Athenian philosophy were taken as imperfect shadowings of a truth soon to be revealed by Christ.

Statius develops the contrast between the goddess Clementia and the gods of power by describing the sanctuary of the temple, the rites held there, and the suppliants who carry them out: "The ritual takes no tax and accepts no burning incense or flow of blood; instead, a dew of tears on its stones, the shorn hair of the mourner as wreath above and for drapery the offcast robe that sorrow has put aside. . . . Image is there none, the divine form is trusted to no mould of metal, for it loves to dwell in minds and hearts" (12.487–494). Statius then sketches the history of the shrine, mentioning but discrediting the legend that the children of Hercules had founded it. He asserts instead that the temple was founded by "visitants from heaven" (*caelicolae*), "whom Athens had ever made welcome."

Medieval glosses on the history of the temple reveal the extent to which it was seen as a type of the church. At least as early as the twelfth century the temple of Clementia was identified with the altar to the unknown god, mentioned by St. Paul in Acts 17:22ff. An especially full version of this gloss, which I find in four manuscripts, the oldest from the twelfth century and northern European, the others from northern Italy and dating to the fourteenth and early fifteenth centuries, says:

> When St. Paul came to Athens to preach, he encountered Dionysius the Areopagite, a very wise man, whom, when he could not convince him, he led round the altars of the various gods, asking about each one. At last he came to this altar and asked whose it was. Dionysius said to Paul: "It is the altar of the unknown god." To whom Paul replied: "The one you call 'unknown' —he alone is known," and Paul began his sermon "In Judaea God is known, his name is great in Israel." [48]

This account of the conversation between St. Paul and Dionysius the Areopagite, which Carlo Landi has suggested was based on a life of St. Denis, [49] appears in the manuscripts of the *Thebaid* as an extension of the older gloss of Lactantius. The Lactantius commentary had provided a summary of the legend, mentioned and then denied by Statius, that the children of Hercules had established the temple of Clementia. [50] The medieval gloss then continues this history into later times, identifying the temple with the famous altar "Ignoto Deo."

This identity of a temple from the age of Theseus with a temple mentioned in Acts appears in at least one commentary on the biblical text as well as in glosses on the *Thebaid*. The *Postils* of Nicholas of Lyra, from the early fourteenth century, include an exposition of the history of the altar "Ignoto Deo" that draws from Statius and Lactantius. Some say, Nicholas reports in his gloss, that the altar was first instituted (and "consecrated") by the children of Hercules, who sought and found refuge in Athens; this report is the origin of the idea that mercy fixed her abode in that city, where an altar was consecrated to her. He uses the term *misericordia* rather than *clementia* when referring to the personified deity, in the manner of the glosses on the *Thebaid,* and he writes "posuisse . . . sedem," echoing Statius's diction: "posuit sedem." He concludes his history by noting that because mercy was not a being known to men, as Jupiter and Mercury were known, this altar was inscribed to the unknown god and it was determined that there should be no sacrifices or oblations except the sighs, tears, and prayers of the wretched who came seeking mercy. He echoes Statius's description in this concluding reference to the rites at the temple, just as he echoes Lactantius's gloss on Statius in his opening references to the children of Hercules.[51]

This tradition of commentary appears in a brief gloss in Boccaccio's *Thebaid* as well. A hand somewhat earlier than Boccaccio's, but later than those of the original scribes for the text and Lactantian commentary, has noted under "Urbe fuit media" (12.481): "quam deus ignotus habebat" (which the unknown god had).[52] Such brief notations seem to have been more common than long glosses such as those in the four manuscripts quoted above, and the shorter gloss appears to have circulated earlier. A notation in a twelfth-century manuscript changes the gender of Clementia to the masculine, presumably with St. Paul's "deus ignotus" in mind, while in the process of explaining at *Thebaid* 12.493 that the Athenians made no image because "deus ille qui illic colebatur ignotus erat" (that god who was worshiped there was unknown).[53] The same phrase appears in a Magdalen College, Oxford manuscript (late twelfth century), and an undated "old gloss" cited by Kaspar von Barth in his edition of 1664 notes that "under the figure [*persona*] of this Clementia, he [Statius] describes wisely and philosophically the nature of the one true god."[54]

The long version of the gloss circulated in a common or set form, ending with mentions of St. Paul's "sermon, 'Notus in Judea Deus.'" This text is from Psalm 75, and it does not appear in Acts 17, where St. Paul is said to have preached on a theme taken from Genesis 1; but it does appear in some of the authoritative commentaries on Acts 17.[55] And finally, we may note that a fourteenth-century *Thebaid* now in Milan draws a further typological association from Statius's temple of Clementia to later figures for the church. Here the glossator says that Statius describes "the altar of Mercy, that is, the first asylum, in whose similitude Romulus made the second. And to this altar came holy Paul with Dionysius the Areopagite, and he began his sermon with reference to it."[56] The asylum of Romulus and Remus figures prominently in St. Augustine's *City of God* as a type for the church (for example, 1.34 and 3.25).

Whether Boccaccio followed Dante in imagining Statius to have been a "concealed Christian" when he wrote of Clementia (in which case the description would appear as a conscious but "closed" or allegorical statement of his faith) or thought of the temple as a feature on the historical landscape of Athens, still standing in the age of the Apostles (in which case it appears to be a historical type of the true church) is not a question that can be determined with certainty. But it is clear that a reader of the *Thebaid* in Boccaccio's time and place would have taken special note of this temple dedicated to a virtue "in hearts and minds" rather than to a god of power. Nicholas of Lyra's remarks in the *Postils* seem especially characteristic of the age, arguing that because this goddess was not known to men as Jupiter and Mercury were, she was called "the unknown god." We have seen that Boccaccio interpreted Statius's "Mars," a "fiction" and a "god of power," as a figurative representation of the forces moving hearts and minds to war. With the temple of Clementia, Statius would seem simply to have abandoned the figurative veil associated with fictional deities to make the moral significance of Clementia explicit. That Clementia's altar is identified with the altar to the unknown god, or that it prefigures the church, vividly reinforces the moral interpretation Statius offers in his formal ekphrasis.

This interpretation of the temple underlies Boccaccio's imitation of the scene, in *Teseida* 2.20ff., that transpires in front of it.[57] When he comes to the scene of Theseus and the Argive widows in the *Teseida*, Boccaccio reduces Statius's description of the temple to a pair of simple references, but he also adds details, such as Theseus's startled and irritated reaction to his first sight of the lamenting women, and the widows' descriptions of themselves, which serve to dramatize the operation of clemency in Theseus. In the *Thebaid*, clemency is described by means of the temple; Theseus himself, after hearing the request of Evadne, is immediately moved by pity for her and her companions. He sets off for the campaign against Creon fired by righteous anger (12.590–592). In the *Teseida*, however, Boccaccio shows him angered at first by the widows themselves, as they interrupt his triumph:

—Chi son costor ch'a' nostri lieti eventi
co' crin sparti, battendosi il petto,
di squalor piene *in atri vestimenti* . . .   (2.26)

[Who are these people at our joyous event with shorn tresses,
beating their breasts, all disheveled in their dark clothing?]

The description of the Argive widows reflects that of the suppliants at the
altar of Clemency, whose tears are offerings on the altar, with "shorn
hair" and "the garments left by a change of fortune":

> *lacrimis* altaria sudant,
> maestarumque super libamina *secta comarum*
> pendent et *vestes mutata sorte relictae.*   (12.488–490)

And the effect on Theseus of Evadne's account is that of Clementia itself.
Their tears have moved their audience to pity ("le qua' con forza avean
messa *pietate* / in ciaschedun di que' baroni attei") and *pietà* enters the
heart of Theseus:

> e greve duol nel cor gli venne quando
> udì de' re la morte   (2.36)

[heavy grief filled his heart when he heard of the death of the
kings]

> . . . tenendo il viso fitto
> nella miseria delle sconsolate,
> da intima *pietà nel cor trafitto,*
> sopra il carro si volse   (2.43)

[fixing his gaze on the misery of the disconsolate women, his
heart pierced by the utmost pity, he turned about in his chariot.]

The diction throughout this passage, and especially the references to
pietà acting in Theseus's heart, recalls Statius's definition of Clementia:
"mentes habitare et pectora gaudet." Boccaccio shows clemency in Theseus as he stands before the temple of Clemency; the principle represented in Statius's description of a building and institution is dramatized
in the *Teseida,* where it acts in the heart and mind of Theseus.

In the conclusion of this scene, another thematic word reappears, carried forward from the earlier representation of Theseus in the garden of
luxury: the struggle with Creon is an example of those praiseworthy

deeds to which Pirithous exhorted his friend. As Theseus calls for his troops to follow him immediately into the field, even though they have yet to return to their homes and enjoy the pleasures of Athens, he appeals to their desire for lasting fame ("per far le vostre memorie famose") and their love of glorious deeds ("ora li cuori all'opre gloriose / vi priego dispognate": 2.45). The "glorious deeds" to which Theseus was called by the dream of Pirithous now have better definition. They are deeds born in a heart disposed to justice and clemency.

Vera: Theban history in the Teseida

Again, the old definition of the *metrum heroicum* distinguishes the "poetic fictions" concerning the pagan gods from the "true" representation of human characters. Further definition of the "true" aspects of epic narrative would specify them to be historical rather than simply credible, but the sense in which epic narration is historical requires some further qualification. Boccaccio himself provides it in his remarks on the *Aeneid* in *Genealogie* 14, when he notes that Vergil describes an encounter between Dido and Aeneas that could not have taken place in history. Both Aeneas and Dido are historical figures, Boccaccio argues, but they did not live at the same time. Vergil brings them together in a fictional encounter because Dido made a "suitable audience" to which Aeneas could recount his escape from captured Troy.[58] The encounter also served to represent Aeneas's moral virtue, for "Vergil's . . . purpose is to extol, through his praise of Aeneas, the *gens* Julia in honor of Octavius; this he does by showing him resolutely and scornfully setting his heel upon the wanton and impure promptings of the flesh and the delights of women." Boccaccio's observation begins with an echo of Servius, who had stated that Vergil's intention is "to imitate Homer and praise Augustus through his ancestors," and like Servius, Boccaccio assumes Aeneas to be a historical figure and the founder of the *gens* Julia; but the "history" of Vergil's narrative is exemplary history with prominent fictional elements employed in it to heighten the exemplary force of historical events.

Medieval prologues to the *Thebaid* reflect the same model of epic narrative, describing the "human characters" in Statius's poem as historical figures embellished somewhat for the purposes of moral and political instruction. Statius's subject is said to be "Theban history," into which he introduces elements of various kinds. For example, the "Scriptum" commentary notes that Statius, "in the manner of a good orator, greatly increases this dissension [between Polynices and Eteocles] so that he might better dissuade the minds of men from fraternal discord."[59] The earlier prologue to the *Thebaid*, "In principio," refers generally to epic poets as "historians": "In the beginning of each historical author, as Servius states . . ." and goes on to define Statius's intention in the *Thebaid* as being "to describe Theban history," so that its memorable example of fraternal strife between princes, with its terrible political consequences, might dissuade the sons of Vespasian from similar evils.[60]

To refine our understanding of the concept of history in the *Thebaid* as it would have appeared in the context of fourteenth-century literary culture, it is useful to note the prominence of the Theban War in medieval chronicles of the ancient world. Boccaccio evidently took a great interest in chronicle literature during the later 1330s and perhaps the early 1340s, that is, while he was composing the *Teseida*. His lively "debate" with Paolino Veneto, a scholar associated with the Neapolitan court during the later 1330s, is preserved in his lustily critical notes on passages from Paolino's universal chronicle.[61] Boccaccio's earlier commonplace books contain long extracts from this and other chronicles and historical writings. The Theban dynasty and the Theban War appear in the authoritative chronicles of Eusebius and Orosius, from which Boccaccio often quotes, while the Theban War is reserved a chapter in Paolino's *Chronologia magna* or *tripartita*.[62]

The place of Thebes in the tradition of universal chronicles may be sketched briefly. Although St. Augustine describes in detail only the histories of Babylon and Rome in *De civitate Dei,* he describes these two empires as examples of a pattern that can be observed in the long succession of other states arising after Babylon and before "Rome, as it were a second Babylon." "All the other kingdoms and kings I should describe as something like appendages of those [two] empires."[63] Writing in the tradition of Augustinian historiography, Orosius added details of those "other kingdoms," including the kingdom of Boeotian Thebes. In his preface to the *Historia contra paganos*, Orosius explains that his work is intended to supplement *De civitate Dei,* by extending its description of the consequences of the Fall into areas and times that St. Augustine himself, for want of leisure, had not discussed. The Thebans appear twice in Orosius's first book, as part of the succession of Babylonian kingdoms. Polynices and Eteocles are mentioned in the second passage: "I omit Oedipus, the slayer of his father, the husband of his mother, the brother of their children, his own stepfather. I prefer to be silent as to how the brothers Eteocles and Polynices attacked one another, each one striving to be the murderer of the other."[64] The authority of Orosius was such that this brief reference assured Eteocles and Polynices a place in medieval universal chronicles. In some of them, their rivalry became especially prominent. The French prose versions of Orosius in the *Histoire ancienne* tradition expanded the brief reference to the sons of Oedipus by interpolating a prose *Roman de Thèbes*. One of the redactions of the *Histoire ancienne* seems to have been made in Naples in the 1320s or 1330s, and copies of the work may be attributed to the scriptoria of that city during the period in which Boccaccio was resident there.[65]

The distinction that medieval commentators on the *Thebaid* would draw between Statius's "historical" human characters and his "fictional" gods reappears in the language of Boccaccio's glosses on the *Teseida*. As has been noted, references to Mars and other pagan gods are often glossed, and the glosses introduced with phrases indicating their special status as "fictions": "Vuole in questa parte l'autore mostrare, poeticamente fingendo" (Here the author wants to show, lying in the manner of the poets: in 1.14); "Scrivono fingendo i poeti che la casa di Marte" (The poets write, lying, that the house of Mars: in 1.15); "Scrivono i poeti che giaccendosi Marte con Venere" (The poets write that, while Mars was in bed with Venus: in 7.25). Such qualifying references to "poets" and to "poetic fictions" are absent from accounts of Theban history in the glosses. In contrast, summaries of "human events" in the *Thebaid* are presented with due attention to their place in a general chronological frame that occasionally includes events outside Greece. Especially revealing is Boccaccio's gloss at 2.10 summarizing the entire *Thebaid*. Boccaccio recounts the events involving the human characters of the poem as if he were quoting from a chronicle, and with no mention of the pagan gods whatsoever. It is a *Thebaid* stripped of its "fictions." Like Guido delle Colonne's history of Troy, Boccaccio's summary separates the "true" human events from the "lies and fictions" of the gods.[66]

Having recovered a definition of epic narrative that was current in Boccaccio's literary culture and that corresponds well with Boccaccio's own references to the principal action of the *Thebaid*, we may turn again to the *Teseida* in hopes of characterizing Boccaccio's imitative design with greater precision than has heretofore been possible. What we see now is a close but not a perfect match between model and imitation. The *Teseida* contains "poetic fictions" just as the *metrum heroicum* does, and Boccaccio's gods correspond closely to those of the *Thebaid*, at least as Boccaccio understood the "poetic fictions" of his source. With his human characters, however, Boccaccio has not reproduced the model of a *metrum heroicum* exactly, instead working an open and evident variation on that model. Unlike Vergil's Aeneas or Statius's Eteocles and Polynices, the principal human characters of the *Teseida* are not "historical"; the main action of the *Teseida*, as it concerns these characters, is not a historical action, in contrast to Aeneas's wanderings or the Theban civil war. It stands clearly apart from Petrarch's *Africa* in the same way. Palamon and Arcite, their rivalry and their tournament, do not appear in any history, ancient or modern; they are entirely fictional, while Aeneas's encounter with Dido or the violent extremes of rivalry between Eteocles and Polynices are fictional embellishments of a broadly historical subject. The invented, verisimilar action of the *Teseida* does, however, represent a variation on the traditional model of epic narrative. Boccaccio does not abandon that model entirely. The rivalry of Palamon and Arcite at once repeats a specific chapter in history, the conflict between Eteocles and Polynices as recounted by Statius; draws explicit parallels between this rivalry and the long series of such disputes in Theban history; and concludes in the apotheosis of Arcite with an equally explicit reversal of that oft-repeated pattern. In sum, "history" is the subject of the *Teseida* in its invented main action by virtue of Boccaccio's open imitation of the *Thebaid*.

Statius in the proemium to the *Thebaid* remarks that the long series of violent deeds against kin goes far back in Theban history, and he also alludes to the repetition of a historical pattern in the course of his narrative, notably in the scene of Manto's rites in *Thebaid* 4, where the prophecies of war on the "fields of Mars" are introduced by references to Cadmus and the *terrigenae,* who were born from the teeth of a serpent sown on that field and who sprang up armed and fighting with one another. The "long series" itself appears in the course of Manto's rites, as the shades of the Theban ancestors appear in Avernus, standing in a lake of blood.[67] In the *Teseida*, Palamon and Arcite themselves recall the "long series" of violent deeds against kin that characterizes the history of their royal family, remarking as well the similarity of their own armed conflict with this historical pattern. Arcite does so in a speech to Palamon in *Teseida* 5 as the venom of Tisiphone is having its first effects, and both refer their own deeds to the historical pattern once again after they have repented of their strife and reestablished the bonds of fraternal affection (*Teseida* 10.36ff.).

The precise position of these fictional Theban cousins in the sequence of Theban rulers is established by Boccaccio in the long gloss at 2.10, which summarizes the "history" in the *Thebaid,* adding a sentence that introduces a new generation:

> e quinci [Teseo] combatté contra Creon e ebbe vittoria e l'uccise. E in questa battaglia furono presi Arcita e Palemone, li quali erano Tebani, e menati ad Attene e messi in prigione da Teseo. (in 2.10)

[and there Theseus warred against Creon and achieved victory
and killed him. And in this battle Palamon and Arcite, who were
Thebans, were taken captive and carried to Athens and put in
prison by Theseus.]

This addition to the Theban royal family and to the "long series" of episodes in their history comes at the end of the episode concerning Eteocles
and Polynices and the Theban civil war as recounted by Statius in the
Thebaid. The narrative of the *Teseida* presents that history in books 1
and 2 much as Statius presents it in the last book of the *Thebaid,* from his
allusion to Theseus's expedition against the Amazons (*Thebaid* 12.519)
to the encounter with the Argive widows at the temple of Clemency, the
expedition against Creon, and the burial of the Argive dead. The references back to that history begin as soon as Boccaccio enters upon his fictional extension of Statius's narrative, in *Teseida* 2.85. Palamon and
Arcite identify themselves as members of the royal house and "descendants of Cadmus" (2.88); the next book opens with a reference to the
destruction of Thebes a year before (3.1) and with an allusion to the early
history of Cadmus and Europa (3.5). Palamon and Arcite define their
own misfortunes as another example of the misfortunes that have long
befallen their royal house (3.36); and Arcite, as he is freed by Theseus,
worries that the terrible consequences of the Theban War will make him
no welcome guest in Greek cities: "two years have not yet gone by since
six great kings were killed at Thebes, because of our deeds" (3.65).

Arcite recalls the series of his Theban ancestors again when he visits
the destroyed city of Thebes (4.12–17), and he is still thinking about the
sins of his city and their consequences for his personal fortunes as Panfilus discovers him in a grove (4.79). And then when Palamon finds him in
the same grove the next morning, Arcite recalls the misfortunes of their
ancestors in even greater detail and explicitly matches the mad violence
between himself and his cousin to the old pattern of Theban internecine
strife. The series of historical episodes in this speech reappears in his
prayer to Mercury in *Teseida* 10, and together these two speeches, with
their catalogs of misfortunes in Theban history, effectively frame the new
episode of fraternal strife in Boccaccio's main action. In the first, Arcite
remarks that when he and Palamon take up arms against each other over
"possession" of Emilia, they will repeat the folly of their ancestors, who
committed acts of violence against their closest kin. Then in the second,
Arcite hopes for mercy on the grounds that his acts have not led to the
terrible consequences of those of his ancestors; moreover that he, unlike

those ancestors, has repented of his strife with Palamon, with whom he has restored their original bond of trust and affection.

Arcite's "long series" of episodes from Theban history begins, in the speech to Palamon as well as the prayer to Mercury, with Cadmus and the *terrigenae* and ends with Eteocles and Polynices. The theme of strife between brothers is noted explicitly by Arcite before the little catalog begins:

> e la fortuna ci ha qui lusingando
> menati con effetti lieti e pii,
> e non Amore, a voler che moiamo
> per le man nostre, come noi sogliamo.   (5.55)

> [And fortune rather than love has led us here, deceiving us with
> gifts of happiness and mercy, so that we will die by our own
> hands, as we are wont to do.]

They seem to be approaching the same dishonorable end of all of their ancestors, from the *terrigenae* to Eteocles and Polynices:

> I primi nostri, che nacquer de' denti
> seminati da Cadmo, d'Agenore
> figlio, ver lor furon tanto nocenti
> che sanza riguardar fraterno amore
> fra loro s'uccisero;
> . . .
> Quai fosser poi fra loro i due fratelli
> d'Edippo nati, non cal raccontare:
> il fuoco fé testimonianza d'elli   (5.57, 59)

> [The founders of our line, who were born from the teeth sown
> by Cadmus, the son of Agenor, harbored such mutual hatred
> that they killed each other, without regard for brotherly love. . . .
> There is no need to recount all that happened later between the
> two brothers fathered by Oedipus: the fire bears witness to them.]

The episodes between these two *exempla* of fraternal strife elaborate the theme of madness leading to violence against the closest kin (Athamas, infested by the rage of Tisiphone so that he killed his own children; Agave, driven mad by Bacchus and the killer of her husband; Oedipus, a patricide), as well as examples of pride (Niobe) and jealousy between rival lovers (Semele).

Boccaccio borrowed this series of episodes from a similar speech in

Thebaid 3, pronounced by "aged Aletes" to the citizens of Thebes after Tydeus has slaughtered the soldiers sent to ambush him in the wood. Aletes consoles the grieving by recalling that "our race has often known sorrow," as the histories of Cadmus and the *terrigenae*, Semele, Athamas, Agave, Niobe, Actaeon, and Dirce bear witness. His tone then turns vituperative as he concludes:

> . . . sic dura sororum
> pensa dabant visumque Iovi. nunc regis iniqui
> ob noxam immeritos patriae tot culmina cives
> exuimus.   (3.205–208)

[such was the sad task of the sisters, so had Jove willed it; but now we strip our country of guiltless citizens, so many eminent ones, for the misdeeds of a cruel king.]

Boccaccio substitutes Eteocles and Polynices for Dirce at the end of the sequence, and he uses the resulting summary of Theban history up to and including the events of the *Thebaid* to suggest that the old patterns are evident in the strife of Palamon and Arcite. He also borrows the concluding sentiment of human responsibility and guilt, but significantly he attributes it to the Theban protagonists themselves, rather than to a courageous old man daring to speak against a tyrant because his life is already near its end.

When Arcite repeats the Theban sequence in his prayer to Mercury, he argues that he has broken the pattern set by his ancestors and accordingly deserves more clement judgment in the afterlife. And because Theseus's intercession in the grove and his strict governance of the "giuoco a Marte" kept Palamon and Arcite from fighting to the death, Arcite can claim in truth that, unlike Eteocles and Polynices, "I did not kill my brother." Although there is a measure of irony to his claims because of the resemblance between his violent rivalry and that which animates the history he is recalling, there is also a most striking difference between Arcite and the pattern of Theban history in his self-knowledge and repentance, which on balance justifies his claims and is, in the poetic fiction of the *Teseida*, rewarded by Mercury.⁶⁸ Eteocles and Polynices had carried their hate for one another to their deaths, and as Arcite remarks it, "the fire bears witness" to such obduracy of heart. Arcite and his cousin, by contrast, in the course of time and in response to Arcite's fatal injury, have come to regret their mutual hatred and to reestablish their original bonds of fraternal affection. As in Aletes' speech, Arcite's prayer to Mercury recognizes the human source of his misdeed:

Se arme furon già per me pigliate
incontro a Palemon, male operai,
e io ben n'ho le pene meritate;
e certo i' non l'avrei prese giammai,
se esso non m'avesse a ciò recato
perch'era, sì com'io, innamorato.   (10.98)

[Whenever I took up arms against Palamon, it was wrong, and
I have justly suffered the consequences; and to be sure, I would
never have taken them up if he had not led me to it, because
he was in love as I was.]

Arcite's courteous excusing of his cousin along with himself reflects the
spirit of reconciliation that has characterized their conversation throughout book 10, conversation that (as Giuseppe Velli has pointed out) Boccaccio casts as a rivalry of "altruistic denunciations and abnegations," a
kind of happy analogue to the other rivalry, which is now at an end.[69]

The "human events" of Boccaccio's narrative of Theban strife conclude
with a reversal in the established historical pattern. His careful matching
of earlier examples of strife in the Theban kingdom with that of Palamon
and Arcite resembles the typological analysis of history in biblical exege-
sis and medieval universal chronicles, in which similarities in historical
action often serve to underscore a final change or contrast. The persistent
identification of Statius's main action in the *Thebaid* with real historical
events in the context of universal history strongly suggests that typology
played a role in Boccaccio's "reading" of his classical source and his composition of a new narrative that mirrors the human events of the *Thebaid*
in a systematic fashion. In his great study of Vergilian imitation of the
Homeric poems, G. N. Knauer has argued that typological understanding
of history is actually present in epic tradition right from the time of the
Aeneid,[70] and there can be no doubt that Boccaccio and his contemporaries read their Vergil and their Statius with an eye for typological correspondences.[71] Boccaccio's master analogy between the course of *historia*
in the *Teseida* and that in its epic source develops like a historical narrative that conforms to a historical archetype, with the meaning of the
foreground action becoming apparent as it is seen against that background. In the conclusion of their fraternal strife, Palamon and Arcite
align themselves with Eteocles and Polynices and a longer history of
Theban *discordia* as in a typological reversal, the contrast underscored
by the fierce funeral flames of Polynices and Eteocles burning in the concluding book of the *Thebaid* while Palamon weeps at his cousin's funeral in *Teseida* 11. In the conclusion of his invented *historia* Boccaccio

gives us two humble Marys reversing the errors of Statius's proud Eves, or more to the point, two figures of brotherly love cast against Statius's fratricides. They have fulfilled Statius's prophecy after Polynices' fall.

Epic narrative and the education of princes

A definition of epic narrative in the terms of Boccaccio's literary culture is a necessary complement to any study of his imitative strategy because it reveals where the imitator has sought to reproduce and where he has sought to transform. Boccaccio's use of the gods as figures for wrath and concupiscence is largely attributable to the influence of his model: the model involved figurative "fables" of this sort, and Boccaccio reproduced them in his poem. At the same time, the *Teseida* clearly involves a measure of transformation in the realm of its human characters, which are not historical even by the medieval definition of that critical term. Boccaccio's allusive narrative of the rivalry between Palamon and Arcite is not an epic narrative but an epic narrative revisited, a fictional recreation of a single epic action. This transformation takes the pattern of action in the *Thebaid* from the realm of politics, focusing on its personal or in the Scholastic term, its ethical aspect. The transformation is represented nicely by Boccaccio's use of the figurative Mars, no longer "homo bellorum" but "homo irascibilis." The alternate ending to the *Teseida*, based on an episode and an apostrophe in *Thebaid* 6, is also governed by this general rule of transformation, for it replaces the Theban civil war with a series of scenes about personal reconciliation, the end of the selfish passions animating the little war. Statius dedicates *Thebaid* 7–11 to the war; Boccaccio has his martial games in one book (8), while *Teseida* 9–11 return the focus to the private causes of the conflict.

This transformation may be described more precisely with the help of medieval prologues to the *Thebaid*, where after addressing "style" and the *metrum heroicum,* the commentators pose the question "to what end the author wrote this work." Servius's answer, in his prologue to the *Aeneid,* is lapidary: to imitate Homer and to praise Augustus. The medieval *accessus* to the *Thebaid* generally adopt and expand this formula. Because the main action in classical epic concerns "human characters" belonging to the class of rulers, the exemplary value of epic narrative serves in the first place as a mirror for princes. But "to praise Augustus" means not only to praise the man himself, and the audience is described in the medieval prologues with reference sometimes to "readers" in general. The two are not, of course, exclusive, the narrative providing specific praise or blame to a prince and generalized moral examples for the larger audience. The force of the latter is only increased by the social status of the exemplary figure in question and the political implications arising from the personal choices of such a person. Boccaccio himself remarks in his defense of Vergil's fictional scenes of Dido and Aeneas that Vergil offered a generalized exemplum of a man who overcomes his concupiscence; and it simultaneously "extols, through his praise of Aeneas, the *gens* Julia in honor of Octavius."

The "Scriptum" prologue to the *Thebaid* refers the moral example of Statius's main action to all readers: "The author's intention in this work is to recall to mind Theban history and the fraternal dissensions between Polynices and Eteocles, and with this utility, that it might strenuously dissuade readers from fraternal discord, once they had seen the bad consequences of fraternal dissension."[72] The "In principio" prologue, however, adds to this general audience a more specific, imperial audience, remarking that some persons had argued that "When Vespasian died, his sons Titus and Domitian burned with such desire for power that they risked fraternal war. To exhort them, the author offered Theban history (so that) having seen what happened to those two brothers, who burned with such desire for rule that they killed one another in battle, they would desist from similar misdeeds."[73] Statius's main action does not praise but blame, or rather warn. Its characters are essentially exemplary: they do not represent Titus and Domitian transposed into an ancient setting but offer a historical example, which may be referred to the strife between these contenders for *imperium* or to others.

Because Boccaccio's model for the human characters of epic narrative defines them as mirrors for princes, the distinctive medieval tradition of writings expressly concerned with the education of young princes offers a useful frame of reference in which to place Boccaccio's transformation of that model. The tradition is long and various, but one treatise stands out for its extraordinarily wide dissemination in the later thirteenth and fourteenth centuries and for the close connection of its author to Naples and Boccaccio. Aegidius's *De regimine principum* was composed in Latin in the later 1270s for the heir apparent to the throne of France, later Philip the Fair, but it found a remarkably broad audience and was translated into all of the European vernaculars.[74] There are several early translations into French and Italian. Its success was probably due to its clear organization, which divides the subject into three parts: "ethics" or private moral education, "economics" or the governing of a household, and "politics" or the governing of a body politic. In his later years Aegidius was a beneficiary of King Robert's patronage, and he dedicated his major work, the second book of commentary on the *Sentences,* to the Angevin king.

Moreover, Boccaccio's revered teacher in Naples, Dionigi da Borgo, was an Augustinian monk like Aegidius, a student of Aegidius's Scholastic philosophy and in a sense the heir to Aegidius's role as the leading representative of Augustinian scholarly traditions.[75]

Aegidius organizes *De regimine* around an analogy that recalls the literary analogy of Boccaccio's *Teseida*. He begins with the microcosm of the prince's moral nature, dedicating the first third of his treatise to "governing oneself," or in his Aristotelian terminology, to ethics. Only after learning to govern the microcosm should the prince move on to govern the macrocosms of household (economics) and kingdom (politics). Boccaccio focuses on ethics in the foreground but uses the systematic allusions to Statius's *Thebaid* to underscore their political implications.

In describing the governance of self, Aegidius employs the same terminology that Boccaccio will use in his description of the motivating passions of Palamon and Arcite in the long glosses on the temples of Mars and Venus. First Aegidius on moral education:

> In this first book we intend to instruct man in governing himself, and since he cannot learn to govern himself unless he knows which motions (of the soul) to follow and which to avoid, we will show how the motions of the soul are ordered, and which command the others. This way we may better learn which motions to follow and which to avoid. We must know in the first place that concupiscence and wrath (*amor, ira*) are the first and most important motions of the soul and that all of the others derive from these two, because everyone is moved in his soul by that which he loves . . . Kings and princes must learn the movements of the soul more than other people, because it bodes ill for other people if they are moved by malice or led to act against reason. And just as they are capable of doing great good for their people when they are moved for the sake of good, so too they are capable of great evil.[76]

In his discussion of the figurative Mars and Venus, Boccaccio draws on a common vocabulary to define the two principal appetites moving Palamon and Arcite:

> To understand (the temples) you must know that there are two principal appetites in every person, called the concupiscible appetite and the irascible appetite. By the first, one desires and takes pleasure in having things which are enjoyable and pleasant

according to one's judgment (which may be reasonable or may be corrupt). By the second, one is troubled: either because one is frustrated in obtaining the pleasant things or they are taken away, or they cannot be obtained.[77]

The moral philosophy represented in Boccaccio's "poetic fiction" has this premise in common with Aegidius. Perhaps not coincidentally, the two works also show a common concern with the primacy of the ethical in descriptions of princely behavior. Boccaccio's translation of the exemplary princes of the *Thebaid* into the smaller scale of the *Teseida* may be defined in these terms. His imitative strategy transforms the *Thebaid*, so as to emphasize its ethical dimension, and uses the *Thebaid* metaphorically to suggest the political consequences of the ethical themes.

Notes to Chapter 3

1. The metrical arguments for the *Thebaid* may be as old as the sixth century; they are printed in the edition of Statius's works by J. A. Amar and N. E. Lemaire (Paris, 1825–1830), vols. 2 and 3; and in Francis J. Magoun, "Chaucer's Summary of Statius' *Thebaid*, II–XII," *Traditio* 11 (1955): 409–420. There were several versions of these verse arguments, and there were also prose arguments for the books of the *Thebaid*, associated with the "Lactantius" commentary. See Robert D. Sweeney, *Prolegomena to an Edition of the Scholia to Statius* (Leiden: Brill, 1969), *Mnemosyne* suppl. octavum, p. 24 and passim. For his verse arguments in the *Teseida*, Boccaccio employs the fourteen-line sonnet in place of the twelve-line hexameters of the Latin verse arguments.

2. On the term *forma tractatus* and its variants in medieval *accessus*, see Richard W. Hunt, "The Introductions to the *Artes* in the Twelfth Century," *Studia mediaevalia in honorem . . . Raymundi Josephi Martin* (Bruges: DeTempel, 1948), pp. 85–112; A. J. Minnis, *Medieval Theory of Authorship* (London: Scolar, 1984), chap. 1 and passim; and for a more discursive view of the term and the habits of thought it may imply, Judson B. Allen, *The Ethical Poetic of the Later Middle Ages: A Decorum of Convenient Distinction* (Toronto: University of Toronto Press, 1982). Also E. A. Quain, "The Medieval *accessus ad auctores*," *Traditio* 3 (1945): 215–264; H. Silvestre, "Le schéma 'moderne' des *accessus*," *Latomus* 16 (1957): 684–689; Bruno Nardi, "Osservazioni sul medievale *accessus ad auctores* in rapporto all'Epistola a Cangrande," in *Saggi e note di critica dantesca* (Milan: Ricciardi, 1966), pp. 268–305; Günther Glauche, *Schullektüre im Mittelalter*, Münchener Beiträge zur Mediävistik und Renaissance-Forschung 5 (Munich: Arbeo-Ges., 1970).

3. Violetta de Angelis, "Magna Questio proposita coram Dante et Domino Francisco Petrarca et Virgiliano," *Studi petrarcheschi* n.s. 1 (1984): 103–209. This magisterial study of the late medieval commentaries on Statius's *Achilleid* examines the texts reflecting this debate on pp. 169–178. So

thorough is the documentation that de Angelis's study casts light on the late medieval glosses to the *Thebaid* as well.

4. *Servii Grammatici qui feruntur in Vergilii carmina commentarii,* ed. Georg Christian Thilo and Hermann Hagen, vol. 1 (Leipzig: Teubner, 1881; repr. 1923), p. 4: "de numero librorum nulla hic quaestio est, licet in aliis inveniatur auctoribus."

5. The illustration is from manuscript Chigi. H.VI.210 of the Vatican Library, a parchment codex (25.2 × 19 cm.) containing the text of the *Thebaid* with marginal and interlinear glosses. It dates to the second half of the fourteenth century and probably comes from northern central Italy. For a description, see Elisabeth Pellegrin et al., *Les Manuscrits Classiques Latins de la Bibliothèque Vaticane,* tome 1 (Paris: Centre National de la Recherche Scientifique, 1975), pp. 355–356. The chapter titles are in red and placed in the text of the *Thebaid,* with a large decorated capital marking the first verse of the chapter, the same scheme followed in Boccaccio's autograph of the *Teseida.* See also here below, note 8.

6. A history of the medieval chaptering of the *Aeneid* and the *Thebaid* has yet to be published, though a set of rubrics for the *Thebaid* may be found in Colette Jeudy, "L'Abrégé de la *Thébaïde* de Laurent de Premierfait," *Italia medioevale e umanistica* 22 (1979): 422–438. The points of division marked by Laurent's rubrics generally correspond to those in earlier rubricated copies of the *Thebaid.* In my experience with *Thebaid* copies of Italian origin, the chapter divisions appear as early as the twelfth century, but are especially common in copies made during the fourteenth. The one copy of the epic to survive from Boccaccio's own library, now Florence, Biblioteca Medicea-Laurenziana, MS Plut. 38.6, is an early twelfth-century manuscript, probably not of Italian origin, with no chapter rubrics or chapter divisions in the text. Later hands, however, have divided the text with large and small paragraph marks. On a fourteenth-century commentator who subdivided the books of the *Aeneid:* Mary Louise Lord, "A Commentary on *Aeneid* 6," *Medievalia et Humanistica* n.s. 15 (1987): 150. Chaptering, the use of graded sizes of capital letters to mark divisions and subdivisions in a text, and the disposition of glosses in manuscript copies of the classical epics were all influenced by the scholastic concept of *ordinatio* and the interest, which increased with the rise of universities in the twelfth century, in using books as reference tools, where something might be looked up. See Malcolm B. Parkes, "The Influence of the Concepts of *ordinatio* and *compilatio* on the Development of the Book," in *Medieval Scribes, Manuscripts and Libraries: Essays Presented to N. R. Ker,* ed. M. B. Parkes and A. G. Watson (London: Scolar, 1978), pp. 115–144.

7. Edvige Agostinelli, "A Catalogue of the Manuscripts of *Il Teseida,*" *Studi sul Boccaccio* 15 (1985–86), pp. 51–52. As far as I know, the only discussion of the *Teseida*'s form that has taken account of the appearance of his classical models is E. H. Wilkins, *A History of Italian Literature,* revised by Thomas G. Bergin (Cambridge, Mass.: Harvard University Press, 1974), p. 104, which mentions the summary verse argument at the beginning of the poem and the marginal glosses, but not the verse arguments of the single books and the chapter divisions. Some manuscripts of the *Teseida*

and the editio princeps (Ferrara, 1475) mark formal similes with the marginal notation *comparatione,* a practice that may also be seen in some late medieval manuscripts of the *Thebaid.*

8. Consider, for example, the following rubrics for the procession of heroes in *Thebaid* 4 and the similar diction in Boccaccio's rubrics for the procession of heroes in *Teseida* 6. I quote from Vatican City, Biblioteca Apostolica Vaticana, MS Chigi. H.VI.210, a parchment manuscript, Italian, fourteenth-century, with verse arguments as well as chapter rubrics:

> 31r: Capitulum 2^m de processu Polinicis.
> 31v: Capitulum 3^m de processu Thidei.
> 32r: Capitulum 4^m de transitu Ypomedontis.
> 32v: Capitulum 5^m de Capanei processu.
> 33r: Capitulum vi^m de Amphiarai processu.
> 33v: Capitulum septimum de processu Parthonopei.

9. "Do genres remain fixed? Presumably not. With the addition of new works, our categories shift." So René Wellek and Austin Warren, *Theory of Literature,* 3d ed. (New York: Harcourt, Brace and World, 1956), p. 227, who are echoing T. S. Eliot's "Tradition and the Individual Talent." Compare Alstair Fowler, "The Formation of Genres" in his *Kinds of Literature* (Cambridge, Mass.: Harvard University Press, 1982), pp. 149–169.

10. Recently repeated by Derek Pearsall, *The Canterbury Tales* (London: George Allen and Unwin, 1985): "It is an epic poem in twelve books, with exactly the same number of lines (9896) as the *Aeneid*" (p. 118). Pearsall may be drawing on Piero Boitani, *Chaucer and Boccaccio,* Medium Aevum Monographs, new series 8 (Oxford: Society for the Study of Medieval Languages and Literature, 1977), p. 10. I cannot determine where the commonplace first took form.

11. I quote from the prologue "In principio uniuscuiusque auctoris," one of the oldest of the medieval *accessus* to the *Thebaid,* which survives in at least four manuscripts. See Appendix 1, below, for the text. Compare also the late fourteenth- or early fifteenth-century *accessus* from Padua, "Scriptum Super Statio Thebaydos," in Appendix 2: "Et est sciendum quod hystoriarum quedam sunt nomina a loco, ut Ylias ab Ylio et Thebais a Thebis; quedam a persona, ut Eneys ab Enea, Odyssea ab Odysseo."

12. *Servii Grammatici,* ed. Thilo and Hagen, p. 4. In the autograph, Boccaccio uses the masculine article with "*Teseida,*" following a medieval custom that understood *poema* to be implicit in the title. See Salvatore Battaglia, *Le Epoche della letteratura italiana* (Naples: Liguori, 1965), p. 342, and the essay by Paul Lehmann cited in the next note.

13. Paul Lehmann, "Mittelalterliche Büchertitel," *Sitzungsberichte der bayerischen Akademie* (1948, heft 4), vol. 1, pp. 54–55; also printed in his collected papers, vol. 5. The *titulus* in Boccaccio's copy of the *Thebaid* appears above the text on the first page (Laurenziana, Plut. 38.6, fol. 1r); it does not seem to be in the hand of the scribe who copied the text on this folio, and it is not in Boccaccio's hand.

14. The argument, developed in several authoritative studies, that Boccaccio

composed the glosses sometime after the poetic text of the *Teseida* (e.g., Giuseppe Billanovich, *Restauri boccacceschi*, 2d printing [Rome: Edizioni di Storia e Letteratura, 1947], pp. 126–127; Alberto Limentani, "Tendenze della prosa del Boccaccio ai margini del *Teseida*," *Giornale storico della letteratura italiana* 135 [1958]: 529; E. A. Quaglio, "Prima Fortuna della glossa garbiana a *Donna me prega*," *Giornale storico della letteratura italiana* 141 [1964]: 347; and recently Bruno Porcelli, "Il *Teseida* del Boccaccio fra la *Tebaide* e *The Knight's Tale*," *Studi e problemi di critica testuale* 32–33 [1986]: 67–68) must apparently be qualified in light of William Coleman and Edvige Agostinelli's thorough reexamination of the manuscript tradition. Boccaccio apparently revised his glosses at least twice, so that the glosses of the autograph represent a final and much longer version than the first two. See above, Introduction, notes 10 and 11.

15. On the style of Boccaccio's prose in the glosses see Limentani, "Tendenze," pp. 524–551; and also the remarks of Piero Boitani, *Chaucer and Boccaccio*, Medium Aevum Monographs (Oxford: Blackwell, 1977), pp. 45ff. and Robert Hollander, "The Validity of Boccaccio's Self-Exegesis in His *Teseida*," *Medievalia et humanistica* n.s. 8 (1977): 163–183. On differences from his models see above, Chapter 1, p. 44 and note 15. Hollander's suggestion that the glosses were added partly to give the poem the status of "instant classic" does not take into account Boccaccio's thoroughgoing imitation of other medieval additions to epic form, such as verse arguments and chapter rubrics, nor the extent to which fifteenth-century commentators such as de' Bassi and the Anonymous follow Boccaccio's lead in adding glosses. But I believe that Hollander's main point is the potential for humor in parody of epic *gravitas*.

16. In the edition of Giorgio Petrocchi, which I quote from the printing of 1975 (Turin: Einaudi, 1975), the stanza reads:

> Questi che guida in alto li occhi miei,
> è quel Virgilio dal qual tu togliesti
> forte a cantar de li uomini e d'i dèi.

Forte is a crux, appearing as *forza* or *forze* in some manuscripts and most modern editions. Authoritative manuscripts read *forte*, however, which may be taken as an adjective used as a noun and meaning "capacity, ability," or as a pure synonym for *forza*, "power." The translation is that of Allen Mandelbaum, *Purgatorio* (Berkeley: University of California Press, 1982).

17. On the adoption of the Servian topics in medieval *accessus*, see Hunt, "Introductions to the *Artes*," p. 94 (Hunt's "type B"), and Minnis, *Medieval Theory of Authorship*, chap. 1.

18. The Servian topics returned to favor in the fifteenth century, especially in Italy (Minnis, *Medieval Theory of Authorship*, p. 230 n.); this tendency is apparent in the *accessus* "Scriptum super Statio Thebaydos" (see Appendix 2, below) and in the topics adopted by de' Bassi for his commentary on the *Teseida* (quoted above, Introduction). The persistence of the Servian model in the special case of *accessus* to the classical epics may be noted in

the commentary on the *Aeneid* commonly attributed to Anselm of Laon (unpublished); for a preliminary list of manuscripts see Christopher Baswell, "'Figures of Olde Werk': Visions of Virgil in Later Medieval England" (Ph.D. diss., Yale University, 1983), p. 362, and the same author's essay on Princeton MS 43 in *Catalogue of the Exhibition: Sixty Bokes Olde and Newe,* ed. David Anderson (Knoxville, Tenn.: New Chaucer Society, 1986), pp. 62–63; as well as in the twelfth-century commentary on the *Thebaid,* "In principio" (below, Appendix 1).

19. *Servii Grammatici,* ed. Thilo and Hagen, vol. 1, p. 4: "qualitas carminis patet; nam est metrum heroicum et actus mixtus, quod constat ex divinis humanisque personis, continens vera cum fictis; nam Aeneam ad Italiam venisse manifestum est, Venerem vero locutam cum Iove missumve Mercurium constat esse conpositum." The phrase "vera cum fictis" is conventional, but Servius's phrase may well echo Horace, *Ars poetica,* 151: "sic veris falsa remiscet" (and so mixes the false with the true), where the reference is also to epic poetry.

20. For the term *ordo artificialis* see, for example, the two prologues to the *Thebaid* in Appendixes 1 and 2, below; and Boccaccio's remarks on the *Aeneid* in his *Genealogie* 14.13: "For poets are not like historians, who begin their account at some convenient beginning and describe events in the unbroken order of their occurrence to the end. Such, we observe, was Lucan's method, wherefore many think of him rather as a metrical historian than a poet. But poets, by a far nobler device, begin their proposed narrative in the midst of the events or sometimes even near the end" (trans. by Charles G. Osgood in *Boccaccio on Poetry,* 2d ed. [New York: Liberal Arts Press, 1956], p. 68). The term appears in Geoffrey of Vinsauf's *Poetria nova,* where, however, it is not applied specifically to epic. See James J. Murphy, *Rhetoric in the Middle Ages* (Berkeley: University of California Press, 1974), pp. 170–171. The *Teseida* does not employ this "noble device."

21. For Thebes in the medieval vision of ancient history, see Robert W. Ayers, "Medieval History, Moral Purpose, and the Structure of Lydgate's *Siege of Thebes,*" *PMLA* 73 (1958): 463–474; and David Anderson, "Theban History in Chaucer's *Troilus,*" *Studies in the Age of Chaucer* 4 (1982): esp. 109–119. On Thebes in chronicles known to Boccaccio, see above, Chapter 1, note 49.

22. Conrad of Hirsau, *Dialogus super auctores,* ed. R. B. C. Huygens (Brussels: Latomus, 1955), p. 17 (*historiographus* and *poeta*); pp. 55–68 (Statius and Vergil).

23. Charles Homer Haskins, *Studies in the History of Medieval Science* (Cambridge, Mass.: Harvard University Press, 1924), contains an edition of Neckham's *Sacerdos ad altare.* Compare the reference to Statius as one of the "historiographical authors" in the beginning of the "In principio" prologue, in Appendix 1, below.

24. I have used the translation of Mary E. Meek, *Historia destructionis Troiae* (Bloomington: Indiana University Press, 1974), pp. 1–3 for Guido's prologue, p. xvii for the translator's comment. Seymour M. Pitcher notes the tendency of medieval sources to describe epic as a variety of historical writ-

ing (*Encyclopedia of Poetry and Poetics,* ed. Alex Preminger et al. [Princeton: Princeton University Press, 1965], p. 243), but his brief summary of medieval views of epic is vitiated by its failure to recognize the influence of Servius. On this influence, see also Allen, *Ethical Poetic,* p. 110, n. 22.

25. That Lucan modified epic conventions in *De bello civili* caused some controversy in Lucan's own day and was noted by Quintilian and Petronius, among others. The important twelfth-century commentary on *De bello civili* by Arnulf of Orléans describes Lucan as a "poet and historian": "Sicut Iuvenalis purus est satiricus, Terencius purus comedus, Horacius in odis purus liricus, non est iste poeta purus, sed poeta et historiographus. Nam historiam suam prosequitur et nichil fingit, unde poeta non simpliciter dicitur, sed poeta et historiographicus" (ed. B. M. Marti, *Arnulfi Aurelianensis glosule super Lucanum* [Rome: American Academy, 1958], p. 4). It is noteworthy that Arnulf says Lucan "did not lie" (nichil fingit) but "followed his history" (historiam suam prosequitur), which recalls the Servian definition "vera cum fictis" while distinguishing Lucan's performance from the standard model. Medieval writers usually include Lucan in the company of Vergil and Statius (e.g., Dante, *Inferno* 4; Chaucer, *Troilus* 5.1792), but a distinction like Arnulf's is common in more detailed commentary. Alexander Neckham includes Lucan with the *ystoriographi* Statius and Vergil, but an anonymous gloss on his treatise comments that Lucan "wrote history, not a poem": "Et nota quod Lucanus non ponitur in numero poetarum quia historiam composuit et non poema" (*Sacerdos ad altare,* ed. Haskins, *Studies,* p. 372 and n.). Cf. Conrad of Hirsau, *Dialogus,* p. 47. Boccaccio follows this tradition in his commentary on *Inferno* 4, noting that many believe him "not to be counted among the poets" because he did not employ a "poetic style" but that of versified history:

> Sono, oltre a ciò, e furono assai, li quali estimarono e stimano costui non essere da mettere nel numero de'poeti, affermando essergli stata negata la laurea dal senato, la quale come poeta addomandava: e la cagione dicono essere stata, percioché nel collegio dei poeti fu determinato costui non avere nella sua opera tenuto stilo poetico, ma più tosto di storiografo metrico.

(Giovanni Boccaccio, *Il Comento alla Divina Commedia,* ed. Domenico Guerri, 3 vols. [Bari: Laterza, 1918], vol. 2, p. 33). The point is that Lucan did not include the "fictions" of the pagan gods along with his "history" of Caesar and Pompey and that he did not employ an "artificial order" (cf. Boccaccio's similar remarks in *Genealogie* 14, quoted above, note 20).

26. The rubrics appear in two fourteenth-century manuscripts, both of Italian provenance: Florence, Biblioteca Medicea-Laurenziana, MS Ashburnham 1032, once in the library of the monastery of Monteoliveto Maggiore (Siena); Wolfenbüttel, Herzog-August Bibliothek, MS 52 Gud. lat. Two rubrics are quoted in Anderson, "Theban History," p. 115.

27. For the Latin texts, see below, Appendixes 1 and 2. In the twelfth-century commentary on the *Aeneid* attributed to Anselm of Laon, the passage from Servius's prologue is restated as follows (I quote from London, British Li-

brary, MS Add. 16380, fol. 2r): "Est autem carmen hoc heroicum constans ex divinis humanisque personis continens vera cum fictis. Nam eneam ad italiam venisse manifestum est. Venerem vero cum iove loquutam. missumve ad didonem mercurium. hoc totum constat esse compositum et ficticium."

28. *Servii Grammatici,* ed. Thilo and Hagen, vol. 1, p. 89: "et sciendum est, inter fabulam et argumentum, hoc est historiam, hoc interesse, quod fabula est dicta res contra naturam, sive facta sive non facta, ut de Pasiphae, historia est quicquid secundum naturam dicitur, sive factum sive non factum, ut de Phaedra."

29. Isidore distinguishes between *historia* or things that actually occurred ("res verae quae factae sunt") and *argumentum,* or verisimilar literary invention ("quae etsi facta non sunt, fieri tamen possunt"), both of which are distinct from *fabula* or literary inventions that could not be true ("quae non factae sunt nec fieri possunt"): *Etymologiarum libri,* ed. W. M. Lindsay (Oxford: Clarendon, 1911), I.xliv.5. Isidore's three definitions are discussed with reference to Dante's historiography in Giuseppe Mazzotta, *Dante, Poet of the Desert: History and Allegory in the "Divine Comedy"* (Princeton: Princeton University Press, 1979), pp. 66–68.

30. *Genealogie* 14.13, trans. Osgood, *Boccaccio on Poetry,* p. 69. In the edition of Vincenzo Romano (Bari: Laterza, 1951), the passage stands as follows: "Per quem Virgilius sentit seu conscientie proprie morsum, seu amici et eloquentis hominis redargutionem, a quibus, dormientes in luto turpitudinum, excitamur, et in rectum pulchrumque revocamur iter, id est ad gloriam" (p. 723).

31. The fifth book of Petrarch's *Africa* contains, in the story of Masinissa and Sophonisba, an imitation of *Aeneid* 4, with Masinissa cast in the role of Aeneas; Petrarch, like Boccaccio, gives Mercury's role to an "outspoken friend," in this case Scipio, who reproves Masinissa for allowing his passions to overcome him and reminds him of his duty (5.519–573).

32. *Genealogie* 14.13, trans. Osgood, *Boccaccio on Poetry,* p. 68. This passage and the one quoted after it are taken from the following:

> Et cum litus Affrum in tempus usque illud a rusticis et agrestibus atque barbaris hominibus incoleretur, ut eum ad personam veneratione dignam deduceret, et equa reciperetur, et cuius hortatu Troianorum casus suosque recitaret, nec aliam preter Dydonem, que, et si non tunc, multa tamen post secula loca illa incoluisse creditum est, comperiens, Didonem, tanquam si iam venisset, eius hospitam fecit, et, ut legimus, eius iussu sua suorumque infortunia recitavit. (Romano, p. 722)

33. *Genealogie* 14.13, trans. Osgood, *Boccaccio on Poetry,* p. 68: "Secundo, quod sub velamento latet poetico, intendit Virgilius per totum opus ostendere quibus passionibus humana fragilitas infestetur et quibus viribus a constanti viro superentur. Et cum iam non nullas ostendisset, volens demonstrare, quibus ex causis ab appetitu concupiscibili in lasciviam rapiamur, introducit Dydonem. . . . Et sic intendit pro Dydone concupis-

cibilem et attractivam potentiam, oportunitatibus omnibus armatam" (Romano, p. 722).

34. *Genealogie* 14.9, trans. Osgood, *Boccaccio on Poetry*, p. 48: "Species vero tercia potius hystorie quam fabule similis est. Hac aliter et aliter usi poete celebres sunt. Nam heroyci, quantumcunque videantur hystoriam scribere, ut Virgilius, dum Eneam tempestate maris agitatum scribit, et Omerus alligatum malo navis Ulixem, ne a syrenarum cantu traheretur, longe tamen aliud sub velamine sentiunt quam monstretur" (Romano, p. 707).

35. Compare his usual designation for epic poets as "heroic" poets, as for example in the passage from *Genealogie* 14.9, cited above, and "lo stilo eroico d'Omero o di Virgilio," in the commentary on *Inferno* 4 (ed. Guerri, vol. 2, p. 33). He also uses the phrase to describe Petrarch's *Africa*. His association of the heroic poem with historical subject matter derives in part from Dante. Boccaccio reports that Dante saw "historical and philosophical truths" in the poems of Vergil and Statius (*Trattatello in laude di Dante*, ed. Pier Giorgio Ricci, in *Tutte le Opere*, ed. Vittore Branca [Milan: Mondadori], vol. 3, 1974, p. 443), while Dante himself referred to the *Thebaid* as the "History of Thebes" (*Convivio* 3.11.16).

36. Petrarch's *Africa* was the most awe-inspiring and discussed of literary works in progress during the middle decades of the fourteenth century. Knowledge of its general design, though none of its text had been published, probably reached Boccaccio as early as 1339 by way of Petrarch's correspondents in Naples, especially Barbato da Sulmona and Dionigi da Borgo. Petrarch was to state in his late *Letter to Posterity* that he had conceived of an epic about Scipio Africanus in 1333, but quickly abandoned the project. He was apparently working on it again by 1338 and had completed a significant portion by the time of his interrogation by King Robert in the spring of 1341 (Thomas G. Bergin and Alice S. Wilson, trans., *Petrarch's "Africa"* [New Haven: Yale University Press, 1977], pp. ix–xiii; E. H. Wilkins, *The Life of Petrarch* [repr. Chicago: University of Chicago Press, 1963], p. 19). In "De vita et moribus domini Francisci Petracchi de Florentia" of ca. 1348, Boccaccio singles out the *Africa* as Petrarch's most significant poem: "et inter alia memoratu dignissima, opus suum illud magnum et mirabile cui Affrica nomen imposuit, eo quod maioris Affricani gesta in eodem heroyco metro monstrentur, ingenio divino potius quam humano creditur compilasse" (ed. A. F. Massèra, *Opere latine minori* [Bari: Laterza, 1928], p. 240). In the same passage, Boccaccio mentions Petrarch's correspondence during the 1330s with Dionigi da Borgo. It is fair to assume that Boccaccio learned of the *Africa* from Dionigi when the latter arrived in Naples, probably in 1337 and certainly by 1339, if he had not heard of it before that time. But he did not see any of the poem until later. In 1341, Petrarch allowed Pierre Bersuire to copy a short passage from the epic, his only willing release of any part of the poem (Wilkins, *Life*, p. 19). The passage describing the pagan gods was used in Bersuire's *Reductorium morale*. It was 1343 before Barbato da Sulmona transcribed a second passage from the unfinished epic and then circulated it against Petrarch's wishes (ibid., p. 42). Barbato copied the description of Mago's death.

37. Boccaccio's gloss on the "casa di Marte" has been discussed by Hollander, "Validity of Boccaccio's Self-Exegesis," esp. pp. 168–170, who suggests an essential consonance of Boccaccio's poetic description and the moralizing gloss in which he interprets it. Hollander notes that Boccaccio did not draw on Lactantius's commentary on the *Thebaid* in composing the gloss, but he does not mention Boccaccio's own commentary on Statius's "domus Martis" in *Genealogie 9.* Victoria Kirkham has identified several likely sources for the definitive terms "irascible" and "concupiscible appetite," which Boccaccio introduces in this gloss. See *"Chiuso parlare* in Boccaccio's *Teseida,"* in *Dante, Petrarch, Boccaccio: Studies in the Italian Trecento,* ed. Aldo S. Bernardo and Anthony Pellegrini (Binghamton, N.Y.: MRTS, 1983), pp. 346–347 n. 37, on other sources.
38. Ed. Romano, p. 447.
39. *Genealogie* 9.3, ed. Romano, pp. 444 (text) and 447 (gloss): (text, citing *Thebaid* 3.424), "Et ut incessus eius ferocitas ostendatur omnis, dicit et alibi Statius idem: Comunt Furor Iraque cristas, Frena ministrat equis Pavor armiger"; (gloss), "Superest de incessu Martis pauca dicere, cuius initium a furore et ira, qui eius comunt cristas, esse videtur, quod his urgentibus absque impetu esse non potest et hoc supra descriptum est, sed hos ideo Martis comere, id est ornatas reddere cristas, id est arma, dicit, ut intelligamus quod cum arma ad inferendam et peragendam pugnam facta sint, tunc splendida videntur cum impetuose operantur."
40. Ed. Romano, p. 446.
41. *Genealogie* 9.3, ed. Romano, p. 446 (commentary on *Thebaid* 7.36–46):

> tempestatum agminumque nymborum, et stridentium aquilonum et grandinum circumdata, ut sentiamus impetus, furores, rabiem, atque rumores et tumultus vacantium bellis. Preterea ferrea describitur domus, ut locorum munitiones, circa que bellum geritur, sentiamus, que ferree sunt, id est armatorum hominum plene, et gladiorum atque telorum; que quidem, eo quod in malum ut plurimum agantur, solis contristant iubar, quia in bonum lux creata sit. Insuper radiorum solis ab armis reflexorum aliquantulum livescit splendor, ex qua livedine aurea solis lux tristari et offuscari paululum videtur.

In *Teseida* 7.30, pp. 454–455 (commentary on *Teseida* 7.30–33):

> Nebuloso dice che è, a dimostrare che l'ira offuschi il consiglio della ragione; il quale intende più giù per lo raggio del sole, il quale dice che la casa di Marte caccia da sé. Per lo ghiaccio intende la fredezza dell'animo dell'adirato, il quale, vinto da questo accendimento d'ira, diviene crudele e rigido e senza alcuna carità. Per li guazi intende le lacrime le quali per isdegno molte volte gli adirati gittano. . . . E dice che ella è tutta d'acciaio risplendente e ha le porte di diamante e le colonne di ferro: per l'acciaio intende la dureza della ostinazione dell'adirato, e questa mostra che sia la copritura della casa, perciò che dice poi che le colonne sono di ferro; e questo acciaio dice che river-

berando caccia da sé la luce del sole, e meritamente, perciò che, se
questo acciaio s'ammollisse tanto che lasciasse passare dentro la luce
del sole, cioè il sano consiglio della ragione nella mente dell'adirato,
ella non sarebbe più casa di Marte, cioè di guerra e di tribolazione, ma
di pace.

42. Ed. Romano, p. 447. Lactantius's commentary on the *Thebaid* points more
explicitly to the relevance of Discordia to the Theban War: "geminum dixit
ferrum tenere Discordiam, quae semper solet duorum inimicitia vel mor-
tibus gratulari, sive propter fratres, quia in hoc bello maxime fratrum discordia proeliatur" (in 7.50; ed. Richard Jahnke [Leipzig: Teubner, 1898],
p. 344). In the context of the *Genealogie,* such a specific reference to the
main action of the *Thebaid* would be out of place. There, Boccaccio is describing the "domus Martis" in general terms, while Lactantius is describing the group of personifications as Statius uses them in the *Thebaid.*

43. Ed. Romano, p. 447. The corresponding gloss in Lactantius simply explains the association of Death with Mars: "quia semper eripit vitam" (ed.
Jahnke, p. 344).

44. See Hollander, "Validity of Boccaccio's Self-Exegesis," esp. pp. 170–173,
on the "casa di Venere." On Boccaccio's use of Venus and Mars as figures
for the concupiscible and irascible appetites, see D. W. Robertson, Jr., *A
Preface to Chaucer* (Princeton: Princeton University Press, 1962), pp. 106n,
110, 260n, 370, 371; Robert Hollander, *Boccaccio's Two Venuses* (New
York: Columbia University Press, 1977), passim; Janet Levarie Smarr,
"Boccaccio and the Stars: Astrology in the Teseida," *Traditio* 35 (1979):
303–332; Victoria Kirkham, "An Allegorically Tempered *Decameron,*"
Italica 62 (1985): 1–23, esp. pp. 2–5 and n. 6; and idem, "'Chiuso par-
lare' in Boccaccio's *Teseida*," pp. 305–351, esp. n. 37. In "The Teseida,
Boccaccio's Allegorical Epic," *NEMLA Italian Studies* 1 (1977): 29–35,
Janet Smarr argues that the allegorical representation extends to the human
characters of the *Teseida* as well, so that Arcite and Palamon represent the
irascible and concupiscible appetites, respectively, and Theseus, who governs them (after a manner), represents reason. She would therefore take
Boccaccio's term "chiuso parlare" in the introductory epistle as appropriate for the human characters of the *Teseida* as well as the pagan gods. I
have suggested in this chapter that Boccaccio's human characters correspond to "storia" in the sequence "storia . . . favola . . . chiuso parlare"
because commentators on the *Thebaid* apply those terms in that way.
Moreover, I would note that irascible and concupiscent passions motivate
both Palamon and Arcite; the language of the poems constantly identifies
them both with "love and wrath" as Theseus does when he comes upon
them in the little grove. Indeed, with help from the general correspondence
between Polynices and Arcite, Boccaccio gives us an exiled Theban somewhat more reluctant to come to arms than is his kinsman. Palamon, who
will pray to Venus, is first to anger (5.2–11), though both cousins are
moved by wrath when they begin their first duel (5.41–43). The slight differences in their characters is described, perhaps with some exaggeration,
by Boitani, *Chaucer and Boccaccio,* pp. 46–49.

45. John Ferguson, *The Religions of the Roman Empire* (Ithaca, N.Y.: Cornell University Press, 1982), p. 73, describes Roman devotion to Clementia in the context of other "divine abstractions" to which temples were built. He notes that Diocletian and Constantine were addressed as "tua clementia."

46. The case was argued by A. W. Verrall at the beginning of this century. He noted that "The adoption of this supplement (whenever first propounded) . . . can be dated with near precision. There is no trace of it in the *Seven Against Thebes*, which indeed would seem rather to exclude it. But about fifty years later it appears complete in the *Suppliants* of Euripides. In this play and in the Children of Heracles by the same author . . . [Athens played the part of] the vindicator of the oppressed and a respecter even of the enemy" ("The Altar of Mercy," in *Collected Literary Essays* [Cambridge: Cambridge University Press, 1913], p. 225). See now John F. Burgess, "Statius' Altar of Mercy," *Classical Quarterly* n.s. 22 (1972): 339–349.

47. See Michele Scherillo, "Il Cristianesimo di Stazio secondo Dante," *Atene e Roma* 11 (1902): cols. 497–506; and especially Carlo Landi, "Sulla Leggenda del cristianesimo di Stazio," *Atti e memorie della Reale accademia di scienze, lettere ed arti di Padova* 29 (1913): 231–266; idem, "Di un Commento medievale inedito della *Tebaide* di Stazio," ibid., 30 (1914): 315–344; and idem, "Intorno a Stazio nel medioevo e nel *Purgatorio*," ibid. 37 (1921): 201–232. Also Giorgio Padoan, "Teseo *figura Redemptoris* e il cristianesimo di Stazio," in his *Il Pio Enea, l'empio Ulisse: Tradizione classica e intendimento medievale in Dante* (Ravenna: Longo, 1977), pp. 125–150.

48. Berlin (West), Deutsche Staatsbibliothek, MS lat. qu. 228 (XIII), fol. 36r; Rome, Biblioteca Vallicelliana, MS B. 30 (XIV), fol. 143v; Padua, Biblioteca del Seminario Vescovile, MS 41 (XIVin), fol. 145v; Florence, Biblioteca Riccardiana, MS 842 (XVin), fol. 105r. Part of this gloss, as it appears in the manuscript in Padua, was published by Landi, "Sulla Leggenda," pp. 231–266. Landi did not know that the same gloss appears in other manuscripts. The text of the gloss is nearly identical in the two fourteenth-century manuscripts from which I transcribe. It is coordinated with the text at *Thebaid* 12.497:

> Cum autem Beatus Paulus Athenas predicaturus advenisset, invenit Dionisium Ariopagatam virum prudentissimum, quem cum non potuisset convincere, duxit eum per aras singulorum [Berlin: aras singulas; Florence: singulas aras]deorum cuius esset inquirens unaquaque [Berlin: inquirendo cuius esset cui; Florence: et inquisivit cui esset, cui]. Tandem ad hanc aram pervenit et cuius esset inquisivit. Cui Dionisius dixit: ara est ignoti Dei. Cui Paulus: quem tu ignotum appellas, solus ille notus est. Et sermonem suum sic incepit: Notus in Iudea Deus, et cet.

49. Landi, "Sulla Leggenda," proposes the *Passio sanctissimi Dionysii* by Hilduin *Patrologia latina* 106, cols. 23ff. The dialogue between St. Paul and Dionysius in chapter 6 of that work is similar in content to the one de-

scribed in these two glosses, but it is rather longer and cannot be said to contain any clear verbal echoes.

50. In *Thebaid* 12.497; ed. Jahnke, p. 479.

51. My paraphrase of Nicholas is based on the following text, as printed in the Basel edition of the *Postils* (Froben, 1501–1502), pt. 6, fol. 195. This gloss corresponds to the lemma "Praeteriens enim, et videns simulachra vestra, inveni et aram, in qua scriptum erat: Ignoto Deo" (Acts 17:23).

> aliqui enim dixerunt quod fuit consecratum et institutum a posteris herculis, qui post eius mortem eiecti de regno suo et potestate, recurrerunt ad auxillium atheniensium per quod restituti fuerunt ad statum pristinum; propter quod dixerunt misericordiam in athenis posuisse sibi sedem, cui consecraverunt aram. Sed quia misericordia non erat aliqua persona qua fuisset nota hominibus sicut Iupiter et Mercurius, . . . illud altare intitulatum fuit Ignoto Deo, et determinatum quod non fierent oblationes et sacrificia nisi de gementibus lachrymis et precibus miserorum ibidem misericordiam postulantium.

Nicholas does not name Statius as his source, but his references to Hercules' children and the rites at the temple of Clementia derive, directly or indirectly, from the *Thebaid*.

52. Florence, Biblioteca Medicea-Laurenziana, MS Plut. 38.6; in *Thebaid* 12.481.

53. Florence, Biblioteca Medicea-Laurenziana, MS Plut. 38.5; in *Thebaid* 12.493.

54. Oxford, Magdalen College, MS lat. 18, fol. 121v. I have not seen this manuscript, and I am indebted to Violetta de Angelis for news of the gloss. Kaspar von Barth, ed., [*Statii Opera*] *quae exstant* (Cygneae, 1664), vol. 3, p. 1505. On von Barth's sources, see Sweeney, *Prolegomena*, pp. 3–4; and O. Clemen, "Handschriften und Bücher aus dem Besitze Kaspar von Barths in der Zwickauer Ratsschulbibliothek," *Zentralblatt für Bibliothekswesen* 38 (1921): esp. 275 n. 2.

55. E.g., Bede (*Patrologia latina* 92, col. 979) and Nicholas of Lyra, *Postils* (Basel ed.).

56. Milan, Biblioteca Ambrosiana, MS M 60; in *Thebaid* 12.497. Further examples may be found in Vatican City, Biblioteca Apostolica Vaticana, MS Pal. Lat. 1717, an early thirteenth-century manuscript containing six books of the *Thebaid* and a number of other works. Immediately preceding the *Thebaid* is Arator's *De actibus apostolorum* (*Patrologia latina* 68, cols. 81ff.) and a summary of the Pauline epistles, among which there is a note on the Areopagus (45r). Although the two texts preceding the *Thebaid* are copied by a different scribe, their association with Statius's work may well reflect the legendary history of the temple "Ignoto Deo." The legend appears in vernacular writings as well. A versified history of Thebes in Venetian dialect of the fourteenth century remarks that the altar of Clementia is the same altar of which St. Paul speaks in Acts (see Paolo Savj-Lopez, *Storie tebane in Italia* [Bergamo: Istituto italiano d'artigrafiche 1905], pp. xxi ff. and 120). Boccaccio refers to St. Paul and Dionysius at *Genealogie* 14.18.

57. Alberto Limentani describes Boccaccio's elaboration of this scene from *Thebaid* 12 as an example of his general tendency "to give greater movement to what he represents . . . and to enlarge the sentiments of his characters," in "Boccaccio 'traduttore' di Stazio," *La Rassegna* 64, series 7 (1960): 231–242, cited by Boitani, *Chaucer and Boccaccio*, pp. 32–33.
58. *Genealogie* 14.13; trans. Osgood, *Boccaccio on Poetry*, p. 68 and, for the subsequent quotation, p. 69.
59. Appendix 2.
60. Appendix 1.
61. Aldo Maria Costantini, "Studi sullo Zibaldone Magliabechiano, III: La Polemica con Fra Paolino da Venezia," *Studi sul Boccaccio* 10 (1977–1978): 255–275 and the bibliography noted there and above, Chapter 1 note 49, especially Giuseppe Billanovich, "Autografi del Boccaccio nella Biblioteca Nazionale di Parigi (Parigini Lat. 4939 e 6802)," *Accademia nazionale dei lincei, Rendiconti*, Classe di scienze morali, storiche e filologiche, 8th ser. 7 (1952): 376ff. Also Costantini, "La Polemica con Fra Paolino da Venezia," in *Boccaccio, Venezia e il Veneto*, ed. Vittore Branca and Giorgio Padoan (Florence: Olschki, 1979), pp. 101–121.
62. I have seen the version of Paolino's chronicle in Vatican City, Biblioteca Apostolica Vaticana, MS Vat. lat. 1960, where his history of the Theban War appears on fol. 56r-v. Paolino makes frequent reference to Augustine's *De civitate Dei* when discussing the sequence of ancient gentile empires.
63. *De civitate Dei* 18.2 and passim, 15–18, where chronological sequence among the gentile empires of the ancient world is established by reference to events in the Old Testament, on the model of Eusebius's *Chronicon*. On Boccaccio's copies of the two works, see Mazza, "L'Inventario," pp. 14, 29–30.
64. Paulus Orosius, *Historiarum adversum paganos libri vii*, ed. Carolus Zangemeister (Vienna, 1882; repr. Hildesheim: Olms, 1967), 1.10.1 (p. 59); English trans. from I. W. Raymond, *Seven Books of History Against the Pagans* (New York: Columbia University Press, 1936), p. 59.
65. Bernhard Degenhart and Annegrit Schmitt, "Frühe angiovinische Buchkunst in Neapel: Die Illustrierung französischer Unterhaltungsprosa in neapolitanischen Scriptorien zwischen 1290 und 1320," in *Festschrift Wolfgang Braunfels*, ed. F. Piel and J. Traeger (Tübingen: Wasmuth, 1977), pp. 71–92; Clem C. Williams, "A Case of Mistaken Identity: Still Another Trojan Narrative in Old French Prose," *Medium Aevum* 53 (1984): 59–72.
66. See above, note 24.
67. *Thebaid* 4.579ff. Chaucer may be alluding to the lake in the hyperbole of Knight's Tale 1660: "Up to the ancle foghte they in hir blood."
68. For the virtuous figures of pagan antiquity recalled in Boccaccio's imitation of an "apotheosis" see Giuseppe Velli, "L'apoteosi di Arcita: Ideologia e coscienza storica nel Teseida," *Studi e problemi di critica testuale* 5 (1972): 33–66. Hollander offers a more gloomy assessment of Arcite's fate in the afterlife, *Boccaccio's Two Venuses*, p. 191, n. 166.
69. Velli, "L'Apoteosi di Arcita," p. 53.
70. Georg Nikolaus Knauer, *Die Aeneis und Homer*, Hypomnemata 7 (Gottingen: Vandenhoeck and Ruprecht, 1964). The argument is repeated in

Knauer's "Vergil's *Aeneid* and Homer," *Greek, Roman, and Byzantine Studies* 5 (1964): 82–83:

> It seems to me as if Vergil had understood the relation of his poem to Homer's epics in a way which can be compared to that of Christian exegesis in understanding the relation between the Old and the New Testament, namely by "typology." The Old Testament was understood as an account of real historic events which represent in an earlier stage the expectations of salvation which are fulfilled in the New Testament. The same event is repeated in the Testament, only on another level, even by way of reversal. This analogy may suggest the reason why Vergil made the Sibyl and Juno declare that the events of the Trojan war would be reenacted, *iterum*, that a new Troy, Rome, would rise—and also the reason why Vergil could found his own characters upon the Homeric. This is *not* an aesthetic or literary interpretation—rather a "historical" one.

71. On typological reading of history, including the histories of the ancient gentile empires, in medieval universal chronicles, see Karl Heinrich Krüger, *Die Universalchroniken* (Brepolis, 1976), esp. pp. 28–29. See also Erich Auerbach, "Figura," *Archivium Romanicum* 22 (1938): 436–489 and often reprinted; Jean Danielou, *From Shadows to Reality: Studies in the Biblical Typology of the Fathers*, trans. Hibberd (London: Burns, Oates and Washbourne, 1960); Henri Marrou, "S. Augustin et l'augustinisme historique," in *La Storiografia Altomedievale*, 2 vols. (Spoleto: 1970), vol. 1, pp. 59–87.

   The thirteenth-century commentary on Lucan, attributed to Arnulf of Orleans, gives evidence of a typological reading of the history in an epic. Berthe M. Marti, *Arnulfi Aurelianensis glosule super Lucanum* (Rome: American Academy, 1958): "Pompey's death has sanctified the land of the Nile as the Crucifixion has made of Calvary a holy place (9.82) and . . . the willingness of a sacrificial animal, considered a good omen by the ancients, may be compared to Christ's self-sacrifice (1.609)" (p. xliii). Compare the glosses on the temple of Clementia in the *Thebaid*, above, notes 45–57.

72. For the text see below, Appendix 2.

73. See below, Appendix 1.

74. Gerardo Bruni, *Le opere di Egidio Romano* (Florence: Olschki, 1936), and his earlier essay, "Il *De regimine principum* di Egidio Romano," *Aevum* 6 (1932): 339–372. By 1932, Bruni had located about 230 manuscripts of the *De regimine*, including translations. The translations began appearing soon after publication of the work: French (1282) and Italian (1288). On Paolino Veneto's compendium in Venetian dialect, see *Le opere*, pp. 358–359. King Robert paid for an illuminated copy of a *De regimine principum*, probably Aegidius's work, in 1310 (Carlo de Frede, "Da Carlo I d'Angiò a Giovanna I" in *Storia di Napoli*, vol. 3 [Naples: Società Editrice Storia di Napoli, 1969], pp. 214–215). On Aegidius's dedication of his commentary on 2 *Sentences* to Robert, see Ugo Mariani, *Il Petrarca e gli agostiniani* (Rome: Edizioni di Storia e Letteratura, 1959), p. 29. A survey of his career

the epic poem was presented as a storehouse of rhetorical and mythologi-cal lore, from which Chaucer drew details to enrich the narrative taken from Boccaccio. The associations of the poem with epic tradition in the matters of narrative structure, theme, and generic form were largely lost to view.

An unfortunate coincidence brought the *Teseida* into critical play as the source of the Knight's Tale in the same period that saw the identifica-tion of Boccaccio's narrative with "romance" and against "epic." When the critical consensus developed in the later nineteenth century that Boccaccio's Palamon and Arcite represented a betrayal of the *Teseida*'s epic form and epic aspirations, its influence was soon felt in criticism of the Knight's Tale, which could be now seen as an exercise in taking the romance out of its epic clothing. Consider the language of W. P. Ker's "Chaucer and the Renaissance," the Clark Lecture of 1912, a year that also saw the second printing of Guglielmo Volpi's *The Trecento* with its succinct statement of Boccaccio's supposed failure. Ker had read his Crescini and probably his Volpi as well:

> Chaucer would not have been attracted so much by Boccaccio's epic if that had been a great heroic poem. But the *Teseide* is really a short novel of the French type enormously magnified and diversified into the likeness of an epic. . . . The story of it we all know, because it is Chaucer's *Knight's Tale*—Palamon and Arcite, the two noble kinsmen. No original has been found for it older than Boccaccio; but either there was a French original which has been lost, or Boccaccio has exactly followed the gen-eral receipt for a short problem story as that was understood by the French.[11]

Several observations may be made here. The first is that Ker, like most Chaucerians after him, has taken the consensus view of Italian criticism of the *Teseida* as his point of departure for discussing the Knight's Tale. What reappear here are not the elements of debate among Boccaccio scholars concerning the sources of the *Teseida*, but their generalized con-clusions about the poem's mismatch of form and content. More impor-tant to note is the related tendency to move the Knight's Tale farther from epic tradition by associating it with Boccaccio's "romance" and against his imitation of epic form. What Chaucer liked, we are led to believe, was not the pretension of "a great heroic poem" but the betrayal of that pre-tension, the "short novel of the French type."

Paradoxically, Chaucer's very evident interest in the *Teseida*—with all

of the respect that it implies—has in the droll course of time and changing literary conventions actually contributed to the decline in the reputation of Boccaccio's poem, at least among students of English literature.
Critical writing on the Knight's Tale in particular has led to a curiously
restricted view of the *Teseida,* because Chaucerians have asked how
Chaucer changed his major source, and they have concluded, perhaps inevitably, that he changed it for the better. The comparison of passages in
"poem" and "source" for the purpose of determining "what Chaucer
did" presents the *Teseida* as a kind of ragbag of narrative motifs and rhetorical topoi awaiting the will of a master tailor. To be sure, this narrow
focus is not without rewards, among them the certain conviction that
Chaucer knew the *Teseida* so well that he could run lines from one book
smoothly together with lines from another as he reworked and recomposed; but it draws attention away from the sophisticated imitative relations between the *Teseida* and the *Thebaid.* And in consequence, the
narrow focus has blocked understanding of Chaucer as imitator. Viewing
the *Teseida* as "source" has tended to restrict critical attention to what
came after, when the imitative design of the Knight's Tale depends on a
reader knowing something of what came before.

   Explicit as well as implicit commentaries on the *Teseida* have a curious
history in Chaucer studies, where most of the commonplace views and
assumptions that emerged in the later nineteenth century have been taken
up not as hypotheses for testing but as statements of fact from which an
analysis of Chaucer's "use" of the poem might begin. There has been a
tendency to exaggerate the poor opinion of the *Teseida* reflected in the
"failed epic" hypothesis, because it so conveniently introduces the argument that Chaucer improved on a loose and baggy monster of a "source."
The remarks of Robert Pratt in his influential essay of 1947, "Chaucer's
Use of the *Teseida,*" offer one of the most striking examples of this tendency. Pratt based his discussion of the *Teseida* largely on Natalino
Sapegno's *Literary History of the Trecento,*[12] the successor to Volpi's volume *The Trecento* in the same prestigious series, whose summary assessment of Boccaccio's epic design followed the general line of argument
traced to Vincenzo Crescini and Francesco DeSanctis. But Pratt does
more than repeat Sapegno's assessment, as the colorful language in his
essay suggests:

>   Thus the plot, the people, and the amorous psychology of the
>   *Teseida* are better suited for a medieval romance than for an
>   epic; and although the romantic and heroic elements in the poem
>   are juxtaposed, they almost nowhere coalesce. Torn between

> presumptuous epic designs and the subjective vividness of his
> own waning amour with Maria d'Aquino, Boccaccio created
> neither an epic nor a pure romance, but rather a leisurely and
> varigated pseudo-epic, lacking in unity and power of theme, de-
> sign, and execution, and lacking in strong characterization, but
> possessing numerous effective descriptions and elevated passages
> of poetry.[13]

The baggiest of baggy monsters. No wonder Chaucer cut the thing by
more than two-thirds! And thank heaven we need not concern our-
selves with this "source" except insofar as Chaucer the master craftsman
made something better of it! All of the features of the "failed epic" thesis
are repeated here with gusto and with the additional suggestion that
Chaucer, in shortening the narrative to the scale of the Knight's Tale, implicitly acknowledged their horrors: the contrast between main action
("better suited for a medieval romance") and the epic form, the assertion
that Boccaccio intended to reproduce the spirit of classical epic and that
the task was beyond him ("presumptuous epic designs").

Pratt's reference to a "waning amour for Maria d'Aquino" in the second sentence requires a note of explanation. One variant on the "failed
epic" hypothesis argued that the epic proportions of the *Teseida* had been
established with the intention of describing the labors of Theseus, but
that something had happened to distract Boccaccio from his plan at the
end of book 2. The version of Boccaccio's biography generally accepted
throughout the later nineteenth and early twentieth centuries provided a
name for that distraction, for it was held that Boccaccio in his youth had
been enamored of an illegitimate daughter of King Robert of Naples, one
Maria d'Aquino. Maria was identified as the "Fiammetta" of Boccaccio's
literary fictions and therefore the person addressed in his introductory
epistle to the *Teseida*. Putting dubious biography together with question-
able literary analysis, the biographical critics of the *Teseida* suggested
that Boccaccio had set out to write an epic in the spirit of the classical
epics, and that he had spoiled that design after book 2 because of a desire
to write about his love for Maria under the guise of the Palamon and
Arcite story. It was Boccaccio's "vivid" memory of the haughty and beautiful Maria that distracted him from a subject more suited to the epic
form and left us with a love story dressed up in Vergilian rhetoric. As
Pratt imagines this literary misbehavior, the "subjective vividness of
[Boccaccio's] waning amour with Maria" caused the would-be epic poet
to leave the straight path of Theseus and stray into the inappropriate
"romantic."

Since the time of Pratt's essay, the existence of a "Maria d'Aquino" has been called forcefully into question, because there is no record of an illegitimate daughter to Robert in any of the histories or genealogies of the Angevin dynasty, even though these writings consistently took note of royal bastards as well as legitimate offspring; and especially because Boccaccio's references to "Fiammetta" are themselves inconsistent, showing all the signs of literary convention rather than biographical revelation.[14] Nonetheless, the "distraction" hypothesis managed to survive Maria's disappearance. In his study *Chaucer and Boccaccio* published in 1977, Piero Boitani takes care to recast his description of the *Teseida* in more prudent literary terms, noting the evidence that casts such doubt on the thesis that Boccaccio had been distracted by a "waning amour." Still, Boitani offered the "failed epic" hypothesis as a point of departure for his analysis of relations between *Teseida* and Knight's Tale, and he too sought a reason for Boccaccio's sudden turn to Palamon and Arcite. Characterizing the long poem Chaucer translated and adapted in the Knight's Tale, he argued that

> The two contrasting forces—the wish to resurrect classical epic
> . . . and the pressure exerted by the experience of two centuries
> of romance (thus the subtitle "about the marriage of Emily")—
> reach an unstable compromise in the *ottava rima* stanza form. . . .
> But there are other features which prevent the author from at-
> taining the dignity which characterizes classical epic: first, as we
> will see later, he is too bourgeois and will therefore break the
> epic intonation of the poem with remarks worthy of the *De-
> camerone*; second, he is too "courtois," too deeply immersed
> in the atmosphere of the love dream to be able to sing only of
> "arma"; he is too lyrical to be tragic. Thus, the classical division
> into twelve books and the fact that the poem is composed (with-
> out the sonnets) of exactly as many lines as the *Aeneid* remain
> superficial features.[15]

In place of Maria's romantic pull, we now have the impersonal push of literary history ("the pressure exerted by the experience of two centuries of romance"), but this kind of romance has the same unhappy conse-quences for Boccaccio's "wish to resurrect classical epic." The crucial as-sumption, that Boccaccio's imitative design was intended to reproduce the "spirit" of classical epic reappears here in all its vigor, leading to a series of observations on the nature of Boccaccio's "failure." When an as-sessment of this kind stands as the point of departure for an investigation of Chaucer's "use" of the *Teseida*, that investigation will almost inevitably conclude that Chaucer's shorter version of "Palamon and Arcite" represents not only an improvement but also an implicit acknowledgment by Chaucer that the main action of the *Teseida* is ill suited to the form and scale of its classical models.

The narrow focus on "what Chaucer did" to the *Teseida* has an unhappy influence on study of the Knight's Tale, for it tends to limit the inquiry to Chaucer's imitation of Boccaccio, while Chaucer follows Boccaccio in proposing an open imitation of the *Thebaid*. Like the *Teseida*, the first Canterbury tale develops an open analogy between the foreground action, involving rivalry between Palamon and Arcite, and the background of Theban history and its final chapter in the Theban civil war. Like the *Teseida*, Chaucer's poem depends for some of its allusive force on the reader's ability to place it in epic tradition and to recognize its variations on the narrative pattern in the *Thebaid*. Chaucer's use of the *Teseida* reflects a strategy of open imitation not of Boccaccio's narrative, but, like Boccaccio's narrative, of Statius's.

The aim of a study such as "Chaucer's Use of the *Teseida*" is to examine what Chaucer translated, what he modified, and what he omitted in composing the Knight's Tale, and the focus remains fixed on that text and its immediate source. The rewards of such a focus are many, but there also comes a cost for excluding the intertextual aspects of the *Teseida*, its allusive narrative, what Boccaccio had "done" to the *Thebaid* in the *Teseida*. If we draw back from the narrow focus on *Teseida*–Knight's Tale to include the longer literary tradition of *Thebaid*–*Teseida*–Knight's Tale, many of the observations by which Pratt characterized Chaucer's "changes" in the *Teseida* show Chaucer *preserving* the imitative patterns that associate the rivalry of Palamon and Arcite with that of Eteocles and Polynices. His use of the *Teseida* is governed by an interest in doing again what Boccaccio had already done before, even while acting within the smaller space permitted by the frame of the *Canterbury Tales*. Moreover, his use of the *Teseida*, the cuts and additions and recombinations, is not testimony to his dislike of the "excess" in his source, but rather to his acknowledgment of its genial transformation of Statius.

Sorting out the intertextual relations of the Knight's Tale along these lines effectively returns the narrative to the epic tradition, where the poem's formal characteristics—four-part structure, mixture of divine and human characters, and so on—suggest it should be. To say that it is written in the epic tradition is not necessarily to call it an epic, but to situate the poem in a tradition of rhetorical forms and narrative motifs to which Chaucer makes open reference and which, to some extent, he expects his readers to hold in mind so as to recognize his allusions and transformations. To say that the poem was written in the epic tradition also frees us of the vague critical term "romance" and offers in its place a critical terminology with some basis in the writings of Chaucer's own literary culture.

Open imitation of the *Thebaid*

Among Pratt's observations on the "improvements" Chaucer worked in the narrative of the *Teseida,* one is especially suggestive in the longer perspective that includes Boccaccio's use of the *Thebaid.* In noting Chaucer's major deletions, which are concentrated in *Teseida* 1–2 and 9–12 and include Theseus's expedition against the Amazons at the beginning and the apotheosis of Arcite near the end, Pratt concludes that "Chaucer commenced th[e] rivalry of the lovers sooner than Boccaccio and . . . rejected all elements of the plot which did not bear upon this central theme." [16] The observation as it stands is accurate enough. But that "central theme" comes from Statius through Boccaccio, not from Boccaccio alone. The observation renders justice unto the *Teseida* only if we lengthen our focus to include the *Thebaid.* In this perspective, the pattern of Chaucer's cuts indicates that he wanted to preserve in his shorter narrative those parts of Boccaccio's invention which carried his systematic allusion to *Thebaid* 1–6.

Several other prominent aspects of Chaucer's use of the *Teseida* also take on a markedly different significance when viewed in this longer perspective. Consider the often-remarked absence of any reference to Boccaccio or the *Teseida* in Chaucer's poem, which instead points the reader to "old" sources in general and to Statius in particular. Modern critics have interpreted Chaucer's silence in various ways, finding in it among other things a sign of anxiety before the figure of a "strong" predecessor; a suggestion that, when and if Chaucer met Boccaccio, the older poet was rude to him; and even an indication that Chaucer owned a copy of the *Teseida* that did not carry the name of its author. It is very improbable, however, that Chaucer could have failed to know who wrote so famous a poem as the *Teseida,* whatever the state of his own copy, and one may well doubt that he worried about Boccaccio's influence on his own creativity. In any case, there is no evidence to support this kind of biographical speculation. Moreover, the absence of any reference to Boccaccio in the Knight's Tale has some practical, literary advantage, for in the longer perspective that acknowledges the imitative design of Chaucer's Italian source, there is a clear distinction between Boccaccio's open allusion to the *Thebaid,* repeated by Chaucer in the Knight's Tale, and Chaucer's very different use of the *Teseida*. From Boccaccio, Chaucer adopts an allusive narrative. There is nothing to gain in the artistic economy of such an imitative design by explicit references to the *Teseida* or its author, because the narrative does not allude to the *Teseida*. It alludes to the history of the Theban civil war as recounted in Statius's *Thebaid,* and it is to the *Thebaid* that Chaucer points us with his epigraph, his references to the long series of misfortunes in the house of Oedipus, and his mention of "Stace of Thebes."

The restraints on length imposed by Chaucer's frame story dictated that he recast the narrative of the *Teseida* in a radically abbreviated form; and as Pratt noted, Chaucer generally omitted elements from his source that did not relate directly to the theme of fraternal strife. Within this general program of abbreviation, Chaucer also did some expanding. His description of the temples, for example, is longer than Boccaccio's, and he altered or rearranged many other passages as well. Whether these changes constitute "improvements" is a subjective judgment and will not concern us here. What can be demonstrated is that Chaucer's alterations generally reflect a concern with preserving and accentuating the *Thebaid*like structure and themes of Boccaccio's narrative. By taking into account Boccaccio's open imitation of the *Thebaid,* we may perfect the observation that Chaucer concentrated his narrative around the theme of fraternal strife by showing that Chaucer rearranged and recast the *Teseida* so as to create another allusive narrative matching the rivalry of Palamon and Arcite with that of Eteocles and Polynices. Consider several representative passages: the opening scene with its theme of Athenian clemency; the simile of Tisiphone; Chaucer's version of "sì poca di cosa"; and the rites of Emilia before the martial games. All show Chaucer changing his immediate source, but doing so according to the spirit of Boccaccio's genial analogy.

(1) The opening scene and the theme of Athenian clemency

The epigraph to the Knight's Tale, "Iamque domos patrias, Scithice post aspera gentis / Prelia, laurigero, etc.," acknowledges the source for the opening 145 verses, which are based directly on *Thebaid* 12.519ff. and Boccaccio's earlier vernacularization of the same scenes in *Teseida* 2.19ff. In his choice for the beginning of his narrative, Chaucer reveals himself to be a keen observer of Boccaccio's use of the *Thebaid.* As noted earlier, Boccaccio's opening is built on the frame of this very passage, *Thebaid* 12.519ff., containing the scene of Theseus's triumphal return to Athens after the campaign in Amazonia.[17] Statius's passage contains only

a brief reference to the campaign itself, but Boccaccio, drawing on the
description of the Argonauts' siege of the Lemnian women in *Thebaid 5*,
replaces the brief reference with a detailed account of the events preceding
Theseus's triumphal return to Athens. These events occupy *Teseida* 1–
2.18. I have also noted above that another early reader of the *Thebaid*
and the *Teseida* seems to have recognized this structural relationship between the end of the *Thebaid* and the beginning of the *Teseida*. Like that
anonymous glossator in Tedaldo's copy of the *Thebaid*, Chaucer returned
to the bare Statian frame of *Teseida* 1–2, taking all of *Teseida* 1–2.18
as a simple elaboration on the brief reference to Theseus's Scythian
campaign.[18]

The constraints of space with which Chaucer deals in his version of the
narrative, and which are frequently remarked by the narrator ("I have,
God woot, a large feeld to ere" [886]; "If that I hadde leyser for to seye"
[1,188]), are apparent in the first scene, that of Theseus's encounter with
the Argive widows. But here as elsewhere Chaucer shortens in ways that
maintain, or even increase, the underlying patterns from the *Thebaid*.
Boccaccio sets up the encounter much as Statius does and over an equally
generous space of verses, beginning with a reference to the end of the
Theban civil war and the destruction of Thebes (2.11), the attempts of
the Greek women to offer burial rites for their dead husbands (2.14), the
vindictive denial by Creon, and their subsequent journey to Athens, city
hospitable to the oppressed.

> Esse non voller da nessuno onore,
> ma solo il tempio cercar di Clemenza
> e in quel con gravissimo dolore
> istanche e lasse fecer residenza.   (2.17)

> [They sought the attentions of no one, only the temple of Clem-
> ency, and in it they took up residence, with their great sorrow,
> tired and dispirited.]

Then Boccaccio turns to the triumphal return of Theseus, the scenes of
Athens welcoming him and Hippolyta, and after the procession reaches
the middle of the city, his encounter with the Argive widows. The entire
sequence, including Theseus's speech to his troops before they set out for
Thebes, spreads into thirty-seven stanzas. In the Knight's Tale it is compressed into a single scene of eighty-one lines, roughly the equivalent of
ten stanzas. There is a very abbreviated description of the triumphal return from Scythia, and there is no speech to the troops after Theseus's

encounter at the temple. The location of the temple is changed from the center of Athens to a place outside the city walls, eliminating the need for a description of Theseus's progress through the city.[19] A place is found in Evadne's speech for explanations of the war and of Creon's ban: "We losten alle oure housbondes at that toun / Whil that the seege thereaboute lay" (936–937).

To say that Chaucer condenses Boccaccio's narrative is to state the obvious, but also to misidentify the idea governing his use of the *Teseida*. For behind Boccaccio's scene of Theseus at the temple of Clemency is Statius's description of that temple and, as I have suggested above, perhaps the medieval tradition of commentary on Statius's description as well. The version of the scene that Chaucer uses to open his Knight's Tale gives full scope to those elements in Boccaccio's narrative which dramatize Statius's representation of Clementia as a goddess "who loves to dwell in hearts and minds." Theseus's initial anger is expressed in a speech a little longer than its Italian original: "What folk been ye, that at myn homcomynge / Perturben so my feste with criynge?" etc. (905–911). While the thematic words "mercy" and "pity" appear more frequently and in tighter concentration during Evadne's response than they do in the corresponding passage in the *Teseida,* they return in Chaucer's description of Theseus's subsequent actions:

> This gentil duc doun from his courser sterte
> With *herte pitous,* when he herde hem speke.
> Hym thoughte that his *herte* wolde breke
> Whan he saugh hem so pitous and so maat. (952–955)

And Chaucer uses them as a leitmotif in his characterization of Theseus, ending the first half of his narrative as it began with a scene of Theseus angry, supplicated, and, on reflection, merciful:

> And in his gentil *herte* he thoughte anon,
> And softe unto hymself he seyde, "Fy
> Upon a lord that wol have no mercy,
> But been a leon, bothe in word and dede,
> To hem that been in repentaunce and drede." (1,772–1,775)

It is language that does not correspond to the parallel passage in *Teseida* 5.92, where Boccaccio's Theseus simply says that likes to be able to pardon ("m'è caro molto il perdonare altrui"), and which reflects Chaucer's development of a figure appearing in Boccaccio's source.

(2) The simile of Tisiphone and the apostrophe to Cupid

The simile of Tisiphone, in which Boccaccio states his equation of the "saevus amor regendi" animating Polynices and Eteocles with the love inspiring rivalry between Palamon and Arcite, survived Chaucer's extensive cutting of his Italian source.[20] I take it as a sign of Chaucer's interest in recreating the allusive style of Boccaccio's narrative that the passage was not preserved as a matter of course in its original form and original context, but recast and resituated at the climax of the scene in the grove. Chaucer recast the simile as an apostrophe, modified the vehicle by replacing Tisiphone with Cupid, and expanded the concluding statement equating the desire for possession of Emelye with desire to possess a kingdom.

Chaucer abbreviated and rearranged the scenes of prison and grove that run from the end of *Teseida* 4 into the middle of *Teseida* 5. In the *Teseida,* Arcite is discovered by Palamon's servant Panfilus (4.79), who then tells Palamon of his cousin's clandestine return to Athens, which leads to Palamon's jealousy, the simile of Tisiphone, Palamon's escape from prison, and his search for Arcite in the grove, with its echoes of *Thebaid* 2 and the ambush of Tydeus in the grove outside Thebes. Chaucer eliminates the role of Panfilus entirely. He has Palamon escape from jail before learning of Arcite's return from exile, but he saves the simile, moving it from the beginning of the sequence in the prison tower to the end of the first battle in the grove. The literary echoes of Allecto visiting Turnus in *Aeneid* 7 and of Tisiphone hovering over the Cadmean towers in *Thebaid* 1, so carefully suggested by Boccaccio when Palamon conceives his jealous rage in the prison tower, disappear with Chaucer's reorganization of these scenes; but the Chaucerian narrative recalls the general pattern of events in the *Thebaid* with even greater precision. Chaucer has moved the beginning of strife back to the very first scene of Palamon and Arcite in the prison tower, so that the armed conflict in the grove simply confirms the theme announced before. This is also the pattern of the *Thebaid,* which announces the strife of Eteocles and Polynices in book 1, before Polynices' exile, and confirms it in book 2 when Tydeus is ambushed in the grove.

His handling of the scene in the grove shows him once again willing to sacrifice small literary echoes while emphasizing the general correspondence between his narrative and Statius's account of the Theban civil war. By chance, Chaucer's Arcite comes to the grove while Palamon, newly escaped, is hiding there. They recognize each other, have words over their rights to "possession" of Emelye, and determine to fight each other to the death (A. 1,451–1,622). Chaucer's version of the encounter is about one-fourth the length of Boccaccio's, and it includes none of the verbal reminiscences of Tydeus's encounter in the grove outside Thebes that characterize the corresponding scene in the *Teseida*. But Boccaccio's allusive *sententia* from the simile of Tisiphone, "signoria né amore stan ben con compagnia," is brought forward and enlarged in Chaucer's version, preceded by two lines of apostrophe:

> O Cupide, out of alle charitee!
> O regne, that wolt no felawe have with thee!
> Ful soth is seyd that love ne lordshipe
> Wol noght, his thankes, have no felaweshipe.
> Well fynden that Arcite and Palamoun.   (A. 1,623–1,627)

The emphatic spread of the translation into two lines is introduced by the two lines of apostrophe and rounded off by its application to the conflict between Palamon and Arcite. One line in the *Teseida* has in effect become five. And although Chaucer does not translate Boccaccio's entire simile, with its reference to the sons of Oedipus, that analogy is carried by the more emphatic equation of rivalry in love to rivalry in "lordshipe" with repetition of the thematic word "felawe." Moreover, in Chaucer's scene, this explicit statement of the analogy is preceded by Arcite's speech on the destruction of the Theban kingdom:

> Allas, thou felle Mars! allas, Juno!
> Thus hath youre ire oure lynage al fordo,
> Save oonly me and wrecched Palamoun.   (1,559–1,561)

and followed by a formal simile characteristic of epic tradition and based on *Thebaid* 4.494ff. (1,638–1,645).

By substituting Cupid for Tisiphone, Chaucer changes Boccaccio's allusion to a specific moment in the narrative of the *Thebaid* into a general reference to the epic as a whole. As noted above, Statius himself characterizes Polynices' longing for possession of the throne as that of a frustrated lover, and the twelfth-century prologue to the epic beginning "In principio" (Appendix 1) describes the rivalry for *imperium* as a burning love (*cupiditas*): "illis duobus fratribus qui tanta imperii exarserunt cupiditate quod se mutuis interfecerant vulneribus" (those two brothers, who burned with such desire for rule that they killed each other in battle).

(3) Chaucer's "sì poca di cosa"

Studies focusing on the Knight's Tale and its Italian source without reference to the *Thebaid* have noted, usually with regret, that Chaucer changed or eliminated most of the scenes by which Boccaccio had given the figure of Emilia some life and complexity.[21] For example, as Arcite leaves Athens in the *Teseida*, he prays for a last glimpse of his beloved and is favored by the appearance of Emilia on a balcony.

> mirando il grazioso giovinetto
> che in esilio dolente n'andava,
> e compassione alquanto gli portava.   (3.83)

> [watching the graceful young man who was sadly going into
> exile, and she had much compassion for him.]

And Emilia's compassion for the exile reappears dramatically when Arcite returns to the court of Theseus, risking death if recognized by the duke. Emilia is the only person at court to make out the features of her admirer under his new beard, and she does not fail to collaborate with him (4.58). Her composure is put to the test, however, when she comes upon the two rivals fighting over her in the grove (5.77–82). Her reactions engage Boccaccio at some length, as in the end she has the poise to recover after the shock and before the rest of the hunting party can see her (5.81).

All of these close-ups disappear in the Knight's Tale, where Emelye is a distant object of desire for the two cousins, never in conversation with them. She even loses her role in the little discovery scene, for in Chaucer's narrative it is Theseus himself who comes upon the two noble Thebans (1,696). But Chaucer's changes in his immediate source are once again made to conform with his open imitation of the *Thebaid*. Early in the *Thebaid*, Statius remarks the disproportion between the rewards of a barren kingdom and the immense price Eteocles and Polynices are willing to pay to possess it. "Pugna est de paupere regno." The fight is over a starveling realm (1.151). The irony, as always in Statius, is bitter. Thousands will die in the civil war. As we have seen, Boccaccio translates the motif into the very different scale and tone of his narrative, where it appears as a comic reflection on the intensity of the dispute between Palamon and Arcite that is out of proportion with their hopes of "possessing" Emilia. It is a delicate task for the narrator, who must suggest the comic disproportion in desire without disparaging Emilia, and he manages it first by reference to her vanity and then, after the personal dispute has threatened to become a civil war, by Theseus's surprised "sì poca di cosa!"—all this for such a small thing. Chaucer in turn develops the topic, but does so by increasing the distance between Emelye and her fond suitors. Theseus is again the character to note the comic irony:

> But this is yet the beste game of alle,
> That she for whom they han this jolitee
> Kan hem therfore as muche thank as me.
> She woot namore of all this hoote fare,
> By God, than woot a cokkow or an hare! (1,806–1,810)

Chaucer keeps away from suggestions that Emelye herself is "sì poca di cosa" and develops the topic entirely around her distance from the whole hot affair.

(4) Emelye's rites

One final example will have to suffice to show the open imitation of the *Thebaid* that governs Chaucer's changes in the *Teseida*. The sacrifices and other rites performed by Boccaccio's Emilia, who wishes to discover the outcome of the battle for her hand (*Teseida* 7.71ff.), are modeled on the rites of Manto in *Thebaid* 4, where the Theban prophetess attempts to discover the outcome of the approaching war between Eteocles and Polynices. The sign received by Emilia in answer to her request then recalls the two struggling flames on the funeral pyre of Eteocles and Polynices at the end of that war. Chaucer not only preserves Boccaccio's description of the rites, but adds to them an explicit reference to Statius:

> Two fyres on the auter gan she beete,
> And dide hir thynges, as men may biholde
> In Stace of Thebes and thise bookes olde. (2,292–2,294)

Theban genealogy in the Knight's Tale

One of Chaucer's little additions to the story of Palamon and Arcite is also suggestive of a broader design to preserve Boccaccio's open imitation of the *Thebaid* and to elaborate again Statius's theme of fraternal strife in a narrative analogous to that of the *Thebaid*. Although Chaucer certainly knew of Boccaccio's encyclopedic *Genealogie*, a work organized around thirteen huge genealogical trees, and was familiar with the legendary his-

tory of England and other modern kingdoms that traced their descent
from ancient peoples such as the Trojans, his own genealogies of the
pagan gods and heroes are few, short, and often puzzling.[22] Take, for example, Proserpyne's oath in the Merchant's Tale, "by my moodres sires
soule" (2,265), a solitary reference that seems to promise meaningfulness
if only we can recall the name of Proserpine's maternal grandfather; or
Criseyde's one reference to her mother "Argive" (*Troilus* 4.762), perhaps
the same "Argyve" mentioned by Cassandra in the next book (5.1,509)
and in any case a person with a surprisingly un-Trojan name. Beyond
these examples, there is little evident interest in genealogy in Chaucer's
literary portraits. His Knight in the *Canterbury Tales* embodies certain
ideals of knighthood but does not represent a specific noble family; the
poet describes him in terms of his character and deeds rather than his
pedigree and coat of arms; a significant preference, reminiscent of the bal-
lade "Gentilesse," in which Chaucer defines nobility in terms of figurative,
not literal descent. This traditional idea appears in the Wife of Bath's Tale
as well, where the wise old hag tells her young knight to prefer spiritual
inheritance to the material kind: "Crist wole we clayme of hyme oure
gentillesse, / Nat of oure eldres for hire old richesse" (1,117–1,118).[23]
Thus when Chaucer draws our attention with some insistence to the "eldres" of a character or characters, as he does in the Knight's Tale, we
shall want to be alert for the wider implications of their family history.

When we are introduced to Palamon and Arcite near the end of the
opening sequence based on *Thebaid* 12.519ff., we are also introduced to
their royal genealogy. This identification is made by heralds, who recognize the emblems on the battle gear of the two wounded Thebans:

> But by hir cote-armures and by hir gere
> The heraudes knewe hem best in special
> As they that weren of the blood roial
> Of Thebes, and of sustren two yborn.   (A. 1,016–1,019)

The scene is, in its specificity, Chaucer's own. He follows the corresponding scene in the *Teseida* (2.85–89) in giving Palamon and Arcite a royal
lineage but not in saying that they are "of sustren two yborn." Boccaccio
has Theseus rather than "heralds" notice their arms and ask them if
they are "of the blood of Cadmus," and this is confirmed in equally general terms. Later, Chaucer also adds a surprisingly explicit reference to
Palamon as "a kynges brother sone" (A. 3,084).[24] Like Proserpine's oath,
these two passages describe a family relation but withhold the relation's

name. Unlike the lonely genealogical reference in the Merchant's Tale, however, these two allusions in the Knight's Tale form part of a series of references to the royal house of Thebes that Chaucer has preserved from the *Teseida*. With the principal characters reminding us that they are descendants of Cadmus and the kings of Thebes in his descent (Palamon at 1,285–1,286 and 1,325–1,331; Arcite at 1,340–1,351 and 1,359–1,361), the two allusions to their specific place in that descent seem designed to provoke speculation. And as it turns out, Chaucer's teasing references to two royal sisters and a king's brother are consistent with the genealogy of the Theban dynasty in Statius's *Thebaid*.

The lineage of the ruling house of Boeotian Thebes appears in a somewhat simpler form in most medieval sources than it does in modern mythological dictionaries, where it has been reconstructed from Greek as well as Latin writings. Lactantius's commentary on the *Thebaid* is representative of the sources from which Chaucer probably learned his Theban history, and may itself have been known to him. The latter part of the Theban succession, which is the part of interest here, is easily reconstructed from the *Thebaid* itself, but Lactantius outlines it anyway: "Laius [the son] of Labdacus, Oedipus of Laius, Ismene, Antigone, Eteocles, Polynices [the children] of Oedipus." Lactantius also traces the earlier history of the Theban line, down to these, its last members in the house of Oedipus. In a gloss on one of Statius's many allusions to the earlier history of the Theban kings, Lactantius gives the entire masculine descent as follows: Jove, Elus [called "Epaphus" by other writers], Belus; Belus had three sons, Agenor, Danaus, and Aegisthus; Cadmus was son of Agenor, Polidorus son of Cadmus, Labdacus son of Polidorus, Laius son of Labdacus.[25] For Chaucer as for Lactantius, the descent from Cadmus to the later kings of Thebes was direct. In the Knight's Tale, Arcite gives the following abbreviated account of his lineage:

> Allas, ybroght is to confusioun
> The blood roial of Cadme and Amphioun,—
> Of Cadmus which that was the first man
> That Thebes gulte, or first the toun bigan
> And of the citee first was crouned kyng.
> Of his lynage am I and his ofspryng
> Of verray ligne, as of the stok roial.   (A. 1,545–1,551)

This compressed version of Arcite's ancestry draws the examples of "misfortune" in Theban history into the immediate background of the

Knight's Tale, along with the recent examples of misfortune in the time of King Oedipus and his sons. It also places Palamon and Arcite in the direct line of these unfortunate Theban kings. Arcite says he is a direct descendant of Cadmus, by "verray ligne," and indeed that he and Palamon are the last of this ancient royal "stok" (1,560–1,561). Chaucer takes this motif more or less directly from the *Teseida,* and it forms part of that series of preserved details that maintain Boccaccio's pattern of allusions to the theme and action of the *Thebaid.* In both the *Teseida* and the Knight's Tale, the fictional Palamon and Arcite have been grafted to a familiar genealogical tree.

Chaucer's addition to the genealogy simply intensifies its allusive force. Because Theseus's siege of Thebes at the beginning of the Knight's Tale took place at the end of the Theban civil war, when Polynices and Eteocles were rivals for the throne, and because Palamon and Arcite are said to be very young when the heralds discover them on the battlefield, Chaucer's genealogical hints point to the royal generation of the Theban War itself. The sisters of Eteocles and Polynices, Antigone and Ismene, are the only "sisters two" in the Theban royal line during that generation. Moreover, they are sufficiently prominent as characters in the *Thebaid* and the other accounts of Theban history to be identified by an allusion to "two sisters" in the "verray ligne" of Cadmus. Chaucer encourages us again to think of Palamon and Arcite as children of the children of Oedipus by means of Theseus's reference to Palamon's father. In view of the chronological setting of the events in the Knight's Tale, Theseus's exclamation that Palamon is "a kynges brother sone, pardee" can suggest only one person, and that is Polynices. His brother Eteocles became king of Thebes after Oedipus; Polynices' own role in the city's history turns on the fact that he was not a king but brother to a king, for it was his brother Eteocles' refusal to share the throne with Polynices that led to the civil war. A close reader of the *Thebaid* would also know of the tradition that Polynices had an incestuous affair with his sister Antigone: Statius mentions at *Thebaid* 11.371 that Eteocles suspects Antigone's loyalty "because of her love for Polynices," and Lactantius's gloss specifies that "it is said that she lay with him."[26] Without saying so outright (and Chaucer seems to prefer not to mention incest outright), our author has invited us to imagine that this Theban affair bore fruit.[27]

This is, I propose, the solution to Chaucer's genealogical puzzle in the Knight's Tale. But the significance of his two references to the parents of Palamon and Arcite has less to do with its "solution" than with the invitation to seek a solution. Chaucer teases our heraldic spirits to consider the leading characters in the recent history of Thebes; like his other, more extensive references in the Knight's Tale to the Theban royal line, these two allusions point our attention back toward the examples of inter-necine strife that have characterized its history. The suggested com-parison between Palamon and Arcite on the one hand and their royal ancestors on the other underscores how they, on a small scale, have re-peated the ancestral pattern.

Chaucer's Theban genealogy elaborates the important theme of frater-nal strife in the Knight's Tale, where they take their place beside other allusions to the events of the *Thebaid,* suggesting comparison between the rivalry for Emelye and the earlier examples of violent rivalry, espe-cially that of Eteocles and Polynices. Consider the context of Chaucer's first genealogical reference: following their unpropitious entrance at the bottom of a pile of Theban corpses, having fallen in the last battle of the civil war begun by Eteocles and Polynices, Palamon and Arcite are imme-diately identified as members of the house of Oedipus, the sons of two royal sisters (A. 1,016–1,019). They are then called "fellows" (mean-ing "companions, comrades") in lines A. 1,030–1,032; "cousins" again (A. 1,081–1,093); "cousins and brothers" (A. 1,131, 1,161); and finally just "brothers" (A. 1,136, 1,147, 1,181, 1,184). All of the terms have cor-responding sources in the *Teseida,* but the frequency of use is much higher in the Knight's Tale. They are "brothers" in that they have sworn a pledge of brotherly allegiance to each other: "thy cosyn and thy brother / Ysworn ful depe" (A. 1,131–1,132).[28] This progression of thematic words, from cousin to fellow to brother, carries us directly into the garden-and-tower scene, where the two kinsmen see the beautiful Emelye. Each desiring to possess her for himself alone, they break their bonds of fellow-ship and brotherhood: "Greet was the strif and long betwixt hem tweye" (A. 1,187) as the narrator remarks at the end of this scene, referring to their verbal battles in a phrase that echoes Statius's thematic word *acies,* while the verbal battles themselves recall the strife of Eteocles and Polynices, who broke fraternal bonds and sworn oaths when they began their dispute for the throne of Thebes. Strife between Palamon and Arcite begins sooner in the Knight's Tale than in the *Teseida;* Chaucer's genea-logical passage, coming as it does at the beginning of this remarkable se-quence of thematic words, points our attention back to the previous generation at Thebes, while in the *Teseida* the same comparison will be suggested by a more leisurely correspondence with scenes in the *Thebaid.*

The same conjunction of "kinship" or "brotherhood" with "strife" ap-pears in the scene at the grove, where Palamon and Arcite first come to blows with each other. Here the genealogical catalog in Arcite's lament for the "confusioun" of his ancestors (A. 1,542ff.) leads directly into Palamon's declaration of implacable jealousy:

> . . . Arcite, false traytour wikke,
> Now artow hent, that lovest my lady so
> . . .
> And art my blood, and to my conseil sworn.   (A. 1,580–1,583)

The narrator's apostrophe to follow, with its explicit likening of rivalry in love and in "lordship," will twice repeat the thematic word "fellow" in the space of five lines. The allusions are, of course, lost entirely on the noble Thebans themselves. With a brilliant touch of comic irony, Chaucer has shown Palamon's jealousy flaring at the moment he recognizes Arcite, and Palamon has recognized Arcite because Arcite has identified himself as the last of the royal line of Thebes.

Love and history

The limited aim of this final chapter has been to redefine Chaucer's use of the *Teseida* so as to take account of the open and systematic allusion to the *Thebaid* developed in the main action of Boccaccio's poem. Taking the longer view of what Boccaccio had done with his major source before Chaucer sat down with the *Teseida* and the *Thebaid* open before him, we have seen that Chaucer's changes in the *Teseida* are governed by a program of open imitation of the *Thebaid*. His art is not an art of "improvements" in the story taken from Boccaccio, but of collegial and respectful collaboration, as Chaucer in the greatly reduced space of his *Canterbury Tales* builds an allusive narrative like the one Boccaccio had built in the more expansive *Teseida*. Like Boccaccio, Chaucer adopts the form of an epic narrative as the first sign to his reader that he would refer our attentions to the epic tradition. The Knight's Tale unfolds within the four-part structure of what the medieval codices presented as a minor or smaller epic, just as Boccaccio had given his narrative the formal characteristics of a twelve-book epic. In condensing, Chaucer focused on the theme of fraternal strife and Boccaccio's recapitulation of *Thebaid* 1–6, cutting most heavily from those portions of the *Teseida* that surround the main action. He also reduced the verbal echoes of Statius's poem, which Boccaccio had woven so densely into the fabric of his diction, heightening at the same time the allusive shape of the narrative itself. The result is an open imitation of the *Thebaid* that is somewhat less literary than the

Teseida, requiring its readers to know only the general shape and legendary subject of Statius's narrative rather than the language of his poetry. In terms of the Servian prologue to the *Thebaid,* Chaucer's narrative alludes to a historical pattern rather than to its literary elaboration. And in this regard, one cannot fail to note that Chaucer had provided an outline of the *historia* in the *Thebaid* at the end of his *Troilus,* where Cassandra summarizes the history of the Theban War in the manner of medieval verse arguments to the classical epic. As was his practice elsewhere, Chaucer had prepared his original audience to understand the allusions of his narrative structure without recourse to bookish glosses.[29]

The critical terms of the Servian *metrum heroicum* are useful for defining the Knight's Tale just as they are for the *Teseida.* While Chaucer's poem should be defined with reference to epic tradition, it cannot properly be called an "epic" or a "mock" epic. Its relation to the classical poems is not primarily rhetorical, having to do with the way the subject is presented, though Chaucer does draw on epic conventions and make some use of high diction or *grandiloquium.* The smaller Knight's Tale is not constructed around a constrast between high diction and low subject matter, as mock epics are; it is not a "Rape of the Lock" or an "Abduction of the Pail" in which distinctly trivial characters and events are presented by means of grossly disproportionate epic machinery.[30] But the poem's design may be defined with reference to classical epic narrative as its formal characteristics were described in the medieval prologues, that is to say a mixture of "fictional" gods and "historical" human characters. Chaucer, following Boccaccio, makes his foreground narrative move like a historical background, presenting an analogue to that history. The result is not properly an epic narrative, but an epic narrative revisited, a transformation of a specific heroic action. The form gives the poet a great deal of freedom in dealing with the historical exempla, not the least of which is the freedom to treat them in a mixed register and with a greater measure of humor than the rhetorical conventions of classical epic poetry—or for that matter historical writing—would allow. It makes possible the translation of legendary events of great political importance into a story in which the emphasis is entirely on the moral or, as we might say, private causes of those events. The epic background is there to underscore the political implications of this smaller history.

Chaucer's fictional analogues present their historical subjects largely shorn of political complications, focusing instead on the private choices that are made and the ethical, rather than political, consequences to which they lead. Political consequences are, of course, present by implication, because the fictions are analogous to historical events. Indeed,

political implications must be present in any example of aristocratic behavior in the literature of a hierarchical society like Chaucer's England,
where the personal affairs of the ruling class so often have immediate
effects on the society it governs. This association is clear in the writings
on the education of princes, which begin with ethics as the basis of "politics." This shift of focus to the more universal, moral issues of historical
events from the local, political ones, comes about largely as a result of
Boccaccio's genial analogy: Generalizing somewhat, we might say that
Chaucer's fictions transform the *metrum heroicum* in that they analyze
historical subjects in terms of human actions motivated by love. In doing
so, Chaucer reflects the medieval commonplace that history is useful as a
repository of moral exempla, to be discussed in moral terms. Moral
terms, then, are to be explained with reference to love. In other words,
Chaucer's recasting of Statius is not an "aesthetic" or literary response to
the *Thebaid* so much as a historical interpretation of a prominent series
of characters and events in the ancient past, a reinterpretation made in
terms of fourteenth-century moral philosophy and the Christian vision of
universal history.

    There is a revealing correspondence between Chaucer's treatment of
Theban fraternal strife in the Knight's Tale and Gower's analysis of the
"divisioun" of ancient empires in his *Confessio*. Gower describes at some
length the effects of division in the succession of ancient empires, including, of course, Thebes and Troy. He states his thesis in rather simple Orosian terms and then adduces examples from both sacred and profane
history to support his case. Following Orosius, whose *Historia contra
paganos* was influential especially in historical writing that concerned itself with ancient history, Gower says that either the sin of a people leads
to division, whence self-destruction soon springs, or God punishes the
sinners: in either case, the fall of a city or empire is the result of moral
choices on the part of its citizens. Gower's chief biblical example is the
Hebrew nation:

> Behold the people of Israel:
> For everewhil they deden wel
> Fortune was hem debonaire,
> And whan thei deden the contraire,
> Fortune was contrariende.   (prologue, 551–555)[31]

The key word throughout Gower's Orosian view of history is "divisioun," or the turning of a house against itself:

> And that [i.e., the Bible] as in conclusioun
> Seith that upon divisioun
> Stant, why no worldes thing mai laste,
> Til it be drive to the laste.
> And fro the ferste regne of alle
> Unto this day. (prologue, 575–580)

"Divisioun" is itself a kind of emblem for sin. It is Gower's shorthand explanation for the continual overthrow of great kingdoms because of the sin of their people. Typological association of one ancient kingdom with another is implicit throughout Gower's analysis, as it is in his patristic and medieval sources. Each city-empire, beginning with Babylon, repeats the pattern of a rise to power in times of personal virtue and political unity, followed by a decline caused by selfishness and the resulting "divisioun." Among the more recent examples Gower cites are Rome (714–768; 830–850) and its successor the Frankish kingdom (769–783); he also sees ominous signs of decline and division in the present day (851ff.). He concludes his review of these fallen empires by explaining "divisioun" in terms of love, which is to say simply that he restates his essentially moral analysis of the "succession of empires" in terms of human motivation:

> And this men sen, thurgh lack of love
> Where as the lond divided is
> It mot algate fare amis. (prologue, 892–894)

A lack of well-directed love, or charity, has caused the succession of "Babylonian" empires to fall. Nor is the message of history without current application:

> And now to loke on every side,
> A man may se the world divide,
> The werres ben so general
> Among the cristene overal,
> That every man now secheth wreche,
> And yet these clerkes alday preche
> And sein, good dede may non be
> Which stant noght upon charite. (prologue, 894–902)

The "world," in Gower's view, was not paying attention to history or the clerks and was headed for a fall.

Like his friend Gower, Chaucer presents the cause of "divisioun" in terms of love, but he does so with reference to only one ancient kingdom and two representatives of its royal house. This perspective allows him to explore the subject in a much less mechanical way than Gower had, even while his historical perspective is based on similar premises. Gower's "divisioun" and Chaucer's fraternal strife both reflect concern with the exemplary value of history, but Chaucer's "history" is presented indirectly, by means of a fictional analogue to the "divisioun" at Thebes at the time of the sons of Oedipus.

Gower's "divisioun" and Chaucer's Theban strife both reflect the tradition of historical writing associated with Orosius's teacher, St. Augustine, and his analysis of Babylonian and Roman history in *De civitate Dei*. It was Augustine, primus inter pares, who established "fratricide" as a central motif in historical analysis and as an emblem of Babylonian cupidity. *De civitate Dei* identifies in Cain and Abel, and then again in Romulus and Remus, type and archetype of that internal "divisioun" which characterizes the succession of empires that stretches from Babylon to Rome:

> The first founder of the earthly city was, as we have seen a fratricide; for, overcome by envy, [Cain] slew his own brother, a citizen of the Eternal City, on pilgrimage in this world. Hence it is no wonder that long afterwards this first precedent—what the Greeks call an archetype—was answered by a kind of reflection, by an event of the same kind at the founding of [Rome]. . . . For there, as one of their poets says when he mentions the crime, "Those walls were dripping with a brother's blood." For this is how Rome was founded, when Remus, as Roman history witnesses, was slain by his brother Romulus. The difference from the primal crime was that both brothers were citizens of the earthly city.   (*De civitate Dei*, 15.5)[32]

This passage not only identifies fraternal strife with the archetypical, "Babylonian" city-empire, but does so with reference to classical epic, Lucan's *De bello civili,* which opens with a reference to Romulus and Remus, and other examples of internecine struggle in Roman history, as prologue to the "divisioun" of Rome during the civil wars. Augustine takes Lucan's subject and draws it into the larger, analytical framework of his historical vision. By fastening on the motif of division and particularly of fraternal strife, Chaucer and Gower reflect something of that historical vision as well, which presents ancient history not only in terms of decline and division, but in terms of love. Augustine defines the citizen of a "Babylonian" or divisive city as a lover: "These two cities [Babylon and

Jerusalem] are formed by two loves: Love of God forms Jerusalem; love of the world, Babylon. Therefore, if you ask what people love, you will discover where they are citizens."[33]

Palamon and Arcite, of course, do not live in Babylon. They come from Thebes. But Augustine's "Babylon" is an abstract type to which historical cities are seen to conform, instead of a single historical city. His analysis of history in terms of the "Babylonian" city and its citizens in terms of love certainly stands behind Orosius and later Gower. To the extent that Chaucer, in writing about Palamon and Arcite, thought of himself as writing about a historical subject, it may well have influenced him also. It is a kind of selfish love or desire to possess Emelye that leads them to their own "divisioun" and to renounce their familial and chivalric obligations to each other. It would have led to their destruction and the end of the Theban royal line as well, had not Theseus come upon them and exercised his just and merciful control for their benefit.

Chaucer's open imitation of the *Thebaid*, or specifically the *historia* in the *Thebaid*, also casts a suggestive light on the position of the Knight's Tale at the beginning of fragment A of the *Canterbury Tales*. Cutting Boccaccio's first two books, as he does, in order to return to the frame narrative at *Thebaid* 12.519ff., Chaucer begins his sequence of tales with a pagan type of the church and with figures of pilgrims, dressed in mourning, who have sought refuge at a kind of national shrine. The Argive widows explain to Theseus:

> And certes, lord, to abyden youre presence,
> Heere in this temple of the goddesse Clemence
> We han been waitynge al this fourtenyght.
> Now help us, lord, sith it is in thy might.   (927–930)

In the account of the Argive widows' journey from Thebes to Athens and the altar of Clemency there is a figure of a pilgrimage by a bereaved nation like that of the Canterbury pilgrims themselves; in the "ire and iniquitee" of Creon, which made their pilgrimage necessary, a shadow of those "Babylonian" forces of division that will be so evident among the Canterbury pilgrims and in the contemporary society their later tales will represent.

It has often been noted that narrative analogy constitutes one of the distinctive features in the first sequence of these tales, which go from the rivals of the Knight's Tale to those of the Miller's Tale and the Reeve's Tale.[34] Each tale develops the theme and narrative motifs of the one preceding it, translating them into a different setting and level of diction. The humor in both of the narratives following the Knight's depends in part on the reader's knowledge of these broadly parodic relations, which is to say some knowledge of the pattern of events in the Knight's Tale. It is usually assumed that the Knight's Tale establishes this pattern of action and that Chaucer cannot use the allusive technique in the first tale itself. But in the longer perspective that acknowledges the imitative nature of Boccaccio's *Teseida,* the sequence of analogical narratives in fragment A may be seen to extend back to the history of Thebes as told in the *Thebaid,* and the technique itself can be attributed to Boccaccio. The sequence of analogies begins before the Knight's Tale. Chaucer's translation of the rivalry for the hand of Emelye into the rivalry for the embraces of Alisoun in the Miller's Tale has an important antecedent in Boccaccio's writings as well. In *Decameron* 7.10, Boccaccio transposes his story of Palamon and Arcite into the popular quarter of Siena, where Emilia's role is taken by a married "donna vaga" named Mita, for whose affections two sworn friends, Tingoccio and Meuccio, find themselves in competition. The first to win, Tingoccio, dies shortly after attaining his bliss, apparently because of his overindulgence. The analogous pattern of events in the *Teseida* is explicitly recalled in Boccaccio's frame story, when Dioneo, who has told the tale, and Fiammetta (of course!) sing "for a long time of Arcite and Palamon." Although there are no verbal echoes of *Decameron* 7.10 in the Miller's Tale, it is tempting to conclude that Chaucer gathered his strategy for imitating the Knight's Tale in the Miller's Tale from the rich fields of Boccaccio's works, just as he adopted Boccaccio's strategy for imitating Statius in the Knight's Tale itself.

Finally, the open imitation of the *Thebaid* in the Knight's Tale adds an important piece to our picture of the influence Boccaccio's learned and classicizing poetry had on the development of Chaucer's art. It has often been noted that Chaucer was largely responsible for introducing the formal simile into English literary tradition and that he followed the precedent of *volgarizzamento* or vernacularization of the classical forms in the works of Dante and Boccaccio.[35] The similes in Boccaccio's vernacular poetry are characteristically learned, in the sense that their vehicles present a vast assortment of allusion to classical myth and history, often demanding quite precise knowledge on the part of the reader who would match the vehicle to its tenor in a way that reveals their similarity. Moreover, Boccaccio extended the technique of the learned simile to the creation of analogous narrative structures, recalling the *Thebaid* in the characters and events of the *Teseida,* the beginning of the *Commedia* in the *Amorosa visione,* and the Trojan narratives in the *Filostrato.*[36] Chaucer is considerably less demanding in his allusions, though he was not beyond offering an occasional teaser, as we have seen in the references to the genealogy of Palamon and Arcite. He is also more sparing in his use of the formal simile itself. But the extension of the learned comparison to narrative structures is highly characteristic of Chaucer's art, and it clearly developed together with his interest in the works of Boccaccio.

The technique appears as early as the *Book of the Duchess*, written in or just after 1369 and generally thought to precede Chaucer's contact with Italian literature.[37] Here, as in the later *Parliament of Fowles*, Chaucer modifies the traditional French model of the dream vision by introducing a classical narrative as prologue. In both poems, he describes the dreamer as reading an "olde book" before falling asleep and gives a summary of the book's contents, the Ovidian "Seyx and Alcione" in the first instance, and Cicero's "Dream of Scipio" in the second. The events narrated in the book and the following dream do not have the same structure, but the juxtaposition invites comparison of their similar themes. In the Wife of Bath's Tale, the story of Midas is introduced and then concluded abruptly with the admonition that the audience "reede Ovide" to learn more. And here too the classical narrative—its themes are deafness and avarice—would seem to have metaphorical application to the Chaucerian foreground.[38] Beside these works in which narratives are juxtaposed, the allusive narrative structure of the Knight's Tale appears to be no more than a variation on a characteristic procedure, borrowed from Boccaccio and adjusted so that the allusions depend less on verbal echoes and more on the shape of the narrative structure itself. Here the classical story is not told but recreated and transformed in a similar sequence of characters and events. It is a variation on Chaucer's earlier procedure for exploring the themes of "olde bookes" by juxtaposition; and it is a variation learned from Boccaccio. Chaucer uses it in the *Troilus*, where his immediate source is again one of Boccaccio's poems, and where the foreground moves like the background of Trojan history, and finally in the Nun's Priest's Tale, where the foreground narrative moves to the pattern of the temptation and fall at the beginning of human history, but recasts it in a thoroughly mock-heroic scale and tone.

Notes to Chapter 4

1. J. Burke Severs reflects the general consensus when he considers *Troilus* and the Knight's Tale among "The Tales of Romance," in *Companion to Chaucer Studies*, ed. Beryl Rowland (New York: Oxford University Press, 1968), pp. 229–246, but warns of the "great variety of medieval narratives which have traditionally been embraced by the term 'romance.'" On medieval definitions of "romance" as a genre (or the lack of them), see the

excellent articles by Derek Pearsall, "The Development of Middle English Romance," *Medieval Studies* 27 (1965): 91–116; and J. C. Payen, *Le Roman*, Typologie des sources du Moyen Âge occidental 12 (Turnhout: Brepols, 1975), pp. 19–29. For a modern definition of the form employed by Chaucer, see Robert M. Jordan, "Chaucerian Romance?" *Yale French Studies* 51 (1974): 223–234. For another generic model, see C. David Benson, "The Knight's Tale as History," *Chaucer Review* 3 (1968): 108–119, which argues that the poem aligns itself with no single generic tradition, but "contains much of the feel and many of the techniques of the . . . chronicle." See also Paul Strohm, "Some Generic Distinctions in the *Canterbury Tales*," *Modern Philology* 68 (1971): 321–328; and idem, "Storie, Spelle, Geste, Romaunce, Tragedie: Generic Distinctions in the Middle English Troy Narratives," *Speculum* 46 (1971): 348–359.

2. Norman Davis et al., *A Chaucer Glossary* (Oxford: Clarendon, 1979) lists three occurrences in addition to those in the Chaucerian translation of the *Roman de la Rose*. See also Jordan, "Chaucerian Romance?" p. 223. The word "romaunce" in *Troilus* 2.100 would seem to refer to a specific work, the *Roman de Thèbes*, a translation or adaptation of the *Thebaid*.

3. Compare Payen's remarks, *Le Roman*, p. 23: "C'est souvent au critique moderne de déterminer si une oeuvre médiévale doit être classée ou non parmi les romans, en fonction et de sa forme et de sa matière. Il y a des critères assez sûrs, mais aucun ne saurait être considéré comme infaillible."

4. See Violetta de Angelis, "Magna Questio proposita coram Dante et Domino Francisco Petrarca et Virgiliano," *Studi petrarcheschi* n.s. 1 (1984): 42–49 on four divisions, and again at 169ff. Interestingly enough, the related debates over the divisions of the work and its state of completion did not necessarily associate the larger number of subdivisions with completion: "anzi le testimonianze che ci pervengono sono nella maggioranza dei casi a favore della compresenza dei due fatti . . . divisione in cinque libri, la più frequente, e morte dell'autore anteriormente alla conslusione dell'opera" (p. 172).

5. de Angelis, "Magna Questio," pp. 155–169 and 175–178 on the Tuscan associations of the debate. Biographies of Chaucer have generally considered his journeys to Italy in light of his translations from works by Dante, Boccaccio, and Petrarch, speculating on his possible encounters with the two latter figures. But his interests would certainly have led him to the company of now less famous teachers of the Latin classics and men of letters associated with the first generations of Italian humanism and the new stir of attention to classical poetry that had followed wherever Petrarch went.

6. I quote from the 1602 edition (STC 5080), *The Workes of our ancient and learned English Poet, Geffrey Chaucer* (London: Adam Islip, 1602), fol. 1. The entire descriptive heading reads as follows: "Palamon and Arcite, a paire of friends and fellow prisoners, fight a combat before Duke Theseus, for the ladie Emelie, sister to the queene Ipolita wife of Theseus. A Tale fitting the person of a Knight, for that it discourseth of the deeds of Armes, and love of Ladies." Ariosto's chiasmic expansion of Vergil's "Arma virumque" had been translated by Sir John Harrington as "Of Dames, of Knights, of armes, of love's delight" (1591).

7. Thomas Morell, ed. *The Canterbury Tales of Chaucer* (London: J. Osborn, 1737), p. 71.

8. Ibid.

9. Thomas Tyrwhitt, ed. *The Canterbury Tales of Chaucer,* 5 vols. (London: T. Payne, 1775–1778), vol. 4, pp. 132–134.

10. The passages are given in James P. Hart, Jr., "Thomas Tyrwhitt (1730–1786) as Annotator and Glossarist of Fragment A of the *Canterbury Tales,* and His Editorial Relations" (Ph.D. diss., University of Pennsylvania, 1971), p. 18 n. 2, with detailed discussion.

11. W. P. Ker, "Chaucer and the Renaissance," printed in Ker's *Form and Style in Poetry* (London: Macmillan, 1928), pp. 64–79; quotation from p. 71. Part of the essay is reprinted in *Geoffrey Chaucer,* Penguin Critical Anthologies, ed. J. A. Burrow (Harmondsworth: Penguin, 1969), pp. 104–111.

12. Robert A. Pratt, "Chaucer's Use of the *Teseida,*" *PMLA* 62 (1947): 598–621; Natalino Sapegno, *Storia letteraria del Trecento* (Milan: Ricciardi, 1958), esp. pp. 286–296. Pratt cites Sapegno in the edition of 1938 ("Chaucer's Use," p. 599, n. 2). For earlier studies of the Knight's Tale and the *Teseida,* see p. 613 n. 58.

13. Pratt, "Chaucer's Use," p. 602.

14. See especially Vittore Branca, "Schemi letterari e schemi autobiografici nell'opera del Boccaccio," *Bibliofilia* 49 (1947): 1–40; for a survey of the scholarship since 1947, Robert Hollander, *Boccaccio's Two Venuses* (New York: Columbia University Press, 1977), pp. 126–127 and 167.

15. Piero Boitani, *Chaucer and Boccaccio* (Oxford: Blackwell, 1977), p. 10.

16. Pratt, "Chaucer's Use," p. 614: "It is well known that Chaucer commenced this rivalry of the lovers sooner than Boccaccio and that he rejected all elements of plot which did not bear upon this central theme. For example, the first two books of the *Teseida,* telling of Theseus's epic conquests, are severely abbreviated, only enough being preserved to bring Emelye, Palamon, and Arcite on the scene, and the detailed epic battles of Book VIII are condensed into a swift and lively skirmish. Thus by a process of careful selection and revision, Chaucer concentrated his narrative on the single theme of rivalry, and only after Arcite's fatal accident does the story as such tend to drag."

    On the Knight's Tale as a narrative in the tradition of epic poetry, see Robert A. Haller, "The *Knight's Tale* and the Epic Tradition," *Chaucer Review* 1 (1966): 67–84; Paul A. Olson, "Chaucer's Epic Statement and the Political Milieu of the Late Fourteenth Century," *Mediaevalia* 5 (1979): 61–65; and now idem, *Chaucer's Canterbury Tales and the Good Society* (Princeton: Princeton University Press, 1986), pp. 61–62. R. W. Hanning, "The Struggle Between Noble Design and Chaos: The Literary Tradition of Chaucer's *Knight's Tale,*" *Literary Review* 23 (1980): 519–541.

17. *Teseida* 2.18–84; Knight's Tale A. 859–1,004. On Boccaccio's use of *Thebaid* 12 as the basis for this passage, see above, Chapter 3, pp. 160–166. It is a part of the Knight's Tale in which Chaucer has frequent direct recourse to the *Thebaid* for his verbal materials. See Boyd A. Wise, *The Influence of Statius upon Chaucer* (Baltimore: Furst, 1911); and Paul M. Clogan, "Chaucer's Use of the *Thebaid,*" *English Miscellany* 18 (1967):

9–31. See also Walter Scheps, "Chaucer's Theseus and the *Knight's Tale*," *Leeds Studies in English* 9 (1976–1977): 19–34.

18.   See above, Chapter 1, pp. 68–70.

19.   I have discussed the location of the temple in "The Fourth Temple of the Knight's Tale: Athenian Clemency and Chaucer's Theseus," in *Studies in the Age of Chaucer: Proceedings*, vol. 2 (Knoxville, Tenn.: New Chaucer Society, 1987), pp. 113–125.

20.   Haller, "The *Knight's Tale*," discusses the simile, the apostrophe, and their classical sources and analogues. See also above, Chapter 1, pp. 45–50.

21.   Pratt, "Chaucer's Use," pp. 613, 615; and Boitani, *Chaucer and Boccaccio*, pp. 135–137.

22.   The following argument also appears in David Anderson, "Theban Genealogy in the *Knight's Tale*," *Chaucer Review* 21 (1987): 311–320.

23.   Chaucer's sources for this definition of "gentilesse" are *De consolatione Philosophiae* 3 prose 6 and meter 6; *Roman de la Rose* 18,670–18,896; and especially Dante's *Convivio* 4.3. The contrast between figurative and literal descent is a prominent topic in medieval Christian writings, beginning with St. Paul and St. Augustine. See D. W. Robertson, Jr., *A Preface to Chaucer* (Princeton: Princeton University Press, 1962), pp. 375–376.

24.   At the end of his speech of consolation, Chaucer's Theseus turns first to Emelye (3,075–3,089) to propose the marriage, and then, briefly, to Palamon: "I trowe ther nedeth litel sermonyng / To make yow assente to this thing" (3,091–3,092). This is notably different from the *Teseida*, where Teseo and Palemone speak to each other at some length (12.20–37) before Teseo turns briefly to Emilia: "Emilia, hai tu udito? / Quel ch'io vo' farai che sia fornito" (12.38). Chaucer's Theseus uses the genealogical reference to persuade, where Boccaccio's Teseo simply commands.

25.   In *Thebaid* 3.286; ed. Richard Jahnke (Leipzig: Teubner, 1898), p. 157.

26.   "Dicitur enim cum eo concubuisse," ed. Jahnke, p. 463.

27.   Cf. Man of Law's Tale, "Introduction," lines 77–90.

28.   In the *Siege of Thebes*, Lydgate refers to them as brothers: "Lygurgus . . . / He was the same myghty Champioun, / To Athenes that kam with Palamoun / Ageyne his brother that called was Arcyte" (ed. Axel Erdmann, Early English Text Society ex. ser. 108 [Oxford: Oxford University Press, 1911], lines 3,521–3,525).

29.   Francis P. Magoun, "Chaucer's Summary of Statius' *Thebaid*," *Traditio* 11 (1955): 409–420.

30.   Following Aubrey Williams's observations on Pope's *Dunciad* and the *Aeneid* (*Pope's Dunciad: A Study of its Meaning* [London and Baton Rouge: Louisiana State University Press, 1955]), we may note that the Chaucerian transformation of the *metrum heroicum* shares one feature of the best mock epics, namely, the exploitation of those serious overtones that arise when trivial events recapitulate an epic action. But the events of the Knight's Tale are not really trivial. They fall in a middle range between low comedy and high epic seriousness, as I have argued in Chapter 2, with reference to the *Teseida*.

31.   On typology in the succession of world empires, see Jean Danielou, *From Shadows to Reality: Studies in the Biblical Typology of the Fathers*,

trans. Wulstan Hibberd (London: Burns, Oates, and Washbourne, 1960);
Robert W. Hanning, *The Vision of History in Early Britain* (New York
and London: Columbia University Press, 1966); and Henri Marrou, "S.
Augustin et l'augustinisme historique," in *La Storiografia altomedievale,* 2
vols. (Spoleto: Centro italiano di studi sull'alto medioevo 1970), vol. 1,
pp. 59–87. Quotations from *The English Works of John Gower,* ed. G. C.
Macaulay, Early English Text Society ex. ser. 81.1 (Oxford: Oxford University Press, 1900).

32. I quote from the translation of Henry Bettenson, *Augustine: Concerning
     the City of God Against the Pagans,* ed. David Knowles (London: Penguin,
     1972), p. 600. Beryl Smalley's comment in *Historians in the Middle Ages*
     (London: Thames and Hudson, 1974) that *De civitate Dei* "was too long
     and rambling to share the immense popularity of his other works. . . . It
     influenced medieval historians through the distorting medium of Augustine's disciple Orosius" (p. 44), would seem to regard those centuries before the twelfth, which are Smalley's main concern in that book. John
     Taylor, *The Universal Chronicle of Ranulf Higden* (Oxford: Clarendon
     1966), states the case for the fourteenth century: "If Eusebius provided universal history with its chronology, Augustine (354–430) supplied it with
     its philosophy" (p. 34). As Smalley herself shows in *English Friars and Antiquity in the Early Fourteenth Century* (Oxford: Blackwell, 1960), the
     English friars Thomas Waleys and John Ridevall wrote an extensive commentary on the work in that century, as did François de Meyronnes and
     Raoul de Praelles in France (see Alexandre de Laborde, *Les Manuscrits à
     peintures de la Cité di Dieu de Saint Augustin,* 3 vols. [Paris: Société des
     bibliophiles 1909]).

33. I translate from Augustine's sermon on Psalm 64:2, *Enarrationes in Psalmos,* Corpus christianorum, series latina 39 (Turnhout: Brepols, 1956),
     col. 823. Cf. *De civitate Dei* 14.28: "In [the Babylonian city] the lust for
     domination lords it over its princes as over the nations it subjugates; in
     [cities which reflect the archetypical City of God] both those put in authority and those subject to them serve one another in love, the rulers by
     their counsel, the subjects by obedience" (trans. Bettenson, p. 593).

34. In addition to the bibliographical notes on thematic unity in fragment I in
     Larry D. Benson, gen. ed. *The Riverside Chaucer* (Boston: Houghton
     Mifflin, 1987), p. 731, see the delightful account of Chaucer's repetition of
     themes and motifs in the tales of the Knight, Miller and Reeve, in Paul A.
     Olson, *Chaucer's Canterbury Tales and the Good Society,* pp. 70–84.

35. W. P. Ker, in "Chaucer and Scottish Chaucerians," remarked that "Dante
     was the first poet to imitate in a modern language the classical use of simile.
     Chaucer is the first English poet to use the epic simile and he seems to have
     taken the suggestion not from Virgil and Ovid but from Dante and from
     Boccaccio, who copied Dante" (*Form and Style,* p. 69; cf. pp. 251–253).
     Useful remarks on the Chaucerian simile may be found in Stephen Knight,
     Rymyng Craftily: Meaning in Chaucer's Poetry (London: Angus and Robertson, 1973), p. 17.

36. See above, Chapter 1, pp. 57–65.

37. Usually dated 1369, but possibly composed as late as 1374. See D. W.

Robertson, Jr., "The Historical Setting of Chaucer's Book of the Duchess," first published in 1965; reprinted in the Robertson's *Essays in Medieval Culture* (Princeton: Princeton University Press, 1980), pp. 235–256. As Howard Schless has recently suggested, there is good reason to believe that Chaucer had some familiarity with Italian literature before his journey to Italy in 1372–1373 (*Chaucer and Dante* [Norman: Pilgrim Books, 1984], chap. 1).

38.   Judson B. Allen and Patrick Gallacher, "Alisoun Through the Looking Glass: Or Every Man his own Midas," *Chaucer Review* 4 (1970): 99–105; D. W. Robertson, Jr., "The Wife of Bath and Midas," *Studies in the Age of Chaucer*, 6 (1984): 1–20. On parallels associating Troy and Troilus, see John P. McCall, "The Trojan Scene in Chaucer's *Troilus*," *ELH* 29 (1962): 263–275; on narrative analogy in the NPT, Mortimer J. Donovan, "The Moralitee of the Nun's Priest's Sermon," *JEGP* 52 (1953): 498–508. The observation that Chaucer's use of classical sources often involves allusive transformation has been nicely stated by Winthrop Wetherbee: "One distinguishing trait of his use of these *auctores* is the tendency to make specific references the occasion for larger structural and theoretic analogies," in "Convention and Authority: A Comment on Some Recent Critical Approaches to Chaucer," *New Perspectives in Chaucer Criticism*, ed. Donald Rose (Norman: Pilgrim Books, 1981), p. 80. Chaucer's learned allusions are discussed as a feature of poetic diction in C. David Benson, *Chaucer's Drama of Style* (Chapel Hill: University of North Carolina Press, 1986).

APPENDIXES

The late-classical commentary on Statius's *Thebaid* attributed to Lactantius Placidus, which circulated widely until the sixteenth century and which provided the basis for most of the line-by-line commentaries compiled in the later medieval period, has no *accessus* or introduction comparable to the prologue in Servius's commentary on the *Aeneid*. At least by the twelfth century, however, prologues to the *Thebaid* had been composed under the influence of the Servian model and other general models for prologues to authoritative texts. Surviving examples of these prologues to the *Thebaid* present a certain variety in detail organized by the stable outline of the conventional topics, beginning with "author" and "title."

Appendixes 1 and 2 contain two such prologues. The first and shorter of the two circulated as early as the twelfth century and survives in manuscripts from thirteenth-century England and fifteenth-century Italy as well as northern continental Europe. The second, found in only one manuscript, offers a striking example of the way the contents of the older prologue could be recast and augmented by a learned writer with access to mythographies and other reference books. It was probably compiled by a *magister grammaticae* in Padua in the later fourteenth or early fifteenth century.

Although it cannot be shown that Boccaccio or Chaucer knew either of these texts, it is only reasonable to assume that both poets were familiar with prologues of this kind and with the traditional definitions of epic poetry articulated in them. Both writers probably encountered teachers' introductions of this sort during their early, formal education.

Appendix 3 gives a transcription of manuscript Plut. 38.6 of the Laurenziana, folio 100r, with Boccaccio's glosses (see Plate 1).

Appendix 1: "In principio uniuscuiusque actoris"

Introduction

The *accessus* to the *Thebaid* beginning "In principio uniuscuiusque
a(u)ctoris" survives in four copies, one from the later twelfth century, two
from the thirteenth, and one from the early fifteenth century. The three
older copies vary considerably as to the text of the prologue, with one,
the manuscript now in Leiden, presenting a severely edited version. In all
four manuscripts, the *accessus* is followed by a line-by-line commentary
based on that of Lactantius and appearing as an independent "continuous commentary," that is, without an accompanying text of the *Thebaid*.

The manuscripts share several other characteristics that may reveal
something of the common archetype. Two of the three older copies are of
northern European provenance, while the third is certainly English and
the fifteenth-century copy is from northern Italy. All three early copies
appear in anthologies with other commentaries on classical Latin poetry,
and in two instances (London and Berlin) these anthologies also contain
the commentary on Vergil's *Aeneid* sometimes ascribed to Anselm of
Laon, a work with which our *accessus* has certain affinities of style and
terminology, including a common reliance on Servius. There is no modern edition of "Anselm" on the *Aeneid,* but many manuscript copies of
the work have been identified, and although the evidence for the author's
name is very weak, there is good reason to believe that it originated in
northern France in the twelfth century. The same may be the case here,
though the evidence for associating "In principio" with "Anselm" on the
Aeneid must be qualified by the observation that the anthologies in which
the commentaries appear together, though certainly gathered in the medieval period, nevertheless contain texts in several hands copied at different
times and places.

The four manuscripts of "In principio" are as follows:

1. Designated "B." West Berlin, Deutsche Staatsbibliothek, Stiftung
    Preussischer Kulturbesitz, MS lat. 2° fol. 34. Parchment; written
    in two columns; late twelfth or early thirteenth century.
    A miscellany of three sections probably of the same origin, per-
    haps from France. The *accessus* and commentary, without a title
    but headed "Sancti spiritus adsit nobis gratia," occupies fols.
    86r–114r. Immediately following it are several short composi-
    tions, including the metrical "Planctus Oedipi."
    Description: Valentin Rose, *Verzeichniss der lateinischen*

Handschriften der Königlichen Bibliothek, 3 vols. (Berlin: As-
cher, 1883–1919), vol. 2.3 (1905), entry 1016, pp. 1304–1308.
See also Robert D. Sweeney, *Prolegomena to an Edition of the
Scholia to Statius* (Leiden: Brill, 1969), p. 22, written while the
manuscript was still on deposit in Tübingen; Birger Munk Olsen,
L'Étude des auteurs classiques latins aux XIe et XIIe siècles, vol. 2
(Paris: CNRS, 1985), p. 563.

2. Designated "L." Leiden, University Library, MS B.P.L. 191A.
Parchment; written in two columns; thirteenth century. A miscellany from the library of the abbey of St. Jacques at Liège.

The *accessus* and commentary are headed with the prayer
"Sancti spiritus adsit nobis gratia," to which a later hand has
added "Glose super Stacium Thebaidos," once at the top of the
first page, once at the bottom of the first column on the same page.
Prologue and commentary occupy fols. 214r–238r of the manuscript, coming at the end of a discrete section (fols. 144–238) that
was copied by two hands and that contains glosses on Lucan's
Bellum civile, a mythography, and, following the commentary on
the *Thebaid,* a copy of the metrical "Planctus Oedipi."

Description: *Bibliotheca universitatis leidensis, codices manu-
scripti,* vol. 3, *Codices bibliothecae publicae latini* (Leiden: Brill,
1912), pp. 92–94. See also Sweeney, *Prolegomena,* pp. 20–21.

3. Designated "Add." London, British Library, Additional MS
16,380. Parchment; thirteenth century. A miscellany, with sections of different format. The portion containing the *accessus* and
commentary on the *Thebaid* is copied in two columns. Marginal
notations elsewhere in the manuscript associate it with Canterbury Cathedral and perhaps Rochester Priory.

Accessus and commentary (fols. 144r–179r) have been given
the title "In Thebaida Statij" by a late hand; the original scribe
has written the prayer "Sancti spiritus adsit mihi gratia" at the
top of the first page and has also added, in the bottom margin
below the first column, "Super Stacium Thebaidos."

Description: Christopher Baswell, "'Figures of Olde Werk':
Visions of Virgil in Later Medieval England" (Ph.D. diss., Yale
University, 1983), app. 2, pp. 362–363. See also *Additions to the
Manuscripts of the British Museum 1846–1847* (London: 1864),
pp. 184–185; Sweeney, *Prolegomena,* p. 21; and R. W. Hunt,
"Studies on Priscian in the Twelfth Century," *Medieval and Re-
naissance Studies* 2 (1950): 12–43.

4. Designated "R." Florence, Biblioteca Riccardiana, MS 842 (*olim*

M III 2). Paper; ii + 117 fols.; early fifteenth century. *Accessus* and commentary on the *Thebaid*. Text in two columns.

An informal manuscript on paper like the one described below, Appendix 2. Except for a few lines in textualis at the beginning of the *accessus*, the script is cancelleresca, with current duct and great variation in letter size and spacing between lines. The bifolia and their gatherings have been mended and recomposed, leaving the collation as follows: A^{10} B^8 C^{12} D^8 E^{18} F^{12} G^8 H^{12} I^4 K^8 L^{6+1} (parchment) M^4 N^6. The last leaf in quire L, parchment, a bifolium from a smaller manuscript with musical notation, was probably employed as the guard leaf before Riccardiana 842 was rebound. The watermarks in the quires preceding the parchment leaf are A–F and L: flower and leaf (Piccard, *Blume* 1421–1431) and G–K: duck (close to Briquet *oiseau* 12098–12099). The reappearance of the flower-and-leaf watermark in L, the quire carrying the end of the commentary on the *Thebaid*, along with the general continuity of text and script at the juncture of quires F and G, leave little room to doubt that quires A–L make up a single copy of the *accessus* and commentary. To this manuscript quires M and N were added (watermark: Oxhead surmounted by a flower, close to Piccard, *Ochsenkopf*, XII, nos. 174–188). They contain a fragment of continuous commentary on *Thebaid* 3.14ff. Probably at the same time, the bifolia were mended and blank leaves (those in G have the duck watermark) were added in several gatherings: B 5–8 = fols. 15–18; G 6–8 = fols. 74–76; N 4–6. The foliation is modern, but an early "99" appears on L6 = fol. 106r, apparently reflecting the number of folios before the blank leaves were added to quires B and G.

The watermarks in the original codex (A–L) indicate an origin in northern Italy ca. 1410–1420; that in M–N northern Italy 1420–1450.

Title: 3r (= A1), "in nomine dei amen / Statii commentaria" and the single word "oratio" left at the top of the same page after trimming.

Description: I have given a fuller description of this codex than the others because no other is available in print. See also Sweeney, *Prolegomena*, p. 20.

Collation of the four texts suggests that B and L are more closely related to each other than to Add or R, an affiliation apparent despite the abbreviated nature of L. Among the readings shared only by Add and R, the most striking are additions at two points: first, after "Sursulus" in the prologue, where Add and R have "ut prediximus [R supradixi] dictus est quasi sursum canens [R cantus]"; and second, after "confusa domus" in the commentary, where Add and R have a long passage beginning "scilicet crudelis Edippus." Both passages are omitted in B and L. Also, Add and R share a distinctive positioning of the passage beginning "Nota tria esse," as opposed to B, while the passage is omitted in L.

Although general statements of affiliation may be made with reference to such shared features, the four copies of "In principio" do not lend themselves to a study of recension. Academic prologues to the *Thebaid* evidently did not enjoy the authority accorded the poem itself, and copyists rephrased, augmented, or abbreviated the prose texts at will. The copy of "In principio" from Liège is a severely shortened version in which the editor has also recast the order and syntax of the text, and the copies of the longer version also show instances of rephrasing and editing. The contrast between B on the one hand and Add + R on the other is the most striking, but there is also significant variation between Add and R, as for example in the passage beginning "Unde finxerunt," which is unique to Add. In many cases, the copyists must have been teachers, and these variations must reflect their personal preferences in style and emphasis.

What follows is not a critical edition of "In principio" but a diplomatic edition of the *accessus* and the beginning of the commentary in Add, normalized for punctuation and capitalization. The orthography of the manuscript has been reproduced, excepting that abbreviations have been expanded silently and the distinction between vocalic *u* and consonantal *v* has been introduced. A few obvious scribal errors have been corrected, the emended words marked by an asterisk while the manuscript reading is recorded in the notes. I have chosen Add for the edition because its provenance is English and its affiliation with R suggests that it represents a version of the *accessus* that also circulated in Italy. Neither Add nor its later relative R offers an especially careful copy of "In principio," but of the two Add must be preferred because it is earlier and on the whole resembles the text in B and L more closely than does R. Moreover, it is somewhat fuller than R, containing the passage "Unde finxerunt . . ." which does not appear in any of the other copies. I have not recorded all variants from R; rather, a light critical apparatus records variants from the B version (and, when it contains a parallel passage, the abbreviated L version) whenever B (or B and L) agrees with R against Add. That is, the critical apparatus seeks only to flag those readings in Add that seem, in light of the limited evidence, clearly to be eccentric.

[Add. 16380 144r]

In principio uniuscuiusque actoris historiographi, ut Servius testatur, hec investiganda diligenter iudicantur. Vita poete, titulus operis, qualitas carminis, intentio scribentis, modus tractandi, materia, finalis causa, quo genere stili utatur, quem actorem imitetur, cui parti philosophie* subponatur. Horum unumquodque eo ordine quo proposuimus exsequamur.* Circa vitam poete hec queri digna perhibemus, a quibus originem duxit, quibus excitavit moribus, unde sit natus, quando et ubi studuit. Legitur itaque actor iste civis tholosanus exstitisse,* nobili patre scilicet Papinio, matre vero Agilina. Burdegali et Nerbone studuit et in Gallias celeberrime rethoricam edocuit. Tandem Romam se transtulit ubi hoc opus composuit. Studuit autem tempore Vespasiani et Titi filii eius, pervenitque usque ad imperium Domiciani, qui minor Tito erat vel est dictus. Fuit igitur morum honestate preditus, acris intelligencie, tenacis memorie, clarus ingenio, doctus eloquio, liberalium artium sciencie feliciter eruditus. Fuit adeo nimie facundie ut de eo meminit Iuvenalis dicens.

> curritur ad vocem iocundam et carmen amice
> Thebaidos letam cum fecit Statius urbem
> promisitque diem. [7.82−84]

Unde et sortitus est hoc nomen Sursulus, quasi sursum canens, eo quod post Virgilium inter ceteros poetas principatum obtinuit* et popularem adeptus est favorem. Nemo enim post eum declamavit; sed opponitur quod Iuvenalis et multi alii post eum fuerant, ergo multi post eum declamaverunt. Non sequitur. Satira enim non solebat recitari. Huius libri talis est inscriptio, Sursuli* Papinii Stacii Thebaidos liber primus incipit. Sursulus ut prediximus dictus est quasi sursum canens et est agnomen. Papinius dictus est a patre et est cognomen. Stacius est proprium nomen, a statu vite sue sic dictus est. Erat enim firmus contra vicia et fortune bifformes eventus neque enim ea blandiente efferebatur, vel contumacius tonante tristis habebatur. Thebais, Thebaidos femininum est patronomi-

---

Editorial emendations in the text are marked by an asterisk, with the corresponding reading from the manuscript given here.

MS] philophie
MS] exequamur
MS] excistisse [cf. R extiterat   B tolosanus fuisse]
MS] obstinuit
MS] sursulii

cum, nomen est Thebane historie. Bene dicitur primus quod sequitur se-
cundus. Sunt enim xii^{cim} libri. Liber dicitur quasi liberans a curis, vel
liberum et expertem curarum expetens, unde Iuvenalis

> quis locus ingenio, nisi cum se carmine solo
> vexant et dominis Cirre Niseque feruntur
> pectora vostra* duas non admitencia curas. [7.63–65]

Unde finxerunt philosophi duos deos esse poetarum, Bacum et Apollinem, per Apollinem sapientiam, per Bacum innueretur temporalium*
sufficienciam. Incipit et dicit quod nil premiserat. Queritur quare tot
nomina in titulo apponantur. Respondemus, ut per ea actore commen-
dato opus reddat autenticum. Qualitas carminis metrum est heroicum et
est hoc metrum continens tam divinas quam humanas personas vera
falsis admiscens. Intencio Stacii in hoc opere Thebanam describere historiam, cuius intencionis diverse a diversis cause assignantur.* Quidam
enim dicunt quod mortuo Vespasiano filii eius Titus et Domicianus in
tantam regni cupiditatem exarserunt quod fraternale odium incurrerunt.
Ad quorum dehortacionem actor iste Thebanam proposuit describere
historiam, et secundum hanc causam talis erit huius intentionis utilitas,
ut viso quid contigerit illis duobus pessimis fratribus scilicet Ethiocli et
Polinici, qui tanta regni cupiditate exarserunt quod se mutuis vulneribus
interfecerunt, et isti a consimili scelere desistant. Verum qui hoc dicunt ex
Suetonio videntur habere, qui in libro de xii^{cim} cesaribus inter cetera de
Tito dicit fratrem suum Domicianum insidiari vite sue desistere nolen-
tem, exercitus adversum se excitantem, tamen noluisse cum* possit oc-
cidere neque seponere, neque in minori honore quam cepisset habere,
sepe autem rogare ut apud [se]* mutua dilectione teneretur, seque suces-
sorem* suum in regno promittere. Alii vero considerantes quod Tito iam
mortuo et Domiciano iam regnum adepto, Stacius hoc opus incepit et ita
nullum esse dehortationis locum, hanc premise causam intencionis assig-
nant dicentes, quod in tempore Domiciani, Romam undique poetas con-
fluere Stacius audierat, ibique ad maximos honores eos provehi, tandem
Romam venit et qualiter populo Romano et imperatori placere possit diu
apud se excogitavit, denique animum suum aplicuit, ut Thebanam histo-

---

MS] nostra   MS] suscessorem
MS] temperalium
MS] assinatur
MS] com
MS] *omits* se [cf. R and B apud se mutua]

riam prenimia annorum vetustate iam pene deperditam describendo* ad
memoriam revocaret, sicque imperatori et populo Romano placeret. Intencio actoris est Ethioclis et Polinicis bellum describere et utriusque partis fautores. Modus materiei tripartitus est, quod nunc historiam tangit,
nunc* figmento subservit poetico, nunc scripto utitur allegorico. Materia
est Ethiocles et Polinices et acies utrinque conferte, vel ut verbis actoris
utamur, *Oedipode confusa domus,* scilicet crudelis Edippus, matris
Iocaste corruptor, Laii patris interfector, Ethiocles et Polinices ceci patris
contemptores, qui regni cupiditate cecati, mutuis vulneribus occiderunt.
Finis ad quem tendit, ut visis utriusque partis incommodis, ne tale ag-
grediamur officium, per quod simile incurramus periculum. Nota tria
esse genera scribendi, humile, mediocre, grandilocum, quibus omnibus
utitur Virgilius, que alii caracteres vocant, alii stilos. In Bucolicis utitur
humili, in Georgicis mediocri, in Eneide alto. Hic autem actor gran-
diloco* genere stili utitur. Hetice supponitur per politicam, quod nobis
informat morum doctrinam. Ethice autem due sunt partes, economica
qua proprie dispensamus familie, economicus enim dispensator interpretatur. Politica est scientia que ad regnum civitatum est necessaria.
Polis enim civitas interpretatur. Quem actorem immitetur ipse docet in
fine, ubi dicit

> Vive precor nec tu divinam Eneida tempta
> sed longe sequere et vestigia semper adora [12.816–817]

per hoc innuens se immitari Virgilium optimum latinorum. Scribit autem
ad laudandum Domiciani imperatoris, non quod de Thebana historia ad
eum quicquam pertineat, sed dicit in hoc opere suum preacuere ingenium, ut postmodum ad fortia eius facta describenda valeat sufficere. Dicit itaque

> tempus erit cum laurigero tua fortior oestro
> facta canam [1.32–33]

Idem in opere Achilleidos, ad ipsum promisit dicens

> magnusque tibi preludit Achilles [1.19]

MS] describendo r [possibly et; but R describendo ad   B deperditam ad]
MS] nunc nunc
MS] grandidiloco [with expunction of the second di]

sed quod et hic et ibi promiserat morte preventus exibere non potuit. Actor iste scri[144ᵛ]pturus* historiam more aliorum recte scribencium, proponit, invocat, narrat. Proponit ubi dicit *fraternas acies,* invocat ubi divinum implorat auxilium, ut ibi *unde iubetis ire dee,* narrat ubi lectione sua inchoat, ibi scilicit *impia iam dextera* et cet. His iam decursis que extrinsecus erant dicenda, ad litteram exponendam accedamus. Ibi convercionem debes incipere. *Pierius calor,* id est musicus amor, id est voluntas scribendi metrice. Muse secundum quosdam Memnoris et Tespie* filie fuerunt, secundum alios Iovis et Memorie, secundum alios Mercurii, que Pierides dicte sunt a filiabus Pieri quas devicerunt. Hic enim mos apud veteres inolevit, ut victoribus nomina victorum imponerentur. *Incidit menti,* id est voluntati mente* *evolvere,* id est evolute describere. Sumptum est a filo, quod fuso involvitur. Historia vero involuta est priusquam narretur, sed narrata evolvitur. Quequam explicata quo ordine res geste sunt mox declaratur. Et ideo dicit involutum, quod totum fuit, evolvere. Nam Iocasta et mater et uxor Edippi fuit, filiorum suorum mater et avia; Edippus vero et filius Iocaste et maritus, Ethioclis et Polinicis pater et frater, quod totum actor explanabit. *Fraternas acies,* quas hinc et inter iunxerunt fratres. Acies nomen est polysemum,* significat enim aciem oculorum et ferri et armatam choortem ut hic; acies est inferiori parte acutus, superiori latus, sed quod gladientes ad bellum sic solent adversibus disponi, ideo acies pro cohorcte ponitur. Sed quia plures fuerant acies fraterne, ut Remi et Romuli, Atrei et Tiestis, alternatim de his qui debuerunt regnare addit, dicens *regna alterna,* id est alternatim quidem possessa, sed quod hi disposuerant quod alternatim in regna sibi succederent.

Variants

qui minor] LBR qui minor Titus dictus est
facundie ut] BR facundie usque adeo ut de eo
multi alii] B multi auctores alii post
             R multi alii auctores post
Unde finxerunt . . . sufficienciam] LBR *omit*
in titulo] BR in titulis
opus reddat] B reditur   R redatur
Intencio Stacii] B Stacii in hoc opere est   R Stacii est

MS] scricturus
MS] et Tespie *interlinear addition* [cf. R Thesperie   B Tespie]
MS] mēe [possibly meae, but cf. B mēe]
MS] polisseñ [cf. B polisenum]

tanta regni] BR imperii
quod se] BR sese
et isti] BR *omit* et
seque sucessorum] BR seque suum fore successorem
iam regnum] BR iam imperium
Nota tria . . . stili utitur] B gives a shorter version of this passage at an ear-
    lier point in the text, following falsis admiscens.
Hetice . . . interpretatur] B gives following exibere non potuit
ad eum] BR ad Domicianum

Appendix 2: A late medieval *accessus* to the *Thebaid* from the library of Pietro da Montagnana

Introduction

THE MANUSCRIPT AND ITS PROVENANCE

Biblioteca Marciana, MS XII.61 is a paper codex written in single columns in a fifteenth-century Italian hand, with corrections in the same
hand. It contains only one text, entitled "Scriptum super Statio Thebaydos" (hereafter "Scriptum"), and a number of blank leaves.[1] A colophon
written in a different hand and ink states that "D[ominus] Petrus Montagnana" assigned and gave ("adscripsit atque donavit") the book to the
monastery of San Giovanni di Verdara, Padua.[2] This colophon includes
the date 1478, establishing a terminus post quem non for the copying of
the text; but as Pietro da Montagnana was a very old man when he made
his will in 1477 and is recorded in documents at Padua as "sacerdos" and
"magister" as early as 1423, there is good reason to believe that this book
and the others came into his possession well before that time.[3] Internal
evidence in "Scriptum" also indicates a much earlier date of composition.

An inventory of the library at the monastery of San Giovanni di Verdara was published by Jacobus Philippus Tomasinus in 1639, "Manu-
scripti codices diversi, qui in Bibliotheca S. Ioannis in Viridario Patauij
asse[r]uantur,"[4] which makes special note, by means of the formula "Donum X" or initial letters, of books given to the monastery. In Tomasinus's
catalog, there are more than forty entries marked "Donum PM" or simply
"PM" for Petrus da Montagnana, which will facilitate the reconstruction
of his private library, though some of that library left San Giovanni di Verdara before 1639.[5] The monastic library itself was removed to Venice and
the Marciana in 1782 or 1784, and its books are recorded in the descriptive catalogs for the Marciana, compiled in the nineteenth century.[6] The
colophon in the "Scriptum" manuscript resembles a number of others in
manuscripts that passed with it to the Marciana, and it is interesting to

note that although Tomasinus indicates the volumes were given to the monastery "ex testamento" or by will, and da Montagnana's will in fact establishes terms for the gift of his library to the monastery, these colophons in Montagnana's books in the Marciana carry dates ranging from 1470 to 1479, suggesting that his library was "assigned" over a period of at least nine years.[7]

Among the books noted as "gifts of PM" in the inventory of 1639 are three commentaries on the *Thebaid,* one of which is almost certainly "Scriptum": "Scriptum in Statij Thebaida Incerti. fol. Donum PM."[8] This title appears in the company of commentaries on works of Vergil by Servius and other, unidentified writers, which in turn make up part of a larger collection that clearly reflects the needs of a grammar teacher with broad humanistic interests, who taught Greek and Hebrew as well as Latin.

DATE AND AUTHORSHIP

The manuscript once belonged to Montagnana, and it is written in a contemporary hand, but that hand is not Montagnana's. The very informal appearance of the manuscript suggests that the book was made for personal reference rather than on commission: although the orthography and abbreviations are uniform throughout, the paper folia are not lined, and the size of the careful, cursive script changes noticeably from one page to the next. The paper carries the common bullshead watermark, which offers no certain terminus ante quem non for the copying (see Briquet 14820 and 14813, with a range of dates from 1423 to 1473). The layout of the pages, and especially the shape and position of large capital letters, is strikingly similar to that in several paper codices written in Montagnana's own hand. Taken together, these features suggest that Marciana XII.61 was copied by a contemporary *magister grammaticae* who had some associations with Padua and with Pietro da Montagnana.

The text of "Scriptum" in Marciana XII.61 seems to have been copied from a defective exemplar, because there are places (for example, on folio 15r) where the copyist left a blank space for missing lines to be inserted later. Further indication that he worked from an exemplar may be seen on folio 5r, where a small blank space in the text is scored through with two horizontal lines and a marginal note states that nothing is missing ("nihil deficit"). The text of the commentary breaks off abruptly on folio 57r, having reached *Thebaid* 4.414. Several blank folios follow. The text would therefore seem to stand at least two removes from the original, an intermediate copy being the source of the lacunae. But the same features could also be explained by the hypothesis that the scribe wrote the commentary, or rather compiled it from several sources. In this case the lacunae would represent his anticipation of materials to be added, and the note "nihil deficit" would represent an instance in which he had at first intended to include more material, only to change his mind. This second hypothesis is less attractive, but it gains some further support from the very informal appearance of the manuscript.

Internal evidence strongly favors a date of composition before about 1420, which would not preclude the possibility that Marciana XII.61 contains the working or autograph copy, but which certainly supports the hypothesis that our scribe copied from an imperfect exemplar. The most significant internal features bearing on the question of date are as follows:

1. "Scriptum" begins with an old-fashioned life of Statius, which refers to the poet as "Tolosanus" or "of Toulouse" in the manner of a medieval *vita Statii*. The *vita* in "Scriptum" must therefore have been copied or adapted before the dissemination of the biographical information in Statius's *Silvae*, which Poggio Bracciolini rediscovered in 1416 or 1417.[9] By comparison, Pomponio Leto correctly identified Statius's place of birth as Naples in the glosses in his copy of the *Thebaid*, MS Vat. lat. 3279, which was copied and annotated in 1470–1471.[10]

2. Although the author shows a certain familiarity with Greek literature, as for example the general references to Homer on folio 2r and the comments on the declensions of Greek proper names on folio 5r, there is nothing in the text to suggest that he knew Greek. He does not quote from Greek authors and does not handle adroitly the transliterated Greek words in a passage he quotes from Fulgentius (folio 4v). Montagnana himself knew, and taught, Greek grammar, and another student of Latin literature in Montagnana's generation or after it might be expected to draw on Greek sources when compiling a new commentary on the *Thebaid*. The same would not, of course, be true of commentators a few generations earlier. Thus, like the "old" *vita Statii* in "Scriptum," this aspect of the work favors an earlier rather than a later date of composition.

3. But not too much earlier. Yet another feature in the text of "Scriptum" suggests a lower limit for the date of composition in the later fourteenth century. The evidence here depends on the fact that the terms employed for the "topics" or "circumstances" in an *accessus* tended to go in and out of fashion.[11] For texts of all

kinds, the Servian topics were generally supplanted in the twelfth, thirteenth, and fourteenth centuries, only to have a revival in the late fourteenth and fifteenth centuries. Because Servius's prologue itself introduced Vergil's *Aeneid,* his sequence of topics appears stubbornly in prologues to Latin epics from all periods, but in the Scholastic period such prologues characteristically added several terms from other, more prestigious models. Now, the *accessus* in "Scriptum" follows the general pattern of Servius's prologue to the *Aeneid,* which is not remarkable; what is remarkable, however, is the scant use it makes of "topics" from any other tradition. It would seem to represent the late medieval "revival" of the Servian model.

The "Servian" prologue is organized around the following terms: (a) the life of the poet; (b) the title of the work; (c) the quality of the poem; (d) the intention of the author; (e) the number of books; (f) the order of the books; and (g) the explanation. The twelfth-century prologue to Statius's *Thebaid* printed above follows the Servian model in general outline, but it also includes the terms "modus tractandi," "finalis causa," and "cui parti philosophie supponatur," which are common in Scholastic prologues. "Scriptum," by contrast, begins with the first of the Servian topics, *vita poetae,* after which the other Servian terms appear, in this order: (b) the author's intention; (c) the quality of the poem; (d) the style of the poem; (e) the order and number of the books; and (f) the title. "Scriptum" does not mention "finalis causa," "cui parti philosophie supponatur," or "modus tractandi" in the *accessus,* though the last term does appear in the subsequent line-by-line commentary (for example, folios 2r and 3v). The absence of such non-Servian terms as were commonly used in prologues of the Scholastic period argues for a terminus ante quem non sometime in the later fourteenth century.

It remains to be noted that "Scriptum" elaborates on the Servian prologue with examples and summaries from the *Thebaid,* from other classical Latin works, from mythographies, and from rhetorical handbooks.[12] This remarkably full treatment continues through much of the commentary's first section. A good example of the author's practice may be seen in his handling of the Servian definition of the *metrum heroicum* or epic form of verse. Servius's *accessus* to the *Aeneid* includes the following passage: "est autem heroicum quod constat ex divinis humanisque personis, continens vera cum fictis; nam Aeneam ad Italiam venisse manifestum

est, Venerem vero locutam cum Iove missumve Mercurium constat esse
conpositum" (ed. Thilo and Hagen, vol. 1, p. 4). The twelfth- or early
thirteenth-century *accessus* to the *Thebaid*, "In principio," follows Servius rather closely but without giving examples from the *Thebaid* in place
of Servius's examples of Aeneas, Venus, Jove, and Mercury: "qualitas carminis est metrum heroicum et est hoc metrum continens tam divinas
quam etiam humanas personas, vera falsis admiscens." [13] "Scriptum," instead, amplifies the general statement with examples from the *Thebaid*,
just as Servius had done with examples from the *Aeneid:* "carmen autem
heroycum constat ex divinis humanisque personis continens vera cum fictis. Nam Polinicem a Thebis, Tideum a Calidonia, ad Adrastum regem
confugisse verum est, nam totum hystorie clamant. Mercurium vero
demissum ad inferos, Layumque ad superos revocatum constat esse fictitium" (fol. 1v). In elaborating the Servian topics, the author of "Scriptum" also drew on the mythographical tradition. One of his sources was
certainly the mythography commonly attributed to Fabius Planciades
Fulgentius, probably composed in the sixth century and often used by
later encyclopedists. The "mystical" or allegorical interpretation of the
myth of Bacchus in "Scriptum" comes from a slightly corrupt text of Fulgentius's mythography, as the following excerpts clearly demonstrate: [14]

> Itaque cum Semele quattuor sorores appellatae sunt, Ino, Auto-
> noe, Semele et Agaue. Quid sibi haec fabula mistice sentiat,
> exquiramus. Quattuor sunt ebrietatis genera, id est prima
> uinolentia, secunda rerum obliuio, tertia libido, quarta insania;
> unde et nomina haec quattuor Baccae acceperunt: Baccae dictae
> sunt quasi uino baccantes, prima Ino—inos enim Grece uinum
> dicimus—, secunda Autonoe quasi autenunoe, id est se ipsam
> non cognoscens, tertia Semele quasi somalion quod nos Latine
> corpus solutum dicimus, unde et ipsa genuisse Liberum patrem
> dicitur, id est de libidine nata ebrietas, quarta Agaue quae ideo
> insaniae comparatur, quod caput filii uiolenta absciderit.
> (Fulgentius, from *Fabula Dionisii*)

> Cuius Semeles tres erant sorores, scilicet Autonoe, Agave, et
> Ino. Quid sibi hec fabula mixtice velit, exquiramus. Quattuor
> sunt ebrietatis genera. Prima est vinolentia; secunda rerum
> oblivio; tertia libido; quarta insania, unde et nomina hec quat-
> tuor Bache acceperunt. Bache dicte sunt, quasi vino vacantes.
> Prima Yno. Ynos Grece vinum dicimus. Secunda Authonoe,
> quasi authonua, id est se ipsam non cognoscens. Tertia Semele,
> quasi semalyone, quod [?] nos latet [*sic*], corpus solutum ap-

pellamus. Unde et ipsa Liberum patrem genuisse dicitur, id est de libidine nata est ebrietas. Quarta Agave, que ideo insanie comparatur, quod capud filii violenta abscidit. ("Scriptum," fol. 4v)

Along with its unusually full references to classical myth and interpretation, "Scriptum" is distinguished by frequent illustrations of rhetorical precepts, such as the discussion of the "prohemiorum offitia" in the *accessus* and the references to ornaments of style in the commentary. Such topics are generally developed without recourse to illustrative examples in Servius and other commentaries. While it is impossible to identify a single source for the author's rhetorical terms and definitions, his phrasing is often close to that of the *Rhetorica ad Herennium*.[15]

THIS EDITION

Although "Scriptum" is very full at the beginning, the author comes to draw more and more heavily on Lactantius's commentary after *Thebaid* 1.46, the beginning of Statius's narrative. Here I transcribe only the first and fullest portion of "Scriptum," namely, the *accessus* and the commentary on the first twelve lines of the poem, which lines include Statius's formal statement of subject and argument. In this transcription, I keep the orthography of the manuscript but normalize its punctuation somewhat, capitalizing proper names and setting off quotations. The copyist relied heavily on abbreviations, which I have expanded silently. The commentator's *lemmata* from the *Thebaid* are italicized, as they are in the manuscript, though I occasionally italicize where the scribe has forgotten to do so. Editorial emendations are set off in square brackets. Additions to the text written in the margins of the manuscript are inserted without comment whenever they clearly belong in the text itself, in other words, whenever they are not glosses. Deletions by the scribe, which are not infrequent in the manuscript, are recorded when notable in the textual notes, set off by angled brackets. Finally, the numbering of the folios in the manuscript begins on the folio before the first page of text and is in error after folio 62. I number from the first page of text (MS 2r = 1r).

Notes to Appendix 2, Introduction

1. The manuscript is described in the catalog of Giuseppe Valentinelli, *Bibliotheca manuscripta ad S. Marci Venetarum . . . codices MSS. latini*, vol. 1 (Venice, 1868); see also Robert D. Sweeney, *Prolegomena to an Edition of the Scholia to Statius* (Leiden: Brill, 1969), pp. 23–24. It is mentioned in Violetta de Angelis, "Magna Questio preposita coram Dante et domino

Francisco Petrarca et Virgiliano," *Studi petrarcheschi* n.s. 1 (1984): 166 n. 113. A passage is quoted in Judson B. Allen and Theresa A. Moritz, *A Distinction of Stories* (Columbus: Ohio State University Press, 1981), pp. 87–88 and n. 6, where the manuscript is referred to as the "Venice commentary on Statius."

2. The colophon in Marciana XII.61 reads as follows: "Librum hunc Canonicis Regularibus Lateranensibus in monasterio divi Joannis Baptistae de Viridaria Padue agentibus, vir venerabilis ac devotus Christi sacerdos et bonarum artium cultor, Grece, Latine Hebraice aeque peritissimus D. Petrus Montagnana optima fide pietatis studio proque salute adscripsit atque donavit, quem quisque legens proficiat primum deinde sit gratus. MᵒCCC-CᵒLXXVIII" (fol. 64v).

3. Paolo Sambin, "La Formazione quattrocentesca della biblioteca di S. Giovanni di Verdara in Padova," *Atti dell'Istituto veneto di scienze, lettere ed arti*, Classe di scienze morali e lettere 114 (1955–1956): 263–280; idem, "Per la Biografia di Pietro da Montagnana grammatico e bibliofilo del sec. XV," ibid. 131 (1972–1973): 797–823.

4. Jac[obus] Phil[ippus] Tomasinus, *Bibliothecae patavinae manuscriptae* (Udine, 1639), pp. 11ff.

5. There is no comprehensive study of Montagnana's library, but studies of single volumes from his collection may be consulted together with the two essays of Sambin: R. W. Hunt, "Pietro da Montagnana: A Donor of Books to San Giovanni di Verdara in Padua," *Bodleian Library Record* 9 (1973): 17–22; A. C. de la Mare, P. K. Marshall, and R. H. Rouse, "Pietro da Montagnana and the Text of Aulus Gellius in Paris B. N. Lat. 13038," *Scriptorium* 30 (1976): 219–225; Giuseppe Billanovich and Emilio Menegazzo, "Tito Livio nell'umanesimo veneto," *Italia medioevale e umanistica* 25 (1982): 313–344, with additional secondary bibliography listed on p. 332, n. 7.

6. Valentinelli, *Bibliotheca manuscripta*, where most of the manuscripts from Montagnana's library are described in chap. 11; but see also vol. 6, p. 45. Carlo Castellani, *Catalogus codicum graecorum qui in Bibl. D. Marci . . . inlati sunt* (Venice: 1895) describes a twelfth- or thirteenth-century copy of the Quattuor Evangelia in Greek, with the characteristic Montagnana colophon on the flyleaf. According to Valentinelli, *Bibliotheca*, vol. 1, pp. 87–88, the monastery of San Giovanni di Verdara was suppressed in 1782 and the books moved to the Biblioteca Marciana in 1784. Thus the manuscript containing "Scriptum" does not appear in the great early catalog of A. M. Zanetti, *Latina et italica D. Marci Bibliotheca codicum manuscriptorum . . .* (Venice, 1741). The monastic library also contained the books of another important bibliophile and scholar of the fifteenth century, Giovanni Marcanova. See Carlo Frati, *Dizionario Bio-bibliografico dei bibliotecari e bibliofili italiani* (Florence: Olschki 1933), p. 331–333; Paul O. Kristeller, *Medieval Aspects of Renaissance Learning* (Durham, N.C.: Duke University Press, 1974), p. 100.

7. Tomasinus, *Bibliothecae*, says of the monastic library, "Est hic Bi[b]liotheca manuscriptis codicibus insignis, qui relicti ex testamento clarissimo-

rum virorum et in primis Petri de Montagnana" (p. 10), but Tomasinus himself notes that Montagnana gave the books at different times: "Iosias Profeta cum glossis, Munus PM 1470" (p. 29); "Comm. Boetij de disciplina scholiarum. Donum PM 1476" (p. 23); "Benvenutus de Imola in Valerium Maximum, fol. Donum PM 1479" (p. 19). Most of the colophons, however, carry the date 1478.

8. Tomasinus, *Bibliothecae*, p. 25.

9. "Scriptum" begins with an "old" *vita Statii*. This brief biography, identifying the author of the *Thebaid* as "Papinius Sursulus Statius" and as "Tolosanus," appears often—though in slightly differing versions—in manuscript copies of the *Thebaid* and the *Achilleid*. Paul M. Clogan, *The Medieval Achilleid of Statius* (Leiden: Brill, 1968), pp. 2–3, prints one rather elaborate version of this medieval *vita*. Throughout the fourteenth century, Statius continued to be identified as "Tolosanus." See, for example, Boccaccio's *Amorosa visione* 5.34 and Chaucer's *House of Fame*, 3.370.

With the recovery of Statius's *Silvae* in 1416 or 1417, it was possible to determine that the poet, named Publius Papinius Statius, had been born in Naples. The traditional *vita* was discredited and soon was replaced by new ones, an early example being that of Palmieri. The old-fashioned *vita* in Marciana XII.61 would therefore suggest that our commentary was composed no later than the early fifteenth century: but some caution is in order, because dissemination of the new biographical information was not complete until later in the fifteenth century, after the publication of the early editions of Statius's works beginning in 1478. At least one set of glosses on the *Thebaid* written in 1462 persists in calling the poet "Tolosanus" (Biblioteca Apostolica Vaticana, MS Urb. lat. 363, fol. 101r).

10. Vladimiro Zabughin, *Giulio Pomponio Leto*, vol. 2 (Rome: La Vita Letteraria 1912), pp. 46–60, discusses this manuscript.

11. R. W. Hunt, "The Introductions to the *Artes* in the Twelfth Century," in *Collected Papers on the History of Grammar in the Middle Ages,* ed. G. L. Bursill-Hall (Amsterdam: Benjamins, 1980), pp. 117–144; also A. J. Minnis, *Medieval Theory of Authorship* (London: Scolar, 1984), pp. 9–39. Minnis, p. 230 n., remarks that "The . . . Servian [model of] prologue enjoyed something of a revival in humanistic commentaries on the poets."

12. The relation of "Scriptum" to earlier medieval commentaries on the *Thebaid* is not clear. Almost all of the earlier line-by-line commentaries, like "Scriptum" itself, contain excerpts from Lactantius Placidus. The author of "Scriptum" probably used a commentary like the one in Appendix 1, for we find in it numerous passages that are similar to passages in this earlier commentary and which do not derive from Lactantius. Moreover, these parallel passages often contain specific references to lemmata from the *Thebaid,* which means that their common source must have been a commentary on that poem. But "Scriptum" does not follow the earlier commentary, at least as we have it in the Berlin and London manuscripts, at great length. The author of "Scriptum" has perhaps drawn from the earlier commentary very selectively and expanded upon it from his own resources.

For another composite work in Montagnana's library, see Mary Louise Lord, "A Commentary on *Aeneid* 6," *Medievalia et Humanistica* n.s. 15 (1987): 147–160.

13. Riccardiana e Moreniana MS 842, fol. 1v; Add. 16380 reads: "Qualitas carminis metrum est heroicum. et est hoc metrum continens tam divinas quam humanas personas, vera falsis admiscens" (fol. 144r).

14. I quote from the edition of R. Helm (repr. Stuttgart: Teubner, 1970), pp. 52–53. Other commentators on the *Thebaid* drew on the mythographers as well. An interesting example is discussed by Carlo Landi, "Di un Commento medievale inedito, . . ." *Atti e memorie della Real accademia . . . di Padova* n.s. 30 (1914): 315–344. Landi is able to demonstrate that the marginal glosses in Padua, Biblioteca del Seminario Vescovile, MS 41, an early fourteenth-century copy of the *Thebaid,* correspond to the text of the Third Vatican Mythographer. The codex described by Landi was probably copied in Verona (p. 138).

15. See below, "Scriptum" note 9.

Venice, Biblioteca Marciana, MS Lat. XII.61
Scriptum super Statio Thebaydos

Autor iste Tolosanus id est de Tolosa civitate Galliarum oriundus fuit.[1] Is etenim celeberrime in Gallia docuit, unde dictus est Sursulus, quasi Surculus id est sursum canens appellatus est. Nam erat optimus rhethor, orator discretus, eloquentie flore Gallias replevit; quod autem sic fuerit Iuvenalis indicat auctoritas sic dicentis:[2]

Curritur ad vocem iocundam et carmen amice
Thebaidos letam cum fecit Statius urbem
promisitque diem, et cet. [*Satires* 7.82–84]

Huius itaque doctrina rhetoricis ornata coloribus, summa laude floruit in Galliis. Postquam vero Alpes transcenderat, Romamque devenit; eius nominis auctoritas non parum amplificata, fama predicante, Domitiani quidem ad aures pervenit. Rome siquidem existens, scriptores pro qualitate carminum ad summos gradus dignitatum sublimare conspiciens, qualiter imperatori Domitiano ac Romano populo placere posset apud se deliberavit. Tandem animum suum ad hoc applicuit, ut Thebanam hystoriam a memoria iam fere, propter vetustatem abolitam, describeret, et ut illud summum discidium Polinicis et Ethioclis prope abolitum ad memoriam revocaret.

Est autem autoris intentio in hoc opere Thebanam hystoriam, fraternumque discidium Polinicis et Etheoclis ad memoriam revocare, et propter hanc utilitatem ut visis incommoditatibus fraterni discidii, lectoribus fraternalem discordiam summo diligentique studio dissuadeat. Hystoriam scilicet itaque Thebanam describendo, Domitiani laudibus imperatoris alludit, non quod aliquid ad ipsum pertineat hystoria, sed in hac hystoria nimirum est quoddam preludium et diligens exercitium ad fortia facta tanti viri describenda. Unde et ipse ait statim:

Tempus erit cum laurigero tua fortior oestro
facta canam. Nunc tendo chelin satis arma referre
Aonia et geminis sceptrum exitiale tirannis [*Thebaid* 1.32–34]

Unde etiam in Statio Achylleidos ait, cum nondum auderet aggredi fortia facta Domitiani:[3]

Et tibi magnus preludat Achilles [*Achilleid* 1.19]

id est ad honorem tui, quasi dicat ut in istis quasi in preludiis exercitatus egregius et laudabilius laudes tuas depromere possim.

Et nota quod in Statio Achilleidos imitatur [folium 1v] Homerum, in hoc autem opere imitatur Virgilium secundum tractatum Eneydos. Utitur igitur carmine heroyco, grandiloquo* stilo, ordine artifitiali. Carmen autem heroycum constat ex divinis humanisque personis continens vera cum fictis.[4] Nam Polinicem a Thebis,* Tideum a Calidonia, ad Adrastum regem confugisse verum est, nam hoc totum hystorie clamant. Mercurium vero demissum ad inferos, Layumque ad superos revocatum constat esse fictitium. Grandiloquus siquidem stilus est qui constat pondere sententiarum et altiloquio verborum; Tulliana[5] siquidem confirmat auctoritas. Altum genus stili esse dicitur in quo ponuntur verba ad* res magnas pertinentia, quecumque materie subiecta sint. Humile genus stili est in quo ponuntur verba ad res parvas pertinentia, quecumque materie subiecta sint. Mediocre quidem est quod in se continet verba muta* nec parvas nec res magnas conplectentia.

Notate quod ordo alius naturalis, alius artifitialis. Ordo naturalis est rerum gestarum expositio secundum eundem ordinem quo geste sunt, ut quoddam primum fit, primo loco narretur, quoddam statim post, secundo loco, et ita deinceps. Artifitialis ordo est quando rerum gestarum

---

Angular brackets mark words or letters written and then deleted by the scribe. Square brackets contain editorial remarks.

MS] grandiloqui
MS] a⟨d⟩ Thebis
MS] ⟨scilicet⟩
MS] muta [emend to "media"?]

fit prepostera expositio, quando quoddam primum fit, secundo narratur loco, quoddam secund[um],* primo exponitur, et hoc ordine hic utitur autor. Nam incipit ubi Edippus peccatum suum recognovit, de patre interfecto, de matre violata, et sibi ipsi oculos excecavit, unde ait:

Impia iam merita scrutatus lumina dextra [*Thebaid* 1.46]

Ibi inquam incepit, cum multa precessissent que summatim et satis oratorie declarat autor. Vere multa precesserunt, nam primum rapta fuit Europa a Iove mutato in speciem tauri; deinde Cadmus exulavit; responsum in Parnaso⁶ accepit; vaccam videns Thebas condidit; in serpentem vertit; filii sui scilicet Athamas et Pentheus regnaverunt usque ad Layum. Hunc Edippus eius filius occidit, matrem eius Iocastam nomine in uxorem duxit, ex qua pignora suscepit, quo comperto, sibi oculos exce [folium 2r] cavit, et ab hoc puncto Statius incipit, quod fere ultimo loco gestum erat; filiis suis imprecatus est; Mercurius Layum ab inferis redduxit; furie fratribus se inserunt; statim discordant ne simul regnare consentiant; exulat Polinices minor; venit ad Adrastum filium Talay et Eurimones.⁷ Similiter et Tideus pro Meleagro fratre suo ab Etholia regione profugus ad Adrastum venerat.⁸ Venientes autem Polinices et Tideus in porticum regis Adrasti, pugna gesserunt. Rex autem accensis luminibus, hos milites regium animum habentes, a lite separavit. Quibus introductis visaque pelle leonis in altero, pelle quidem apri in altero, responsorum rex ipse recordatus est. Argyam Polinici, Deyphilen Tideo desponsavit; turbantur nuptie per casum clipei in templo Palladis. Iam annus transivit; officium legationis suscepit Tideus; licentiam bellorum Argya a patre impetravit; Amphyaraus progreditur; fontes ex[s]iccantur;* Langya sola remanet; Olphetes moritur; Ligurgus; ludi Archemori, id est principi[i]* mortuorum, celebrantur; singulos tractatus de omnibus facit; nimiis* vulneribus occurrit; Adrastus fugit; Creon sepulturam vetuit; matrone Theseum qui Hyppoliten Amazonum reginam secum duxerat, imploraverunt; hic Theseus singulari certamine Creontam [sic] occidit, et eius regnum suo continuavit. Et hec breviter est materia. Patet igitur totius hystorie summa.

Et notate quod satis ydonee quasi quadam prefatione prescribitur breviter partiendo in tria, scilicet in propositionem, invocationem, et nar-

---

MS] secunde [? or] secundo [?]
MS] exiccantur
MS] principi
MS] Mimus [or] Nimus

rationem, prohemiorum offitia eleganter ex[s]equendo,* nam lectores benivolos, dociles, et attentos facit.⁹ Proponit ubi dicit *fraternas acies,* et ibi reddit dociles. Invocat ubi dicit *unde iubetis,* et cet. et tunc attentos facit. Narrat ibi, *impia iam merita,* et ibi facit benivolos. Vel ubi proponit de qua re dicturus est, sibi attentos; ubi invocat, benivolos; nam tunc quodammodo* manifestatur modus tractandi et in modo tractandi sunt semper lectores benivoli, in narratione vero dociles. [folium 2v]

Titulus talis est: *Papinii Statii Sursuli Thebaydos liber primus incipit.* Papinius a cognatione dicitur. Statius, proprium nomen eius fuit. Sursulus quasi Surculus, id est sursum canens, quia post Virgilium inter alios poetas obtinuit principatum, et est agnomen, quia ab eventu. Thebaydos a Thebis civitate, de qua hystoria est, et declinatur hec Thebays, -dis vel -dos, id est hystoria de Thebis. Et est sciendum quod hystoriarum¹⁰ quedam sunt nomina a loco, ut Ylias ab Ylio et Thebais a Thebis; quedam a persona, ut Eneys ab Enea, Odissea ab Odisseo.

Dicit itaque *Pyerius calor,* id est musicus ardor, quasi dicat voluntas scribendi. Pyerides Muse, secundum quosdam filie Iunonis, secundum alios Iovis et Melpomone[s].¹¹ Iovis enim dicitur iuvans vis et est ingenium. Ingenium enim iuvat ad sciendam. Melpomone dicitur multam meditationem faciens permanere. Bene ergo Pyerides dicuntur filie Iovis et memorie, nam per Musas et ingenium excitatur et recognita firmissime memoria retinentur.

Incidit, id est venit in mentem. *Evolvere,* id est explanare *fraternas acies* et quia multe fuerant fraterne acies, utpote inter Thyestem et Atreum, Meleagrum et Tideum, ideo distinguendo manifestat cum dicit vel addit *alternaque regna,* id est alternatim disposita inter Polinicem et Ethyoclem, non quod uterque regnasset sed quoniam ita dispositum erat inter illos, ut alter uno alter altero anno regnaret et per hoc aperte determinat regnum Thebanorum.

Decertata, id est debellata. *Profanis odiis,* quia frater fratri mortem intulit; vel *profanis,* id est procul a fano quoniam interfectis contra naturam fratribus, Creon sepulturam interdixit; vel *profanis* quia tunc flamme rogi quasi bellum commoventes vise sunt pugnare, profanum enim odium est quod post mortem durat; vel *profanis,* id est talibus odiis quod aliquis hominum de his non deberet loqui. More boni oratoris illud discidium miro modo aggravat, ut melius fraternalem discordiam a men-

---

MS] exequendo
MS] quoddammodo

tibus hominum dissuadeat. Et etiam incidit mee menti velle *evolvere*, id est evolute explicare,* *sontes Thebas*. *Sontes* quia filius patrem interfecit, matris thorum violavit. Satis igitur ydonee atque [folium 3r] proprie posuit autor *evolvere*, nam omnia erant involuta. Nam unus eiusdem frater erat et pater, maritus et filius; una eadem uxor et mater. Exquisite siquidem unum vocabulum posuit autor, scilicet *evolvere*, omnia talia designans. Attentos in propositione fecit, sceleris atrocitatem applicando, et de quibus acturus sit rebus designando. Et notate quod miro modo a fraternali discidio deterreret cum ne sermo inde fiat vehementer persuadet.

Unde iubetis. Hic invocat et quoniam multa erant Thebane hystorie principia, ne vitium incurrat nimis remota narrando, satis eleganter Musas consulit,* quibus incipere debeat, vitans illud vitium a Tullio reprehensum, ne ab ultimo repetatur, unde Horatius:

Nec bellum gemino Troianum orditur ab ovo [*Ars poetica* 147] [12]

Hoc quantum ad principium narrationis. Similiter in fine huius voluminis observat precepta que pertinent ad finem narrationis, unde Tullius, ut ne ad extremum prodeatur; quod bene Statius in fine observavit, dicens:

Et mea iam longo tetigit ratis equore portum [*Thebaid* 12.809] [13]

Dicit itaque *unde iubetis ire,* id est a quibus iubetis incipere o vos Muse.

Dire gentis, unde ait *sontes, primordia,* scilicet *Sidonios raptus;* fabulam tangit per transitum: Europa filia fuit Agenoris regis Sidonie, fama pulcherrima, a Iove nimis amata. Quadam vero die dum inter patris armenta spatiaretur, Iupiter, in speciem thauri mutatus, inter armenta incedens Europam rapuit; ultra mare devexit. Cadmus eiusdem Agenoris filius missus est a patre ut eam quereret, cui pater interdicit reditum in patriam nisi illam invenisset. Abiit; quesivit; non invenit; in patriam non rediit; Thebas constituit; et hoc est quia dicit *Sidonios raptus.* Vel *Sidonios raptus,* id est Sidoniorum stuprum, quia Iupiter filiam regis Sidonis stupravit, unde Virgilius:

. . . rapti Ganimedis honores [*Aeneid* 1.28]

id est stuprati, ita exponit Servius. [14]

Inexorabile, quia nec prece nec pretio potuit Agenor flecti, ut Cadmus

---

MS] id est evolute explicare [appears in margin]
MS] Musas ⟨invocat⟩ consulit

repatriaret, nisi Europa inventa. *Longa retro,* non, inquam, repetam a raptu Europe, nec a pacto [folium 3v] Agenoris inexorabili; et merito, nam si hoc fecissem, *longa retro series* esset, id est a nimis remoto principio incipere. Hic reddit benivolos in modo tractandi, et vitat illud vitium, ne a longe repetatur; *series,* id est narrationis inchoatio, nimis remota a principio est. Ita dico *si expediam,* id est si exponere incipiam. *Agricolam operti Martis,* id est Cadmum cultorem agri in quo seminavit dentes serpentis sulcis opertos, in quo statim nascentes armati bellum inter se commiserunt. Omnesque interfecti sunt preter quinque, qui postea cum Cadmo muros Thebanos constituerunt, unde quinque superstitibus, quorum fuit unus Echyon. *Agricolam,* dico, *trepidum,* nam timuit ne milites de terra nascentes cum eo vellent manus conferre. *Condentem,** id est abscondentem; *prelia,* id est preliantes; *infandis sulcis,* terribilibus et inauditis.

Et longa est retro series. *Si penitus sequar,* id est si per singula velim ex[s]equi* et exponere. *Quo carmine,* id est genere cantillene, *Amphion iusserit Tyrios montes,* id est Tyrios lapides. *Accedere montes,* id est ad muros Thebanos. Anthyopa fuit filia regis Atheniensis, nomine [N]icthei,[15] quam Lycus rex duxit in uxorem, et ea contempta aliam superduxit, scilicet Dyrcen; que timens ne a rege sperneretur, et Anthyopa duceretur, fecit dictam Anthyopam in carcere poni, et multis tormentis ibidem affligi. Iupiter ad Anthyopam in carcerem descendit, et cum ea concubuit. Ex ea duos filios habuit, scilicet Zethum et Amphyonem, qui postea Lycum occiderunt, et Dircen novercam suam indomitis equis tractaverunt, usque adeo mutata est in fontem sui nominis vel paludem iuxta Thebas.[16] Amphyon autem musicus erat optimus, Zetus vero venator. Iste siquidem Amphyon sui cantus dulcedine lapides ad muros Thebanos currere fecit, quod nichil aliud est quam istum Amphion[em] * eius admirabili discretione atque facundia, homines tardos et stupidos more bestiarum sibi vitam propagantes ad humanum et divinum cultum or[e] * duxisse, atque ad civitatem constructionem reduxisse; montes appellamus homines incultos, stupidos et tardos instar montis.

Etiam *longa est retro series si expediam,* id est quibus causis contingere. *Graves ire,* id est novitie. *Bacho in menia,* id est infra menia, scilicet cognata Bacho. Bachus enim fuit filius Semeles, que fuerat Cadmi, et ideo cognata, et cet. Bachus siquidem optinens victoriam de popu-

---

MS] *il. di. cod.* [emend to "illum dico *condentem*"?]
MS] exequi
MS] Amphion
MS] ora

lis Indie, iam quasi [folium 4r] in numerum deorum reputatus apud
Thebas cum triumpho rediit. Populus autem Thebanus, cum mira alacri-
tate illi venit obvius. Unde Pentheus, de tanto honore collato Bacho indig-
nans, nuntios suos misit ad sacrificium quod institutum erat Bacho, ut
sibi Bachum vinctum adduceret. Nuntii recesserunt; Bachum non invene-
runt. Acestem sacerdotem Bachi adduxerunt, deinde non misit nuntios,
sed Pentheus ipse ivit ad sacrificium; evenit ut Bachum vinctum adduceret. Illi autem sacrificio quattuor sorores interfuerant, scilicet Autonoe, Agave eius Penthei mater, Semele mater Bachi, et Yno, que Bacho
stimulante, facte furibunde, Pentheum advenientem aprum esse putave-
runt, et totum discerpserunt; et primum mater eius Agave illum invasit, et
hoc est unde *graves ire.*

    Quod fuit opus seve Iunonis, id est hoc totum contingit, Iunone im-
movente. Vel potest legi quod erit capitulum per se, quod fuit *opus seve
Iunonis.* Nota quod Iupiter Semelem filiam Cadmi adamavit et rem cum
ea egit, ex qua Bachum genuit. Iuno anxia hoc percepit, unde vultum
Beroes nutricis Semeles simulavit, ad Semelem devenit. Inter multa alia de
Iove mentionem fecit, optans ut cum ea Iupiter rem egisset. Nam dicebat
multas castas mulieres deceptas esse per deos mentientes et se deos confir-
mantes, sed falso; ex cuius verbis commota Semele et dubita[n]s,* quesivit quomodo secure scire posset an esset Iupiter, an non. Cui Iuno
mentita similitudinem Beroes ait: Pete ab eo, ut eo modo agat tecum rem,
quomodo cum Iunone, et dic ei ut iuret per Stygiam paludem antequam
hoc petas. His dictis, Iuno recessit. Iupiter rediit; voluit agere cum Semele. Illa recusavit, dicens eum non esse Iovem, cui Iupiter ait: pete a me
quicquid volueris et impetrabis et iuro Stygyam paludem. Illa autem pe-
tiit, ut eo modo secum ageret quomodo cum Iunone agebat. Iupiter voluit
vocem reprimere, sed verbum eius erat irrevocabile, quia per Stigyam
paludem iuraverat. [folium 4v] Assumptis igitur fulminibus cum ea concubuit; Bachum ex ea genuit.[17] Cuius Semeles tres erant sorores, scilicet
Autonoe, Agave et Ino.

    Quid sibi hec fabula mixtice velit, exquiramus. Quattuor sunt ebrieta-
tis genera. Prima est vinolentia; secunda rerum oblivio; tertia libido;
quarta insania, unde et nomina hec quattuor Bache acceperunt. Bache
dicte sunt, quasi vino vacantes. Prima Yno. Ynos Grece vinum dicimus.
Secunda Authonoe, quasi authonua, id est se ipsam non cognoscens. Tertia Semele, quasi semalyone, quod* nos latet [*sic*], corpus solutum ap-

---

MS] dubitas
MS] quoddam [?] [emend "latet" to "Latine"]

pellamus. Unde et ipsa Liberum patrem genuisse dicitur, id est de libidine nata est ebrietas. Quarta Agave, que ideo insanie comparatur, quod capud filii violenta abscidit. Liber ergo pater dictus est, quia vini passio liberas mentes faciat. Yndos vero devicit, quia hec gens vino sit valde dedita, duabus scilicet de causis, sive quod fervor solis eos faciat potatores, sive quod ibi sit falernum vinum, id est montanum, cuius vini tanta est virtus, ut vix quilibet ebriosus toto mense sextarium bibat, unde Lucanus:

> Indomitum Meroe cogens spumare Falernum [*De bello civili,* 10.163]

Aqua enim omnino domari non potest. Maroni nutriendus Dyonisus datus est, quasi Meroni. Mero enim omnis nutritur vinolentia. Hic et tygribus insidere dicitur, quia omnis vinolentia feritati semper insistit, nam "tunc pauper cornua sumit," [18] sive est quia vino effere mentes mulceantur. Unde et dicitur Lyeus, quasi lenitatem prestans. Iuvenis vero ideo pingitur, quia puerilem ebrium efficiat. Ideo nudus, quia ebrietas secreta denudat.

Notes to "Scriptum super Statio Thebaydos"

1. On the *vita Statii,* see above, p. 241 and note 9.
2. This quotation from Juvenal is part of the traditional *vita Statii.* In the manuscript all quotations of verse are written out as prose, without line divisions. Marginal notations such as "Iuvenalis" here and "Tullius" below (see note 5) appear regularly in the manuscript when authorities are cited in the text.
3. The Teubner edition (ed. A. Klotz) gives: ". . . magnusque tibi praeludit Achilles."
4. The passage is modeled on Servius, *In Verg. Aen. I Praef.* (see introduction to this appendix, pp. 236–238), itself an echo of Horace, *Ars poetica* 151; cf. also *Thebaid* 10.113.
5. Cicero, *De Oratore* 5.20: "et grandiloqui, ut ita dicam, fuerunt cum ampla et sententiarum gravitate et majestate verborum."
6. I.e., at Delphi; Ovid, *Metamorphoses* 3.8–9, says simply that Cadmus went to the "oracle of Phoebus": "[Cadmus] Phoebique oracula supplex / consulit."
7. "Son of Talaus and Eurimone," namely, Eurynome, though the form Eurimone is common in medieval sources, e.g., Boccaccio, *Genealogie* 2.41: "Adrastus Argivorum rex, unde ait Lactantius, fuit filius Thalaonis et Eurimones" (ed. Vincenzo Romano [Bari: Laterza, 1951], vol. 1, p. 96). Most Greek sources give Talaus and Lysimache, but our commentator is follow-

ing the tradition of Lactantius, as does Baccaccio. See Lactantius *In Theb.* 1.391 and 5.18.

8. Lactantius, who says that Tydeus was exiled from Calydon because he killed his brother Menalippus (*In Theb.* 1.403), refers to Meleager as Tydeus's grandfather rather than his brother. Thus our commentator's assertion that Tydeus killed "his brother Meleager" cannot derive from Lactantius. Although most mythographies count Meleager and Tydeus as brothers, or half-brothers, sons of King Oeneus of Calydon, only the treatise known as the First Vatican Mythographer says that Tydeus killed Meleager: "Meleagrides, sorores Meleagri, illum a fratre Tydeo interfectum, intolerabiliter flentes" (198, ed. Bode, p. 60).

9. The terms are conventional, the phrasing close to that of the *Rhetorica ad Herennium* 1.4; see also Quintilian, *Institutio oratoria* 4.1.5. A fragmentary commentary on the *Thebaid* in Vat. lat. 3280, copied in a twelfth-century hand, remarks at *Thebaid* 1.1ff. "prologu[s] . . . reddit nos atentos b[en]ivolos dociles" (fol. 103v).

10. Medieval *accessus* frequently described epics as *historiae:* see for example Alexander Neckham, "Sacerdos ad altare," in Charles Homer Haskins, *Studies in the History of Medieval Science* (Cambridge: Harvard University Press, 1924), p. 372; and Conrad of Hirsau, *Dialogus super auctores,* ed. R. B. C. Huygens (Brussels: Latomus, 1955), pp. 16, 54ff.

11. Manuscript reads Melpomone. The Muses are usually said to be daughters of Mnemosyne.

12. Horace, *Opera,* ed. E. C. Wickham (Oxford: Clarendon, 1967) reads: "nec gemino bellum. . . ."

13. The Teubner edition (ed. Klotz) gives: "et mea iam longo meruit ratis aequore portum."

14. Servius, *In Aen.* 1.28 (Thilo-Hagen ed. vol. 1, p. 23): "*Rapti* stuprati, ut est *rapta Garamantide nympha.*"

15. Manuscript reads Victhei. This version of the myth of Antiope and Dirce seems to be corrupt in at least two other details as well: first, Nycteus, according to Hyginus (*Fab.* 7) and later mythographers, was a king of Thebes, not Athens; and second, Dirce was killed when tied to a bull, not to horses.

16. The fountain is an important feature of the legendary geography of Boeotian Thebes. See, for example, Ovid, *Metamorphoses* 2.239ff. and Statius, *Thebaid* 2.322ff. MS reads *iusta* for *iuxta.*

17. The following interpretation of the fable of Dionysus is a close paraphrase of Fulgentius, *Mythologiae* 2.12 (ed. R. Helm, p. 53); see introduction to this appendix, pp. 238–239.

18. This phrase seems to be a quotation or proverb, inserted by the commentator. It does not appear in Fulgentius's fable of Dionysus, which is the source for this passage, or in the corresponding passage of the Third Vatican Mythographer (12.3), which is an elaboration of Fulgentius (ed. Bode, pp. 244–245). The phrase finds a close analogue in Horace, *Odes* 3.21.18 (an address to a wine jar): ". . . et addis cornua pauperi" (line 18).

Appendix 3: Boccaccio's glosses on *Thebaid* 7.666–687

Florence, Biblioteca Medicea-Laurenziana MS Plut. 38.6

Parchment; text of the *Thebaid* in one column with the commentary of Lactantius as marginal and interlinear gloss; early twelfth century, except folios 163–164 and 173–178, which are thirteenth century; folios 43, 100, 111 and 169 are fourteenth century, in the hand of Boccaccio.

Descriptions: *Mostra di manoscritti, documenti e edizioni, Sesto centenario della morte di Giovanni Boccaccio* (Certaldo, 1975), vol. 1, pp. 155–156; Birger Munk Olsen, *L'Étude des auteurs classiques latins aux XIe et XIIe siècles,* vol. 2 (Paris: Editions CNRS, 1985), p. 535.

There follows a transcription of *Thebaid* 7.666–687, with accompanying glosses, from folio 100r of the manuscript. Folio 100r is reproduced in Plate 1. I have arranged the transcription in the manner of the original whenever possible, but in some cases the location of an interlinear gloss is indicated with an asterisk and the gloss itself is transcribed in the right margin. I have transcribed the text of Statius's poem as it appears in Boccaccio's copy, adding an apparatus that records the substantial variants from the edition of D. E. Hill, *P. Papini Stati Thebaidos Libri XII* (Leiden: Brill, 1983), pp. 187–188.

Florence, Biblioteca Medicea-Laurenziana, MS Plut 38.6, fol. 100r, lines 1–22 (= 7.666–687)

	nos *per semelem*	*propter baccum*

666   Gens sacrata sumus. gener huic est iuppiter urbi

propter hermionem filiam eius   *nos*

     Gradiuusque socer. bachum haud mentimur alumnum

          herculis   *illi*   *euneo*   *herculis almene filius*

     Et mangnum alciden. iactanti talia frustra   *thebis altus fuit.*

        mangna   *tĕ ·p· n*

     Turbidus aeria capaneus occurrit in hasta.

           mangnam   *summe*   *diluculo*   *ab*   (*) *ille erat talis*

     (*)   ·*a*·   ÷

670   Qualis ubi primam leo mane cubilibus atris

         ·*b*·

     Erexit rabiem. et sevo speculatur ab antro

·i· iuuenis sine cornubus   *·i· cornu*
Aut ceruum / aut nondum bellantem fronte iuuencum

uenatoris
In fremitu gaudens licet arma gregesque lacessant

canes   *non formidat futura*
Venantum predam uidet et sua uulnera nescit

675   Sic tum congressu capaneus gauisus iniquo

astam
Librabat mangnam uenturam mole cupressum

·a·   *·b·*
Ante tamen quid femineis ululatibus inquit

o eunee   *bacus*
Terrificas moriture uiros? utinam ipse ueniret

·i· ad honorem cuius   *o tu eunee*
Cui furis. hec tyrijs cane matribus et simul astam

campaneus   *hasta*
680   Expulit; illa uolans ceu uis non ulla moretur

haste   *super*   *transiuit*
Obuia. uix sonuit clipeo. et iam terga reliquit;

ei   *mangnis*   *fragoribus*   *quod erat super clipeum*
Arma fluunt. longisque crepat singultibus aurum

·b·   *fregit*   *·a·*   *o*
Eruptusque sinus uicit cruor occidis audax

tu dico   *bachi.hoc dicit propter tigres que erant prima cura*
Occidis aonii puer altera cura liei

·a· o eunee   *·b· montes*
Martia te fractis planserunt ismara tyrsis;

montes   *(*)*   *(**)*   *(*) in ariete ad cuius similitudinem*
Themolos. te nisa ferax·theseaque naxos.   *hec est facta*
                                                    (**) insula quam theseus deuincit

(***)

fluuius indorum   *(***) Bachus debellauit habitantes*

Et thebana metu iuratus in orgia ganges   *iuxta gangem eosque coegit iurare*

per sua orgia.

Hill: 673   In fremitu] it fremitu
      676   mangnam] magna
      685   Martia] marcida
      686   Themolos] te Tmolos

INDEX OF CITATIONS FROM THE *THEBAID* AND THE *TESEIDA*

This index does not include material from the appendixes.

GENERAL INDEX

University of Pennsylvania Press
MIDDLE AGES SERIES
Edward Peters, General Editor

Edward Peters, ed. *Christian Society and the Crusades, 1198–1229*. Sources in Translation, including The Capture of Damietta by Oliver of Paderborn. 1971

Edward Peters, ed. *The First Crusade: The Chronicle of Fulcher of Chartres and Other Source Materials*. 1971

Katherine Fischer Drew, trans. *The Burgundian Code: The Book of Constitutions or Law of Gundobad and Additional Enactments*. 1972

G. G. Coulton. *From St. Francis to Dante: Translations from the Chronicle of the Franciscan Salimbene (1221–1288)*. 1972

Alan C. Kors and Edward Peters, eds. *Witchcraft in Europe, 1110–1700: A Documentary History*. 1972

Richard C. Dales, *The Scientific Achievement of the Middle Ages*. 1973

Katherine Fischer Drew, trans. *The Lombard Laws*. 1973

Henry Charles Lea. *The Ordeal*. Part III of Superstition and Force. 1973

Henry Charles Lea. *Torture*. Part IV of Superstition and Force. 1973

Henry Charles Lea (Edward Peters, ed.). *The Duel and the Oath*. Parts I and II of Superstition and Force. 1974

Edward Peters, ed. *Monks, Bishops, and Pagans: Christian Culture in Gaul and Italy, 500–700*. 1975

Jeanne Krochalis and Edward Peters, ed. and trans. *The World of Piers Plowman*. 1975

Julius Goebel, Jr. *Felony and Misdemeanor: A Study in the History of Criminal Law*. 1976

Susan Mosher Stuard, ed. *Women in Medieval Society*. 1976

James Muldoon, ed. *The Expansion of Europe: The First Phase*. 1977

Clifford Peterson. *Saint Erkenwald*. 1977

Robert Somerville and Kenneth Pennington, eds. *Law, Church, and Society: Essays in Honor of Stephan Kuttner*. 1977

Donald E. Queller. *The Fourth Crusade: The Conquest of Constantinople, 1201–1204*. 1977

Pierre Riché (Jo Ann McNamara, trans.). *Daily Life in the World of Charlemagne*. 1978

Charles R. Young. *The Royal Forests of Medieval England*. 1979

Edward Peters, ed. *Heresy and Authority in Medieval Europe*. 1980

Suzanne Fonay Wemple. *Women in Frankish Society: Marriage and the Cloister, 500–900*. 1981

R. G. Davies and J. H. Denton, eds. *The English Parliament in the Middle Ages.* 1981

Edward Peters. *The Magician, the Witch, and the Law.* 1982

Barbara H. Rosenwein. *Rhinoceros Bound: Cluny in the Tenth Century.* 1982

Steven D. Sargent, ed. and trans. *On the Threshold of Exact Science: Selected Writings of Anneliese Maier on Late Medieval Natural Philosophy.* 1982

Benedicta Ward. *Miracles and the Medieval Mind: Theory, Record, and Event, 1000–1215.* 1982

Harry Turtledove, trans. *The Chronicle of Theophanes: An English Translation of anni mundi 6095–6305 (A.D. 602–813).* 1982

Leonard Cantor, ed. *The English Medieval Landscape.* 1982

Charles T. Davis. *Dante's Italy and Other Essays.* 1984

George T. Dennis, trans. *Maurice's Strategikon: Handbook of Byzantine Military Strategy.* 1984

Thomas F. X. Noble. *The Republic of St. Peter: The Birth of the Papal State, 680–825.* 1984

Kenneth Pennington. *Pope and Bishops: The Papal Monarchy in the Twelfth and Thirteenth Centuries.* 1984

Patrick J. Geary. *Aristocracy in Provence: The Rhône Basin at the Dawn of the Carolingian Age.* 1985

C. Stephen Jaeger. *The Origins of Courtliness: Civilizing Trends and the Formation of Courtly Ideals, 939–1210.* 1985

J. N. Hillgarth, ed. *Christianity and Paganism, 350–750: The Conversion of Western Europe.* 1986

William Chester Jordan. *From Servitude to Freedom: Manumission in the Sénonais in the Thirteenth Century.* 1986

James William Brodman. *Ransoming Captives in Crusader Spain: The Order of Merced on the Christian-Islamic Frontier.* 1986

Frank Tobin. *Meister Eckhart: Thought and Language.* 1986

Daniel Bornstein, trans. *Dino Compagni's Chronicle of Florence.* 1986

James M. Powell. *Anatomy of a Crusade, 1213–1221.* 1986

Jonathan Riley-Smith. *The First Crusade and the Idea of Crusading.* 1986

Susan Mosher Stuard, ed. *Women in Medieval History and Historiography.* 1987

Avril Henry, ed. *The Mirour of Mans Saluacioune.* 1987

Maria Menocal. *The Arabic Role in Medieval Literary History.* 1987

Margaret J. Ehrhart. *The Judgment of the Trojan Prince Paris in Medieval Literature.* 1987

Betsy Bowden. *Chaucer Aloud: The Varieties of Textual Interpretation.* 1987

Felipe Fernández-Armesto. *Before Columbus: Exploration and Colonization from the Mediterranean to the Atlantic, 1229–1492.* 1987

Michael Resler, trans. *EREC by Hartmann von Aue.* 1987

A. J. Minnis. *Medieval Theory of Authorship.* 1987

Ute-Renate Blumenthal. *The Investiture Controversy: Church and Monarchy from the Ninth to the Twelfth Century.* 1988

David Anderson. *Before the Knight's Tale: Imitation of Classical Epic in Boccaccio's Teseida.* 1988

Robert Hollander, *Boccaccio's Last Fiction:* Il Corbaccio. 1988